Democratic Processes in the Secondary Classroom

ROSALIND M. ZAPF, Ph.D.

Edwin Denby High School
Detroit, Michigan

Englewood Cliffs, N. J.

PRENTICE-HALL, INC.

1 9 5 9

PRENTICE-HALL EDUCATION SERIES
Harold Spears, *Editor*

© 1959 BY
PRENTICE-HALL, INC.
ENGLEWOOD CLIFFS, N.J.

LIBRARY OF CONGRESS
CATALOG CARD NO.: 59-6534

TO THE BOYS AND GIRLS IN MY CLASSES WHO
HAVE MADE MY TEACHING YEARS UNBELIEVABLY WONDERFUL.

PRINTED IN THE UNITED STATES OF AMERICA

19800

Preface

Recollections of my own difficulties in the years that I have taught classes on a democratic basis have made me very aware of the problems that face teachers engaged in helping boys and girls learn the skills of democratic living. This book is an attempt to review the techniques which, over the years, have proved to be helpful to me and to others with whom I have come in contact. An attempt has been made to give an over-all picture of a democratically functioning class, its purposes and its daily procedures, as well as the classroom atmosphere within which these activities thrive. Material has been recorded which will give practical assistance in initiating such a program, in developing methods for furthering pupils' ability to work together in groups, and in selecting and solving problems for study by means of pupil-teacher planning techniques. It is hoped that the examples given will aid the classroom teacher in developing with his pupils the skills, techniques, and attitudes of democratic operation.

The reader will recognize that he cannot possibly do everything suggested in this book with any one class. Nor can he necessarily follow the suggestions in the exact order in which they appear in the book. Some are in operation simultaneously. For example, the techniques of learning to work together, as well as the basic skills of communication and social grace, will be developed in conjunction with a great many other activities.

Whenever possible a number of methods of achieving a desired goal have been described in order to give the teacher an opportunity to select that which best fits his needs. Many of these will, in all probability, not be used exactly as described. They will serve as suggestions on which a teacher can build his own procedures, trimmed to meet his own particular situation. The quest for better methods is a never ending one. Just when one thinks he has found *the* way of solving a difficulty, he finds a better way. This makes teaching in a democratic class exciting and stimulating.

Examples which have been written in dialogue form are, with the exception of that found in Chapter 10 and the Appendix, not verbatim, but are as close to the original as it is possible to write from notes and memory. The names used throughout are fictitious. If the names of persons in this book bear any similarity to those of actual persons, the similarity is purely fortuitous.

All photographs were taken in classrooms at Edwin Denby High School, Detroit, Michigan. They were taken by the Press Picture Service specifically for this book.

Rosalind M. Zapf

Acknowledgments

It is impossible to name all the people who have contributed to the development of the material in these pages, or to identify most of the sources of ideas on which the procedures described have been built. I am sincerely grateful to all the teachers across the country with whom I have talked, and whose classes I have visited, for their suggestions, ideas, and their enthusiasm, and to *The Fund for the Advancement of Education, Ford Foundation,* for making such visitation possible. These contacts have contributed in no small amount to the writing of this book.

In particular I should like to express deep appreciation to:

The late Leigh G. Cooper, under whose leadership the Denby core program was initiated and whose strong support gave me courage when it was needed most.

Irvin Wolf, whose continuing administrative support has provided freedom to experiment in the area of democratic procedures.

Fred J. Mulder, to whom I could always bring my problems and whose keen thinking helped me to find solutions to many difficult situations.

My colleagues, Helen Beaumont, Marion Howell, Ann Marie Laird, Genevieve Morger, William Robinson, as well as former core teachers, who, over the years, have shared so generously their own methods and procedures, and through whose deep and abiding concern and courage has developed Denby's core program. I should especially like to express my appreciation to Genevieve Morger for the endless hours spent in discussing the problems of democratic procedures.

Clara Olson, who read sections of the manuscript and contributed valuable suggestions.

Ann Bogdan, who reproduced the drawings in the Appendix.

Jenine Kemp, who spent many hours transcribing the tape recorded material in Chapter 10 and in the Appendix.

My pupils, both the members of the former core class who participated in the discussion recorded in Chapter 10, and all those others in whose papers and class discussions I have found examples of the various techniques described.

Theodore Rice, who conducted the interview recorded in Chapter 10, and who gave invaluable suggestions concerning the writing of this chapter.

More than anyone else, W. Clark Trow, who read the manuscript and without whose assistance this book would have been poorer by far. He was my chief critic and chief supporter, and I am deeply grateful for the time and thought he has given to this book.

R. M. Z.

Contents

CONTENTS   vii

5   A Problem to Work on   161

6   Solving a Problem   198

7   Reporting to the Class   240

8   Relationship with Parents   278

9   Emphasizing the Basic Skills   315

*Democratic Processes
in the Secondary
Classroom*

1

A Democratic Classroom In Action

You HAVE A FEELING OF WARMTH AND FRIENDLINESS as you walk into Miss Randall's room. Of course, the room is well lighted, but so are others you have visited, and it is no different from them in shape, size, or general equipment. It may be that the bright yellow window boxes filled with plants and flowers and the colorful bulletin boards against the green walls help to create the feeling. Or it may be the laughter and gay bantering of the pupils as they come into the room before the class starts. Perhaps it's Nancy's cordial greeting. Nancy is the class chairman to whom Miss Randall introduces you, and who finds a place for you at one of the tables. You feel welcome.

You notice that there is none of the subdued strain, nor the electricity in the air that is found in many well-behaved, well-"disciplined" classes. Nor, on the other hand, is there the rowdy anarchy that is sometimes mistaken for democracy. Instead, there is a feeling of enthusiasm and eagerness, the kind that is produced by young people engaged in activities that they enjoy.

You have wanted for some time to visit a classroom in which the teacher not only believes in the concept of democratic class activity, but has put the theory into operation. Such terms as "pupil-participation" and "pupil-teacher planning," which are so widely used in educational circles, have haunted you. As they

3

are talked about, however, you have realized that many teachers, both beginners and those with years of experience, accept the concept of pupil participation in the learning that takes place in the classroom, but are frequently at a loss when it comes to putting this concept into practice. You have heard, and have yourself asked, many questions:

What are democratic practices?
How can they be developed?
How does one initiate such procedures?
How is a class organized?
How is subject matter selected?
How do pupils learn to work in groups?
How much freedom should pupils have?
What is the role of the teacher?
Can such practices be used only in special classes such as core or basic living?
Can they be used with pupils of low intelligence? Of high intelligence?

So today you are visiting Miss Randall's class. It is a ninth-grade group of thirty-two pupils who meet together two consecutive class periods each day throughout the year. In the school program, this time would usually be assigned to two separate classes, English and social studies.

The conference you had with Miss Randall previous to your classroom visit made you aware of the fact that there is more to the process of kindling the minds of pupils through the medium of a democratic classroom than meets the eye. It is not as simple an affair as you had thought. She explained to you that in such classes much emphasis is placed on learning the skills of democratic citizenship that are generally considered to be essential for all people living in a democratic society. "We are, therefore, concerned with the whole area of human relationships," she said.

You were given a mimeographed sheet listing the assumptions made by the teachers who have classes like this one; these assumptions form the basis on which they are developing their program.

You glance again at the sheet and realize that, although brief, it contains the results of many hours of group consultation:

A. The primary common concern of citizens in a democratic society is to isolate the problems that arise out of group life, to give these problems adequate study and consideration, and to arrive at wise and equitable decisions concerning them.
B. An education that will adequately prepare one to participate in this type of democratic action will require more than *studying about* the nature of government and the problems of democracy. It will require a real opportunity to learn and practice the skills and techniques of democratic citizenship.
C. These skills and techniques we believe to be:
  1. The ability to think cooperatively with one's fellows.
  2. The ability to work cooperatively with others in the solution of common problems.
  3. The ability to utilize the best techniques for solving problems.

"These skills and techniques," said Miss Randall, "are the goals toward which we are working with our classes. In brief, the essence of this method of teaching is to arrange opportunities for pupils to work in situations in which they can realize the purposes that are fundamental in the education of people living in a democracy, namely, thinking and working together, and cooperatively meeting problems on a rational basis. This necessitates giving boys and girls as many opportunities as possible to make decisions which are of importance to them and which, because of this importance, seem to them to be worthy of their consideration."

With this briefing in mind, you look about you and note signs of the machinery that helps to develop an active, problem-solving group of boys and girls. There are more shelves of books than are usually found in a classroom, a filing cabinet, several cardboard file drawers, a well-stocked magazine rack, a number of wall maps, and a screen for film projection. A small exhibit case contains a collection of sea shells. Across the back of the room are four tables. The pupils' desks are of the usual type, with chair attached, but they are not arranged in rows all facing in one direction. Instead, on either side of the room three rows of seats face each other across a wide aisle. Pupils are also sitting, two at each table, across the back of the room, thus forming a modified hollow square, the side toward the chalkboard being open except for the teacher's desk. Your sketch of the seating arrangement looks as is shown in Figure 1.

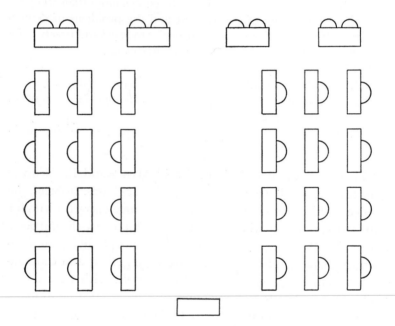

Figure 1. A workable seating arrangement.

On a large bulletin board, headed by the words, *How Does a Telephone Work?*, are drawings of the parts of a telephone. These, you learn later, have been prepared by a group studying the differences between the operation of the telphone and the telegraph.

That there is order and method in working out class problems is obvious from a study of an outline on the front bulletin board, printed large enough so that it can be read across the room:

Steps in Solving a Problem

1. Define the problem
2. Make a plan
3. Prepare a preliminary bibliography
4. Gather information
5. Share information
6. Reach a conclusion
7. Report to the class
8. Discuss solution with the class
9. Evaluate work done

The boy next to you explains the check marks in front of the first three items. "That means that we have completed the first three steps in solving the problems we are working on. When we finish a part we check it off. We have been gathering our information for the last week and a half, but we haven't finished that yet. So there's no check mark in front of number four. We have that list up there to remind us of what we need to do, and to keep track of how much we have finished."

Across the back of the room on a long, narrow bulletin board is a series of drawings, each representing a different social situation that teen-agers are likely to meet. Under each is a brief description of the situation, together with the words used by one of the figures in the picture. The heading for the series reads: *How Would You Say It?*[1] A small bulletin board at the front of the room has the heading, *Have You Heard?* Under this are notices of school activities, advertisements of a recommended film, an exhibit at the Art Center, and a newspaper clipping of the day's television programs.

Two sections of the chalkboard at the back of the room contain schedules of classroom activities for the week, one apparently for this class and the other for a 12A class that presumably meets in the same room at a different period. The ninth-grade schedule is surrounded by painted clowns in brightly colored suits and caps. The twelfth-graders used capped and gowned seniors as their motif. "Jill painted the clowns with chalk paint," the boy seated

---

1 Taken from booklet, *How Would You Say It?*, prepared at Edwin Denby High School, Detroit, Michigan.

next to you explains, "because that will wash off. Each week we write our plan in the schedule spaces with chalk."

While you have been looking around the room the bell has rung, the chairman has called the class to order, and pupils have settled into their seats. The minutes of the previous meeting are read by the secretary, corrected, and accepted, and the chairman turns to the affairs for the day.

NANCY

Jack, do you have any announcements about the library books?

JACK

Yes. Alex, did you bring your book back today? Dick is waiting for it and it was due yesterday.

ALEX

Here it is. I'll check it in with you later.

JACK

One more thing. Bill brought in the magazines that the group on "Religions of the world" was asking about. He says they may be taken home, so you can sign them out just the same as you do a room library book.

NANCY

Thanks, Jack. Miss Randall, do you have any announcements?

MISS RANDALL

Just one. The exhibit material for the "Weather forecasting" group has arrived. It's in the cupboard. You can get it whenever you are ready for it.

NANCY

Anything else? If not, let's get going. According to our schedule we will continue work on our problems today. Are there any who need to go to the library? (*A number of pupils indicate that they wish to go.*) All right. Will you get your library passes from the secretary? (*Several hands are now in the air, and* NANCY *nods to* JIM.)

JIM

We need to have two tables pushed together today, because Miss Blair is coming in to help our group plan how to present the play we wrote about the telephone. She is going to bring in some large charts. So we will need extra room.

NANCY

Well then, will those of you who usually sit at the two tables near the window give up your space today? You can move down in this corner where the telephone and telegraph group usually meets. Angela?

ANGELA

Three of us need to go to the visual-aids office today. O.K.?

Nancy nods and the class begins to move. Individually and in groups, members make the needed preparations for their work. It is somewhat noisy, but things are getting done. Seats are pulled into better positions for working, and small groups settle down in different places in the room. The two tables, pushed together to form a square working space, are ready as Miss Blair comes in and begins to unroll her charts. The class librarians are busy opening book cupboards, and clipping and picture files. The box of exhibit material is brought out, and another table is bargained for in order to have room to spread the objects out so that the group may examine them. You overhear two girls near you:

EVELYN

Will you water the plants today? I don't want to miss the plans my group is making with Miss Blair.

JANE

Sure, I'll do it.

And in a few minutes the window boxes have had their daily care.

Nancy comes to you and explains that there are five groups in operation at the present time, each working on a different problem. "These are their plans," she says, giving you some papers. "I thought you might like to see them." From the group plan sheets you see that the five problems are not at all alike.

1. What is the difference between the operation of the telephone and the telegraph?
2. How are weather forecasts made?
3. How are the religions of the world alike and different?
4. What is life like in Japan?
5. How should teen-agers act on different kinds of dates?

As you move from one group to another, you realize that not only does each group have a different problem, but each is developing the solution in a different way. You stop at the table at which the weather forecasting group is examining its exhibit material.

AL

This thing is the barometer.

RUTH

How does it work?

CURT

Well, we ought to be able to figure it out, because we studied the chart in the science book.

AL

Some way it doesn't look like the chart I drew in my notebook.

FRANCIS

There are two kinds of thermometers here just like we read about.

RON

Sure—a Fahrenheit and a Centigrade. Let's see if we can read them.

FRANCIS

Let's get those science books out again and compare the charts with the real thermometers and the barometer.

MISS RANDALL (*joining the group*)

Maybe you will want Mr. McDonald's help. If you do, be sure to see him early enough so that he has plenty of time to make his plans.

AL

That's a good idea. But let's see how far we can go by ourselves first.

The group working on the dramatization dealing with the invention of the telephone is hunched so close together that you hesitate to push yourself in. But snatches of excited discussion come to your ears:

——Tony would make a swell Alexander Graham Bell!
——How can we get whiskers on him?
——But Bell wasn't so old when——?
——Well, how old was he?
——. . . a screen for a wall.
——Miss Randall's desk could be the work table.
——Mike and I can build a . . . !

Some pupils are not seated in groups but are working individually. A number are reading. Others are reading and taking notes. "We keep our information on these three by five inch index cards," says the boy at whose desk you have stopped for a moment. "The name of the book and the author goes on the top line. Then a title that describes what the note is about is on the next line. The note should be in our own words. And then we put the number of the page on which we found the note at the bottom." He grins up at you ruefully and says, "It isn't easy to put it in your own words. I have trouble with that."

Miss Randall has suggested that you might like to follow the two groups of pupils that have left the room. Before leaving, however, you stop for a minute and look around. The room is far from silent, but is, without doubt, one of the busiest classrooms you have ever seen. Pupils are moving about to get books from the shelves, or clippings or pictures from the files, or to use the dictionary. Some are working alone, some in pairs, some in groups. The telephone-telegraph group is excitedly pointing out how and where the scenes for their dramatization can be laid. A number of individuals have gone over to the table containing the weather forecasting instruments and are asking questions. The teacher has been moving from one group to another giving help wherever it is needed.

But now she turns to you. "I'll go with you to the audio-visual aids office," she says. "I always try to make myself available at least once during the period to pupils who are out of the room. I may not be needed, since we have a most helpful person in charge of audio-visual aids, but I like to be on hand just the same."

As you enter the office you see that Angela and Carl have just finished looking at a filmstrip. "It's on Japan, Miss Randall, and it's interesting, but it doesn't tell enough. We've read about a lot of things that don't show up on the filmstrip at all. I don't think we can use it in our presentation," says Angela.

"What did you think about it, Carl?" asks Miss Randall.

"I don't know either," Carl says. "It's a good filmstrip, but I don't see how we can use it."

"Let's thread the machine again and look at the first few pictures. Maybe there is a way that you could weave it into your presentation but not just show it all by itself," says the teacher. As Angela turns to the first picture, Miss Randall asks, "What do you know about the subject of that picture in addition to the information given in the caption?" But Angela cannot seem to think beyond the picture.

Carl, however, suddenly sees a possibility. "Sure, Angela, don't you see? Pat has lots of material on that. He could tell whatever fits that picture as we show it. Turn to the next one, Miss Randall. There, see? You know about that one yourself and you can tell it when this picture is shown. And there are several others that I read about, too. When we have no information to add to a picture we can just read the caption. Let's bring the whole group down here and plan how to do it. What do you think, Angela?"

"I guess you're right. I just couldn't see how we could use the filmstrip, but it sounds as though it would work that way. Can we all come down tomorrow, Miss Randall?"

"If it's all right with Miss Dennis, I don't see any reason why you couldn't come." Then she turns to Ann who has been leafing through a film catalog. "Any luck, Ann?"

"Well, there are two films that sound as though they would be good for our group on teen-age problems. Miss Dennis says that she will order them, and when they come our group can come down to preview them. I'm ready to go back to class. Are you, Angela?"

"Yes, we're ready, too."

On the way to the library, Miss Randall says that it is difficult for boys and girls to learn to use films, filmstrips, and recordings to advantage. "Sometimes," she says, "the whole class takes time out and practices taking notes from a recording or a film. It is not easy at any time for pupils to learn to be selective, and it is much more difficult when the information slips by quickly as it does on a film or recording."

The seven pupils in the library are busy and do not need Miss Randall's help. They smile as she comes in. One crooks a finger at her, and, as she comes to his table, he shows her, in an atlas, a map that was just what he wanted.

To another she says, "Isn't that book pretty difficult to understand?"

"Yes," says Richard, "but when I can't get it, Art helps me to read it."

"Good," says Miss Randall. "I brought two books to class that I think will help you and I forgot to give them to you. When you are ready for them, tell me."

Betty and Janet are working with the *Readers' Guide,* and Barbara is at the card catalog.

It is nearing the end of the class period, and you walk back to the classroom. As you come into the room, you see that the chairs and tables are back in order, the exhibit has been put away, and the cupboards are closed. As the bell rings and the class leaves the room, there is the same eager chatter you noticed at the beginning of the period, together with many "good-byes" both to you and Miss Randall. The warmth and friendliness are still there.

"Do you think you can stand another class after lunch?" she laughs, as the last pupil goes out of the room. "Mr. Warren has his twelfth-grade class in the next room this afternoon, and I believe this is the day for their business meeting. I think you would enjoy seeing them."

You are sure that you want to see this phase of classwork, so, after lunch, Miss Randall introduces you to Mr. Warren. In the few minutes before the class comes into the room, he tells you that these pupils are in their senior year and have had experience in a democratically operated class all through high school. He has been their teacher for the last three years. "It takes time for pupils to learn to operate the way they do," he says, "and these are just normal young people—a few who are outstandingly bright and some with relatively low intelligence ratings. The greater part of the class, of course, is spread between the two extremes. About one third of them plan to go to college."

The room is as pleasant and cheerful as Miss Randall's. One bulletin board contains charts indicating salaries, necessary training, and qualifications for a wide variety of jobs, pictures of people at work, and a sample letter of application for a job. On another is the caption, *Is College for You?*, and underneath it these questions:

> Why do you want to go to college?
>
> Is college training necessary for the work you want to do?
>
> What does your high school record indicate about your chances for academic success?
>
> Do you enjoy studying?
>
> Have you taken the proper courses to fit you for the college work you want to do?

The weekly schedule is painted on the chalkboard as in the room you visited earlier. You smile to yourself as you see that these seniors have used Father Time as their theme. A tenth-grade schedule has little green elves dancing about.

Seating arrangements are different from those in the previous room. Small, individual tables are placed end to end in the shape of a closed, hollow square; the chairs are not attached. Pupils take their places around the outside of this square.

As they come into the room, you see evidences of the same friendly relations among the pupils and between pupils and teacher that you noticed in the other class.

"Hello Mr. Warren, remember what day this is?"

"Sure, Sid," he says. "This is the day you are going to collapse at my feet!" The class laughs, and, although you do not know their special joke, the feeling of friendship is in the words and tone of voice of both boy and teacher, and in the laughter of the class.

The chairman calls the meeting to order. He tells the class they will have more time than usual today to discuss the problems they are concerned with, since the committees held their meetings yesterday instead of during the first part of the business meeting period, as is usually done. He then calls for the minutes of the last meeting. The secretary presents the following minutes:

> The business meeting was called to order by the chairman, Dave Elman, at 1:20. The minutes were read by the secretary, and were ac-

cepted. The treasurer's report showed eighty-five cents in the treasury. The librarian reported that all books were accounted for.

The Planning Committee presented its suggested plan for the week. The plan was accepted by the class.

The Current Events Committee named Jean, Allen, Emma, and John as the discussion leaders for the following week. Articles selected for discussion were to deal with national affairs.

The Social Committee suggested that before the end of the semester we spend an evening singing at the convalescent home where we carolled at Christmas. Questions were raised as to when we could do it and what we could sing. Mr. Warren suggested that the committee call the home and find out whether a visit at this time would be possible. After some discussion, Carol made a motion that the problem be turned back to the committee for more careful study. Ben seconded it. The motion was carried.

The Ways and Means Committee had no report.

The meeting was adjourned at the end of the class period.

Respectfully submitted,

ELLEN ANDRE

CHAIRMAN

Are there any corrections? If not, the minutes stand approved as read.

Kathy, will you report your committee's suggestions for next week's schedule?

(KATHY *goes to the chalkboard on which the committee recorder has written the plan shown below.*)

	First Period	Second Period
Monday:	Complete note taking on problems (both periods)	
Tuesday:	Organize material and plan outline	Current events—Discussion on city affairs
Wednesday:	Discuss and decide on new method of presenting data to class	
Thursday:	Free choice	Prepare oral presentation
Friday:	Committee meetings	Business meeting

KATHY

We think we've left something out, but can't see what it is. Does anybody know what it could be?

JOHN

It looks all right to me. No—wait! What week in the term is this?

ELLEN *(checking in the book of minutes)*

It's the twelfth, and next week is the thirteenth.

JOHN

Then next week is the time to do our evaluations for our report cards. We have to have a period in there someplace.

KATHY

That's it.

JEAN, ALLEN, BOB *(all together)*

How about Thursday? One period on Wednesday. Wednesday——!

CHAIRMAN

Wait a minute. One at a time or we can't hear you. Allen?

ALLEN

I think we could use one of Wednesday's periods for it.

JEAN

That doesn't seem right. That discussion will take two periods and we have a free choice period on Thursday that can be used.

JACK

I move that we change the free choice period to an evaluation period on Thursday.

SID

I second the motion.

CHAIRMAN

Any further discussion?

(The motion was then put to a vote and passed. There were no further changes and the plan was accepted and recorded on the chalkboard schedule.)

CHAIRMAN

Roy, what about the Current Events Committee?

ROY

The four people who are to serve as discussion leaders have already been notified. They are Jack, Sharon, Marie, and Tony. The topic will be city affairs. Let's all watch the newspapers this week so that we can pitch in on the discussion.

CHAIRMAN

What about the Social Committee?

JENNY

Well, we've talked quite a bit about singing at the convalescent home once more before we graduate. You remember that at the last meeting Mr. Warren suggested that we call the home to see how they would feel about our coming before we made any decisions. Doris called and they said we would be very welcome. They would really like to have us come.

In our committee meeting we discussed what we could take as little gifts—you know—as we did at Christmas. We took the fruit and the cellophane packages of home-made cookies then. Oh yes—and a fifty cent gift for each patient. And we had a Santa Claus. But it's almost summer now. So—we don't just know how to do it. Ron thinks we can do the same thing as at Christmas, but the rest of us aren't so sure. But, before we talk about all that, wouldn't it be a good idea to find out whether the class really wants to take on this project or not?

CHAIRMAN

That sounds like a good idea. It would be a waste of time to make plans and find out later that only a few are interested. Will those of you who want to go please raise your hands? That's—twenty-nine. How many are not in favor of going? That's—two. And two are absent. Well, it looks as though most of us want to go. Then I guess we can go ahead with plans.

JENNY

Now what about taking things for the patients?

JUDY

I think the cookies are just as good an idea now as at Christmas.

GAYLE

But the little gifts are so Christmasy. Can't we do something else?

HERB

The fruit idea is still all right, too, isn't it? Of course, there won't be a Santa Claus to take the stuff around to the people, but what's the matter with us? We look all right, don't we? Of course we're not as fat and handsome as he was!

(*The class laughs and* PAUL *says:*)

Well, I'm not as fat and handsome either since I took those pillows out and the grease paint off!

BEVERLY

And what will we wear? We certainly don't want the big red bows and the bells.

GAYLE

No, but we could——

CHAIRMAN

Wait a minute. Let's settle one thing at a time. The question we are working on is what we can take to these people.

BEVERLY

O.K.

ARLENE

This may sound silly, but I think the old people at the home would like it. How would it be if we made little bouquets of spring flowers, one for each one?

JUDY

I like that.

JENNY

Me too.

HERB

What would they put them in?

KEN

How could you carry them?

JOYCE

Who would give them out to the people?

PAUL

Where could we get them?

MR. WARREN

How much would they cost?

JUDY

Could we see how many like the idea of little bunches of flowers? In that way the committee members will know whether or not to go ahead with the idea. If the class is in favor of it, the committee can have some answers to the questions that have been asked by the time of our next meeting.

CHAIRMAN

That sounds sensible. How many like the flower idea? —twenty-seven. How many do not? —four. Can we leave this question at this point and move on to other business? I think we've given the Social Committee plenty to work on.

JENNY

Yes, we'll really get on the job now that we know we are going and something of what we want to do.

CHAIRMAN

There isn't much time left but what about the Ways and Means Committee?

BEN

We considered two suggestions that were made by members of the class. Both have to do with changes in procedure in our business meetings. Since there is so little time left today, could our committee be given the time for reporting immediately following the Planning Committee's report at the next meeting?

CHAIRMAN

That seems fair enough. In that way you won't run the risk of being cut off again. We'll put you in that spot at our next business meeting.

Mr. Warren, is there anything that should be brought up?

MR. WARREN

At our next meeting will we be able to have a report on the field trip plans for the combined 12B and 12A classes? Rita, you and Gerry have met with representatives from those classes, haven't you?

RITA

Yes, but we are going to have another meeting on Tuesday. We'll have more information next Friday.

(*As the bell rings,* DAVE *says:*)
The meeting is adjourned.

As you drive away from the school, you try to analyze the differences between the classes you have just seen and many others with which you are acquainted. The pupils themselves were little different from those you have known, for these classes were not outstanding in ability and quite obviously there were the usual number and kinds of problems within the pupil group.

The seating arrangement was certainly different from what is found in most classrooms, for, although many rooms today are equipped with movable seats or individual tables, they are seldom placed so that pupils are able to see many of their classmates face to face. From your observation of the business meeting in the senior class you realize that, when a class discussion was in progress, such an arrangement greatly facilitated pupil-pupil discussion since the focus was on other pupils rather than on the teacher.

Although such a seating arrangement greatly increased the possibility of pupil participation, you suspect that a more important difference lay in the purposes toward which both pupils and teachers were consciously working. The goals obviously required the acquisition of facts relating to a body of subject matter. But there was more involved. Their goals included the development of skills and techniques of democratic living, of working together in small and large groups. This, too, constitutes a subject matter, a discipline not of factual knowledge only, but of interrelated events, of behavior, in which the test of success comes in the doing.

As you think about it, you realize that a still more important difference between the classes you have observed today and many others you have seen was the degree of pupil participation in making important decisions in the classroom. Even the class goals were not imposed by the teacher. Pupils were following their self-determined purposes. The subject matter studied, and it was worth-while subject matter, had been selected by pupils and teacher together, and had value and meaning, since it served to achieve the purposes that the class members had identified. A pupil committee took the responsibility for planning the week's schedule; elected officers started the class on the day's work; a group of pupils went to another teacher for special help in dramatizing its material. Individuals expressed their opinions freely in the business meeting; in fact, twenty-one of the thirty-one pupils present took an active part in the discussions. Still others, although silent today, participated by making choices either for or against questions that were put to a vote. Some of these had served on the various committees as well.

And then you remember the laughter of the senior class when Mr. Warren said, "Sure, Sid. This is the day you are going to collapse at my feet!" You remember the chatter between pupils as they came into the room, and the ring of pupils around the teacher, each with something he was eager to say.

The classroom climate was different from that in most classes you have seen. The pupils had freedom, yet it did not become license. The ninth-grade room, in which boys and girls were working in groups, was noisy, but it was the noise of people working. The senior business meeting gave everyone an opportunity to participate, but was orderly and businesslike. It was a permissive climate that clearly had built-in, self-imposed limitations.

Along with this freedom there was a lack of tension. Pupils expressed themselves freely and easily, agreeing or disagreeing, but obviously saying what they felt and believed, not what they thought the teacher wanted them to say. There was a willingness to try new ideas even though they might fail. It was "safe" to try them. There was security for the boys and girls in these classrooms.

As your thoughts turn to the teachers of these classes you recall Miss Randall's explanation of the role of the teacher:

In classes such as these the teacher is not solely a dispenser of knowledge. In general he plays three roles, no one of which is separate and distinct from the other two. He is, above all, a participating member of a class, taking part in all of the activities carried on in the classroom as one of the group. He must be willing to be more nearly an equal member and less the dominating teacher.

At times it is necessary that he be the educational expert or the consultant. In this capacity he is charged with the responsibility of helping the class find methods of realizing its goals, of helping it find ways to solve its problems. He also helps pupils see the implications of their discoveries in terms of a wide variety of other problems, thus broadening their horizons. He contributes of his knowledge and experience as it can be useful to the class. As a member of the group, however, he must be able to see his suggestions ignored or changed at times and must be able to admit that he doesn't know the answers to all questions.

In addition to these two roles the teacher is a guide and counselor to the members of his class. He not only helps pupils to understand other people, but to know and understand themselves and to evaluate their own growth. Above all, he is their friend, an adult to whom they can safely come with their problems.

Classes at the secondary level in which you are most likely to find such pupil participation in classroom learning as you have just observed are those that come under the heading of core, basic living, general education, common learnings, or unified studies. In general, these classes combine or replace English and social studies, forming a two-hour block of time in the school day. In many places, especially in the junior high school, these are combined with science, thus forming a three-period block of time. This does not mean, however, that no democratic procedures, no pupil-teacher planning, can take place in other classes. The techniques described in the following pages, although largely drawn from the writer's experience with core classes, may well be applied to any class in which the teacher, in addition to teaching subject matter, recognizes the need for helping pupils learn the skills of democratic living.

2

Getting Under Way

THERE THEY ARE. THIRTY-FOUR NEW FACES—A FEW
friendly glances, but many withdrawn and distant; some obviously frightened; but all of them waiting to see what the new
teacher is going to say, how he is going to sound, what he is going
to do. What the teacher does and says in those first days and weeks
will determine to a large extent the degree of success he will have
in developing a democratically functioning class. This is his opportunity for laying the foundation for a good working relationship between himself and the members of his class.

There are many things that need to be done in these early
weeks of the semester, but the teacher's first concern is to help his
pupils adjust as easily and rapidly as possible to the new situations
and problems they are facing. He must help them to orient themselves to the new class, and, if they are new to the school, help
them to feel comfortable in their present school home. If the class
is composed of pupils who were in the same school the previous
year, and who have even perhaps been in classes together, there
will, of course, be no need for orientation to the school, since they
know their way around the building, know the local rules and
customs, and have already formed many friendships.

For the first semester pupils, however, every thing and every
person is new and strange. They will need help in becoming acquainted with one another, with their teacher, and with the

the ticket by saying that he couldn't ride elevators. Then they laughed again when the teacher told them that the elevator was a freight elevator.

At the close of the two periods she said, "I know that I am going to have trouble recognizing all of you when I pass you in the hall. Won't you help me by saying 'Hi, Miss Raye,' when you see me?" As these ninth-graders went out of the room, she stood at the door and said, "Good-bye" as they went past her. Several waited after class to ask questions as the result of her friendliness. The first step had been taken.

The degree to which a teacher allows his pupils to become acquainted with him makes a difference in their attitudes toward him. Young people frequently have strange conceptions of the life a teacher leads. Nothing amazed the writer's students more than the fact that she lived with her mother, that she lived in a house rather than an apartment, that she cut the grass and washed dishes. Knowledge of such simple facts tends to establish common ground between the teacher and boys and girls. Such information is not imparted all at once on a given day nor necessarily to the entire class, but it comes to light as it fits an occasion. It may arise during an informal chat with several boys before class when one is bemoaning the fact that he has to cut the grass after he gets home from school.

"I know how you feel because I have to cut my grass tonight, too," says the teacher.

"Do you cut grass?" comes the astonished question.

"Of course. It's quite a job isn't it?"

"Gee, I didn't think you did things like that." And a bond, very small, but very real, had been established.

An eighth-grade general education teacher came to school one morning and announced the birth of a daughter. He wondered whether his boys and girls would like to suggest names for the baby, since he and his wife couldn't decide on one. He would not promise to choose one of these but would appreciate some help. Needless to say the response was tremendous. The class felt that it had a stake in the whole family and a closer relationship was established between pupils and teacher.

Such occasions are usually wholly unplanned, but the teacher can well be alert to make use of them when they present themselves. This does not mean that a teacher should spend any considerable time talking about himself and his activities. Neither is there any need for him to enlarge on personal facts about himself. But the simple, everyday things that boys and girls experience themselves give them a feeling of kinship and belonging.

Orientation of pupils to one another

A second phase of orientation involves the establishment of good relationships between the boys and girls themselves. Many times a child is acquainted with no one in the class, or at best only one or two, a situation that should not be allowed to exist any longer than is made necessary by the mechanics of enrolling pupils in the class.

There are a number of get-acquainted techniques, one or more of which can be used, the choice depending somewhat on the age of the pupils and on the numbers in the group. One that almost any age responds to is the use of *Howdy tags.* Before coming to class the teacher prepares as many tags as he expects to have pupils in his class. These are most attractive and usable when made of vari-colored construction paper approximately 6 by 9 inches in size with irregularly cut edges. With a brush pen or heavy, dark crayon the word, *Howdy!,* is printed at the top. In the upper right-hand corner each tag is given a number from 1 to 35, if that is the number of pupils expected. Immediately below the word, *Howdy,* the following is written in ink: *My name is*————.
A line is then drawn across the entire tag. Below this line, numbers from 1 to 35 (or whatever number of pupils is expected) are written in two columns, using both front and back below the level of the line that has been drawn across the tag. A straight pin is fastened to the upper section below the number. The tag will appear as shown in Figure 2.

Figure 2. A *Howdy tag* for the first day.

When ready to use the tags each pupil is asked to write his name on his own tag following the words, *My name is* ——————. He folds it on the straight line across the card, tears the top piece off, and pins it on himself. Each boy and girl then takes the lower section and goes to everyone else in the room, asking each pupil to sign his tag. When signing a tag, a child signs in the space following the number that appears in the upper right-hand corner of his own name tag. For example, if Bill's number is 17, he signs each pupil's *Howdy tag* after the number 17.

It is important to make this as informal a period as possible. True, it may be noisy, but the benefits derived from it will more than compensate for the noise. A time limit may be set if desired, thus putting urgency into the picture and increased effort to complete the list. By the end of the activity, each child will have spoken at least one or two words to every other child in the room.

This scheme also provides an opportunity for the teacher to

Figure 3. *Howdy tags* help pupils get acquainted.

mingle with the class members on a much less formal basis than is usually possible. If he, as well as his pupils, fills out a *Howdy tag*, he, too, will speak directly to every pupil. It also gives him an opportunity to observe the reactions of pupils to one another. There is sometimes the girl who stays seated and lets everyone else come to her, or the boy who is so busy poking people he has no time to get names on his card, or one who is very efficient in getting his card filled, moving swiftly from person to person. Some of these actions can be identified in Figure 3. In themselves, such behaviors are relatively unimportant, but they serve as first clues to understanding these pupils.

Another technique for helping pupils become acquainted is the use of the pupil-pupil interview. There are many ways that this may be carried out. A simple method is to divide the class into two sections, count off identically in both groups and have number one in the first group pair off with number one in the second, number two in both groups pair, and so on. If there is an odd number present, the teacher serves as one of a pair in order that no one may be left out.

There may be a need to break through the feeling of strangeness before interviewing begins. In this case, matching halves of cartoons will serve to pair pupils off as well as to give them an opportunity to mingle informally with their classmates. These are simple to prepare but they must be ready ahead of time. A series of newspaper cartoons, such as *Bobby Sox* or *Dennis the Menace,* will serve the purpose. Each cartoon is mounted on paper, then cut in half in zig-zag fashion. Each pupil draws a half and must find the person having the matching half. The two become partners for interviewing. The simplest method of all, of course, is to pair pupils off according to their seating positions, two people seated next to one another forming a pair, each interviewing the other.

The interview itself should be quite simple, perhaps having each person able to introduce his partner to the class, tell from what school he came, what he likes to do in his spare time, and some interesting or humorous incident that happened to him last year or since he came to this school. Such a list arouses interest best when developed from suggestions made by the class members. This also provides one of the first opportunities for class participation in planning an activity. The question, "What things would you like to know about other people in our class?" will set this in motion.

It is well to suggest that each pupil jot down on paper the information he obtains from his partner in order that he may not forget it. A time limit of ten minutes is usually sufficient for the interviews. Each person then introduces his partner to the class. To insure against confusion of names during the introductions, each pupil may be provided with a colored sheet of construction paper on which he prints the name of his partner with heavy, dark crayon. As he introduces him to the class he pins the name tag on him. In this way the class members have an opportunity to associate the name with the face of the pupil.

The introductions also provide an opportunity for the teacher to observe his group and unobtrusively record his observations. Which pupils find it difficult to speak to the class? Which have no difficulty telling their stories? Does one have a speech defect? Does another seem to have eye trouble? Is this one really angry or does he just sound that way? He must also be ready with small talk as the introductions proceed. He can not just sit back and listen and write, but must be a participating member of the entire proceedings. He must be alert for places where a bit of humor will help, or where oil needs to be poured on troubled waters. For example, he must catch the tone of voice and the frown when a boy who is introduced as, "Dick," says, "I want to be called Richard now." The teacher can remark, "Richard it is. As we get older we have the right to be called by our whole name." The frown disappears and from that day on Dick is Richard in this class.

In a tenth-grade class that was composed of members from four former classes the teacher suggested that each of the four groups meet separately, selecting a host or hostess to serve as the person to introduce the members of the group to the rest of the class. Each group could decide for itself the things that were to be told, the only requirement being that more information than just the names be given. It was a successful and satisfying experience to the class.

The use of name tags during the first two weeks is a simple and effective means by which both pupils and teacher may come to associate names and faces. In too many classes, even in those that are supposedly functioning democratically, the members cannot call more than half a dozen of their fellow classmates by name at the end of a semester. It is important for the self-esteem of each individual that his classmates call him by name. If name tags are to be used they should be ready for use on the second day. They should be large enough so that they can be read across the room. Since older pupils frequently reject the idea of pinned-on name tags, one of the most satisfactory types is made to stand on the desk or table in front of the pupil. It should be made of paper heavy enough to hold its shape, preferably light in color, and made from a sheet approximately 9 by 12 inches in size. This is folded in half lengthwise, thus making it possible to set it upright on the table. The name is printed or written with either a dark, heavy crayon or brush pen.

Name tags, or "dog tags" as they are often jokingly called, are picked up by the pupils from the teacher's desk at the beginning of the class period each day and returned at the end of the period, thus assuring their presence on the following day. A frequent check may be made by the teacher relative to the number of his classmates each pupil can name. A quick and easy way to do this is to say to the class at the beginning of a period, "How many can name every person at the first two tables?" Three or four pupils are then given an opportunity to prove their naming ability. To stimulate further learning of names, he may say, "By the end of the period today let's see how many of us can name everyone at the third and fourth tables as well as the first two. While we are doing other things today, let's also study the name tags and try to learn the names of these people." The wise teacher will remember, too, that it behooves him to do this chore also, since otherwise he may be caught in the trap of having some boy or girl ask him if he is able to name these people. Use of such name tags can usually be abandoned after a week or two.

Another means of facilitating the association of names and faces and of becoming acquainted with everyone is the use of a large seating chart drawn on the chalkboard. Many classrooms have movable seats and pupils are, of course, not always seated in the same places throughout the class period. In most classes, however, they are seated in a specified arrangement for at least a part of each period. It is this semi-permanent arrangement that is used for this activity. At the initial appearance of the chart on the chalkboard it has no names recorded on it. Each class member makes a copy of this on paper that will fit into his notebook, or the teacher may prepare mimeographed copies. A period is spent in having each pupil go to the board and write his name in the space that represents his seat. If inter-pupil interviews have not been made, each boy or girl may also tell the class something about himself, such as, what school he came from, what he likes to do in his spare time, or some interesting or humorous incident that happened to him either last year or since coming to this school. Again, such a list should be decided upon by the class in terms of the things they would like to know about other pupils. As the names are recorded on the large seating chart, each pupil writes them on his own chart, so that when it is completed he has available at all times the names and seating places of the entire class. It is amazing to see how often these charts are referred to as the semester proceeds.

Preparing a *Who's Who* bulletin board has high interest for all except the upper high-school grades. On a 5 by 8 inch index card, preferably colored, or on a half sheet of construction paper, each pupil presents information concerning himself, the items to be included having been decided upon by the class. In order to make it as interesting as possible, he pastes a recent snapshot of himself on the card, then illustrates his information in any way he may wish—more snapshots, line drawings, stick figures, cutouts from magazine illustrations, anything that will help his classmates to visualize what he is telling about himself. The following items are usually included: family members, address, pets, nickname, and special interests or hobbies.

A class period spent in planning the cards and making rough sketches for them provides an opportunity for getting acquainted and sharing ideas, especially if the pupils work in pairs or small groups. It goes without saying that the teacher makes a card for himself, since he, too, is a member of the class.

An alternative method is to have pupils make cards for one another. Each person draws a name from a hat, interviews this individual, and then makes a card illustrating the information he has obtained. Each person furnishes his interviewer with his picture for the card.

A completed card is shown in Figure 4.

Figure 4. A *Who's Who* card ready for the bulletin board.

The individual cards are mounted on a bulletin board when finished, with a heading such as *Who's Who in 218?* The amount of interest in the board is unbelievable. It is one of the few exhibits that continues to draw marked attention day after day.

In many classes a wide cross-section of nationalities is represented. One of the initial approaches to developing understanding and acceptance of one another may be an activity dealing with this factor. A technique used successfully with younger boys and girls calls for a drawing on a large sheet of paper of a tree with many limbs spreading from its trunk. Each limb is labeled with the name of a different country. The children cut small circles out of colored paper to represent fruit. Each child writes his name on a circle and fastens his piece of fruit to the limb of the tree representing the country of his father's birth. A second tree may be made to show the countries in which the mothers were born.

Older children are interested in the same information. Each pupil may be asked to consult his parents for information about the names and native countries of his parents, grandparents, and great-grandparents, and then to construct a family tree. With the help of the teacher, this information is made into attractive posters, exhibited on a bulletin board, and used as the basis for a class discussion of the nationalties represented in the class.

A similar technique that may be used through the ninth grade is the preparation of a map on which class members indicate with gummed stars the places of their own birth. Usually a large United States map is sufficient, although in certain localities a world map will be necessary. This always arouses a great deal of interest, especially if each pupil tells a little about the areas that are far from the town in which the school is located. A map serves equally well as the large tree to represent places of birth of parents.

Seating arrangements. The ease with which pupils become acquainted with one another depends to no small degree upon the seating arrangements that are possible in the classroom. If, as in too many classrooms, the seats are bolted to the floor in rows facing the front of the room, it is difficult to develop a feeling of belonging among the class members. For a pupil who can only see the back of the head of the person seated in front of him, or, sitting in the front rows can see no one without turning around, there is little likelihood of making many friends or feeling at ease with most of the members of his class. At best he becomes acquainted with the few who are sitting directly around him.

It is also important to recognize that when seats are arranged in straight rows, front to back, the most logical place for a pupil to look is toward the teacher or the chairman at the front, and thus the person addressed in a discussion is the teacher or chairman. It ceases to be a *class* discussion, and becomes a teacher-to-pupil-to-teacher, or chairman-to-pupil-to-chairman conversation. As a further result, it then seems only important that the *teacher* or *chairman* hears what is said, with much of what pupils are saying being inaudible to the other pupils throughout the room. In this situation the teacher or chairman becomes the dominant individual in the classroom rather than an equal participant in the class activities. Where at least some of the pupils are facing each other there is a much greater degree of give and take between class members, a lessening of the dominant status position of the teacher or chairman, and a much greater interest on the part of pupils in what their classmates are saying. As a natural consequence of this, there is greater insistence on hearing what is being said. It has become the pupils' personal concern to know what is going on.

This is not to say that group feeling is impossible to achieve under a formal seating arrangement, but a great deal of additional effort is required. One principal with imagination had all the seats unscrewed, rearranged them, again in rows but at angles, and placed a large table in the center. Since there was a city ruling that seats must be fastened in place, she had them bolted down again, but they were in much more usable positions. Pupils could see many more of their classmates.

In a room equipped with desk and seat combinations that need not be bolted to the floor, or with chairs with broad writing arms, a variety of arrangements is possible. If the class is relatively small, a circle is excellent. If the number in the class makes this difficult, placing seats in two rows around three sides of the room and facing toward the center is an easy working arrangement. This leaves the chalkboard wall open for special use. In some rooms the fourth wall is used for seating as well, with all sides facing center.

Tables are being used in increasing numbers. These are frequently small and intended to be used by one person. They may be arranged in a U shape along three sides of the room or in a hollow square along the four sides of the room. Pupils are seated on the outside of the U or square, in this way facing their classmates. When small group work is in order, a number of tables may be combined to form a large working space. Larger tables are frequently used also and may be similarly arranged. The new trapezoidal tables, shaped so that when each is placed next to another in one order they form a continuous line and placed in a second order form a small circle, have become very popular and are extremely useful. In classrooms where tables are not available, many teachers have had plywood circles cut approximately five feet in diameter. These are placed across desks and furnish the large flat surface needed for many activities.

Orientation to school

The degree to which a classroom teacher should assume responsibility for orienting the members of his class to the school depends upon the activities conducted by the school as a whole to help new pupils become acclimated.

It depends, too, upon the size of the school and the degree of familiarity that pupils have both with the school and their fellow classmates previous to entering. The suggestions in the following pages must of necessity be trimmed to fit the actual situation in which the teacher operates.

In many schools the student council assumes the task of acquainting first-year pupils with the school plant by conducting small groups on tours of the building. Or perhaps it presents an assembly program at which pupils meet the principal and other members of the administration. It may prepare a handbook in which are recorded the school rules, the school songs and yells, as well as a plan of the building indicating room locations and any other information that new school members should know.

To the extent that such a program is conducted for all new pupils it obviously becomes less important for the classroom teacher to carry out this phase of orientation. If, however, little is done by the school, the teacher of a group of boys and girls who are to function well in a democratically operated classroom will do well to plan activities that will help them in the initial steps toward good school adjustment. If pupils feel secure in their total school situation, the teacher will have a far greater chance of helping them achieve success and satisfaction in the classroom.

The beginning of orientation to the school lies in the teacher's offer on the first day to help with difficulties boys and girls may be having in locating various places in the building. If there is no response from his pupils, he would do well to ask more pointed questions: How are they going to go from the present classroom to the next? Does everyone know exactly where all the classrooms are in which his classes meet tomorrow? Friendly and interested questioning will bring forth the problems or difficulties pupils are having.

Bulletin boards containing material to arouse interest in the school can be used to advantage. A heading such as: *Do You Know Where These Places Are?* starts the ball rolling. Such questions as the following may be used for this:

Where is the nurse's office?
Where is the bookstore?
Where is the "Lost and Found" office?
Where is the public telephone?
Where is the gymnasium?
Where is the swimming pool?
Where is the main office?
Where is the auditorium?
Where is the cafeteria?
Where can you keep your bicycle?
Where is the locker office?

An attractive display may be made by combining the questions with pictures cut from an old yearbook. Discussion of these questions and their answers will raise a host of others.

Verbal methods may be supplemented by other ways of helping class members become familiar with their school. It may be possible to enlist the aid of an older class in serving as hosts and hostesses on guided tours of the building, dividing the class into small groups of six or seven. Or the teacher, himself, may conduct a tour with the entire class, although this is frequently not as satisfactory as dividing the class into smaller groups.

If older pupils serve as guides, a planning session should be held with them in order that each may know exactly what is expected of him. This should include plans for moving around the building in such directions that groups may avoid reaching the same places of visitation at the same time. It may also be necessary for them to make special arrangements to visit certain areas, for example, to obtain permission to visit the swimming pool, the auditorium, a science laboratory, or a shop. Some time should be spent in helping the older class members recognize the purposes of such a trip in terms of developing a friendly feeling on the part of the new pupils as well as orienting them to the physical plant.

A happy experience for all involved was one in which each member of a tenth-grade class served as host or hostess to one of the members of a new ninth-grade class. Each host conducted his own guest on a tour of the building. The names of the members of the new class were written on slips of paper and drawn one by one by the tenth-graders, thus enabling each to know his guest by name. A list was prepared of the hosts and their guests and posted in both rooms. Thus, it became definitely a person-to-person activity. Many of the older boys and girls maintained an interest in the new pupils for a long time afterward.

If school handbooks that contain a floor plan of the building are available, these may be used to assist boys and girls new to the school in finding their way around. If no floor plan is printed, and the building is simple enough to make this possible, a plan may be drawn on the chalkboard to serve as a basis for planning a trip around the building. If a trip is completely impossible, such a floor plan is an invaluable source of data in answering pupils' questions.

Another effective bulletin board display deals with a different type of information. It might be headed: *Do You Know?* or, *How Many Can You Answer?* and contains such questions as the following:

How many pupils attend our school? _____

How many first-year pupils (or whatever year this class may be) attend our school? _____

How many teachers are there in our school? _____

What is the principal's name? _____
What is the assistant principal's name? _____
For whom was our school named? _____
When was our school built? _____
What is the name of our school paper? _____
What is the name of our yearbook? _____
What is the name of our school song? _____

Each question has a line drawn at the end of it in order that the correct answer may be filled in at the time these questions are discussed.

There are usually members of the class who can answer some of the questions. If, however, certain questions cannot be answered, a committee may be appointed to find the information and report back to the class. The committee will probably need help from the teacher in determining where it can obtain the needed information but from there on can operate on its own.

A technique used by a ninth-grade core teacher to stimulate her boys and girls to gather as much information as possible about their school goes by the name *Dragnet*. Using the television program, *Dragnet,* as her stimulus, she makes a game of it, implying that her pupils are detectives, and assigning them the job of collecting every fact about the school that they can possibly find. They may use any sources they wish—reading the handbook, asking questions of teachers and other pupils, or personal observation—the only stipulation being that each item must be a fact that can be proved. A time limit, usually three or four days, is set. At the end of this period each brings his list to class.

This is a day well worth watching. In the excitement of assembling and counting the number of facts they have collected, which sometimes runs well over a hundred, there is much good natured bantering among pupils, and they come to know one another on a friendly basis. Sometimes the class is divided into small groups, the members of each group telling one another all the unusual facts they have discovered. Sometimes everyone in turn is given an opportunity to tell his most exciting discoveries to the entire class. As their teacher walks among them, answering questions, helping to count, friendly and at ease with her pupils, they come to recognize her human qualities, to understand her better, and to accept her as one of them. She in turn gains valuable information about her class.

A sample of the teacher's observation notes on such a day reads:

GROUP OBSERVATIONS

1. The class members in general have formed closer relationships with one another than I had thought. (I can ease off on pupil-pupil orientation.)

2. The class seemed to revolve around four pupils, Jill, Helen, Bill, and Mike, breaking into informal groups with each one of these as a center.

3. Class members as a whole were much interested in the items everyone else had collected. No one seemed to be pushing himself into the limelight.

INDIVIDUAL OBSERVATIONS

1. Jane had a long list of items. When those around her wanted to name hers as the longest she tried to get her paper back and said, "No, please don't call mine." Her face was very red.

2. Jeannette has a very loud and rough voice. Sue and Helen "shushed" her several times, but she just shrugged her shoulders.

3. Ruth and Joe took no part in any phase of the activity. When I suggested to Joe that he work with Bill or Jim, he half rose from his seat, but sank back into it and stayed by himself. Ruth said, "I'd rather work alone."

As can readily be seen, the *Dragnet* activity served more than the purpose for which it was originally created.

Sometimes plans are made for acquainting all pupils new to the school with the extracurricular activities available to them. In one school, tables are arranged in the gymnasium, each bearing the name of a club or special activity. Two or three members are seated at each table to answer the questions of the newcomers as they circulate around the room. This is preceded by a short program presented by the various clubs demonstrating activities characteristic of their particular group. If there has been no school-planned orientation to the extracurricular activities, some effort should be made in the classroom to bring clubs and athletic activities to the attention of the pupils. It is vital to build a "we" feeling in the class, but in addition they should be helped to see that "we" are a part of a larger whole, namely the entire school with all its activities.

Again, a bulletin board display can serve as a springboard for action. Pictures of club groups and activities, athletic groups and their activities, cut from an old yearbook are attractive and exciting. The heading might read: *Which Would You Like to Know About?* Those activities for which no pictures are available may be listed in large print at one side of the board, perhaps headed: *Here Are Some More.* The class discussion of the contents of the board starts with a sharing of the information pupils already have about the clubs and athletic activities. There will be many about which they know little or nothing and about which they would like to know more. If a school has a large number of extracurricular activities, there will probably not be enough class time for all of them. The class and teacher together select the six or seven in which the majority of the pupils are interested. The teacher will, of course, help individuals find information concerning any club, even if it is not one of those selected by the class.

The mechanics of selection can be handled by preparing a typed list of all clubs, which is passed from pupil to pupil and on which each checks his one or two first choices. Another method is to ask each pupil to write his choices on a slip of paper. These are then compiled into a single list. A third method is to name each club in turn, asking pupils to vote for their two choices by a show of hands. The votes are counted for each club and those receiving most votes are selected.

After the activities about which the class wishes information have been selected, ways of getting the information wanted are considered. The class might invite club representatives to come into the room during the class period and tell about the clubs of which they are members. Or, perhaps they would prefer to select committees that would report back to the class later.

During the discussion of these possible methods it becomes clear that letters of invitation will have to be written if the first method is selected, or letters requesting interviews if the second. When the decision has been made as to which method of getting information is to be used, the class turns to the matter of writing letters.

This task furnishes another experience in working together in groups. The class is divided into small groups, each of which has the responsibility for writing a letter to one club. The possible contents of such letters are decided upon by the class and written on the board. A sample list is as follows:

1. Who we are
2. What we want to know
3. Why we want to know these things
4. When our class meets
5. Where the person can send an answer

A ninth-grade teacher, using the method described above, went one step farther. When arrangements had been made for various club representatives to visit the class, she helped each letter-writing group to select one of its members to serve as host or hostess to the person invited. The host or hostess met the representative at the door, introduced him to the class, and as he left, thanked him on behalf of the class for taking time to come.

Orientation of teacher to pupils

In order to be of help to pupils in developing the ability to work together, a teacher needs to know as much as possible about each child's beliefs and prejudices, about his interests and values. He needs to know how the pupil reacts emotionally to different situations, what his physical condition is, and how well he handles himself socially. He needs to know and understand the home life out of which these characteristics grew. It is as important to know about these matters as about the child's intellectual abilities. Such knowledge does not come overnight nor as the result of the use of any one technique. It is of slow growth and requires continuous search on the part of the teacher. Some of it comes from the pupil's records, some of it from the observation of his reactions in many different situations, some of it from specifically planned techniques, and some from direct conversation with the child himself. Each bit of information added to that already obtained gives a teacher better understanding of the child's daily behavior and a better chance to serve wisely as a guide and helper.

School records. School records vary from system to system, some being complete cumulative reports from the time the pupil entered school to the present. Others are meager records of attendance and scholastic achievement. However, in almost any system it is possible to obtain certain basic facts about each pupil.

1. What is his chronological age and how does it compare with that of his classmates?

2. What is his intelligence rating?

3. How does his reading ability compare with his chronological age?

4. How does his reading ability compare with that of his classmates?

5. Where does he stand with respect to mathematical aptitude? Mechanical aptitude? Clerical aptitude? Other special abilities?

6. What has been his record of scholastic achievements? What were his strong points? What were his weak points?

7. What has been his health pattern? What illnesses has he had? Are hearing and vision normal?

8. Have previous teachers recorded any helpful information?

Such data should be assembled by the teacher for each pupil in the class in order that it may be at hand when needed. By themselves the answers to such questions are not sufficient to give a very complete picture of an individual. They are, however, a good place to start.

Observation. Every teacher "observes" his class every day. Unfortunately, he only too often does not take the time to record these observations. True, no teacher can both teach and record every occurrence that takes place in his room, nor can he record an item for every child every day. He can, however, learn to be selective and, with a small pad at hand, jot down a few notes each day on those behaviors that seem significant.

First observations of a class are usually quite general and relate to the reactions of the class as a whole. Teachers' comments to one another about new classes are in this vein at the close of the first day of a semester:

TEACHER A

My class seemed very alert and anxious to get underway.

TEACHER B

Mine certainly wasn't. They just sat. I tried to be friendly and welcome them, but there was no response.

TEACHER A

Mine looked pleasant and smiled as they went out or said good-bye as they passed me.

TEACHER C

That new class of mine is a wild bunch. I'll have my hands full, I know.

TEACHER B

Well, even though there was no response to my welcoming efforts, mine certainly followed directions well in making out their cards and information sheets. They were slow but they did the job.

Even in the first few days, however, individual pupils begin to stand out. There is the boy who on the first day asks a dozen questions; the girl who, during the *Howdy tag* activity, remains in her seat and lets everyone else come to her instead of joining the others in going from person to person; the one who quickly looks away when you smile at her in the hall. Then there is the girl who enters into the first group activity so wholeheartedly, and the boy who says he doesn't want to be called Dick anymore, but prefers Richard. These are not profound observations, but they should be recorded, for they are possible clues to understanding the unknown personalities in this class.

Too often a teacher continues to be satisfied with generalized judgments about the class as a whole that obscure the individuals within it. "When we show films my class explodes." Does the *whole* class explode? Or are there certain individuals who make it seem as though the entire class has burst apart at the seams?

"My class is wonderful on free-reading days. Everyone enjoys it." Does *everyone* enjoy it really? How about Joe, who quietly holds a book in front of him but never turns a page? Or Mary, who changes books every ten or fifteen minutes? Or Bill, who is reading a book but rubs his eyes until they are red?

Such items should be recorded under the name of the individual together with the date of occurrence. It is not long before a series of items has been recorded for a number of boys and girls. Samples from several such records follow:

GARY DAYTON

September 13:

First free-reading day. Made no effort to find a book. Sat in his seat and looked out of the window. 15 minutes later went to book tables, picked up three or four, thumbed them, yawned, looked out of window. At 3:35 (30 minutes after class had started) Gary took a book and went to his seat. Did not read.

September 19:

During small group work Gary did not take part. Just sat and looked around.

September 22:

In small random group, Gary was the only boy in a group of girls. He refused to move his seat in close enough to the other members to participate when they asked him to join them. Later I suggested that he move in closer. Nothing happened.

September 28:

Free-reading day. Spent twenty minutes thumbing books. Took one on F.B.I. to his seat. Read steadily all the rest of the period. Took the book home.

September 30:

Brought the F.B.I. book back. Said he liked it. Brought in samples of his own fingerprints, which he had made at home to see how they compared with those in the book.

TOM WEST

September 15:

Tom stammers but makes an effort to participate. Long pauses between groups of words.

October 3:

Volunteered to copy a page of material needed by the class on the board.

October 4:

Took an active part in small group discussion—as near as I could tell—without stammering.

October 9:

I noticed that he squints when he reads things on the board, but when I asked him whether he could see the board all right he was very emphatic in his "Yes." (I must watch and check on his health record.)

October 10:

Checked health record. Vision normal.

November 14:

I met Tom's father at Parent Night meeting. He said, "I suppose you have your hands full with that boy of mine." I said, "Tom is one of the finest boys I've ever had." His father said, "Well, with that speech trouble he's sure hard to handle." (I had better make a home visit.)

The question that is so frequently asked is "What should I record?" For the teacher attempting to keep anecdotal records[1] on a non-research level the answer is to record what a child does in many different situations—in the library, during a class discussion, in a small group, in the hall, before class, after class, in an audience situation—not everything, of course, and not all pupils every day, for that is quite impossible. It may become clear that

---

[1] Helpful material on making anecdotal records may be found in the following:
Association for Supervision and Curriculum Development, *Fostering Mental Health in our Schools,* 1950 Yearbook (Washington, D.C.: The National Education Association, 1950), pp. 184–202.

The Staff of the Division on Child Development and Teacher Personnel, *Helping Teachers Understand Children* (Washington, D.C.: American Council on Education, 1945), pp. 1–41.

more extensive records on certain individuals are needed. This may become apparent not only through observation of behavior that attracts attention but also from the blank page under a child's name in the observation records. An example of this is the following:

BILL SMITH

September 8:

No smile during his introduction of the person he had interviewed. Spoke quietly without looking at anyone.

October 25:

I suddenly realized that I have been completely unaware of Bill day after day. It is as though he were not present.

A month and a half had elapsed with no item recorded for Bill. Rather intensive observation was needed here.

Questionnaire. One of the simplest methods of obtaining background information about boys and girls is the use of a questionnaire. The following sample is long, but does not actually take a great deal of time to answer. It might be broken into sections such as those questions dealing with the child himself, those dealing with the family pattern, and those dealing with the home. These could be duplicated separately and be given on different days.

Name_____ Birth Date_____ Grade_____

1. I live with:

   a. my parents_____   e. my stepmother_____
   b. my mother_____   f. my stepfather_____
   c. my father_____   g. my guardian_____
   d. my grandparents_____   h. others_____

2. Names of schools I have attended:

   a. _____
   b. _____
   c. _____
   d. _____
   e. _____

3. I have a job.

   a. Yes_____
   b. No_____

4. The type of work I do is: _____

---

5. I like the work I do.
    a. Yes _____
    b. No _____

6. I work an average of _____ hours each week.

7. My income from my job averages each week approximately:
    a. between 5 and 10 dollars _____
    b. between 10 and 15 dollars _____
    c. between 15 and 20 dollars _____
    d. more than 20 dollars _____

8. My allowance from my family is:
    a. _____ per week
    b. None _____

9. Names of clubs or organizations I belong to outside of school are:
    a. _____
    b. _____
    c. _____
    d. _____

10. Names of clubs or organizations I belong to in school are:
    a. _____
    b. _____
    c. _____
    d. _____

11. I play:
    a. tennis _____   f. baseball _____
    b. basketball _____   g. hockey _____
    c. golf _____   h. swim _____
    d. track _____   i. others _____
    e. football _____   _____

12. I belong to an organized team.
    a. Yes _____
    b. No _____

13. The average amount of time I spend in these sports per week is _____ hours.

14. Outside of sports I enjoy the following hobbies:
   a. _____
   b. _____
   c. _____
   d. _____

15. On the average I attend _____ movies per week.

16. I spent last summer at:

   a. working _____   f. cottage _____
   b. summer school _____   g. home _____
   c. camp _____   h. others _____
   d. church school _____   _____
   e. travel _____   _____

17. My future plans include completing:
   a. 10th grade _____   d. business school _____
   b. 11th grade _____   e. college _____
   c. 12th grade _____   f. others _____

18. The type of work I hope to follow when I leave school is _____

_____

19. I was born in _____

20. My father was born in _____

21. My mother was born in _____

22. Both of my parents are living.
   a. Yes _____
   b. No _____

23. If the answer to #22 is yes, my parents are:
   a. living together _____
   b. separated _____
   c. divorced _____

24. Besides English we speak _____ at home.

25. My father has completed:
   a. less than the 8th grade _____   c. high school _____
   b. 8th grade _____   d. college _____

26. My mother has completed:
   a. less than the 8th grade _____   c. high school _____
   b. 8th grade _____   d. college _____

27. During the past five years we have moved ——— times.

28. Our home is:
    a. owned by us _____
    b. rented by us _____

29. We live in:
    a. single home _____   d. rooming house _____
    b. two family flat_____   e. other_____
    c. apartment house _____

30. We have _____ rooms in our home.

31. There are _____ people living in our home.

32. The people living in our home include:
    a. parents_____   d. grandparents _____
    b. brothers _____   e. relatives _____
    c. sisters _____   f. roomers _____

33. The number of children in our family is _____

34. My father works at _____

35. The type of work he does is _____

36. My mother works at _____

37. The type of work she does is _____

38. We have the following electrical appliances in our home:
    a. radio _____   h. television_____
    b. refrigerator _____   i. garbage disposal _____
    c. automatic washer _____   j. air conditioner _____
    d. automatic dryer_____   k. dehumidifier _____
    e. iron·_____   l. others_____
    f. vacuum cleaner_____   _____
    g. deep freeze _____   _____

39. My family has ——— automobile(s).

40. I usually eat dinner with:
    a. both parents _____   d. whole family_____
    b. one parent_____   e. by myself _____
    c. brothers and sisters _____

41. I usually eat breakfast with:
    a. both parents·_____   d. whole family _____
    b. one parent _____   e. by myself _____
    c. brother and sisters_____   f. I don't eat breakfast_____

42. On Sundays I attend:
    a. church _____
    b. Sunday school _____
    c. both church and Sunday school_____
    d. I do not attend _____

43. We subscribe regularly to the following newspapers:
    a. _____
    b. _____
    c. _____

44. We subscribe regularly to the following magazines:
    a. _____
    b. _____
    c. _____

45. My parents use a library card.
    a. Yes_____
    b. No _____

46. I use a library card.
    a. Yes_____
    b. No _____

47. My parents often attend:
    a. concerts _____
    b. stage plays _____
    c. lectures_____
    d. art exhibits _____
    e. operas _____

48. Other interests of my parents are:
    a. cards_____
    b. bowling _____
    c. bingo _____
    d. billiards, pool_____
    e. movies_____
    f. ball games _____
    g. races (horse, auto)_____
    h. others_____
       _____
       _____

49. I have taken trips with my family to:
    a. _____
    b. _____
    c. _____
    d. _____

50. List the names of your brothers and sisters who live at home in
    the order of their ages. Include yourself in the list.

	Name	Age
a.	_____	_____
b.	_____	_____
c.	_____	_____
d.	_____	_____
e.	_____	_____
f.	_____	_____
g.	_____	_____

Items that are pertinent in a certain community may be substituted, some may be added, or some may be deleted. There is no magic in a particular set of questions. The point is to obtain as much information as possible.

Another form that has been developed and used over a period of years is much simpler. It is mimeographed on 5 by 8 inch cards, half on one side and half on the other, and can largely be filled out by the pupils.

Name _____ Address _____ School _____

Birthdate _____ Sex ___ Age ____ Telephone _____ Course _____

Name: Father _____ Mother _____

Ages: Sisters _____ Brothers _____

Other Occupants in Home _____

Birthplace: Father _____ Mother _____ Child _____

Occupation: Father _____ Mother _____ Child _____

Other Schools Attended: _____

Special Interests: _____

Special Achievements: _____

Clubs—Extracurricular: _____

Have participated in: Band _____ Orchestra _____ Glee Club _____
Drama _____ Others _____

Jobs Held: _____

Extensive Trips: _____

Serious illnesses you have had: _____

_____

Additional information: _____

Autobiography. In addition to the questionnaire method of collecting information there are many helpful techniques that may be used to give the teacher a more complete understanding of his pupils. One that is frequently used is the autobiography. This should not be asked for until a truly friendly relationship has been established between pupils and teacher. It is usually well to let a month or more elapse before asking a class to do this, since if done too soon only surface facts will be recorded.

Such an assignment should be written in a situation as free from tension and pressure as possible. Boys and girls must feel free to express their feelings, to tell about the things that have been important to them in their lives. To get really spontaneous and worth-while data it has always seemed to the writer that an autobiography should not be considered an English assignment, a "composition," which is to be corrected and red-penciled and graded. Pupils should be urged to do a careful piece of work, but they should know before writing it that its worth is not to be judged by its sentence structure but by its contents. They should know that its purpose is to help the teacher become better acquainted with them in order that he may be of more help to them during the year. Boys and girls should also know that whatever is told in the autobiography will be held in strictest confidence. Under no circumstances should this be violated.

To help pupils in planning such a piece of work, an outline of its contents can be worked out by the class. A sample outline developed by a ninth-grade class included the following items:

1. Divide description into the following parts:
   a. From birth to five years
   b. From five years to ten years
   c. From ten years to now
2. Things to be included:
   a. Things I remember or have been told about where I lived
   b. Things I remember or have been told about school
   c. Special things I remember or have been told about the kind of person I was or things I did

d. Things I did that I especially enjoyed or especially disliked
e. Who my friends were
f. Activities that I took part in
g. Pets I had
h. My hobbies
i. Trips I took
j. My family

In order that boys and girls might know that their papers had been read, an eighth-grade teacher wrote a short letter to each pupil responding to various items recorded in the autobiography.

Writings of pupil. Much light is shed on a pupil's thinking, his attitudes, beliefs, and values by studying other papers he writes. If the topics he is asked to write about are within his world and he has developed a trust in his teacher, he will express his feelings quite honestly. A series of five or six short papers, spaced at one- or two-week intervals, preferably no more than a page in length, is better than one or two that are required to be much longer. Titles that frequently yield much in the way of information about the writers have been listed by a ninth-grade teacher. From this list, shown below, he selects those that seem to him would be most suitable for shedding light on the values and beliefs of the members of his class.

1. If I Found Ten Dollars
2. The Person I Admire Most
3. Things I Like and Don't Like About School
4. What I Like to Do in My Spare Time
5. Is Reading Fun?
6. How I Spent Yesterday
7. How I Would Spend Twenty Dollars
8. What I Like to Do Least Each Day
9. My Best Day Last Week
10. My Worst Day Last Week
11. The Funniest Thing That Ever Happened
12. A Boy I Know Skipped School
13. When I Grow Up
14. Three Things I Wish For Most

Completing a short story. A technique that is intended to give the teacher further insight into the attitudes and feelings of boys and girls is initiated by presenting the beginning of a story.[2] Pupils are asked to complete the story in any way they wish. Many teachers have used this device, building their own situations to suit their specific needs. An example of such an unfinished story is as follows:

1. Bill was waiting for the bus to take him to school. He did not look very happy as he stood there kicking stones out into the road. A neighbor, standing near him, said, "What's the matter, Bill?"

Bill looked up scowling and said, "If a fellow just didn't have to go to school."

What made Bill feel like this?

This story was finished in the following manner by two ninth-graders. Both reactions proved to be definite leads to the personal problems of the two children involved.

a. Maybe Bill is not as smart as his classmates and he can't keep up with them. And maybe when he gets his report card his parents keep him in all the time because of the marks he got. And yet he tries his hardest.

b. Bill doesn't like school because he is very shy and the boys don't talk to him. When anyone comes near him he turns and walks away. The reason he turns away is that he gets all flustered and scared when he meets people. But he wants to have friends.

Other story beginnings are:

2. As Mary came out of the store with a big bag of groceries in her arms, a girl who was in a hurry to enter, bumped her arm and the bag crashed to the ground. The girl _____

3. Bill had a date and wanted to use his brother Jim's car. He had told Sue that he would be at her home with the car at 8 o'clock. When Jim came home he said that he needed the car himself. Bill was angry and _____

---

2 Technique developed by Horace Mann-Lincoln Institute of School Experimentation, Teachers College, Columbia University.

4. Karen usually had her homework ready on time, but last night there had been a math assignment and a long history assignment. Her mother and father had gone out for the evening and she had had to put her two sisters to bed. She completed the history work but not the math. When she came to school she _____

A similar technique uses pictures to stimulate reactions. This, too, has been developed by the Horace Mann-Lincoln Institute of School Experimentation; the pictures, planned for special purposes, were posed for and photographed. However, it is quite possible to select magazine pictures that will serve a similar purpose. Such a picture should be mounted on background paper and should either be large enough to be seen by all or should be shown by means of an opaque projector. Depending, of course, upon the subject, the directions might be to tell the story of what is happening in the picture, to tell what the people are saying to one another, what one person is thinking, or what you would do in this situation.

Having boys and girls keep diaries of their activities during a week end, Saturday and Sunday, is another method of collecting data. They record exactly how, and where, and with whom they spend their time during the two days.

If a class remains with the same teacher over a period of several semesters, it is necessary to devise some method of keeping up to date on the activities, plans, thoughts, and feelings that are important to each member. It is not enough to have at hand the data accumulated at the time each pupil first entered the class. He has changed in many ways in the course of a year. Some of these changes are obvious, of course, but many are not.

A simple method that has been of great value has been the maintenance of a personal folder for each pupil. Some time during the first semester each pupil writes as completely as possible on each of the following four topics:

1. My Autobiography
2. My Plans for the Future
3. My Spare-Time Activities
4. Myself as I See Myself

These papers are placed in the folder, serving as a source of information as the teacher needs it. Toward the end of the year, time is set aside for bringing these up to date. A paragraph is added to each, indicating any changes that have taken place. If there has been no change, the pupil makes a statement to this effect. The paragraph is dated. The same procedure is followed at the end of each succeeding semester. Other kinds of data may be included in such a file as well, perhaps an essay dealing with the pupil's feelings about school.

Another is a mimeographed sheet with the heading, *As I See Myself in Class.* The page is divided into three sections, with space for writing under the first two. The three points to be considered are:

1. Things I often do to help our class.
2. Things I often do to hinder class progress.
3. The way I see myself in class:
   _____ Very helpful almost always
   _____ Quite helpful many times
   _____ Helpful some of the time
   _____ Seldom helpful
   _____ Never helpful

This, too, is dated, and a new one completed each semester.

Pupils take a tremendous interest in the contents of their files. They are always amazed at the changes that have taken place since the last writing and are eager to bring the records up to date. Such comments as these are frequently heard: "How could I have been so silly!" "I had forgotten that I felt like that." "I certainly didn't know where I was going last year at this time." "I think I've grown up a lot since the last time we looked at these."

An eleventh-grade teacher who had had the same pupils for several years used another method to bring her information about her boys and girls up to date. As one part of this program she asked them to answer the following question. In presenting it she read it aloud to them, discussing its points as she moved along.

Within each of us there are many desires, many things we wish we were able to do that we feel we are incapable of. There are many things, too, that we wish we knew about, because we feel that knowing them would make our lives more satisfying to us. We seldom tell people about these things because we are afraid others will laugh at us. Perhaps we think they are such little things that we hate to ask about them. Perhaps they are so deep within us that it is hard to find words for them.

Yet these desires are important parts of our lives, and we keep on looking for answers to them.

If it were possible for you to *learn to do* or to *know* any four things this semester, what would be of the most importance and value to you? These may have to do with *any thing* or *any persons* or perhaps have to do with *yourself*.

Explain what you mean by each statement as carefully and fully as you can.

Responses to this covered a wide range and were not always limited to things they would like to learn to do or know. A few of the items listed were as follows:

1. I'd like to get a steady girl friend.
2. I would like to have the knowledge to be a good construction worker, such as a brick layer, so I could help my dad.
3. I wish I could carve a big statue out of wood.
4. I would like very much to know how to make a happy home, one where the father and mother do not argue constantly and where the children are raised in love. I want to know this so I will not make the same mistakes as my parents.
5. I would like to have both a mother and a father, but as it is I have just my mother. I wouldn't want to trade or anything. I just would like to have both a father and a mother to live with.
6. Something that I'd like to know is why I am afraid to face the world. I'm afraid to go out and meet different people. How can I overcome this? I am not shy.

Conferences. As early in the semester as possible, the teacher should find time to talk individually with each boy and girl. Too often conferences are held only at such times as a pupil is in difficulties instead of serving as a friendly move on the part of the teacher toward better understanding of a pupil's interests and problems. What can be talked about? His feelings about his school; something he has done well in class; a question he has asked; a paper he has written on "The Funniest Thing That Ever Happened"; his plans for the future; his friends; his hobbies; other classes he is enjoying; an interesting point he made in his autobiography—*anything* will start the ball rolling. There will probably be more serious points that the teacher will want to discuss, questions he will want to ask, but the initial step is to make the pupil feel at ease and to realize that he and his welfare are important and of concern to the teacher.

And what can be learned through such conferences? It is the extra item, the information that is seldom recorded on a paper-and-pencil questionnaire that comes to light during a friendly talk with a boy or girl. Through conferences with his tenth-grade pupils, a teacher added to his information about several of them as follows:

He knew that Mary's mother had died two years previously and that she was the oldest of three children. But through talking with her he discovered that Mary kept the house in order, cooked the meals, and managed her younger sisters during the daytime. He also learned that she idolized her father and worked hard so that he would see that they did not need a stepmother.

Steve's papers were unusually well written, but only in talking with him did the teacher discover that Steve's real joy was writing poetry.

Nick's records showed that his school grades were low. They also showed that he was the younger of two boys. But the records could not show the feeling of inadequacy and the resentment that burned in Nick each time a teacher or his parents compared his brother's successes with his own failures. This was discovered through the conference.

Home visits. The establishment of a good relationship between the teacher and the home will be considered in Chapter 8. Methods of initiating home visits and techniques of carrying them out will be examined. But it would be remiss not to indicate its importance at this time, since contact with the home is a further means of obtaining information that will be helpful in working with a pupil. Whenever it is possible, a visit to each home should be made, for it is only through such visits that the background of a child really comes alive. His responses to written and oral questioning give a picture that is never really accurate or complete. Such visits not only clarify differences in cultural and economic background between the pupils in the class, but help a teacher to estimate to a degree how and why a child's values and attitudes differ from his own. Too frequently a teacher's expectations and aspirations for his pupils are based on his own cultural and economic standing rather than on that of the boys and girls he is teaching.

Group social patterns. A knowledge of the peer-relationships of the boys and girls constituting a given class is of vital importance to the teacher. It cannot be accurately gauged by observation alone. Recently the writer listed for her own interest the names of the boys and girls in her eleventh-grade class whom she considered to be outstanding leaders, that is, pupils who influenced the thinking of the group. She then asked class members to name those pupils whom they considered to be their leaders using the same definition of a leader. The results were enlightening. The teacher had listed nine pupils. Of these nine, four were not named by anyone in the class. Of the eight listed by more than half of the class as leaders, five were also on the teacher's list. The other three were individuals whom the teacher had not even vaguely suspected as having influence on the class.

The Social Distance Scale[3] is one means of discovering the feelings of boys and girls toward one another, or the general social structure of a class. Pupils indicate their feelings toward each of their fellow classmates under one of five headings:

---

[3] E. S. Bogardus, "A Social Distance Scale," *Sociology and Social Research,* Vol. 17, 1933, pp. 265–271.

Ruth Cunningham and Associates, *Understanding Group Behavior of Boys and Girls* (New York: Bureau of Publications, Teachers College, Columbia University, 1951), pp. 171–174.

1. Would like to have him as one of my best friends.
2. Would like to have him in my group but not as a close friend.
3. Would like to be with him once in a while but not often or for long at a time.
4. Don't mind his being in our room but I don't want to have anything to do with him.
5. Wish he weren't in our room.

From the responses it is possible to determine the degree to which each individual is accepted by the group and, in turn, the degree to which he accepts others.

A sociogram[4] is a further means of making the social structure of the class observable. As was indicated previously, adults are frequently unable to see accurately the interrelationships that exist in a class of thirty-five teen-agers. The girl who is everything that a teacher could wish for, responsive, friendly to the teacher, always completes the tasks assigned, and has many good ideas, may well be without friends in her peer group. The boy who is an endless nuisance to the teacher may be a very popular individual with his classmates. A sociogram will indicate a variety of such situations. It will point out the popular members of the class, the *stars*. It will also indicate the pupils who are not selected as friends by any member of the class, the *isolates*. It will show which pupils are bound together in *subgroups* within the class, or perhaps two people who have formed a mutual friendship to the exclusion of all others.

Sociograms may be constructed in response to a variety of questions. A "friendship chart" uses the question: *Which people do you consider as your best friends in this class?* Others may be made on the basis of such questions as: *Which boys and girls would you like to work with? Sit with? Go to the movies with?*

4 Ruth Cunningham and Associates, *Understanding Group Behavior of Boys and Girls.* (New York: Bureau of Publications, Teachers College, Columbia University, 1951), pp. 154–171.

Helen Hall Jennings and Associates, *Sociometry in Group Relations.* (Washington, D.C.: American Council on Education, 1948), pp. 31–37.

J. L. Moreno and Helen H. Jennings, "Sociometric Control Studies of Grouping and Regrouping," *Sociometry Monographs,* No. 7. Beacon House, 1947, pp. 20–29.

The number to be named is usually limited to three. Pupils should feel free to name less than three if they wish, however.

Such data, assembled into chart form, presents a picture of the structure of the class at the time and serves as a basis not only for understanding the relationships between class members, but also as a direction signal to the teacher, pointing out the needs for special help and guidance.

The class structure, however, is not static, but shifts relatively frequently. For this reason it is well to repeat the procedure later in the year. By doing this it is possible to discover whether the techniques used to bring an isolate into a better relationship with his classmates have been successful; whether the stars have remained stars; what shifts have taken place in the subgroupings; whether some pupils have lost their positions in the class and in turn, become isolates. The new sociogram then becomes a lead to further assistance to the class as a whole and to its members individually.

Standardized tests. A variety of standardized tests are available, the results of which will assist the teacher in obtaining a better understanding of the interests, problems, and personalities of his pupils. Among these are the *SRA Youth Inventory,* the *Kuder Preference List,*[5] the *Mooney Problem Check List,*[6] and the *California Test of Personality.*[7] To serve the purpose of gaining insight into a child's feelings and problems the total score on such a test is frequently of much less value than an analysis of the individual responses he has made to the test items. It is no great help to a teacher to know that the pupil's score on a personality test places him in the 20th percentile. It is helpful, however, to know that he feels that people do not think he has good ideas, that people are not interested in him, that most people can do things better than he can, and that folks do not seem to think he will be a success. These may explain to some extent his behavior in the

---

[5] Science Research Associates, 57 West Grand Avenue, Chicago, Illinois.

[6] The Bureau of Educational Research, Ohio State University, Columbus, Ohio.

[7] California Test Bureau, 5916 Hollywood Boulevard, Los Angeles, California.

classroom. These are clues to the direction in which a teacher can move.

Tests of this nature, like the autobiography and the sociogram, should not be used until good rapport has been established between pupils and teacher. If given before this point has been reached, many boys and girls will give the answers they think the teacher wants. The tests should not be used until the teacher is sure that pupils feel "safe" to answer as they truly feel, that is, until the test presents no threat.

Orientation to the course

A phase of orientation only too frequently by-passed in the rush of getting a class under way is that of orientation to the course itself, its purposes, its over-all procedures, and its limits. The initial approach should be made during the first day or two, even though much that is said at this time will not be remembered. Continuous effort must be made throughout the year to help pupils become increasingly aware of the things they are trying to achieve in the class. Many of the problems that arise are due to the fact that pupils have lost their sense of direction, and teachers have failed to help them to reorient themselves.

The initial orientation to the course will probably involve no more than a brief explanation of the purposes for which the class is organized. If there are no limitations in terms of required subject matter to be covered, the teacher might say:

One of the most important things you will learn to do in this class is to work with other people in solving problems. These will be problems that you feel are important. You will help in choosing them and in deciding how you will study them. The class will often divide into small groups, and each group will study a different part of the problem.

Working with other people and solving common problems is something that everyone living in a democracy must be able to do. We used to think that such things could be learned from a book, but now we know that we need a chance to practice them if we are really going to learn to do them. So, in this class you are going to practice methods of working that are useful in democratic living.

An introduction, of course, must fit the actual situation. If there are certain prescribed limits, such as the requirement of staying within the field of American history, or if there are certain units that must be covered, this information should be included in the introduction. To the preceding explanation the teacher would for example, then add words to this effect:

In addition to the problems that you select for yourselves, there are two areas of subject matter that you are required to study this semester. These are *World Geography* and *Natural Resources of Our State*. However, you will help decide how the class is going to study these. It would be a good idea for each of you to be thinking about this and deciding what you would like to know about each of these subjects.

The initial orientation may well be accompanied by a mimeographed page giving relatively the same data as has been stated above. Pupils should be asked to take these to their parents since they may have difficulty explaining what the course is about. This is especially important when the course goes under the title of general education, core, basic living, or any other term not known to parents.

There are several films available that can be helpful in further orientation of a class to the types of procedure that are possible in a democratically functioning class. The film, *Practicing Democracy in the Classroom*,[8] and the filmstrip, *A Core Curriculum Class in Action*,[9] both have a wealth of suggestions. In addition to such films, orientation material can be developed by a creative teacher. A junior high school core teacher who was interested in photography took pictures of class activities each year. These were converted into slides and used with later classes. Black and white enlargements serve many bulletin board needs both at the orientation period and throughout the semester. These are all used, however, to best advantage at a later time, preferably at the time the class is planning its organization.

---

[8] Encyclopedia Britannica Films, Incorporated.
[9] Audio-Visual Utilization Center, Wayne State University, Detroit.

Conclusion

Orientation is a continuous and on-going process, never wholly completed, since there are always changed situations to become oriented to, as long as class and teacher remain together. The time devoted to specific, initial activities in this area will, however, not exceed two weeks with most classes. Some activities, for example the writing of an autobiography, the making of a sociogram, or taking a personality test, will not be a part of the two-week program, but will be carried out at considerably later dates. There are others, such as responding to incomplete stories, conferences, or home visits that will be spread throughout the semester.

Orientation activities should be selected with care, thought being given to such items as the age and sophistication of the class members, the degree of their acquaintance with one another, and their knowledge of the school and its activities. With a class new to the school, activities should be selected in each of the four phases of orientation—pupil to teacher, pupil to pupil, pupil to school, and pupil to course. For pupils who have been in the school previously it is possible to omit orientation to the school. It may or may not be possible to omit orientation of pupils to one another depending upon how well they are acquainted with one another. However, the orientation of the pupil to the teacher, and the teacher to the pupil, as well as orientation to the purposes and procedures of the course, should be as carefully covered as with a new class. A well-planned period of orientation, with activities selected to meet the needs of the class, is a firm foundation on which to build.

3

Working in Small Groups

THE ACTIVITIES OF SMALL GROUPS HAVE BEEN RE-
ferred to in the previous chapter a number of times. Such groups,
in many places called committees, have come to be an accepted
part of democratically functioning classrooms. The present
chapter is concerned with procedures that are helpful in developing the skills needed in working together in such groups. The
problem-solving aspects of the activities—the selection of a problem, planning for its solution, collecting and assembling data,
presenting such data to the class—will be considered in later
chapters.

The group skills and problem-solving abilities actually develop
together, the former serving as a means for improving the latter.
It is not possible to set aside a certain number of weeks to be devoted to the learning of group skills *per se,* and then expect them
to function when needed. They must be learned little by little in
relation to solving the problems with which pupils are concerned.
With the exception of the initiating steps, the techniques described in this chapter apply to no particular time in the year, but
are used as it becomes clear that the pupils need help in understanding and developing certain aspects of the process of working
in groups in order that they may function more effectively.

If small-group procedure is to have value, it is necessary to do
more than merely seat a group of five or six pupils together and
expect that some kind of magic will bring the desired results.

Working in a small group will have value for its members only when teacher and pupils are clearly aware of the purposes for which the group technique is being used, and if they develop increasingly greater understanding of the interpersonal relationships involved in working in such a situation.

Group work is not a cure-all or an end in itself, but is a procedure that should be used when it meets the needs of a given situation. It is not a technique to be used every day and for everything. It must further be recognized that boys and girls need continuous help in learning *how* to work in groups, and that growth in ability to work with other people is a very slow, but rewarding, process.

Reasons for using small group procedure

Let us consider some of the major purposes for using small groups in a classroom. The purpose that pupils recognize most readily is that such procedure is a means of solving a problem more thoroughly than any one individual can do by himself. A problem such as *How well is Detroit meeting the recreational needs of youth?* has many facets, and boys and girls quickly see that no one person can obtain all the information needed in the time available. The logical solution is a division of labor.

Without question, a second important reason for using small-group procedure is to give pupils experience and practice in solving problems together. This means that, confronted with a question to which they wish to find an answer, a group of pupils will have an opportunity to develop the skills and techniques needed to solve the problem cooperatively. This is more than a knowledge of the steps to be followed in the scientific solution of a problem. It also involves more than having each member assume responsibility for a portion of the work and then proceeding individually from this point on. It is much more than voting and accepting the will of the majority. It includes the development of such skills as the ability to share one's ideas and experiences with a group, a willingness to consider with an open mind the ideas of others, a real concern for the beliefs of the minority, an ability to recognize and subordinate one's own prejudices and biases, and an attempt to consider each contribution as it affects the problem. Properly viewed, the process demands recognition of the personal worth of each member of the group and of each individual's responsibility in the work of solving a common problem.

A third purpose in using small group procedure is to give opportunity for the personal involvement of every pupil in the activities of the class. Through this personal involvement the members of a class are brought into closer and more realistic relationship with their classmates. The social experiences of each individual are thus broadened, giving him greater opportunity to find truly congenial friends among his classmates as well as to develop skills for adjusting comfortably to a wide variety of people. It increases his range of ideas, since each group with which he has contact offers him the results of new and different experiences. These ideas may become a part of his own thinking and being in a very real sense when he has formed a personal bond between himself and his group-mates that is both intellectual and emotional.

The closer relationship resulting from small-group work produces a more closely knit class. As its members achieve better understanding of one another through working in many different small groups, they become welded together, forming a unit ready to move ahead as a whole. Evidence of this is given in the following evaluation written by a tenth-grader after a semester in a core class in which small-group work was a usual part of class procedure.

I think our class has grown a great deal since September. We are no longer individual pupils with a teacher, but a class and teacher all working together. We are able to get things done faster and smoother than at the beginning. We give more attention to the suggestions of our classmates and take part more freely in class discussions. We are working together now and not against each other.

Class unity is evident also in the demand for class social activities outside of school, such as parties, picnics, and hikes. A further indication of the feeling of "togetherness" that develops in such classes is found in the numerous reunions that are held by classes that maintain close associations for years after they have left high school. The girls of a core class in a large city high school, graduating in 1949, have come together for a social evening every few months since their graduation, frequently bringing babies and husbands, and always inviting the teacher. As they have said, "We all belong together."

How often should small-group procedure be used?

The question of the frequency with which small groups should be organized depends upon many things. In general, it would be safe to say less frequently at the first of a year in a class that is beginning to function democratically, and more frequently later in the year. For classes that have had no previous experience with this type of procedure, the first attempt at small-group work may not be a very happy experience, but as pupils grow in their ability to handle themselves in the situation, develop a safe and secure feeling about it, they themselves want more of it.

The teacher's own security is also a factor in determining how often small-group procedure should be used. It matters little how long a teacher has taught school, nor for that matter how long he has used democratic techniques. Each class is different, and until he has a fair understanding of the social, emotional, and intellectual patterns of these boys and girls, has sensed their span of attention in relation to certain types of activities, and has learned to plan in accordance with their needs, he should not overdo small-group activities. It is better to have pupils work in groups relatively infrequently at first, and make a careful analysis of what takes place each time, than to overload them with experiences that neither they nor the teacher understand.

Although it is true that small-group activity is one of the best ways we know of helping pupils learn how to work with others, it is not the only way. Small groups should be set in motion only when these will best achieve the particular purpose toward which a class and teacher are working. Only too frequently classes are divided into groups when there is nothing to be gained by so doing. Perhaps a single small committee reporting back to the class at large would be much more worth while, or perhaps a period spent in general class discussion would serve the purpose far better.

There is also no value in spending time in small groups if the question is so simple that a quick consideration by the class will achieve the solution. A question of the choice of a day on which to show a particular film does not require organization of groups. If, however, the problem is relatively complex, one for which as many ideas as possible are needed, it is well to use the small-group technique in order to involve everyone. Where some pupils have shown insecurity and fear of expressing themselves before the class, small groups should be used frequently, since they will usually talk more readily with a few than with many. Each situation needs to be examined carefully before the decision to use small groups is made, and both teacher and class must learn to judge whether this procedure will best serve their needs at any given time.

Methods of grouping

There are various ways in which a class may be divided into small groups. Among those used most frequently are: (1) random grouping, (2) grouping by choice of topics or area of work, (3) grouping by sociometric methods, (4) grouping by free choice of persons, and (5) grouping by teacher or committee. The method used should be determined to a large extent by the purpose for which the groups are organized or by peculiar situations that may exist within a particular class.

Random grouping. Random grouping is an excellent method of dividing a class if the activity is a short-term operation. Let us suppose that the class had just viewed a motion picture film. Previous to showing the picture, the program committee presented several questions for consideration. The class members had jotted down their reactions during the showing and interest was keen. A general class discussion would be possible, of course, but only a small number would be able to participate in the time left in the class period. A more satisfactory method would be to divide the class into groups, thus giving almost all members an opportunity to express their views and to hear those of others. Random grouping is most satisfactory in such a situation, since each group is carrying on exactly the same activity and will be in session for a relatively short time.

The process of random grouping is simple. The chairman or teacher determines the number of groups that seems advisable. If a class consists of 35 pupils, perhaps seven groups of five each would be satisfactory. Starting at one point in the room pupils count off by sevens (the number of groups desired): 1–2–3–4–5–6–7. Then the counting is repeated until each child has a number. All pupils with the number 1 are in the same group, all with the number 2 are in a second group, all with the number 3 in a third group, and so on. The first few times that this method is used it is well to avoid confusion by having all pupils with the number 1 raise their hands or stand, then all with number 2, then 3, until each group has seen its membership. The chairman or teacher then designates the meeting place in the room for each group.

Each time the class is divided on a random basis it is well to start numbering with a different person. Direction of counting should be changed as well, perhaps counting across rows or tables instead of up and down. Unless the direction of counting is changed as well as the person with whom counting is started, the same members will constitute each group each time. It is important that group membership shift, in order that pupils have the opportunity of becoming acquainted with a greater number of their classmates.

Grouping by choice of topics or areas of work. When a number of problems, topics, or sub-topics need to be considered at the same time, the use of a small group working on each is a

logical method. Let us assume that a class has made the decision
to study an area that they have called *What Is Our Community
Like?* They have listed the following as sub-topics, each to be
developed by a separate small group:

1. Recreational facilities
2. Housing conditions
3. Work opportunities
4. School conditions
5. Transportation facilities

In such a situation it is hoped that each child will select an area
that is of concern to him. Indication of choice by hand-raising is
seldom satisfactory, since in this situation a pupil frequently
makes his choice on the basis of acquaintance with those whose
hands are up, rather than by considering the relative appeal of
the different problems.

In order to help boys and girls to make their choices on the
basis of the value and interest to them of the area to be studied, it
is important to plan procedures in such a way that pupils may
see the possibilities of the various problems. If, for example,
there is a choice between five different problems, or five sub-
topics of a single general problem, a teacher's first step should
be to help his class see the ramifications of each. Time should be
taken to consider the questions that might be answered and the
activities that might be carried out under each, in order that
pupils may realize some of the implications.

As an example, let us suppose class members are making a
choice between the five sub-topics listed above. These may be
written in a row across the top of the chalkboard. Under each
are then listed some of the questions that might be answered by
studying this topic, as well as possible activities. Teacher and
pupils both contribute to these lists, no effort being made to
organize the items of any given list or to make them fit together.
This is simply an attempt to see some of the problems that lie
within this area.

A sample list for one topic follows:

RECREATION IN OUR COMMUNITY

Questions:

1. What kinds of recreation are open to teen-agers in our community?
2. Who plans a recreation field?
3. How are recreation fields or community houses paid for?
4. How many people use Chandler Park? the YMCA? the YWCA?
5. How could we get more recreational facilities in this community?
6. How much does a recreation center cost?
7. What other kinds of recreational facilities are there in our community?
8. How much do the churches help?

Possible Activities:

1. Trip to a community house.
2. Write to Recreation Department for information.
3. Make a survey of the use made of a recreation field.
4. Interview someone at the YMCA and at the YWCA.

A similar list is made for each of the other topics. Following this, each pupil writes his choice of an area for study on a sheet of paper, giving his reasons for his selection. It is well to have pupils make both a first and second choice, in order to make it possible to balance the numbers in the groups, although it is certainly not necessary to have an equal number in each group. Organization of groups may then be made by a committee of pupils, or by the teacher, and reported back to the class on the following day.

Sociometric grouping. Many teachers prefer to divide a class into groups on a sociometric basis. It is an especially good method to use with an insecure class, possibly one in which a number of boys and girls need the safety of having at least one person whom they know in their group. To a large extent, however, this method precludes selection of a particular topic or problem. It is excellent when all groups work on a common problem.

The technique for using this method is to ask each child to list, perhaps on a 3 by 5 inch card, three pupils with whom he would like to work. The promise should be made and kept that each child will be in a group with at least one of the three he has listed. Groups are then arranged by the teacher, using the data supplied on the cards. Whenever this method is repeated, new choices of working companions are made in the same manner. It is important that each set of cards be filed for comparison with later choices. If, by chance, choices remain very much the same a second time, it is well to plan an activity in which random grouping is used in order that pupils may become acquainted with a greater number of their classmates and so develop a wider range of possibilities for choice.

Free choice of persons to work with. A method somewhat similar to the sociometric approach, but which has many dangers not inherent in the latter, is that of having pupils make their choices of people to work with, on an invitational basis. Several things tend to happen when this method is used. There is always the child who is not asked to join any group. No matter how cleverly a teacher manages to get a group to invite him to join them, he—and there may be three or four—is an outsider looking on at the time of forming the groups. The damage has been done and often cannot be easily corrected.

Another potential danger lies in the formation of groups of pupils who work willingly and well with one another, but develop into small cliques that grow away from the rest of the class, thus destroying the unity and common understanding that should exist in a democratically functioning class.

A third difficulty arises when groups are either too small or too large. Two girls wish to work together but with no one else. Another group turns out to have twelve members, because certain individuals are very popular and, since these pupils are wanted by several groups, all have joined forces. This situation can be remedied, of course, by an agreement with the class that groups cannot be smaller than a certain number, perhaps four, nor larger than a certain number, perhaps seven. The limitation itself, however, can cause frustrations and emotional disturbances so that groups do not get off to a smooth start.

Assigned grouping. Once in a great while it may seem wise, because of some particular situation, to carry out an activity with groups designated by a committee of class members or the teacher. A tenth-grade class, for example, was having trouble. Some members felt that small cliques had formed and that the members of these were not considerate of the rest of the class. The boys and girls in the so-called cliques recognized that something was wrong, but they felt that they were not welcomed by the rest. The class finally reached an impasse where no one could see anyone else's point of view. Progress came to a halt.

The teacher stepped into the situation with a proposal that she select an activity with which no one in the class had had much previous experience and that this activity be followed for three weeks. She further proposed that the class select a committee of five to organize small groups in such a way that each group would be, to the best of their knowledge, a cross-section of the class. The situation was bad enough so that the class members saw the proposal as a possible way of breaking down the barriers that had arisen between them. They agreed to try it, and a committee was selected. The work of the committee was a labor of love, for it took hours of out-of-school time to complete it. Since the class had agreed to this procedure, they accepted the grouping despite the fact that almost everyone found himself working with people with whom he had been arguing violently.

The activity selected by the teacher was a hand-craft project. Each group was asked to select an outstanding occurrence that had taken place in this class during the past year. Having made the selection, the group members were asked to work together in illustrating it—by a model, a chart, a mural, a set of slides—any method that would show the incident or activity clearly. Practically no one was adept at such craft, and all had to learn from the ground up. But after the first stunned silence they set to work.

In the course of the three weeks their genuine amusement at their own amateur efforts, their very real appreciation of heretofore unknown abilities of other boys and girls, their tremendous interest in the products of other groups, and their pride in their own successes carried them over the hump. They came out of the experience with a completely changed viewpoint toward their fellows. Once more the class moved ahead as a united group.

In this case, the method used in dividing the class had a specific purpose, and was accepted by the class because they recognized the problem they were facing. There are not many situations in which the assignment of pupils to specific groups by either a committee or a teacher would seem justified. It is a method to be used relatively infrequently.

Starting group work

If pupils have never participated in group work in a classroom before, the first experiences can be extremely frustrating and discouraging unless the teacher has made his plans carefully. The first two or three times the process should be almost wholly teacher directed. By that time the simple, initial steps of the pattern have become established, and pupils begin to operate automatically on certain general procedures.

For a first group experience, the problem for consideration or the activity to be carried on should be very clear cut and precise. It should be of such a nature that it can be accomplished in a relatively short period of time. Let us assume the class is new to the school and, as a part of the orientation unit, the teacher has decided to use small groups as a means of having boys and girls become acquainted with one another. Before groups are formed the teacher explains precisely what each group is to do. As he talks, he writes the main points on the chalkboard so that pupils may refer to them later. He might say:

Each person in your group will tell his name, and his nickname if he has one. You will tell the things you like to do in your spare time, and any special hobbies you may have. And since you are all new to our school, tell something interesting that you have seen or that has happened to you since you came here.

You have each been given a 3 by 5 inch card. When the person on your right tells about himself, jot down the information on the card. Later you will introduce this person to the class.

When groups have assembled, several pupils should be asked to repeat the directions, and any questions should be answered. For the first few times the groups should be kept small, four or five pupils to a group at the most. For a first experience it is frequently wise to form groups by having boys and girls seated near one another move together, in this way having less general room confusion and less mental confusion on the part of the pupils. Random grouping may also be used, however.

The teacher should urge the pupils in each group to move their seats close to one another. Their closeness gives a sense of unity. In addition to that, in the ordinary classroom, it is necessary that group members be seated close together in order that they may hear everyone else in the group, a point of vital importance in group activity. The teacher must also be alert to the need to use room space to best advantage. Groups should be scattered as evenly as possible throughout the room.

As soon as groups have assembled, the teacher moves from group to group, *appointing* a chairman in each. He says little about the work of the chairman, merely indicating that he is more or less a "key man" in the group. This presents the idea of chairmanship to a group without asking it to carry out the selection of such an individual at a time when they are already sufficiently confused. The next time small groups are used the teacher again appoints a chairman in each, being careful to select a different person. By the time group procedure has been used twice in this way, groups should be ready to select their own chairman.

When initiating small group operation, a time limit for the activity should be set, anywhere from five to fifteen minutes, depending upon the task at hand. It should be relatively short the first few times. If the teacher sees that a group has finished before the allotted time, he should help the members check their data for completeness, and then help them decide on a further activity that may be carried on for the remaining time. In the orientation activity a group might well add to the information its members have collected about one another. They might decide to find out where they live, or how many brothers and sisters each has, or whether any of them have pets. Thus, boys and girls begin to learn that there is always a further step that may be carried out. If no further activity seems feasible, it is better to call the group out of session and help members select activities as individuals, than to have them form a habit of sitting in groups with nothing to do. If, on the other hand, groups are moving well but need more time, this should be granted. It is not always possible to estimate in advance the exact amount of time needed to complete a piece of work, since what is adequate for one class may be insufficient for another.

During the time that groups are in session, the teacher moves from one to another answering questions or sitting with a group for as long a time as he is needed. He must not remain aloof, but should be a helpful and friendly part of all groups. He should, however, be careful not to participate too much nor insist that his approach to a problem is best, but should help group members to clarify their own thinking and find their own solutions. This does not mean that he refrains from expressing his opinions or from giving information that will be helpful to the group. It does mean, however, that he gives these only as a member of the group, leaving pupils free to use them as they see need for them.

A ninth-grade teacher participated in the following manner with three groups that were busy with the problem of interviewing one another concerning the schools they had come from, their families, and their hobbies:

GROUP I:

All were bent over the table listening to what Bill was saying. Joe was writing the information on a 3 by 5 inch card. As Miss Dobson approached, several looked up but immediately turned back to Bill. Joe said, "Wait a minute, Bill. How do you spell that?" Several attempted to spell "aquarium" but were dubious. Joe turned to the teacher with, "Miss Dobson, how do you spell it?" The teacher spelled the word and the group immediately continued with the interview. She moved on to the next group.

GROUP II:

At a second table interest was high. The members looked up at Miss Dobson as she pulled up a chair and joined the group.

"John has a chemical set and so do I. Boy! Are we going to have fun!" said Dave.

"Mary lives only three blocks from me and we both just love ice skating. Isn't that wonderful?" said Joyce.

"Everyone in our group has a little brother. I think that's funny."

Miss Dobson slipped out of her seat smiling and said, "Sounds to me as though this group is moving ahead in great shape."

GROUP III:

But this group had bogged down, in fact had not even really gotten under way. It was obvious that help was needed here. The chairman was at a loss as to what to do. One member was working on her algebra homework. Two were talking about the World's Series, and the fifth was just sitting.

The teacher smiled in as friendly a manner as she had when she was with the highly successful Group II. "How much time does this group still need to finish the job?" she asked.

The chairman squirmed, Carol slipped the algebra book under her desk, and the boys fell silent.

"Are you having trouble? Can I help?" asked Miss Dobson.

The chairman burst out with, "We can't get started because the boys won't help."

Russ glowered at her and retorted, "It's the chairman who won't help. The chairman is supposed to ask everyone about himself."

Norine objected with, "No. Everyone is to ask his neighbor."

Then Jay chimed in, "Which neighbor? There's one on each side of me."

"The chairman should do it because the chairman is going to introduce everyone to the class."

Obviously the directions given at the beginning had not "taken" with this group, despite the care the teacher had given to clarification of both problem and procedure.

"Let's read the directions on the board together in order to be sure that we all understand what's to be done and how to do it. Would you read them out loud for us, Jay?" Miss Dobson spoke quietly and in a friendly tone of voice.

When Jay had completed the reading he said sheepishly, "I guess I didn't listen very well when you told us what to do."

And Russ said, "Me too. Come on Jay, you're on my right. I'll write down what you tell me and then I'll tell Norine about me and she can write that down. Do you have a nickname?"

Miss Dobson quietly left the group and moved on while Group III went to work with a vengeance.

The working period is followed by a reporting session in which each group reports its findings to the class. In the example given, the reporting would be in terms of an introduction of his neighbor to the class by each member of the group. In other situations the usual procedure would be to have a representative of each group, probably the chairman or recorder, report to the class the conclusions reached by his group. These conclusions should, if possible, be discussed by the class as a whole.

One of the most important phases of group procedure, and one that is only too frequently omitted, is the evaluation of the experience itself. Even the first group sessions should be evaluated in some simple manner. Perhaps, in these early attempts, ten minutes spent in a general class discussion is sufficient. Such questions as the following will stimulate discussion.

1. What did you like about working in a group?
2. What troubles did you have in working together?
3. What do you think your group could do better if you were starting over again?

Such simple questions are sufficient as a beginning. After a second activity, carried out in small groups, such questions as these may serve as the basis for evaluative discussions:

1. In what ways were you more satisfied with the way your group worked today than you were last time?
2. What difficulties did you have this time that you did not have last time?

No names should be mentioned. Boys and girls may need a great deal of help in making their statements objective and keeping personal feelings in check. It is the teacher's leadership that will determine the tone of the evaluation session. His calm and friendly appraisal of situations will go far in setting the stage for a similar approach on the part of the pupils.

When a class has had two or three experiences in small-group work, it is time to introduce the idea of having each group select one member who will serve as a recorder of the group's activities. This may already have been suggested by some alert boy or girl as a means of keeping track of what is being accomplished. The work of a recorder should be clearly understood by everyone. A ninth-grade class in which recorders served a very real purpose made, over a period of time, the following decisions relative to what would be expected of them:

1. The recorder keeps a daily log of group activities.
2. He records plans that are made.
3. He records changes in plans.
4. With the help of the group he makes out a weekly progress report.
5. He records any questions or difficulties the group may have.
6. He brings up to date a member who has been absent.
7. He gives the daily record to the teacher at the end of the period.

Such a list does not develop all at one time. Perhaps the only purpose that a beginning class can see in having a recorder is to have someone keep a daily record of group activities. As time goes on, however, and groups work for longer periods of time on more involved problems, further responsibilties are discovered for the recorder and these are added to the original item.

The question is frequently raised concerning the teacher's ability to keep abreast of the activities of pupils working in groups. It is true that with classes of 30 to 40 pupils he cannot work with every child every day. Insofar as possible he should, of course, make an effort to spend time with each group daily, although at times even this may be impossible. The daily activity record, however, turned in by the recorder, serves as a very valuable link between teacher and groups.

The class that developed the list cited above expected the records to be read and returned to them the following day with any suggestions the teacher might have to offer and with answers to questions that pupils had not found opportunity to ask in class. This method kept him in contact with all groups even though he was not able to spend an entire period with any one. It gave him excellent leads as to which groups were operating well and, at the moment, did not need his help. Those whose daily records showed poor functioning were the ones to which he could turn his attention first on the following day. It also made it possible for him to help groups in locating material that they did not seem able to find. The daily reading of group activity records is not a difficult chore, since, if six groups are in operation, there are only six reports to be read.

The following are group logs written later in the year by the recorders of two groups, one indicating that a group had experienced a very unsatisfactory day, whereas the other is a record of a profitable day.

LOG OF GROUP I

Our Group Problem:

What changes have taken place in transportation in the last 100 years?

Our Progress Today:

We planned to use our class period today in sharing the information each of us had collected during the last three days. But we didn't get very far because Jim forgot to bring his notes. Barbara and Betty did not have much material, because they tried to use the *Readers' Guide* to find magazine articles and they had forgotten how to use it right. Richard brought two books home from the public library on diesel engines, but he couldn't understand them. We tried to help him today, but we could not understand them either. Pat had read a lot and told us about his material and I had read quite a lot too.

Questions:

1. Where can Richard find out about diesel engines?
2. How do you use the *Readers' Guide?*

Log of Group II

Our Group Problem:

What part does the United States play in the operation of the United Nations?

Our Progress Today:

The job we had today was to make plans for getting visual-aids materials that would help us to illustrate our information when we make our report to the class. We each took a part of the job and were out of the room the first part of the period. Then we came back and talked over what we had found out.

Steve and Mary went to the Visual-Aids Office and checked on films that we could use. They brought back the names of six films. The group decided on two of these. When they come we will preview them and if they are good we will show them to the class. Steve went back to the Visual-Aids Office and ordered them.

Bob and Kathy checked the list of materials we could get from the Children's Museum. The group decided on five charts and a set of pictures. Bob went back to the Visual-Aids Office and ordered them.

Allen went to the library to see if there were any pictures available, but there weren't.

We think we did a good job.

Questions:

1. Miss Jones, do you have any pictures of the United Nations building?

2. Where can our group preview the films?

Obviously the kind of assistance needed by the first group is very different from that needed by the second. Probably the teacher would need to spend a considerable amount of time with Group I. Richard and perhaps one or two others need help in finding material at their own level of understanding. Betty and Barbara—and probably the others—need help in reviewing the use of *Readers' Guide to Periodical Literature*. They also need help in deciding whether information on their topic is likely to be found in periodicals. Jim's forgetting his notes needs to be checked. Were they forgotten because he was having difficulties collecting data and they weren't very satisfactory even to himself? Or was it just a slip, such as any of us make once in a while?

Group II can have its questions answered quickly. A suggestion might also be made that they record in the log the names of the films and the material ordered from the Children's Museum. A pat on the back for a job well done is in order as well.

Later group work

By the time that boys and girls have worked in groups five or six times they have become accustomed to the general procedure —the method of dividing the class, moving seats into small circles, selecting chairmen and recorders, reporting results to the class, and evaluating their experiences. They have the surface techniques in hand. It is necessary now to move them on to some of the more difficult aspects of group work. They must be helped to see and understand to some degree the interpersonal relationships involved in working in a group, what constitutes good group procedure, and what roles individuals must play in order to make this a satisfying and functioning experience. These are difficult concepts to grasp, both for the pupils and for the teacher, and, at best, they are of slow growth.

Characteristics of good group work. With most classes it is possible by this time to use the pupils' experiences with small-group work as the basis for a general class discussion directed toward the question, "What are the characteristics of good group work?" This will not result in a perfect list either in language or content. It will, however, have meaning to the pupils, since it is their own and is in accord with their own development and understanding of group process at this time. A sample list recorded at approximately this stage follows:

1. Everyone should take part in the work.
2. One person shouldn't do all the talking or boss the others.
3. Take turns talking. Everyone should listen to what other people say.
4. Don't get angry just because you don't agree with what someone else has said.
5. Don't argue just to win your point.
6. Everyone should stick to the subject.
7. Be sure we know what we are to do.

It is possible to see from this list some of the problems these boys and girls were having in working together, namely lack of participation, domination by one person, lack of attention, anger, and wandering from the problem under consideration. The teacher added a point that dealt with general participation aspects of a good group discussion. It was done in the form of diagrams in which small squares represented group members as shown in Figure 5. The lines and arrows represented the direction of discussion.

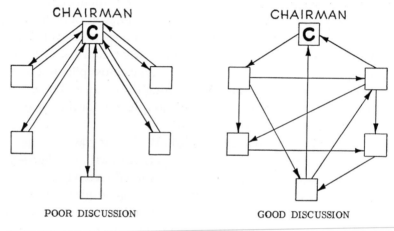

Figure 5. Group discussion diagrams.

The list of good group characteristics was printed on a large chart with a felt brush pen and placed in a conspicuous place on the wall in the classroom so that it could be easily referred to at any time. Space was left on the chart for later additions, and as time went on, the class was able to draw further items from their experiences to supplement the original list. For example, it was later discovered that some boys and girls thought they should never express disagreement. A discussion clarified this point, and the class added two more items to its list as follows:

8. When you don't agree with someone's ideas, say so, but explain why you don't agree.

9. If you do agree with someone's ideas, say so. If you can add a reason why this idea is good, be sure and do it.

Such a list can serve as a check list for group evaluations. Time should be set aside at intervals for this purpose, perhaps ten or fifteen minutes on Friday may be used for a quick review of the week's successes and failures. At other times, a more complete analysis of group activity may be made by using one or more of the following methods.

Group evaluation later in the year. Such evaluations will become more complete as pupils become accustomed to the process. The following is an evaluation made by a group of tenth-grade pupils at the close of a unit of work.

For a number of weeks the class had been divided into seven groups, each investigating a different problem. Each group of pupils had reported its data to the class and was about to make a final evaluation of the successes and failures experienced as its members had worked together toward the solution of their common problem.

The goals relating to group work, which had been set by the class earlier in the semester, were written on the chalkboard by the class chairman. These were as follows:

1. Accept responsibility for doing your share of the work.
2. Select leaders who are going to do a good job.
3. Pay attention to persons who are speaking.
4. Use class time to advantage.
5. Share your information with group members.
6. Take an active part in making group decisions.

On the basis of these goals, each pupil wrote an analysis of the group in which he had worked. At the end of twenty minutes the seven groups assembled to compare the notes of the members. Each group then prepared a group analysis, a list being made of all activities that the members agreed had been good, and a second list of all activities that they considered to have been poor. A sample analysis follows:

We Agree on These Points

Good Points

1. Everyone carried out his share of the work. We all helped to solve our problem.

2. We got together at least one day each week and compared notes and books, and questioned things we did not understand. We contributed information and material to each other in the group and to persons in other groups as well. When giving our reports we sometimes gave each other notes. We were very free with our information.

3. Everyone helped in deciding how we were going to solve our problem and how we were going to present it.

4. In presenting our reports everyone knew his material.

5. We used our time well. We didn't fool around too much. We didn't go to the library just to see our friends. We went for material. We worked.

Bad Points

1. We listened when other people were talking, but sometimes they were not talking about the topic.

2. We chose a good leader, but we sort of pushed her into it.

3. We did not vary our reports enough. We did not plan this very well. We could have made them more interesting by using visual aids, drawings, skits, or radio scripts.

When the group analyses were completed, each group was asked to rate itself as *Very good, Good, Fair,* or *Poor,* on the basis of the analysis it had made of its own activities. The pupils in the group cited above rated themselves as *Good.*

Bulletin board picture analysis. The list of characteristics of good group work is also useful as a basis for a picture analysis that the teacher may make. To represent the members of a group it is most realistic to have photographs of boys and girls of approxi-

mately the same age as the pupils in the class in which they are
to be used. It is not wise to use pictures of pupils in the class,
since their fellow classmates will find it difficult to react objec-
tively to them. One snapshot each of six pupils, taken at desks in
a schoolroom, and enlarged to 5 by 7 inches or thereabouts,
makes a satisfactory basis for this particular bulletin board lesson.
If this is not possible, use squares of colored paper and draw, or
have a pupil draw, a face on each one. These are placed on the
bulletin board in a circle, as pupils would be seated in an actual
group.

As the teacher moves from group to group, he cannot help but
hear discussions that indicate excellent group progress and again
he hears things that show that a group is having difficulties. After
listening to the groups in action long enough to sense various
problems, the teacher selects a situation that will lead the class
to consider some of its own strengths and weaknesses in group
work. It is not wise to use names of boys and girls in the class
either in the bulletin board illustration or in the discussion that
follows. Insofar as possible, even the words the teacher has heard
should be changed so that they serve the purpose he is trying to
achieve, but do not point a finger too strongly at any individual.
He writes each of the statements made by pupils in the selected
group with heavy, dark crayon or a felt brush pen on an 8 by 11
inch sheet of paper. Each of these is then thumbtacked near one
of the pictures and joined to it by a narrow strip of paper or a
piece of cord or yarn. Each is then given a number that indicates
the order in which the various parts of the conversation took
place. Figure 6 is a picture of such a bulletin-board analysis of a
group situation.

In order to involve all class members in a consideration of the
problem, each pupil is asked to study the situation carefully for
a few minutes, and then to list on paper as many items as possible
in response to each of the questions:

What do you see that is good?
What do you see that is not good?

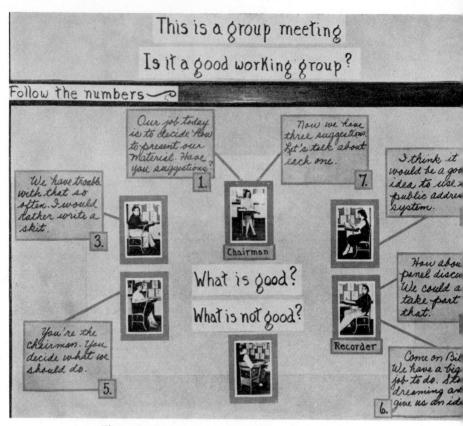

Figure 6. Picturing group activity on the bulletin board.

A later study of these papers will also indicate to the teacher the degree of progress pupils are making in understanding group activity. At the time, however, a general class discussion follows in order to bring out the important points. In the situation pictured the good points are as follows:

a. The chairman has stated the problem clearly.

b. Three members made worth-while suggestions.

c. The objection raised to using the public address system was based on experience.

d. One member tried to draw the silent and inattentive member into the group.

e. The chairman moved the group on to the next step.

The weak spots lay in the inactive member and in the member who did not want to take any responsibility, but wanted the chairman to make the decision.

The discussion should then be directed toward a consideration of what the various members of this group could have done to overcome the weakness within the group and to strengthen its good points. It is not enough to analyze a situation, since this is but part of the solution. Possible action steps to improve it should be developed by the class. The discussion may well be followed by having each pupil make a copy of the positions of the group members in the illustration, then indicate what each person *could* say which would lead toward a solution of the difficulty.

Almost any situation may be captured by this method. Perhaps another would involve the following conversation:

MEMBER 1 (*chairman*)

MEMBER 2

Let's get going.

MEMBER 3

I think we could get some ideas from Mr. Smith.

MEMBER 4

I don't like Mr. Smith. Did you know he made Joe stay an extra hour yesterday? I don't think that's fair.

MEMBER 5 (*talking with* MEMBER 6)

That was a swell party last night, wasn't it.

MEMBER 6

Oh, I don't know. I didn't think much of it. I left early.

Here there are many obstacles to a satisfactory work period:

a. The chairman is inactive.

b. Two members are discussing an activity between themselves that is not connected with the problem.

c. One member is wasting time by bringing in an item that is wholly beside the point.

d. Only two members are trying to get the group into action.

Groups frequently find it very enlightening—and also find it fun—to make pictures of this sort of their own activities. It is sometimes very helpful to have each boy and girl prepare one that he feels represents his group, allowing time afterwards for comparisons within each group. Growth in understanding the group process as well as growth in understanding one another results from this.

Use of an observer. A technique that can be used in a variety of ways is the use of an observer in each group. It is an assignment that should be rotated within a group in order to give each member the opportunity to look at the activity of the group in a more objective way than is possible when he is a participating member. It is also important that not just the better students carry out this activity. Unless everyone takes a turn at this, it is likely that distrust will arise between group members and the observer, thus destroying the value of the technique.

A very simple method is to have each observer answer questions such as the following:

1. Did the members of the group work steadily on the problem?
2. If not, what happened to slow them down?
3. If they worked steadily, what did different members do to make things run smoothly?
4. Did the group complete the work it planned to do today?

A series of such questions may be developed by pupils and teacher together from the list of characteristics of good group action, such as those described on page 88. For ease in using, the questions may be mimeographed, with perhaps a 3-inch space following each one, in which the recorder may write. Here again, individual names should not be recorded at any time.

In order to help all class members understand how to make an observation, it is a good idea to have a practice period or two. A volunteer group may serve as the practice group carrying on a regular group meeting for perhaps ten or fifteen minutes at the front of the room. The rest of the class members, each with a copy of the questions, serve as observers. Following the practice period, the observers discuss their reports and ask questions about the procedure. A second practice period, using another group, may then be run in order that those who were in the demonstration group the first time have an opportunity to be observers. Such a second practice period is not a loss to those who are now observing for a second time, since the discussion period should have given them new insights and ideas that they can now check. In this way each child has had at least one experience previous to carrying on the activity within his own group.

A second type of observation may be made by recording the amount of participation of the various group members. Large sheets of $\frac{1}{4}$-inch cross-section paper are necessary for this. One sheet is given to each group observer. He assigns a number to each member. These numbers, rather than names, are written one below the other on the left hand side near the top of the sheet. Lines are then drawn across the entire sheet, one above the first number and one below the last number, thus framing the area of the page within which the observer will place his record. A duplicate of this is made below it, leaving perhaps five spaces between the two. In this way the observer need not stop to prepare the additional record form during the discussion.

As the group gets under way, he places a small cross (x) in the square following the number of the boy or girl who has spoken first. With the next statement he moves his pencil to the second column, placing a cross opposite the number of the person who was second to speak. This is continued for each statement made by a member of the group, moving one column further each time. Thus the order in which participation has taken place is indicated on the chart. As pupils gain skill in this technique they are able to record another item. They may use a cross in a circle $\otimes$ to indicate discussion that has nothing to do with the problem being considered by the group, thus recording negative activity as well as helpful participation.

When using this type of recording, it is well not to let it extend over too long a period of time, twenty-five minutes at the most, ten to fifteen minutes being much better. It serves as a sampling rather than an endurance contest. A bell, tapped at five minute intervals, signals the observer to draw a vertical line at these points. Such divisions will enable the group to study its record with greater ease. At the conclusion of the discussion, the observer connects the crosses, moving across the page from column to column. At times there will be more than one cross in a column; one of these crosses is perhaps encircled. The extra one may be indicated outside of the line of direct communication as shown in Figure 7.

At the bottom of the sheet the observer records the number of times each member participated, as well as the number of times each one spoke of something that had nothing to do with the problem. When this is completed, the group members study and discuss their record, and the conclusions they reach are recorded on the observation sheet. When this method is first used, rather specific questions, perhaps such as those listed below, serve as guides. Later, pupils will not need these and can draw conclusions without them.

1. Did all members of your group take part in the discussion?
2. Did any member of your group take no part in the discussion at all?
3. Did any member of your group take part only a few times compared with the others?
4. Did any member take too large a part in the discussion?
5. Does your chart show any time when two people kept the discussion just between themselves?
6. Were there many statements that were a hindrance to your group?
7. Considering the entire chart, both helpful and hindrance contributions, were you satisfied with the performance of your group?
8. Are there changes that your group feels it ought to make in order to do a better job?

All group members acting as observers. Although the following technique is not observation in the same sense as the pre-

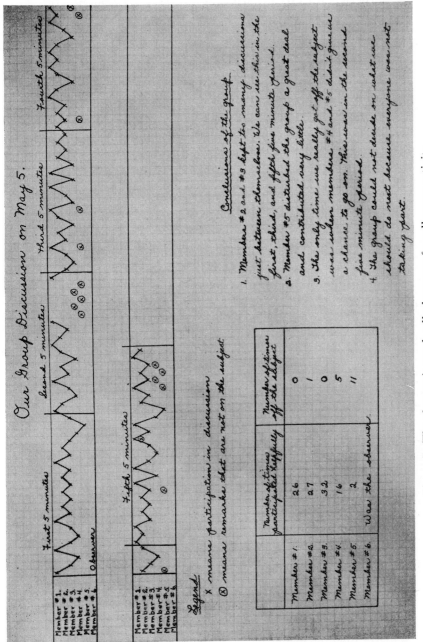

Figure 7. The observer's graph tells the story of small group activity.

viously described methods, it may be so named when giving directions. At times it is well to give everyone an opportunity to describe his own group. At the beginning of a group session, the teacher asks each person to observe closely the activities and contributions of the members of his group. The chairman of the group assigns a letter, A, B, C, D, and so forth, to each person, and in the descriptions written by the members these letters are used instead of names. A general description may be written in response to a direction such as this:

Recall the things that took place in your group today. Describe these in the order in which they happened to the best of your ability. Use the assigned letters instead of people's names.

Instead of a general description such as this, more pointed questions may be used. These questions are placed on the board before group work is begun, in order that pupils may know what to watch for.

1. How well did the members of your group listen to the ideas of other members?

2. How many questions were asked about the reports given by others?

3. Was there a discussion about the report? If so, what was it about?

4. How often did each member take part in the work of the group?

5. Are there other things you noticed about your group?

The responses made by an individual in an eighth-grade class to such questions were as follows:

My Observation of My Group

C gave a report on Jenny Lind. The number of times each person participated in the discussion after the report was finished was:

$$A — 8$$
$$B — 1$$
$$C — 10$$
$$D — 5$$
$$E — 7$$

Everyone listened to C's report except B. B just sat and tried to get A to pay attention to him, but A did not do it.

E asked a question concerning the meaning of a word. D asked a question about a statement in the report which he did not understand. A asked several questions about things she did not understand. C answered the questions.

The discussion was about musicians. We talked about why musicians played the instruments they did, and how much money they earn, and how much training a musician needs. We talked about people who sing and who write music.

In the beginning we couldn't get started because A, C, B, and D (I was D) were all talking at once. But it was all right after we got started.

The group seemed to enjoy C's report. I know I did. But B made fun of everything that we said and this made me angry.

Several things may be done with such reports as these. They may be exchanged within the group and compared. Such a comparison helps pupils to understand that no two people see a situation in exactly the same way, and that one person may react in one way to an occurrence whereas another person reacts in an entirely different manner. Each becomes aware of situations that are disturbing to others and to the progress of a group, as well as those that are helpful to the group. Alone, he might have missed these points. It is sometimes good to ask each group to write a composite of the five observations as an incentive to discussion. The observations may also be collected and several drawn out for general class discussion. It is especially for the latter use that letters instead of names are important.

Observation of entire class. The observation technique may also be used to advantage during a class discussion in order to help pupils recognize some of their problems. In this case, the group is considered to be the entire class. Three persons are selected by the class or appointed by the chairman to serve as observers. Each is given a class seating chart large enough so that notations may be made on it. Each is also given an envelope containing directions and materials which he will need.

The envelope given to one observer contains fifty small triangles with a base of approximately ¾ inch, cut from green paper. The directions enclosed are as follows:

In the proper space on the seating chart mark an X each time a member of the class makes a helpful suggestion, or gives any needed information, or discusses the problem being considered.

The envelope given to the second observer contains fifty circles approximately ¾ inch in diameter, cut from orange paper. The directions enclosed are as follows:

In the proper space on the seating chart mark an X each time a member of the class asks a question.

The envelope given to the third observer contains fifty ¾ inch squares cut from red paper. The enclosed directions are:

In the proper space on the seating chart mark an X each time a member of the class says something that has nothing to do with the problem being considered, or talks to his neighbor without concerning himself with the class problem.

The teacher should meet with the three observers for a few minutes in order to be sure that they understand what is to be done. The remainder of the class does not know what the observers' directions are. The observers should then be seated so that they can see the whole room easily, but are not conspicuous.

Previous to the class period, the teacher has prepared a bulletin board on which the observers' data will later be recorded. Blank 4 by 6 inch index cards are arranged on the bulletin board, or fastened to the chalkboard with scotch tape, in the same order as the seating chart used by the observers. Each card represents a pupil, but no names are recorded on these. The heading may be: *How Would You Describe Our Group Today?* or, *Was It a Good Group?* or, *What Does This Show?*

At the conclusion of the discussion period, each observer fastens one of the colored pieces of paper enclosed in his envelope to the proper index card on the bulletin board for each X on his seating chart, one observer using the top third of each card, one the middle third, and one the lower third. Scotch tape or paste serve equally well for fastening the colored pieces in place. The legend is then added to the board in order that the

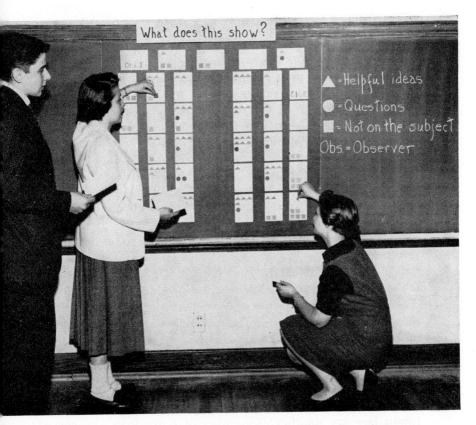

Figure 8. Observers record the participation in a classs discussion.

entire class may know the meaning of the picture that is being formed. Pupils completing such an observation record may be seen in Figure 8.

The value of this technique lies in the class discussion that follows the completion of the picture of the observations. In order to involve all members of the class and to assure the development of the maximum number of ideas, each pupil is asked to study the picture carefully and to write a description of what it shows about the class on this particular day. The interpretations put upon the data vary. The following samples refer to the observation data shown in Figure 8.

99

1. This diagram shows that all the people sitting in the two rows directly across the aisle from one another participated better than those in the outside rows. I think this goes to prove that we all talk better when we are facing each other.

2. This indicates to me that some people are not in the discussion at all. There were only nine who spoke frequently enough to be called active participants. We must be losing many good ideas. It also seems to me to mean that if a small group carries the discussion they are possibly also influencing the decisions of the class too much.

3. Most of the people who participated are sitting near each other, and the ones who didn't participate are sitting near others who didn't. If they were mixed together, I think we would have a lot more participation. The people who were off the beam most were in the outside rows together.

4. This shows me that there are some people who do most of the talking and participating, while others sit back, relax, and just listen. Then there are also the people who take part only once or twice. This shows me that many people in the class are putting the responsibility on someone else's shoulders instead of doing the job themselves.

All of these points were bases for heated discussion. The result was a class decision to move chairs into one large circle whenever a lengthy discussion of a problem was due, so that all might face one another. A number of individuals also agreed with the class that they would function better seated away from certain people and that they should take it upon themselves to sit somewhere else during discussions. Others volunteered to put forth more effort. The same observer technique, used at a later time, showed a marked improvement in participation and in quality of discussion.

Understanding of roles played in a group. Ability to work well in a group increases as the pupil develops an understanding and acceptance of the roles that must be played by the group members. In his first experiences he is working blindly, as are all the members of his group. By chance, the experiences may be happy ones; by chance, they may not be. As various evaluative techniques are used, he becomes aware of the fact that when certain things are done in a group, for example when everyone participates, good results are usually achieved. Conversely, he becomes aware of the fact that when some members of a group do not contribute, the results are less satisfactory. It is necessary, however, to help him see that participation or non-participation has many facets, that all contributions are not equally valuable, nor do they bring the same results. He must come to recognize the varying parts each member of a group plays in the success or failure of the whole group. This includes recognition of the roles he himself plays.

There is little value in initiating the concept of group roles in the terminology used by students of group dynamics. It is necessary to start with words, ideas, and situations with which pupils are familiar. Unless a beginning is made in a recognized situation, the concept will be merely a "lesson" to be learned by rote, and not an experience that leads to understanding and changing behavior.

A technique that has been highly satisfactory involves the use of the bulletin board again. Several days prior to this activity, the teacher prepared a set of fifteen 8 by 11 inch colored construction paper sheets, each of which appeared as shown in Figure 9.

The fifteen sheets were then mounted on the bulletin board with the heading: *What Roles Do You Play in Your Group?*

The bulletin board aroused much interest but, although many questions were asked, the teacher gave the class no answers until he was ready to use it. His introduction to the concept of group roles was as follows:

TEACHER

You have all seen many movies and television plays, and you know that in these each actor has a special part to play. He performs in certain ways because he represents a certain kind of person. We say that he has a role, or a part, to play. Everyone in a movie has a role to play.

In our families, too, we each have roles. For example, in most families one of the father's roles is that of the breadwinner for the family. What would the mother's role be in most families?

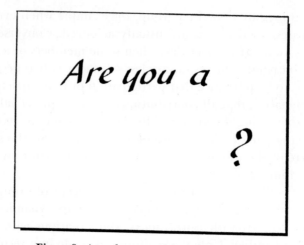

Are you a

?

Figure 9. A card prepared for group role study.

MAY

The home keeper?

TEACHER

That's right. Are there other roles that members of your family play?

STEVE

My sister helps support us. My father and my sister both work. My father works at the post office and my sister is a clerk in a store.

TEACHER

Then in your family two people have the same role, except that they carry it out in different ways. What other roles do family members have?

SAM

My brother and I are the odd-job guys around our house. We cut the grass or run errands and things like that.

RUTH (*laughing*)

My brother is the family pest. He always gets into everyone else's things and teases my sister and me.

SUSAN

Well, my little sister is the family borrower. If my older sister or I can't find our beads or hankies or belts or anything, we always know who is wearing them.

TEACHER

It sounds as though you are saying there are roles that are helpful to your family and some that are not. Is that what you mean?

RUTH

Yes. Only my brother isn't always a pest. Sometimes he does awfully nice things for us. And sometimes we have a lot of fun with him. He makes us laugh.

SUSAN

My sister does too.

TEACHER

Does that mean that the people in your families take different roles at different times?

After a moment's thought, heads began to nod vigorously and hands were flying. The class spent some time considering examples of this. The teacher then turned the question toward himself, asking the class whether he played the same role all the time or different roles at different times. They concluded that sometimes he was a dictator, such as when he gave orders, sometimes a discussion leader, sometimes a question-asker, sometimes an interest-starter, sometimes he gave information, sometimes he was a helper.

He then picked up group observer records that had been written the day before. As an introduction to the one he had selected for consideration, he said:

When we work in groups we all take roles, too, just as the members of a family do, or as I do when I am with you in class. Yesterday each of you wrote a record of the activities that took place in your group. I am going to read one of these to you. Let's see whether we can figure out the kinds of roles people were taking. Will you listen very carefully and on a piece of paper write all the different things that people did in this group?

He then read the observer record quoted on page 96. When the reading was completed the following comments were recorded on the board:

1. People listened.
2. B sat.
3. People asked questions.
4. C answered questions and told his report.
5. B made fun of things and made people feel little and silly.
6. C kept things going.
7. Pupils talked all at once.

The teacher then suggested that they could give names to these roles. For example, perhaps they could call the first item *listeners*. The second immediately became *sitters*, but was rejected because the class decided that everyone sat during a group meeting. Eventually it became the *do-nothing* role. The list as completed for the record became:

1. Listener
2. Do-nothing
3. Questioner
4. Information giver
5. Belittler
6. Leader
7. Blocker

Through the use of other observer records, the following were added to the original list:

8. Know-it-all
9. Idea giver

The teacher then turned to the bulletin board headed *"What Roles Do You Play in Your Group?,"* which had been ready for use for several days. Each of the nine roles that had just been identified was printed on one of the sheets reading, *Are you a ———?*

Since fifteen sheets had been prepared and only nine roles had been identified, there were six blanks. The next time small groups were in session class members were asked to identify the roles that were played in their group, and to watch for roles that had so far not been mentioned, recording what the person did, but not mentioning the names of any individuals. At the

Figure 10. Developing recognition of group roles.

end of twenty minutes, the teacher called for a break in group
activity and new roles were identified. To the nine already
listed the following were added:

10. Fence sitter (can't make up his mind)
11. Shy guy
12. Peacemaker
13. Wisecracker
14. Summarizer
15. Complainer
16. Objector

A class at work at such a bulletin board is shown in Figure 10.
Such a listing of roles is, of course, only a first step toward an
understanding of group process. It is, however, in terms that

105

even quite young boys and girls can understand. That they do understand is very clear, since the teacher, in moving from group to group, hears such remarks as, "You read that article, Joe. You be the *information giver* for that."

"Stop being a *know-it-all*. We've got a lot of *idea givers* in this group."

"Make up your mind what you want to do. You can't just be a *fence-sitter*."

"Isn't it time that somebody is a *summarizer?*"

Introduction to group roles through sociodrama. Another technique that may be used for developing recognition of group roles is the sociodrama. The initial introduction to group roles may be made through the discussion of various family roles and teacher roles as described previously on pages 101–103. As a lead into the sociodrama the teacher might say:

When we work in groups we all take roles too, just as the members of a family do, or as I do when I am with you in class. Today I am going to ask six of you to act out a small group meeting. Each one will be assigned a different role to play. The rest of the class will not know what these roles are but will watch carefully and try to identify them.

Six boys and girls are then selected to serve as the participants in the sociodrama. To each of these the teacher gives a slip of paper on which he has written the role this individual is to portray. Any six roles may be selected, but it is good to see that for an initial performance there are represented both roles that are helpful and those that are a hindrance to a group. The slips given to the role-players do not *name* the role, but describe how the boy or girl is to behave in the group. The following six work well in this situation.

1. You think that you know all the answers. No matter what anyone says you have a *better* idea. You seldom wait for others to finish explaining their ideas, but always have something to say that you are sure is better. You always let people know that you think your ideas are best.

2. You have good ideas. You suggest things that are practical and

can be worked out. If the group does not approve of one idea you try another.

3. You can never make up your mind. One minute you think an idea is good, the next that it isn't good. You do not have any special reasons for changing your mind. You just cannot decide.

4. You are a person who raises questions about the problem you are working on. If you do not see how a plan would work out, you ask questions about it. If you do not understand a person's point, you ask a question.

5. You are a person who tries to smooth out disagreements among members of the group. If two people argue, you try to show how both may be right. You calm people down. You are friendly and understanding.

6. You object to the ideas that are presented. Even if they seem to be good ideas, you object to them. Nothing is right.

In selecting pupils to portray these roles it is good to choose those who are able to carry them out, yet not to select people who fit certain roles too perfectly. For example, a chronic *know-it-all* or *objector* in real life situations may feel himself, and sometimes truly find himself, being held up to ridicule before his peers if he is assigned such a part to play. There should be no possibility of hurt feelings involved in the demonstration.

The problem to be worked on by the six members participating in the sociodrama is told both to group members and to the audience class members. It may be any problem that can be discussed on the spur of the moment and about which the pupils have sufficient information. As an example, the following is a possibility:

The core classes have been asked to furnish an exhibit for Education Week for the school exhibit case in the main hall. This group is meeting to decide what to put in the case.

A well-known school problem serves admirably for such a demonstration, since pupils are aware of the problem and have many suggestions. Such a one might be the following:

There is great difficulty in serving everyone during the lunch hour. This group is a Student Council Committee which is meeting to discuss ways in which the system of moving through the cafeteria can be improved so that everyone may be taken care of.

The six participants are given three or four minutes together, perhaps in the hall, to consider the problem to be discussed. They are asked, however, not to divulge to one another their individual roles. During this time the teacher asks each member of the audience to list the names of the members of the demonstration group on a sheet of paper, leaving space between names. He instructs them to watch the presentation carefully and to record the type of participation of each member.

The demonstration group is seated in a circle so that they can be observed by everyone. Since the problem is not an actual one and there has been no time to prepare for such a discussion, the teacher must watch closely in order to cut it short in case the participants run out of ideas. Usually ten or twelve minutes is sufficient time.

The discussion that follows the sociodrama brings to light the observations of the audience. These are listed on the board for each role played. The following is a sample of such a list.

Role 1:
    Made smart remarks.
    Knew all the answers.
    Gave some information.

Role 2:
    Gave many good ideas.

Role 3:
    Couldn't make up his mind.
    Was shy.
    Was afraid.

Role 4:
    Asked good questions.

Role 5:
    Did not say much.
    Made people feel better when there was trouble.
    Just sat quietly most of the time.

Role 6:
Objected to everything.

General Statements:
All but Number 1 listened to what was going on.
Some people, such as Numbers 1, 3, and 6, kept the group from
moving ahead.

The members participating in the sociodrama were then
given a chance to say whether they felt that the observers had
recorded their roles accurately or not. This gave each an opportunity to justify his actions and tended to make several feel
much better about the remarks made by the observers. For example, the boy taking Role 3 said, "It wasn't that I was shy or
afraid. I just couldn't make up my mind sometimes how to go
about not making up my mind." The good-natured laughter
that followed this made Bill feel much better about what seemed
to him to have been failure to fulfill his role completely. Sue,
who had Role 5, said that the reason she just sat quietly most of
the time was because there was so little trouble for her to smooth
out.

From the discussion that followed there developed a list that
obviously included more than the teacher had planned when he
set the six roles in motion. This list was:

Wise guy	Shy guy	Objector
Know-it-all	Questioner	Listener
Information giver	Peacemaker	Blocker
Fence-sitter	Do-nothing	

Thus, the class had identified eleven roles that are frequently observable in the functioning of a group. As he turned to his own
working group, each pupil carried with him a copy of these
roles, which he used as a check list for identifying the roles
played as his group proceeded. To this list each added any
other roles that he perceived in operation but which had not
been previously identified. These were added to the original
class list, and the entire list was recorded on a large sheet of
poster board and placed on a bulletin board where it served as

a basis for evaluation from time to time. Space was left on the sheet for the addition of other roles that would be identified throughout the year.

The individual's own roles. A further step in helping a child to improve his ability to work in a group is to assist him in identifying the roles he, himself, takes. Up to this point, he has been busy watching his fellow group members. Now it is time for him to watch himself.

At the beginning of a period in which pupils will be working in groups, the teacher asks each child to watch his own activities and to identify the different roles that he plays. At the end of fifteen or twenty minutes, group work is halted long enough to have each pupil write a description of his own behavior during this period. The following are samples of such descriptions written by eighth-graders:

> I was sort of a *blocker* and a *do-nothing* both but I helped in part of the discussion. A few times I talked to Ed and I blocked by doing this. I was a *do-nothing* when I looked at the bulletin board with pictures on it and didn't think about what was being said. But I was an *information giver* part of the time, too.

> I was a *leader* when I led the discussion for a little while. I was a *know-it-all* when I stopped someone's opinion very fast and thought my opinion was better and told the group so. I was a *peacemaker* when I changed the subject when two people were arguing. And I was a *questioner* when I asked Bill what he meant by what he said.

Another method serving the same purpose of helping pupils identify their own activities in a group is to duplicate the list of roles as developed by the class, allowing space between the items. These lists are given out to the class members on a day that they will be working in groups. Each pupil is asked to record under the proper heading his own action in any role that he plays and to number these consecutively. In this way a picture of the sequence of activities is developed.

Such self-descriptions serve as the basis for a class discussion relating to the shifts an individual makes from one role to another resulting from the changing requirements or conditions of the group within which he is operating. If there is good rapport between class members, it will be possible to ask for volunteers to describe the changes they made from one role to another and to indicate, as far as possible, what caused them. Another method is to collect the descriptions and to draw a series of them at random to read to the class. Names, of course, should be withheld. When using this method, it is possible to develop only hypothetical reasons for the shifts in roles, and the discussion must be on the basis of the conditions that would logically cause such role-changing.

Self-descriptions serve also as data for teacher conferences with those who are having difficulties becoming functioning members of a group. The teacher cannot, however, depend wholly on such check lists or self-descriptions. He must be alert at all times to the activities of the members of his class. Some may need help in recognizing the roles they are taking. Others need help in developing an understanding of their own behavior in terms of causes and effects. Still others need help in changing from undesirable to desirable roles, or in enlarging their field of operation to include more active roles or a wider range of roles.

On a more technical level

In some high schools the same pupils remain in a democratically functioning class for several years under the guidance of the same teacher. With these more mature pupils, who have had considerable experience in analyzing their group work, both in small groups and in the class as a whole, it is possible to achieve more complete understanding of the interaction between members of a group and to develop new concepts of the various group roles. They can be helped to see that certain roles are necessary in order to maintain the unity of the group itself, that others are needed in order to fulfill the task assigned to the group, and that still others serve no purpose other than to satisfy the individuals who are playing them.

The need for moving into this next stage frequently arises without prompting or pushing by the teacher. It may grow out of questioning by an individual or a small group. It may develop from a class discussion of some group activity or problem. The stage may also, of course, be set by the teacher.

The eleventh-grade class described in the following pages had, since the tenth grade, been aware of and worked within the limits of the sixteen group roles recorded previously. These were:

Listener	Idea giver
Do-nothing	Fence-sitter
Information giver	Shy guy
Belittler	Peacemaker
Leader	Wisecracker
Blocker	Summarizer
Know-it-all	Complainer
Questioner	Objector

A discussion among four pupils set the class members thinking in a new direction. The conversation was as follows:

NED

What do you call a person who starts things moving in a group?

JILL

What did he do?

NED

He gave us the idea of making colored slides to illustrate our report on colonial schools. We hadn't even thought of illustrating it.

JACK

Then he's an *idea giver,* isn't he?

NED

I suppose so, but in some way it seems to me that it was more than that. It wasn't just any old idea. It was an idea that really got us started.

BARBARA

I know what you mean. I was in that group too.

NED (*turning to the teacher*)

What would you call that role, Mr. Lane?

TEACHER

From what I've heard you say I think I'd call him an *initiator*.

JACK

But that isn't on our list.

TEACHER

No, but that list only included the roles we were able to recognize. There are really quite a number missing.

JACK

Aha! Maybe that's why I can't always fit the things people do into that list. I couldn't figure out why it wouldn't work.

A general class discussion followed, Ned leading off with a description of what had happened in his group and following this with a summary of the talk the four pupils and the teacher had had. In the discussion that followed, statements were made and questions were asked that indicated that these boys and girls were ready to move ahead. Some of these were:

There are different ways of giving ideas to a group. Sometimes you just tell what you think about something that has been said.

Sometimes you give an example to explain a point. That's giving an idea, too.

What do you call a person who says that he agrees with an idea?

Isn't the *shy guy* important sometimes? He's a *listener* and you need listeners.

There are different kinds of *questioners,* too. Some people say an idea in a question. In our group Mary asked, "Couldn't we each write our own part?" What she really meant was, "Let's each write our own."

Some questions ask for information.

Some questions ask what other people are thinking about the problem.

Isn't an *objector* a *blocker?* And how about the *know-it-all?*

The teacher decided that the time had come to present more complete and accurate data concerning the roles that people play in groups. For the following class period he prepared three mimeographed sheets. On one of these he listed the following six roles under the heading, *Group Building Roles:*[1]

1. *Encourager*
   Praises or expresses agreement with ideas of others.
2. *Harmonizer*
   Is the peacemaker in disagreements.
3. *Compromiser*
   Gives up part of his own idea in order to meet others in the group "half-way."
4. *Gatekeeper*
   Keeps discussion moving along either by drawing quiet members into it or by suggesting a time limit for individual participation in order that all may take part.
5. *Standard setter*
   Expresses standards that he thinks the group should live up to.
6. *Follower*
   Serves as an audience in a group discussion.

On the second sheet he listed the following twelve roles under the heading, *Group Task Roles:*

1. *Initiator*
   Suggests new ideas or new ways of doing things.
2. *Information seeker*
   Asks for facts about the point being discussed.
3. *Opinion seeker*
   Asks how others feel about the point being discussed.
4. *Information giver*
   Gives facts that are authoritative or relates own experiences about the point being discussed.
5. *Opinion giver*
   States his own opinion about the point being discussed.
6. *Elaborator*
   Gives examples or explains the meaning of the point being discussed.
7. *Coordinator*
   Shows how different ideas or activities of different members fit together.

---

[1] Kenneth D. Benne and Paul Sheats, "Functional Roles of Group Members," *The Journal of Social Issues*, 4:2:42–47, Spring, 1948.

8. *Orienter*
   Summarizes ideas. Points out that the group is not working on its problem.
9. *Evaluator*
   Points out how well the group is working according to work standards that were accepted by the group.
10. *Energizer*
    Prods the group to action or decision.
11. *Technician*
    Helps by doing things for the group—distributing materials, arranging seats, and so forth.
12. *Recorder*
    Keeps a record of group suggestions, decisions, and activities.

On the third the following six roles were listed under the heading, *Individual Satisfaction Roles:*

1. *Blocker*
   Disagrees with others beyond reason. Blocks progress.
2. *Recognition seeker*
   Calls attention to himself by boasting or by acting in unusual ways in order to make himself "top man."
3. *Aggressor*
   Makes others feel small. Shows envy by taking undue credit. Picks on others.
4. *Playboy*
   Cracks jokes, indulges in horseplay, or expresses lack of interest.
5. *Dominator*
   Asserts authority or superiority. Interrupts others. Insists on his right to attention. Gives orders.
6. *Help-seeker*
   Looks for sympathy from others.

The following day, each pupil received copies of the three lists. The teacher reviewed briefly the discussion of the previous day and then turned attention to the lists of group roles. He pointed out that a great deal of work has been done in recent years in the study of how groups operate, and what makes some work well whereas others are unable to accomplish anything. He said further that people who have made such studies have identified many roles that the person not trained for this might not recognize. It has also been determined what effects these roles have on a group.

The remainder of the period was spent in a discussion based on what happens in a group when an *encourager* role is taken by someone, or a *harmonizer* role, or any of the others on the first list. The generalization drawn from this analysis was that these roles made a group feel better, made a group pleased to be together, or, in other words, as the heading indicated, built a group.

As they moved to the second list, they saw at once that these were roles that helped a group to complete its task. The third list was felt to be well named, since they saw clearly that none of these roles either helped to build the group or to accomplish the work that needed to be done. The only persons who derived any satisfaction from such roles were the individuals who played them.

Plans were made to discover how many of these roles were actually operating in this class. Since the problem facing them at the next business meeting was a consideration of how to do a better job of keeping up to date with current news, they felt that this discussion would be an excellent opportunity for checking themselves, since the class would be operating as a group trying to solve a problem. It was decided to make a tape recording of the meeting, which could be played back later for analysis.

The plan was carried out and the tape was played back on the following day. It was run through twice, the first time to review the discussion as a whole, to give pupils the opportunity to identify people, and to get the usual giggles and familiar remarks of "Is that the way I sound?" out of the way.

The second playback was for purposes of analysis. In order to involve everyone in the process, the class decided to divide into four groups, each of which was assigned to listen for a different set of group roles, one group listening for evidences of *Group Building Roles,* one for the first six of the *Group Task Roles,* one for the second six of the *Group Task Roles,* and one for the *Individual Satisfaction Roles.* Each pupil prepared a large sheet of paper for recording his findings, listing the roles, and leaving space for writing after each one. As a role was identified the statement that had been made was recorded as completely as possible under the name of the role. It was not necessary to identify the individual who made the statement.

At the completion of the playback, the members of each of the four groups assembled to discuss the data collected and to make a composite of the individual records. The combined report of the group on *Group Building Roles* was as follows:

GROUP BUILDING ROLES IN OUR DISCUSSION
Statements Made by Group Members

Encourager

  1. I think that's a good idea. (*This was said four different times.*)
  2. Jerry's mimeographed sheet was a big help.
  3. I like that.

Harmonizer

  1. I don't think Ruth meant it the way we took it.

Compromiser

  1. Nine pupils wanted everyone to buy a subscription to *Time* magazine, while most class members wanted to use the daily newspaper. The nine agreed to stop arguing for *Time* magazine when the rest of the class agreed to subscribe to *Scholastic* magazine.

Gatekeeper

  1. What do you think, Ray?
  2. Let's give everyone a chance to say what he thinks by not going into too many details in our suggestions.
  3. We haven't heard from Janet or Shirley yet.

Standard-setter

  1. I think we ought to move along since we agreed to complete this part by the end of the first period.
  2. Didn't we agree to let the committee members give their ideas first?
  3. One person talking at a time is the rule.

Follower

  1. You couldn't hear the "followers" on the tape, but we remember that many people listened during the discussion.

The *Individual Satisfaction* roles were conspicuous by their absence, which was to be expected since this was a discussion that all knew was being recorded. Since it had been recognized that these were not helpful roles, any normal tendencies to play them were sharply self-curbed for the day.

If a tape recorder that will pick up clearly the voices of such a large group is not available, the same technique may be used without it by assigning four individual observers to record the roles taken throughout the actual discussion. Either method should be followed by a careful study by the class of the observer records.

Following the establishment of the new list of group roles, opportunities should be given from time to time for small groups and the class as a whole to measure their own interactions against this list. The tape recorder again is a helpful means of doing this. It is an especially good procedure when a group (small group or entire class) recognizes that it is having difficulties in solving its problems. By playing the tape back, a group may check its work to see what roles that are needed were not being carried out by any member, or, conversely, what roles were being played that were hindering the progress of the group. The lists of roles serve as yardsticks.

Concept of leadership. The original list of group roles included the term *leader*. That this was not to be found in the more extensive list caused much confusion and questioning. How can a group operate if it doesn't have a leader? Was this role omitted by mistake? Isn't the chairman the leader?

At the close of a class period that had been spent working in groups of nine or ten, a sheet of paper was given to each pupil on which the following three questions had been mimeographed, with space left for writing after each one.

Who were the members of your group?
Which of these acted as leaders in helping the group to progress?
What did they do?

The answers to the third question served as the springboard for the discussion the following day. Eleven items were listed one or more times in response to this. These were as follows:

1. Tried hard to keep the group working at its problem.
2. Made new suggestions that were very good.
3. Asked the group to make a decision.
4. Summarized the ideas that had been suggested.
5. Asked questions that made us think about what we had read.
6. Asked us for our opinions.
7. Gave information that the group needed.
8. Tried several times to evaluate how far our group had come.
9. Got everyone into the discussion.
10. Reminded us that we only had a half hour to work on this.
11. Told us how he felt about our ideas.

This summary was written on the chalkboard in order that it might be at hand throughout the discussion. The teacher pointed out that these were all quite different ways of behaving, that trying to keep a group working at its problem was obviously not the same as telling how you feel about an idea. Yet, both had described a leader. He then suggested that the pupils refer to the three lists of group roles and identify each of these eleven activities. They had no difficulty, and reached agreement quickly on the following roles as names for the eleven descriptions.

1. Energizer	5. Information seeker	9. Gatekeeper
2. Initiator	6. Opinion seeker	10. Standard setter
3. Energizer	7. Information giver	11. Opinion giver
4. Orienter	8. Evaluator	

To their amazement they found only one duplication of roles, the *energizer*. Ten different roles had been listed. The class was asked to study this list of roles carefully, then to write an answer to the following question: *How do you account for the fact that leaders have been described in ten different ways?*

For some this was too difficult, and they were unable to draw any conclusions. Several said that something was wrong, that a leader should have just one role, namely, to keep the group moving. This idea, however, sparked the proceedings, and the class generally came to the conclusion that this is exactly what a leader does, but he keeps the group moving by operating in many different ways.

The teacher reminded them that not just one person had been named as leader in each group, but that in the first group six out of ten members had been named, in the second four out of nine, and in the third seven out of nine; in other words seventeen people had been classed as leaders out of a total of twenty-eight, yet only three were chairmen of the groups. Again, several said that something was wrong, that each group had to have *a* leader, not four or five.

However, there were a few who saw an answer in the data before them.

BILL

Then it isn't just one person in a group who keeps it moving.

KATHY

And there isn't just one way to do it.

BARBARA

Oh, I think I see it. A leader can be anybody in the group ——

KATHY

Yes. It depends upon what he does. If it's what the group needs right at that minute, the group moves ahead and he's the leader for the time being.

STEVE

That's it. That's why so many people were named as leaders. Each one helped us get ahead at a different time.

Recognition of this does not come to an entire group at the same time. It is, however, a concept that is very satisfying to young people when they become aware of it. It gives recognition to a person's actions in a group—his question may be the helpful one, his suggestion, his example, his compromise, his word of agreement—any one may help a group to progress. They begin to see that no contribution, if it is aimed at solving the problem, is too small to present.

Conclusion

Ability to work with other people in solving common problems is of slow growth. The necessary skills develop only as an individual increases his understanding of the activities that take place within the groups in which he participates. It is a step by step growth. His own experiences in working with others must precede each attempt to verbalize the process, for the words can have meaning only as they shed light on his own interaction with others in a group. However, the experiences *must* be *verbalized,* in order that they may be interpreted and clarified. Continuous participation in group activity without help in understanding what is taking place is often meaningless and completely baffling to a pupil. Many teachers say that group activity is not successful in their classes, and that they have given it up entirely. Usually, in such instances little or no effort has been made to help pupils learn *how* to work in groups nor how to interpret their experiences. The result has been that, without a sense of direction, the groups disintegrated and accomplished little, either in terms of ability to work with each other or in solving problems.

Helping boys and girls learn to work in groups is often discouraging. We expect and hope for so much more skill than can possibly develop in the length of time we have a class. We fail to recognize that a year is not very long and that, even if there has been considerable growth, we are not always observant enough to see it.

4

Moving Into Pupil-Teacher Planning

Sᴛᴀʀᴛɪɴɢ ᴀ ᴄʟᴀss ᴄᴏᴍᴘʟᴇᴛᴇʟʏ ᴏɴ ᴀ ᴘᴜᴘɪʟ-ᴛᴇᴀᴄʜᴇʀ planned basis on the first day is for most teachers similar to stepping off into space. There is nothing to hang on to. It is usually safer to make a slower approach, to start with teacher-directed activities and, as boys and girls show ability to accept minor responsibilities, to work from these to activities planned by pupils and teacher together. Many boys and girls have had no previous experience in planning classroom activities, whereas others have had such opportunities in varying degrees. However, in a new class situation, with a new teacher and new classmates, even the latter are frequently thrown badly off balance.

Introduction to pupil-teacher planning

A unit or two planned largely by the teacher will serve as a bridge leading from the teacher-controlled classroom to pupil-teacher planned procedures and activities. Such a unit gives a teacher an opportunity to determine the degree to which the class is ready for democratic procedures, and allows him to introduce pupil-teacher planning techniques slowly and in accordance with the ability of pupils to accept the responsibilities involved. This avoids plunging a class into problems with which they cannot adequately cope. Such units also serve to build a common background of experience and understanding for all members of the class, and it becomes unnecessary either to rely on or to blame pupils' past experiences for their present level of understanding and acceptance of democratic ideas and values.

A unit planned for this purpose is introduced by the teacher. It initially moves forward as the teacher directs and for the purposes determined by the teacher. However, as the unit proceeds, opportunities can be presented for small choices and decisions to be made by the class members. In the first few of such decision-making situations, the teacher states the limits of the choices. Perhaps he says, "There is a film illustrating this point which I would like to have you see. Does Monday or Tuesday seem better to you for this?" Or perhaps at another time he says, "We can use either a filmstrip or a recording, both of which tell this story. Which do you think would be better?" Another example of early pupil-teacher planning is given in the description of pupil-pupil interviews in Chapter 2, in which it was suggested that boys and girls participate in planning the activity to the extent of preparing the list of things they would like to know about their classmates, a list that would be used in conducting the interview.

An opportunity for making a choice of another type develops from such a question as, "Which procedure do you think would be better to use for this, small group discussions or a class roundtable discussion?" As decision making is increasingly ably handled, the problems should gradually deal with more important matters, and the opportunities for making them should be more frequent.

The teacher holds the reins but loosens them as time goes on. If he finds he has let go too far, he must tighten his hold again, always, however, remembering to relax control again very shortly. There is the temptation to maintain an authoritative hold because "the class operates so much more smoothly when I tell them what to do." This is probably true, but the measure of a democratic classroom is not necessarily the smoothness of operation, but the growth shown by pupils in taking responsibilities upon themselves. Many teachers, too, are afraid to let go because, inversely, they are afraid they may have to back up and start over. It is an affront to their teaching ability. They do not realize that helping boys and girls learn to operate in a pupil-teacher planned classroom involves an endless estimating of when it is possible to loosen further the reins of teacher control, and when it is temporarily necessary to tighten them, in other words, judging when pupils are ready to take certain responsibilities and when they are not. It is important to recognize that such "backing and filling" is a necessary part of progress.

The period of time spent in orienting the boys and girls to one another and to their school as described in Chapter 2 is an example of a first unit, initiated by the teacher and having the activities almost entirely planned by the teacher.

Unit on democratic living. A second unit that further serves as a bridge from the teacher-directed classroom to that planned by pupils and teacher together is one dealing with *Democratic Living.* This may well be used in a social studies class, a combined social studies and English class, a core or general education class. In this unit, too, more and more decisions are made by the pupils, although the over-all plan is made by the teacher. In addition, while working on the unit, the class is introduced to further techniques and procedures that are an integral part of a democratically operating class. They become familiar with a wide variety of methods of operation, which they will use at later times. Under the teacher's guidance the boys and girls learn to work with more assurance in small groups, to conduct circle discussions and panel discussions, set up committees for carrying out special jobs, plan an agenda for a day or a week's work, and to evaluate their progress.

Through the unit dealing with the democratic way of living, the teacher tries to develop an understanding of the meaning of democracy, its strengths and its weaknesses, and a growing faith in its values. It has seemed to the writer that one of the reasons many so-called democratic classes have not lived up to expecta-

tions has been the fact that the pupils, and sometimes the teacher, have not developed a clear concept of, nor belief in, the underlying principles of democratic life. Unless such knowledge and faith develop, the methods and techniques of operating are cold and sterile, and they will bear no fruit in lasting behavior of the participants.

An approach to democratic living has been made by some teachers through a study of the history of democracy from its earliest times to the present. Others have traced its development in our own country. Still others have approached it through a study of our government. It has always seemed to the writer that too frequently such approaches become merely factual studies, which, valuable as they may be, are drained of their applications to the immediate lives of the boys and girls in the classroom.

A method that involves all of these, but on a less academic basis, starts with each child's own concept of the meaning of democracy. Each pupil is asked to write a paragraph in which he explains what the word *democracy* means to him. If these are written in class, the pupils may be asked to take them home and talk them over with their parents, and to bring them back to class for discussion on the following day.

The meaning of democracy to many boys and girls is expressed by the familiar words, "government of the people, by the people, and for the people." There is little or no attempt to think beyond these words or to interpret them. Others quite frankly admit that they have little idea of its meaning, as is shown in the following ninth-grade paper.

I really don't know the real meaning of democracy. I think it has something to do with the state but I don't know. If I really knew what democracy is I could write about it.

Many, however, try to reach beyond the usual words. Several examples taken from the same class follow.

I haven't a very good idea of what the word itself means, but I have a little idea about it. Democracy to me means the world as one. It

means the friendship of the world together. In a country it means people getting along with each other.

Democracy means thinking for yourself. When you are twenty-one and can vote you can vote for the person you think is best. And when you decide how to do things without being influenced by someone else you are being democratic. If you fight something that you think is wrong, even if other people think it is right, you are being democratic.

Democracy is saying what you please, doing what you please, and living as you please.

Democracy is something that is intangible. You can't see it and you can't eat it, but every citizen of our country has it. Democracy is all our freedoms like freedom of religion, freedom of the press, and freedom of speech.

It was obvious to the teacher that if this class was to be built on a basis of democratic principles a more common understanding must be established than was evidenced by the diverse ideas expressed in the papers.

On the day designated for consideration of these ideas, the teacher used the technique of a class roundtable discussion. Seats —all thirty-five of them—were swung into a large circle around the edge of the room as a means of giving every child an opportunity to talk with his classmates on a face-to-face basis. It had the further advantage of moving the teacher out of the central position, since he sat in the circle with his pupils. In this way it could become truly a class discussion.

Each pupil had his own paper at hand in order to minimize the stage fright that comes to many boys and girls when they are facing their peers and trying to express ideas for which it is difficult to find words. The papers could be referred to at any time.

After several ideas had been expressed and had been discussed, it became obvious that the class was so eager for discussion that only a few ideas would be touched upon. The teacher proposed that all discussion be withheld until each pupil had had an opportunity to present his definition. He appointed a boy to write these on the board.

There were, of course, many duplications that were not listed. The final list of definitions was as follows:

Democracy means:
1. Freedom of religion
2. Freedom of speech
3. Freedom of the press
4. Government of the people, by the people, and for the people
5. Something to do with the state
6. Thinking for yourself without being influenced
7. A place where no one can stop you from doing what you want
8. Everyone has an equal chance to get a job
9. Getting along with others
10. People can do what they please
11. People can live as they please
12. All people are equal
13. A government that the people have elected
14. Have education for everyone

The discussion waxed hot and furious. Little question was raised about items 1, 3, 9, and 13. All others were battled royally, pro and con. In a democracy you *can* say just what you want to. No, you can't, because if it isn't true a libel suit can be brought to court. You can think for yourself, but other people have a right to try to influence you—that's what advertising is supposed to do. You *can't* do just what you want to, because we have laws and police and courts. Besides, what would happen if *everyone* did just as he wanted to? It would be a mess. You have to consider other people besides yourself. And it isn't true that everyone has an equal chance at a job. A Negro doesn't. People *can't* live as they please. Many summer resorts will not accept Jewish people. What's wrong with that? The resort owners have a right to have the people they want in their own resorts, don't they? But all people are equal, so why should some be kept out because of their religion? We believe in freedom of religion, don't we?

Almost every boy and girl participated in the merry-go-round discussion, and it was not always easy for the teacher to keep feelings from getting out of hand in the three class-periods that were

necessary to cover the points on the list and give everyone a chance to express his views. He participated by helping to clarify points that were made and by helping boys and girls to understand each other without anger. In addition, he recorded items mentioned and points made which gave rise to further questions or which had not been either well or completely handled.

Toward the end of the third period of discussion, despite the fact that it could have well continued for several more, the teacher called a halt with this statement, "We have been discussing the meaning of democracy for three periods. I wonder whether you feel as I do that before we can reach an agreement we need some factual information. For example, you have repeatedly referred to our Bill of Rights. Do you know what these rights are and where you would find them listed?"

The class looked a bit sheepish and one boy said, "I think it's in the Declaration of Independence but I don't really know what it says."

"No, it's not in the Declaration of Independence," said the teacher. "In order that we may have better information than we now have on several subjects that have been mentioned, are there some of you who would volunteer to take a special assignment? I will write the list of items about which we seem to need more data on the board. That will give you a chance to make a choice."

This was the list:

1. United States Constitution
2. Bill of Rights
3. The Puritans and freedom of religion
4. How our government operates
5. Federal ruling relating to Negroes and whites in schools; Federal ruling relating to Negro rights of housing
6. Emancipation Proclamation
7. Democracy before the time of the American colonies
8. Freedom of the press

Eight pupils volunteered to collect the needed information and report back to the class by the end of the week. The teacher suggested that the encyclopedia might be a good place to start collect-

ing information on some of these subjects. For others he volunteered to meet with the pupils in the library and give them
assistance in finding the information they needed. Another procedure might have been to divide the class into small groups,
assigning one topic to each group. Since, however, the purpose
was to collect information as quickly as possible, the teacher
chose to use the individual method.

At the beginning of the next class period a film, *Defining
Democracy,*[1] was brought in by the teacher. He introduced it in
this way.

> Yesterday the word *dictatorship* was used a great deal in your dis-
> cussion on the meaning of democracy. You pointed to it as being the
> opposite of democracy, but you did not make clear in what ways a
> dictatorship is different from a democracy. Today I have brought a
> film called *Defining Democracy,* which tells about democracy and
> despotism. *Despotism* is another word for dictatorship. This film will
> help us see how democracy and dictatorship differ from one another.

The film is based on the principle that as the people of a community increasingly share their power and share their respect
with all groups and individuals, they approach a democracy. As
they place power in the hands of fewer and fewer people, and as
they show respect for only certain groups of people, they approach despotism. The graphs used in the film to show shifts in
these two aspects of democracy, shared power and shared respect,
were used as a basis for further class work. A mimeographed
sheet, as shown in Figure 11, was prepared by the teacher.

On successive days these sheets were filled out in class. The
first time the blank space in the heading was filled in with the
word *City*. Pupils were asked to draw a heavy line across each
column to show the degree of democracy that they believed
existed in their city, in terms of shared power and shared respect.
Below the chart they were asked to explain in detail their reasons
for placing the lines at such points. These ratings, as recorded by
different individuals, were then discussed. Examples of shared

---

[1] Encyclopedia Britannica Films, Incorporated.

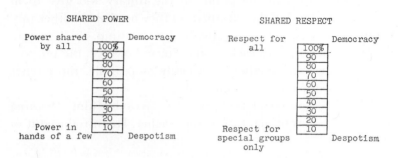

WHAT ABOUT OUR_____?

Figure 11. Democracy or despotism.

power and shared respect, drawn from their own and their families' experiences, were reported. Many examples showing lack of these characteristics were presented as well.

The same procedure was followed by writing the word *Club* into the heading of a second sheet. This might be a school club, a church group, or any club to which the child belonged. A third approach was made by filling in the blank with the word *Home*. This last, it is obvious, can only be used if good rapport has been established between teacher and pupil. The reactions were discussed in class as before.

The fourth area for consideration was the *School*. With only a few exceptions, the school was rated extremely low in both shared power and shared respect. In fact, it was considered quite a joke even to be asked about these points in relation to school. The discussion included such comments as the following:

The teacher is the boss. You have to study what she tells you to.

If she gives you a chance to do anything it has to be done just the way she says.

You *have* to go to school until you're sixteen. Nothing democratic about that.

The teacher makes the rules in the room and the pupils have to obey.

In some classes we have had class officers but the teacher told them exactly what to do.

But in our class we helped plan a party once and it was a good party too.

My mother says I should respect the teacher.

I held the door open for Miss Smith and she didn't say "Thank you."

Mr. Raymond is always friendly to everyone in the class, not just to a few.

Everyone says we should respect the teacher, but no one ever says the teacher should respect us.

When feelings are as sharply defined as this, it is necessary to move cautiously toward the idea of developing a democratic structure within a class. A first step was to help the boys and girls review their past schoolroom experiences more carefully from the standpoint of activities in the planning of which they had really had a share. When they stopped to think about it, most found a great many. In this review the question was also raised concerning the lack of respect teachers were said to have for their pupils. Here, too, they found that they had made a generalization that fit only a few of their teachers.

The teacher then asked a question:

Let's pretend for a few minutes that this class was being run on a democratic plan. What could you do in a democratically operated class that you cannot do if the teacher always makes the decisions? Jot your ideas down on a piece of paper.

The class looked stunned for a minute, and then went to work with a gleam in their eyes that augured ill for autocratic procedures. The list as finally agreed upon was as follows:

1. We could make the rules for the class.
2. We could help decide what the class will study.
3. We could say what we think without having to agree with the teacher.
4. We could help plan any special activities.

The discussion through which this list was arrived at had been fiery. There were a few who argued that if it were a democratic class the teacher could have no part in any decisions. There were also those few who tried hard to include such items as the right to come into the room or stay out of the room as they wished. This led to a consideration of the teacher's responsibilities both to the school administration and to parents, in other words, to the limits within which it is possible to operate democratically in a classroom.

The class was pleased with its final list and was all set to move into operation. The teacher, however, suggested that perhaps there was another side to be considered. Was democracy only *freedom* to do things? For example if they had the *right* to help make the class rules, did they not have some *obligations* in this area? They were quick to see that it would be necessary to live up to such rules and to make rules that would be helpful to the class as a whole. A list of obligations was developed by the group that read as follows:

1. We must make rules that will help the class.
2. We must live up to the rules.
3. We must choose worth-while subjects to study.
4. We must have good reasons for the ideas we express.
5. We must give others a chance to express their ideas.
6. We must plan activities that will help the class.

Through the discussion of these rights and responsibilities, a fifth item was added to the list of rights, namely: *We could vote the way we think is best.* The following item was also added to the list of responsibilities: *We must take an active part in all class activities.*

At this point the teacher felt that it would be well to give the class a preview of some of the activities that other classes operating on a democratic basis had undertaken in the past. He showed the film, *Practicing Democracy in the Classroom,*[2] and the film-

---

2 Encyclopedia Britannica Films, Incorporated.

strip, *A Core Curriculum Class in Action*.[3] The discussion that followed pointed to similarities and differences between the pictured classes and their own.

Having established the rights and responsibilities that boys and girls would have if the classroom were operated on a democratic basis, and having looked ahead to possible activities, the teacher asked them how they felt about actually organizing their class democratically. Were the rights worth making an effort to achieve? Would they be willing to accept the obligations they had listed? The pupils were eager to make the decision at once, but they were asked to go home and think about it, to write out their reactions to the idea and to bring the answers to class the following day.

Without exception they wanted to try it. The lists of rights and obligations were printed by a committee on large sheets of poster board and posted in the room to remind themselves of the decision they had made. And the class was on its way.

Organization of the class

Class organization involves a number of things. There are class officers to be elected. Rudimentary knowledge of parliamentary procedure must be learned in order to carry on class business. The operation of a business meeting is itself a new experience to many. Some classes feel the need to write a class constitution that serves to summarize the rules and regulations pupils have set for themselves and to define their own particular class organization.

Election of officers. To boys and girls of almost any age the outstanding mark of a democratic classroom is the election of class officers who are responsible for class operation. For this reason, the election of officers is an excellent place to start in the organization of a class. The number of officers needed depends upon the number and kinds of jobs that need to be done in the classroom. Frequently pupils see only a few at first: a chairman to conduct the class meetings, a clerk to take attendance, and a

---

3 Audio-Visual Utilization Center, Wayne State University, Detroit.

secretary to record the class activities. This is a good beginning. It is unnecessary, even unwise, to push a group into acceptance of a large number of officers for whom at the moment they see no purpose and for whom there may be no work. Later, as various officers are absent, pupils come to realize the need for assistants. And if there is a room library they soon see that they must have a librarian or two. When money is collected for any special purpose—fees, a party, book fines, or perhaps a small gift or a card to a member of the class who is ill—the importance of having a treasurer comes to light. These are the times to fill such new offices.

If, as sometimes happens, this is a class in which it is difficult to draw more than a few pupils into a general discussion, the teacher may be eager to use a method that will assure participation of as many class members as possible in deciding what class officers are needed. This should be an activity in which every pupil has a part. For example, each pupil can be asked to list in one column the things that he feels need to be done in the room in order that activities may run smoothly. In a second column he is asked to list the name of an officer to fulfill this duty. The teacher might start it off like this:

Things to be Done	*Officer*
Calling the meeting to order	President

When the lists have been completed, the class is divided at random into small groups of five or six, and a summary list is compiled in each. The groups will need help in deciding on a method for making such a compilation. If not given assistance, they may simply collect the individual lists, give them to a recorder, and spend the period in conversation having nothing to do with the group problem. This is intended to be a period for sharing ideas and should be so used. A few minutes time, before moving into groups, spent in planning *how* to share their ideas and reach some agreements is worth far more than time spent in scolding them after a wasted period. For example, they may decide that:

1. One person at a time will read one of his ideas to the group.

2. This will be discussed by the group.

3. If the group feels that it is a good point, it will be recorded on the summary list. If it is not accepted it is not recorded.

4. Each person in turn then reads one of his ideas and each is treated in the same way as the first.

Group summary lists are then reported back to the class as a whole at the end of ten or fifteen minutes, and a master list is recorded on the chalkboard that represents the thinking of the entire class. In accepting reports from groups, it is good to record one item from each group, then a second item from each group, and so around and around until all different points have been made. If this is not done, one group may "steal the thunder" from the rest and they, having nothing to report, are not involved enough to maintain concern for the problem. The method described may result, of course, in a relatively long list of offices to be filled.

Taking suggestions from the floor is another possible procedure. Boys and girls give suggestions from the lists they have prepared individually and these are recorded on the board. Many, however, will not volunteer their ideas in this situation, so, not only are good ideas lost, but some pupils feel that their written work was a waste of time since it was not used.

The class next decides which of the suggested offices are really needed and what are the exact duties of each officer to be elected. This can be done by means of a general class discussion of the list on the board, or it can be assigned to a committee that reports its suggestions to the class. A further question that must be considered is the length of time each individual is to hold office. The class then proceeds to conduct its election. A class in process of carrying on an election is shown in Figure 12.

At a later time, perhaps at a second or even a third election, the teacher will do well to raise another important question with his class: Do the pupils feel that it is important to get the best possible people into elected positions in order that the class may run smoothly or do they feel that it is important to give as many boys

Figure 12. A class elects its officers.

and girls as possible the experience of being a class officer? The
reactions to this question will vary widely from group to group.
However, whatever the decision is at this point, by the time a
class has had two or three groups of officers they come to see that
some persons have held offices very well who, at the time of election, did not seem well qualified. Insofar as possible, it is good to
move in the direction of having many pupils have a hand at some
time or other in the administration of the class. If the emphasis
is placed too strongly on selecting people seemingly best qualified

to fill the positions, frequently only the intellectually brighter pupils, or those who are already strong leaders, are elected and re-elected, since these seem to class members to be the best.

Many boys and girls wish desperately to be elected to an office and never quite make the grade. An eleventh-grade pupil wrote on a confidential list of *Wishes:* "I wish more than anything that sometime I would be elected chairman of our class. That would be tops for me." A semester later she was chosen as chairman and made an excellent one. She had been by-passed for this office five semesters although she had been an active member of a number of committees.

A later chairman of the same class was a very quiet, unassuming, but capable girl. Her election was a distinct surprise to the teacher. However, a conversation that was very enlightening was overheard between Ann and a fellow class member at the Christmas party at the teacher's home. The teacher had played the record, *Getting to Know You,* from *The King and I*[4] as a way of expressing her feelings about the class. At one point the words are:

> Getting to know you, getting to feel free and easy—
> When I am with you, getting to know what to say.
> Haven't you noticed? Suddenly I'm bright and breezy—
> Because of all the beautiful and new things
> I'm learning about you day by day.

The group, seated on the floor around the fireplace, had picked it up and sung it over and over. Later Ann and Dell were washing dishes in the kitchen, and Ann was heard to say, "Funny, isn't it, but that's the way it is with me, too. Now that I'm chairman, I'm getting to feel free and easy, and I'm getting to know what to say, and I *do* feel bright and breezy. I guess it's really because I *am* learning things about all of you every day." Had the emphasis been placed on electing only those whom the class members felt

---

4 Copyright © 1951 by Richard Rodgers and Oscar Hammerstein 2nd, Williamson Music Inc., owner of publication and allied rights.

were best qualified, neither of these girls would have been chosen. Yet both were excellent chairmen.

A point that would seem to be unnecessary to make, but which is frequently violated by the teacher is that, the class having elected officers, they should be given opportunities to function. No matter how long a teacher has worked in a democratic classroom, he must watch himself to see that he does not take from pupils the rights of their offices. Too often a chairman waits for the teacher to tell him what the teacher wants done, even though a schedule for the week has been planned by the class. Or perhaps the teacher says to the treasurer, "Let me have the money. I'll take care of it." On reading days he tells the librarian which group is to go to the bookshelves first, second, and so forth, instead of giving the librarian an opportunity to fulfill this responsibility. Unless the officers are free to assume their obligations, the election has been wholly a sham.

Parliamentary procedure. A question is frequently raised relative to the use of parliamentary procedure. Many teachers feel that parliamentary rules must be followed in detail, and that a violation of such rules negates democratic activity. If one is only interested in the surface aspects of democratic skills and techniques, it becomes necessary to follow rigidly the rules of order. If, however, it is the spirit and feel of democracy that is of vital concern, it is quite possible to operate with a minimum number of rules, at least at the beginning. It is not long before boys and girls become aware of the fact that some pattern of operation needs to be established if they are going to carry on any reasonable amount of business.

When this happens they can be introduced to parliamentary procedure either through the film, *Parliamentary Procedures in Action,*[5] or through such a book as, *So You Were Elected,* or *Robert's Rules of Order.*[6] The film deals with a high school

---

5 Coronet Films.

6 Virginia Bailard and Harry C. McKown, *So You Were Elected* (New York: Whittlesey House, 1946).

Henry Martyn Roberts, *Robert's Rules of Order* (Chicago: Scott Foresman and Company, 1951).

dramatics club conducting a meeting and follows parliamentary procedure in detail. From discussions of these sources, decisions can be reached as to the pattern the class will follow. A ninth-grade class decided upon the following plan as its order of business during a business meeting.

Order of Business:
1. The meeting is called to order by the president.
2. The minutes are read by the secretary.
3. The list of absent members is read by the clerk.
4. The old business is completed:
    a. Committee reports
    b. Other unfinished matters
5. New business is considered.
6. The meeting is adjourned.

The class then considered the procedures of business meetings as shown in the film and books on parliamentary procedure. In addition, several pupils attended various school club meetings and reported to the class the different methods of carrying on a meeting. From these, with the help of the teacher, they prepared a simple model plan for a business meeting to serve as a guide. This was duplicated and a copy given to each pupil.

A BUSINESS MEETING[7]

PRESIDENT

The meeting will please come to order. (*He waits until everyone is quiet.*) The secretary will now read the minutes of the last meeting.

(*The secretary reads the minutes.*)

PRESIDENT

Are there any corrections or additions?

[If not, the president says, "The minutes are accepted and approved as read."]

[Any correction of the minutes should always suggest a better way than the one used by the secretary. The following procedure is followed if a correction is made.]

---

7 William Clark Trow and Rosalind M. Zapf and Harry C. McKown, *Getting Acquainted With Your School, The Junior Citizen Series* (New York: McGraw-Hill Book Company, Inc., 1951), pp. 33–34.

FIRST PUPIL

Mr. President.

PRESIDENT

Mary.

FIRST PUPIL

I suggest that instead of just saying, "Miss Brown made a few announcements," the minutes should report what the announcements were.

PRESIDENT

Will someone make a motion that the minutes be accepted as read and corrected?

SECOND PUPIL (*after he has addressed the chair and has been recognized*)

I move that the minutes be accepted as read and corrected.

THIRD PUPIL (*after he has addressed the chair and has been recognized*)

I second that motion.

PRESIDENT

It has been moved and seconded that the minutes be accepted. All those in favor of the motion raise their right hands.

(*The hands are counted.*)

PRESIDENT

Those who are opposed raise their right hands.

(*The hands are counted.*)

PRESIDENT

The minutes are accepted. The report of the clerk will now be given.

CLERK

The absentees are ———— (CLERK *reads the names of absent pupils.*)

PRESIDENT

Is there any unfinished business?

[Reports or other matters that were left over from a previous meeting are considered.]

PRESIDENT

Is there any new business?

[Reports or other matters that were not brought up in previous meetings are considered.]

PRESIDENT (*at the close of the period*)

Will someone move that the meeting be adjourned?

FOURTH PUPIL (*after he has addressed the chair and has been recognized*)

I move that the meeting be adjourned.

[This motion is handled in the same way as the motion to accept the minutes.]

PRESIDENT

The meeting is adjourned.

[The meeting is not over until it has been adjourned.]

Some weeks later, complaints were being made by a number of pupils that the plan of procedure decided upon by the class was not being carried out. They felt that there should be an evaluation of some sort. A committee of four was appointed by the chairman to figure out a way to do this. They prepared a bulletin board display that served as the basis for an evaluation of the business meeting procedure as carried out by the class. A copy of the order of business and a copy of the well-conducted business meeting that had been prepared by the class was posted under the heading: *How Would You Rate Our Business Meetings?* In addition, the following questions were printed with a brush pen on a large sheet of poster board:

How Well Are We Carrying Out Our Decisions?

1. Does the president call the meeting to order?
2. Does the secretary read the minutes of the previous meeting?
3. Are these minutes corrected when there is a mistake in them?
4. Do pupils wait to be recognized?
5. Does the president count the number of pupils in favor of a motion and those who are opposed?
6. Is the list of absent pupils read?
7. Is old business completed before new business is taken up?
8. Is our meeting always properly adjourned?
9. How could our business meetings be improved?

These questions could have been considered by the class in a general discussion and suggestions for improvement in procedure made. However, since the business meetings were truly functioning very poorly, the committee members felt that every pupil should be involved in the evaluation. They suggested that, in addition to placing the questions on the bulletin board, a copy of the same questions, with space left for writing after each one, be duplicated and given to each boy and girl. When the pupils had completed the questionnaire, the class was divided into random groups of five or six each. The job assigned to each group was to consider the responses of all its members and, insofar as possible, reach agreements on answers to all of the questions. These group agreements were then reported to the entire class, recorded on the chalkboard, and discussed by the class as a whole. In this way every pupil was involved, and the possibilities for recognition of the weak spots were increased enormously.

As a result, the class decided to have two persons serve as observers at each meeting who would report at the end of the class period on the success or lack of success in terms of the rules the class had established. This tended to keep them on their toes and very much aware of the techniques they were using. The business meetings improved tremendously.

A class constitution. Invariably there is a class member who insists that the class must have a constitution. In some groups the idea catches fire and nothing will do but that all important data relative to the organization of the class be put into the form of a constitution or bylaws. In other classes the idea does not take hold at all. Some classes have written constitutions in the ninth grade and, by amending them as the need for change arose, have lived by them through the twelfth grade. In others they have been useful for a short time only.

If a class wishes to write a constitution, it is good to take class time to consider what items are generally found in such a document. A copy of our national or state constitution placed in the hands of each class member is a simple but effective method of doing this. A committee may be appointed or elected to draw up the class constitution, or the entire class may work on it, different sections being developed by different groups. Upon completion, each section should be presented to the class for changes, rejections, approval, and final acceptance. It should then be duplicated in order that each member may have a copy at hand.[8]

A tenth-grade class, in its second year in a democratically functioning classroom, was having serious difficulties in operating. There was endless bickering about decisions that were made. The secretary's minutes did not satisfy the members. They finally spent many days listening to and discussing a proposal made by one of its members relative to the establishment of a *Ways and Means Committee*. The proposal was that this committee undertake, as part of its job, to assemble in written form all rules and regulations the class had established, keep clear records of all items dealing with the organization and operation of the class, and any special procedures pertaining to particular situations, such as elections, changes in membership in certain committees, and so forth. The idea was accepted. The class, in the succeeding years, turned to this committee for help whenever things went wrong, and looked to the records of this group as the guide for all procedures. They had, in effect, established a set of bylaws. *The Ways and Means Committee* members were considered next in importance to the chairman and were always elected immediately following the election of the vice-chairman, who was automatically chairman of the committee.

Daily and weekly planning

One of the important skills that must be developed in a class that is to function democratically is the ability to plan. It is needed in many different situations—in mapping out a day's or a week's work, in the development of an over-all arrangement of work for the semester, in deciding how to study a problem, how to collect data, how to share information, or how to present data to the class; in fact almost anything that is to be done must be planned. For this reason it is necessary to provide frequent opportunities for developing this ability.

In the following pages considerable attention will be given to

---

[8] A sample constitution may be found in the Appendix.

procedures for assisting pupils in setting up a skeleton outline for the semester's work and in using such an outline when developing specific weekly activity schedules. Without a long-term plan that gives direction to the activities, there is the danger that the class, remaining on a day-to-day basis, will operate only in terms of answers to the question, "What should we do tomorrow?"— without consideration of what has preceded or what should follow. This is an untenable situation. Activities are more than likely to lack continuity; they are pieces that do not fit together. Frequently they lack purpose. And in a short time the procedure fails to satisfy the pupils. A second danger lies in the chance that when boys and girls cease to find this type of planning satisfying, or when they run out of ideas, the teacher will take over the job and, as in the first few weeks, select the daily activities. It then ceases to be a democratic class.

As has been indicated, the activities of the first week or two are determined almost entirely by the teacher without consulting the class. During this time it is good procedure to list the day's agenda on the chalkboard at the beginning of the period in order that pupils may see clearly what is to be done and, in turn, recognize how much has been accomplished by the end of the period. Within a very short time pupils should be given opportunities to assist in planning the day ahead. The secretary should take over the teacher's position as daily recorder of the activities decided on for the following day, and assume responsibility for writing these on the board at the beginning of the next class period.

Having completed any introductory unit, such as an *Orientation* unit, a *Democratic Living* unit, the election of officers, and the organization of classroom business procedure, class and teacher together should look ahead to the semester, or the year, as a whole and prepare an over-all plan that will indicate the kinds of activities in which the class will participate, as well as the approximate amounts of time to be devoted to the major items during the course of each week.

If there are no required units, the pupils may need to be reminded that one of the purposes for which this class has been established is to help them learn to work together in order to solve problems to which they are really eager to find answers. This means, of course, that a part of the time will be spent in working on problems they will help to select. If certain items, such as specific subject matter content or specific units, are required to be taught in this course, it is important that these be listed when the semester planning is being done. Pupils should be aware of the limits within which they may have freedom to make choices and to understand how much time is available for additional activities.

To set semester planning in motion, each pupil is asked to list the *kinds* of activities that he feels it is important for the class to participate in during the semester, in addition to the study of topics that they will help to select or in addition to any required areas. The technique described previously may be used to summarize these lists, namely, to divide the class into random groups, the members of each group considering the individual lists and coming to agreement on the items that seem most important to them. The recorder for each group then reports the final list to the class as a whole. A sample list recorded from a ninth-grade core class planning session included the following:

1. Study topics selected by the class and teacher together. (This item was written on the board by the teacher before pupils made their individual lists.)
2. Learn about current happenings.
3. Have movies for fun.
4. Read stories.
5. Have business meetings.
6. Have parties.
7. Time to do as we please.
8. Take field trips to interesting places.
9. Time to do homework for any class.
10. Class discussions on problems about which class members are concerned. (This item was contributed by the teacher.)

Through a discussion of the items on this list, pupils clarified the point for themselves that class time was not a play time. This is shown in the final list by the change in their approach to the use of movies, the shift in the use of a free choice period, and the elimination of time to do homework for any class. The revised list was as follows:

1. Study topics selected by the class and teacher together.
2. Current happenings.
3. Movies.
    a. Current events movies.
    b. Movies to go with topics studied.
4. Free reading.
5. Business meetings.
6. Social events.
7. Free choice time (*to work on any project for this class*).
8. Field trips that help us understand our class work better.
9. Class discussions on special problems about which class members are concerned.

The allocation of time to all of the activities listed was difficult, but it was finally decided to use four or five periods per week of the ten-period class for work on problems, dividing the time between the topics of their own choosing and any special problems that they felt should be considered in class. They further decided to spend one period each per week in free reading, a study of current happenings, and a business meeting. Films and field trips, as well as any other items that would be needed would be fitted into the periods to which nothing had been assigned. Whenever more time was needed for a specific activity, the schedule would be adjusted to meet this. Social events would be planned as the class was ready for them, and would probably be held in after-school hours. Free choice time was omitted. As blocked out by the class, the general schedule appeared as shown in Figure 13.

There is a danger that must be recognized in such a blocking of future time. If it is considered by either teacher or pupils to be a rigid, absolutely unchangeable thing, life in the classroom can become very difficult and frustrating. If, however, it is viewed as a flexible plan that can be changed as the need arises, it serves to give direction without forcing every week into exactly the

OUR OVER-ALL SEMESTER PLAN

	Monday	Tuesday	Wednesday	Thursday	Friday
1st Period	Work on Problems		Work on Problems	Work on Problems (Some weeks open)	Free Reading
2nd Period	Work on Problems	Current Events	Work on Problems		Business Meeting

Figure 13. The over-all semester plan.

same mold. There are times when it is necessary to plan only one problem work-period on Monday but two on Thursday, or four problem work-periods in a row on Tuesday and Wednesday. If a current events film is available on Wednesday, but not on Tuesday, it would be sad indeed to omit the film because a rigid schedule made it imperative to devote a period to current events on Tuesday. The only period that this particular class considered inviolate was the Friday business meeting. This remained in the same spot all year. The others were shifted to fit the needs of the moment, although the amount of time spent on each remained relatively constant.

As the weeks went by, the class found that time was needed for many things that no one had thought of in the early stages. The teacher was well aware of many of these but allowed the class to make its own discoveries of its needs as they arose. Some of these activities were:

1. An extra reading period for a special purpose
2. Help in writing reports
3. Help in note taking
4. A discussion period on a crucial school problem
5. A sociodrama to clarify a classroom situation
6. Evaluation sessions
7. A special film
8. A library period for help in using the *Readers' Guide*
9. Discussions of, and practice in, group techniques

10. Planning periods for special activities
11. An extra business meeting

The class also discovered that working on problems had many meanings. Under this heading they might be doing any of the following:

1. Selecting a problem
2. Planning for work on problems in small groups
3. Collecting data
4. Sharing information
5. Planning a presentation
6. Presenting information to the class
7. Evaluating the success of the group
8. Evaluating their personal success
9. Writing reports

They found that if each day's schedule did not indicate exactly what activities were to be carried on it did not present a clear picture. A fully developed plan for a specific week might be as shown in Figure 14.

Planning committee. Up to the time of the completion of the over-all semester plan, the daily schedules have been made through the combined efforts of the class as a whole and the teacher. When the general procedure is clear, most classes object to the amount of time that must be taken each week for this. If it should happen that no pupil approaches this problem other than with grumbling about the time required, the teacher can raise the question as to how else it can be done. Usually some boys and girls see the possibility of having a committee work out the weekly arrangement of activities, thereby saving the class a great deal of time. If no one makes such a suggestion, however, it may be necessary for the teacher to suggest trying a *Planning Committee* for a few weeks. Such a group can be appointed by the chairman, or elected, whichever seems best to the class.

A tenth-grade class, accustomed to the use of such a committee, decided that it should be composed of representatives from the small groups in operation at the time. As a new problem was

Figure 14. A planning committee at work.

selected and new groups were formed, a new Planning Committee automatically came into being. This method provided information useful in planning, since each member was aware of the needs of his own group.

At the beginning of any class period during which the Planning Committee meets, the committee chairman asks the class and the teacher whether there are any special items that need to be included in the following week's schedule. Such items are added to the list of activities continuing from the present week, and the committee goes to work organizing these data into a workable plan. Frequently, when there are difficulties, an alternative schedule is prepared by the committee. The two are presented to the class at the business meeting.

At no time should the Planning Committee be considered to have the final word. Although the committee members have made considerable effort to weigh the various possibilities, and see to it that all important items are included, such a plan must be approved by the class in order to go into effect. Sometimes it seems to require as much time as when the plan was prepared by the class as a whole, but, in general, as the committee learns to anticipate the objections and agreements of the class it moves much faster. Without an opportunity for the class to approve or reject, the committee members can become a dominating group, and the weekly activities will be their choice and not those of the class.

Such a plan should be posted in the room, so that it is available at all times. This may be done on a large sheet of paper or recorded on the chalkboard. In some rooms the artistic talent of class members is utilized, and a schedule is painted on the chalkboard with colored chalk paint. The weekly plans are written in with chalk and erased with a cloth or paper tissue, thus leaving the basic painted form untouched.

The selection of the design for such a painted schedule form can be made on a contest basis, although the only prize awarded is the privilege of painting the winning picture on the board. Everyone with an idea for it prepares a drawing, or, if a boy or girl has no artistic ability, but has an idea for a schedule form, he asks someone to draw it for him. These drawings are exhibited on a day agreed upon, and the selection is made by the class. True, the selected picture may not seem either artistic or appropriate to the teacher, but, after all, he had his chance too, and if for a semester he has to look at a cat sitting amid five balls of yarn (five days' plan spaces are needed) or a bilious sea serpent blowing five bubbles, let him remember that there are worse things, especially when the class is tremendously proud of the results!

Establishing class goals

On one of the first days of the semester, the teacher spent considerable time explaining to the pupils the general purposes of the democratic type of class. However, by the time officers are elected and the class is organized many have completely forgotten the initial statements. The explanation will probably need to be repeated. This is a good time, too, to review with the class the activities of the past weeks, and to identify the democratic procedures that have been used and the democratic ideas that pupils have come to understand. An eighth-grade class listed the following:

1. We worked in small groups.
2. We had class discussions.
3. We had business meetings.
4. We helped decide things we wanted to do.
5. We elected our officers.
6. We learned from the movie that in a democracy you have to share the power.
7. We learned that in a democracy you should respect everyone.
8. We got acquainted with each other.
9. We learned about our school.
10. We learned that in a democracy you have rights and also responsibilities.

The discussion of these class activities was pointed toward the establishment of class goals to be formulated in terms of the pupils' own experiences and on their own level of development and understanding.

TEACHER

That looks like a pretty complete list. It seems to me that we have been busy people. Maybe it's time we stopped to see which of these worked well and which didn't. Any suggestions as to where we can start?

STEVE

I think our class discussions are real good.

JERRY

Well, the business meetings are pretty good, but when we work in small groups, sometimes it works and sometimes it doesn't.

BILL

Yeah, like the times when only one or two people get down to business and the rest fool around.

MARY

That isn't any worse than when one person talks all the time and doesn't give anyone else a chance.

JOE

Sometimes those small groups don't work because people are afraid to say what they think because someone makes fun of everything that's said. Those are the times I just keep still.

TEACHER

It sounds as though there are some things we need to be careful about when we are in small groups. Let's make a list of them. Will the secretary write them on the board? What's one item to start us off?

PETE

Give other people a chance to talk.

BILL

Do your share of the work.

JOE

Don't make fun of people's ideas.

ANN

Stick to the work that has to be done.

SUSAN

Take part in the group discussion.

TEACHER

Any more?

BILL

Yes. I think those small groups won't work unless everyone tries to understand everyone else's ideas. People always want things to go their own way. Everybody's idea can't be best.

TEACHER

What about Joe's point of not making fun of people's ideas? Does this have something to do with Bill's remarks?

JOE

I think Bill and I mean the same thing, only I said what you shouldn't do and Bill said what you should do.

RUTH

I agree with Joe and I think Bill's is the way to say it.

[Item 3 is changed to read: Try to understand other people's ideas.]

TEACHER

Are there any others that you think should be added?

MARY

Maybe mine isn't so good, but I think there is another one that should be on the list. Be friendly toward everyone.

DICK

Sure it's good. That's important.

TEACHER

Any more?

[No further response.]

TEACHER

Let's look at the list now.

1. Give other people a chance to talk.
2. Do your share of the work.
3. Try to understand other people's ideas.
4. Stick to the work that needs to be done.
5. Take part in the group discussion.
6. Be friendly toward everyone.

Have you been in a group where people have done some of these?

SUE

I have.

JERRY

Me too.

TEACHER

What happened?

SUE

Well, in one group I was in everyone was friendly and it made it easy to take part in the discussion. I didn't want to change groups.

JERRY

I was in one group where everyone worked without fussing and we stuck to it until it was done. Boy, did we ever get things done fast!

TEACHER

Is there any other activity that we carry on in class where these things are just as important as when we are working in small groups?

JOY

I think we need to do those things when we are having a big class discussion too.

TEACHER

Is Joy right?

[A general nodding of heads followed.]

TEACHER

Any other?

MAE

We ought to do those things when we have a business meeting, too.

TEACHER

Well, if they are so important for small-group work and for class discussions and for business meetings, would you think that these are some of the things we should especially try to learn to do this semester?

STEVE

I guess we'd better learn how to do them or we can't work in groups or have discussions or business meetings.

SUSAN

I think we could do a lot better if we really tried to do the things on the list.

TEACHER

Let's watch ourselves for a week. At the end of that time we can decide whether these are some of the goals we really need to work toward this semester.

No two classes will establish exactly the same set of goals. The items included will depend on the activities in which pupils have been involved, on the time of the semester at which the idea of goals is introduced, and on how clear a picture pupils have developed of democratic action in their classroom. If it is presented too early, boys and girls have little to draw on but their earlier years of classroom experiences or the generalized statements made by the teacher, such as "learn to work together." If not introduced until after a topic has been selected and worked through, many more items will be included than in the example given. It is quite possible, however, to establish general class goals relatively early in the semester, later adding others, such as things to work toward in taking notes, or writing reports, or presenting reports to the class. These may be added at the time that they become important to the class members.

Another approach to the development of a goal list is more direct. Pupils are asked to respond in writing to the question, "What things do you think we ought to be able to do, or to do better, by the end of the semester?"

The class is then divided into random groups, each group discussing all of the items on the lists of its members. Each group is asked to develop a list of points on which its members agree. These are reported to the class and recorded on the chalkboard. A thorough class discussion will eliminate many items as being not important enough to place on a list of class goals. The final list should include those items whose importance is generally agreed upon by the members of the class.

This list should be duplicated so that each pupil has a copy at hand in his notebook. It is also helpful to record the goals on a large chart hung in the room for easy reference. The following is the completed goal list as compiled by the eighth-grade class described in its early stages of goal setting.

THINGS WE WANT TO LEARN TO DO

In Class Discussions or Small-Group Work:
1. To give others a chance to talk
2. To take responsibility for doing our share of the work
3. To try to understand other people's ideas
4. To stick to the work that needs to be done
5. To take part in the group discussions
6. To be friendly toward everyone
7. To share our information with others

In Working on Topics:
1. To collect material from many sources
2. To take accurate notes
3. To have sufficient material to solve the problem
4. To select material that fits the problem

In Presenting Material to the Class:
1. To organize material so that it is smooth

2. To present reports without reading notes or paper
3. To speak clearly
4. To use correct English
5. To make material interesting to others

In Written Reports:
1. To use correct English
2. To include our own ideas
3. To spell correctly
4. To write neatly

With some groups an individual goal list in addition to the class goals may be developed, or an extra item or two for each individual may be added to the class list. This would include items that individuals recognize as their own personal weak spots in which they see need for improvement. It may be a personality problem that the pupil needs to do something about such as:

To hold my temper
To make pleasant remarks instead of being sarcastic

On the other hand, it may deal with a more academic difficulty, such as:

To write in complete sentences
To write so that people can read it
To get my work in on time

Items such as these will probably not be listed at the beginning of the term, but only as situations arise throughout the semester that bring the problems into focus and as the pupil sees their importance.

Use of a goal list. The list of goals prepared and accepted by a class should be used frequently. It should never be considered as a completed task and as an end in itself. If it is used merely as a wall decoration or a page in a notebook, it will soon be forgotten, and the time spent in developing it will have been largely wasted.

It serves as a guide when undertaking various activities and as a means of evaluation when the activities have been completed. Using the sample set of goals recorded on pages 155–156, let us suppose boys and girls are preparing to present their topic ma-

terial to the class. The five items under the heading, *In Presenting Material to the Class,* are reminders that they have agreed to have their material well organized, to present it without reading it from notes or paper, to speak clearly, to use good English, and to make their material interesting. This will probably mean that at first they will need help in organizing data and in finding ways to make it truly interesting, and they will certainly need encouragement in their attempts to tell their stories to the class without reading them. They will, however, have goals to strive for that are their own, and can judge for themselves to what degree they are succeeding in achieving them.

When difficulties arise in a small group, the goals relating to small-group work may be used for evaluation, and the areas of difficulty identified by group members themselves. The list may also serve as a basis for evaluation when difficulties arise in the class as a whole. It may also be used periodically as an over-all means of evaluation for reporting progress to parents. This use of the list will be described in detail in Chapter 8.

Unit goals. Goals may be constructed in form other than the over-all semester approach described above. Many teachers prefer to develop a new set of goals in connection with each new unit of study. There is much to be said in favor of this technique. Goals will fit the specific situation better, and they are more apt to fit the changing needs of maturing boys and girls. Probably the major objection to this method is the time required for developing a new set of goals so frequently. There is a compromise, however. An over-all list of goals may be developed, limited perhaps to seven or eight items. These are automatically made a part of each set of unit goals, with items that pertain strictly to the new unit being added to the original list.

A tenth-grade class functioned for a year in this fashion. Their basic list was:

Working Together for the Good of the Class:
  1. Respecting each individual and his ideas
  2. Accepting responsibility for work
  3. Sharing ideas pertaining to the problems at hand

4. Giving full attention at all times to the person speaking
5. Contributing worth-while ideas to discussions
6. Carrying out plans on time

For a rather unusual unit that involved the painting and decorating of their classroom they added the following:

Decorating Our Room:
1. Do as accurate and careful a job as possible in decorating our room.
2. Learn more about planning a decorating job.
3. Learn more about color and color combinations.
4. Learn more about using materials such as paper, paint, brushes, etc.
5. Learn how to combine the ideas of individual people and to reach a satisfactory conclusion in each small group.
6. Learn how to combine the small group solutions into a final class solution.
7. Base our conclusions on accurate data.

Using this same technique, a ninth-grade class in an early unit on *Conservation of Natural Resources* added the following to its basic list:

1. Learn facts about conservation.
2. Learn to use the library:
    a. Use of card catalog
    b. Use of magazines
    c. Use of encyclopedia
    d. How to take books out
    e. Rules of the library
    f. How to choose the right book
    g. How to find pamphlets and clippings
3. Learn how to record our information.
4. Develop ability to express our ideas on conservation in writing.
5. Develop ability to express our ideas on conservation orally.

Changing a goal list. A goal list is not sacred. A class should feel that it is quite possible to add to it, change the wording of any item, delete one that no longer seems to have meaning, or change the form of a single point, section, or even the entire

document. Such shifting is especially valuable if the class continues with the same teacher for several semesters. No class should continue a second semester without a careful re-examination of its goals. Boys and girls are a semester older and have an additional semester of experience behind them. The new goals should point the way to still wider experiences.

Conclusion

The activities described in this chapter need not all be carried out within the first few weeks. A number of them can be developed at a later time. If a class decides to write a constitution, work on this can be carried on over a considerable length of time in periods not assigned to problem work. The same is true of making a painted form for the weekly schedule on the chalkboard. The development of parliamentary procedure will more than likely be an outgrowth of the class' experiences in conducting a number of business meetings, and so will appear later.

The Planning Committee, too, may not evolve for quite some time. The establishment of goals, although best developed fairly early, may be held off for a few weeks, especially if it seems that the class needs a shift away from an activity such as this, since it involves considerable class discussion. A restless class will not do a good job. While still completing activities dealing with organization, it is possible to move into the area of selection of problems for study much sooner than the contents of this chapter might lead one to believe.

Pupil-teacher planning is often misinterpreted. To some it means giving pupils freedom of choice without limits, which is *laissez-faire* or license, not democracy, and can only result in a chaotic classroom situation. To others it means presenting the teacher's plans in such a way that pupils will agree to them. This is an autocratic procedure even when benevolently handled, with pupils learning only to figure out what the teacher wants and then to follow blindly. Neither of these is a means of developing a democratically functioning class of boys and girls who are learn-

ing to make wise decisions and to share both power and respect with others, the teacher included.

It is quite true that a certain predetermined foundation has deliberately been laid during the first few weeks, but it is a foundation upon which the class may now safely build its democratic future. In the first weeks there has been little pupil-teacher planning. It was largely teacher controlled but gradually moving in the direction of shared planning. It is only by starting with schoolroom experiences and procedures with which pupils are familiar that it is possible to move on to a new concept of operation.

By the time a class has examined the ideas of democracy, has decided upon its rights and responsibilities within the classroom, has organized, elected its officers, and has established its goals, it has had the opportunity to make many decisions. Boys and girls have gradually come to see the teacher as a member of the group, older and more experienced, a person with many ideas to share with them, but also willing to consider and work with them on their ideas and plans. Class activities are now not planned by the teacher, nor planned solely by the pupils, but teacher and pupils are learning to plan and work together.

5

A Problem to Work On

IN THE PREVIOUS CHAPTERS LITTLE HAS BEEN SAID
about actual subject matter. The emphasis rather has been on
methods of initiating procedures for developing the basic skills of
democratic living involved in working together on common
problems. It is, of course, necessary, if one is to learn to use such
procedures, and to become skillful in applying them, to solve real
problems.

The word *problem,* as applied to educational method, is somewhat loosely used, but tends to follow the dictionary definitions:
a question proposed for solution, specifically, (1) a question propounded for academic discussion; (2) a perplexing question or
situation.[1] It may be a controversial question to be debated, or
it may be any question to which an individual or a group wishes
to find an answer, for example, "How does a telephone work?"
or "What was life like in ancient Egypt?"

The problems selected for class study, as well as the methods
used in selecting them, depend in part on whether or not there
is a required course of study. In many classes, particularly those
listed as core, basic living, or general education, there are no
prescribed areas of study, textbooks, or other subject matter
limitations. In such classes, problems may be selected by teacher
and pupils cooperatively, the process of selection itself being
considered a valuable learning experience. In other classes,

---

1 *Webster's New International Dictionary of the English Language.*

broad problem areas are designated by the teaching staff on the basis of research on adolescent growth and development and on the societal needs of adolescents. In some school systems, specific areas are assigned to different grade levels, whereas in others any area on the list may be selected at any grade level.

An example of areas that are designated for a given grade level is the following, a series assigned to ninth-grade core classes in Prince George's County, Maryland:[2]

1. Democracy—A Balance between Rights and Responsibilities
2. Living Together in Prince George's County
3. Finding Our Place in the World at Work
4. Achieving and Maintaining Good Family Relationships

An example of a series designed for use at any grade level (7–12) is that developed at University School, The Ohio State University.[3]

1. Problems of School Living
2. Problems of Healthful Living
3. Problems of Communication
4. Problems of Government
5. Problems of Producer-Consumer Economics
6. Problems of Conservation of Resources
7. Problems of Values and Beliefs
8. Problems of Human Behavior (Understanding Self and Others)
9. Problems of Conflicting Ideologies
10. Problems of Education
11. Problems of Occupations (Selection and Preparation for)
12. Problems of a Developing Cultural Heritage
13. Problems of Social Relationships in a Rapidly Changing Society.
14. Problems of Living in the Atomic Age

The most common classroom practice is to limit the problems to one area, American history for example, or civics, or English

---

2 Board of Education of Prince George's County, *Handbook for Core Teachers* (Upper Marlboro, Maryland, 1955), p. 8.

3 The Faculty of the University School, *A Description of Curricular Experiences* (Columbus, Ohio: The Ohio State University, 1956), p. 18.

literature. But no matter how rigid the restrictions, it is possible to use some pupil-teacher planning of both content and method of study, the amount of such cooperative planning increasing as the limits of the subject matter that may be covered and of the materials that may be used are widened.

A further determining factor in the selection of problems, and a very pertinent one, is the degree to which the teacher is willing to accept the values and purposes of the democratic process. If he has faith in cooperative procedures, he will use pupil-teacher planning techniques in the selection of study problems as much as possible within the imposed limits of the curricular structure.

Establishing criteria

A preliminary step in all classrooms in which pupils have any degree of choice is the establishment of criteria for the selection of problems. Such criteria serve as a yardstick against which the worth of suggested problems can be measured. Unless time is taken to determine the points that should be considered in selecting problems, pupils will only too often make choices with little or no serious thought, and will base them solely on their momentary or immediate interests. As a consequence, many dissatisfactions are likely to arise as the unit progresses.

Both pupils and teacher should cooperate in developing a list of such criteria. Although the number of suggestions pupils can make may be small at first, or may be lacking in clarity and definiteness, a beginning should be made before the first problem for study is selected. The list can be revised throughout the year as pupils recognize the need for improvement. In a ninth-grade class in which there were no subject limitations in the choice of problems, the teacher introduced the idea of criteria in this manner:

Since we are ready to suggest problems to investigate, we need to decide how we are going to know whether or not the problems that are suggested are worth taking time to work on. When you go into a store to buy a coat, you consider a number of things before you buy it. You may say to yourself, "Is this the kind of coat I need? Is it warm enough? Is it well made? Do I like it? Is it the right color? Is it different from my last one? Can I afford it?" If the answers to these questions are satisfactory you are likely to buy the coat, but if not, you do not buy it.

Such questions are called *criteria*. They are standards by which we decide whether to buy or not buy. For our choice of problems for study, we need standards, or criteria, also; otherwise we may select a topic which will have little or no value for us. What are some of the things you think we ought to consider in choosing a problem?

The initial list that resulted from the class discussion following this introduction included only the following items:

1. It should be one that will be of value to us now or later.
2. It should be something that we are interested in.
3. It should be something that we haven't studied before.
4. It should be one for which there is enough material.

The fourth item was suggested by the teacher because of former experiences with problems for which little or no material was available. It was introduced as follows:

TEACHER

Is there another point that we ought to include? What would happen if we selected a problem and then could not find enough material to help us solve it?

BILL

We'd be out of luck.

MARY

We would have to start all over and choose another problem.

JANE

I suppose we would just have to do the best we could.

JOE

Well, that isn't any good. We would be wasting a lot of time and not getting anywhere.

TEACHER

What could we do to avoid such a situation?

GERRY

Couldn't we go to the library and check on how much material we could get before we chose a topic?

JOE

Sure! We should only choose a topic if there is enough material. That could be another one of our crit—cri—criteria!

TEACHER

Does that sound reasonable?

Heads nodded all around the room and the point was added to the list.

By the time a second unit was being selected, pupils realized that the meaning of the first criterion on their list was not clear, since it could be interpreted in so many ways. The list was revised several times so that at the end of the year it was in this form:

CRITERIA FOR SELECTING A TOPIC

1. It should be one that will be of value to us now and/or later. This means:

    a. It should help us to understand the world in which we live.

or . . . b. It should help us to understand ourselves.

or . . . c. It should help us to understand adult life and its problems.

or . . . d. It should help us to understand the connection between life in the past, our present life, and life in the future.

2. It should be something we really want to know about.

3. It should be something we haven't studied before or which we want to know more about.

4. It should be broad enough so that many may work on it, but not so broad that it cannot be completed.

5. It should be one for which materials are available.

6. It should be one that will help us achieve our goals.

An introduction to criteria in the manner described above is equally useful if the problem is to be selected from a specific area. Let us assume that choice is limited to the area of *Con-*

servation of Natural Resources in our State. The need to establish criteria for problem selection is the same. The only difference lies in the addition of a reminder of the limits of choice by saying for example, "Our problem this time will be in the area of *Conservation of Natural Resources in our State.* What are some of the things you think we ought to consider in choosing a problem to study in this field?"

Problems based on expressed concerns of pupils

In a class for which there are no specific subject-content requirements, it would seem to be a simple matter to select a problem that would meet the criteria established by the class. Yet this is one of the most difficult aspects of pupil-teacher planning. It is not easy to bring to light the questions that are of real concern to pupils. At age four and five, a child is agog with questions; adults cannot answer them fast enough. But as the years go by, there is a strange lessening in the number of questions he asks, especially in the classroom. As a rule he seldom has an opportunity to participate in planning the subject content that he is to study. He is *told* what to study and how to study it, and his questions dry up or, if he asks them, they are too often bypassed because they are "not in the lesson." As he approaches adolescence, he has scores of questions to which he wants and needs answers, but he is not sure enough of himself and of the changes that are taking place in his physical and emotional reorganization to state his questions. He is not sure that these are acceptable, nor is he sure that others have similar problems. And so he says nothing. Many of his difficulties he cannot recognize clearly enough to bring to a verbal level. They remain hidden, unless he is given help in probing for them.

A further difficulty in selecting problems lies with the teacher rather than the pupil. Many of us who are attempting wide use of pupil-teacher planning have had most of our school experiences in classrooms where we were *told* what to study. It is a pattern we have grown up with, and now that we are in the teacher's role, we feel, even when we don't want to feel this way, that it is our job to *tell* our pupils what to study. We have a guilty feeling that we are perhaps not fulfilling our obligations unless we do.

We are also often disturbed by the nature of the problems selected by immature pupils. To us, as adults, they seem trivial and not worthy of class time spent on their solution. Without doubt this is sometimes true. But perhaps we should remember that:

> All experience is not educative, since some may not enhance the individual for effective living. The teacher must realize that sometimes the learner has to go through unprofitable experiences because he cannot at the moment accept the idea that the experience he wants is not enhancing. Patience during unprofitable experiences is only part of the teacher's art in leading the learner to more profitable experiences. It is in the nature of a detour on the way to goals which will ultimately enhance the learner.[4]

However, the use of the list of criteria that has been developed by the class will do much to eliminate carelessness in choosing problems. The criteria should be considered carefully each time a new problem is selected. At the conclusion of the unit, it is important that the class consider the value of the experience they have had in working on it. In the light of the same criteria, has it proved to be a wise choice or not? If not, how can they avoid a poor selection another time?

Many problems, however, in which pupils express concern and which seem to be a waste of time to us who are much older are by no means trivial to teen-agers. We sometimes need to recall our own interests at a similar age in order to appreciate their importance. Then too, a transitory, surface interest may be the wedge that will bring to light the child's more basic problems and needs. By starting with an area in which he is interested, he can be helped to find his real concerns and to open many doors of knowledge and experience that he might otherwise have by-passed. Furthermore, he will learn the techniques

---

4 Earl C. Kelley and Marie I. Rasey, *Education and the Nature of Man* (New York: Harper and Brothers, Publishers, 1952), p. 76.

and skills of problem-solving more successfully when dealing with a problem that he is eager to solve than when struggling with one that does not seem important to him.

Discovering areas of concern and interest. In Chapter 2 considerable time was spent in describing methods by which a teacher may become acquainted with his pupils. The information assembled through the use of these techniques serves as one of the earliest means of discovering some areas of concern and interest from which problems to be studied may later be developed. The autobiography, the questionnaire, responses to unfinished stories or pictured situations, individual conferences, home visits, all give leads that should not be overlooked.

A section of a teacher's notes taken from such sources was summarized as follows:

1. Four boys have gone on hunting trips with their fathers.
2. Three expressed their enjoyment of camping and fishing.
3. One spends his summer on a farm and wants to be a farmer.
4. One writes poetry, and three like to write stories.
5. Drawing or painting is the spare time occupation of one.
6. Five have cameras.
7. Two have model railroads.
8. Six enjoy making models—planes, trains, boats, etc.
9. Four have trouble at home with brothers, sisters, or parents.
10. Twelve express the hope that they will make new friends in high school.
11. Eight of the girls are beginning to date. Six wish they could.
12. Four express distaste for school.
13. Three wish they could read better.
14. Two boys want to be pilots, three girls want to be airline hostesses.

In addition to information such as this, derived from statements written earlier by the pupils, the development of an "I wonder" list is most helpful as a means of involving the entire class in the establishment of a list of problems that might be selected for study. Two weeks before problems were to be selected, the teacher made the following assignment:

As you know, it will not be long before we will be ready to select our problems for study. During the next two weeks I would like each of you to watch for things that you read, or hear, or see, or feel that you do not understand, or that you wonder about. Let's call it an "I wonder" list.

When you read a newspaper or a magazine article which you do not understand, write the subject or a question about it on your list.

Listen to people talking on the bus or in stores, and to your family and friends. Listen to the radio and television. When things are said that you do not understand, or that you wonder about, add them to your list.

Use your eyes as well. When you see things taking place in school, outside of school, on television, or at home that you don't understand, jot them down.

Watch your own feelings. What things bother you in different situations at school, at home, or with your friends? Record these on your list.

Your ideas will help us build a list of topics that are of real importance to you. So, for two weeks keep a record of the things you read, hear, see, or feel that you wonder about.

The lists resulted in a total of 116 questions that could be grouped under the following headings:

Teen-agers	Religions
Personality	Armed forces
World problems	Strikes and arbitration
Science	Marriage
Politics	Racial problems
Health and safety	School problems
Crime	Inventors and their inventions
Money problems	Russia and communism

A few of the questions asked were:

1. Why is it so hard to find a really true friend?
2. Why do movie companies make movies about teen-agers that make all teen-agers look like juvenile delinquents?
3. If all countries in the world want peace why do they continue making weapons?
4. How can weather predictions be made days ahead of time?

5. How can power come from the sun?

6. How does a picture on a television screen come from the studio to the screen?

7. Does smoking really harm a person?

8. Why is there so much crime these days?

9. What are the stars made of and what are their shapes?

10. Why is the price of an article higher in some stores than in others?

11. Why do prices on meats change from one week to another? Sometimes they are higher and sometimes lower.

12. Why are people in favor of segregation?

13. How do great inventors like Edison think of their inventions and how long does it take to develop them?

14. Where does slang originate? Where do new words come from?

15. Why can't I get along with people?

The 116 questions, under their respective headings, were mimeographed, and copies were given to the members of the class, in order that they might see the questions that were of concern to their fellows. Such a list serves as a source of ideas for problems that might be studied by the class. In addition, it gives pupils confidence to add any questions of their own that they had originally been hesitant about including.

Frequently, failure to find satisfactory problems lies in the fact that a teacher does not utilize the information he has at hand relative to each individual, and that he fails to help pupils identify areas in which they have questions. In such a situation, he has recourse to direct questioning only. Although response to the question, "What are you interested in studying?" often yields little of value, this question, too, has its place, and should not be overlooked; it can be used from time to time.

The selection of the first problem for study was brought into focus through the establishment of the criteria for problem choice. The first attempt to make such a choice, if it is to be well done, will not be easy, nor will progress be rapid. For many pupils, even the idea of participating in selecting a problem to study is difficult to accept. For this reason, it is good to move one step at a time. The teacher of the ninth-grade group we have been following said:

Yesterday we decided that there are four things we will need to consider when we select a problem to study. We said that it should be a problem that will be of value to us now or later; that it should be something in which we are interested; it should be something we haven't studied before; and it should be one for which there is enough material. At the end of the period I gave each of you a copy of the questions that were asked by the members of this class on the "I wonder" lists. I asked you to think about these overnight and to jot down any of the topics that you thought fit our criteria. You were also to add any topics that were not on the list but which you thought should be included. How many of you found at least one topic that you felt met our criteria and therefore would be a good one to study? ——Good!

I will give each of you an index card. Write your name on it and then list the topics that you think fit the criteria.

The index card has, of course, no special merit except that there seems to be something important about an index card to eighth- and ninth-graders. The simple device of giving each pupil a 3 by 5 inch card for some strange reason lends increased importance to the activity. In addition to this, it is a means of filing the suggestions for comparison with later lists.

While the class was filling out the cards, the teacher wrote the following on the chalkboard:

Various class members have said they are interested in the following activities or have these problems. Would you like to add any of them to your list of topics?

hunting	aviation
fishing	model building
camping	model railroads
farming	getting along with the family
writing poetry	making friends
writing stories	dating
drawing and painting	improving reading ability
photography	

Thus, fifteen additional possibilities were presented. Since the original contributors were unidentified, it was easy for a pupil to add such an item as *getting along with the family* to his list without having anyone know that it was his biggest problem.

After a few minutes spent in completing their lists, pupils were divided into random groups of five pupils. Each group was asked to discuss all of the suggestions of its members, checking them against the criteria and eliminating those that the group agreed did not warrant consideration.

The following day, the class list of suggestions was compiled on the chalkboard, the recorder of each group presenting those areas that had been acepted by his group. As has been suggested earlier, it is good to record one item from each group in turn, then a second from each, and so on until all have been recorded. Opportunity should be given at the conclusion of group reports for any individual to add a topic that has perhaps been rejected by his group but which he is still convinced fits the criteria and which is very important to him. It is quite possible that, had he been in another group, it would have been accepted. It is also possible that as the list was being compiled a topic came to mind that had not been thought of previously. The final list, including several suggested by the teacher, contained forty-two items.

1. Radar	15. Life in the sea
2. Michigan	16. Boats
3. Holidays around the world	17. Myths and legends
4. Japan	18. Tropical fish
5. Prehistoric times	19. Travel
6. Cars	20. Guns and other weapons
7. Animals	21. Hunting and fishing
8. Space travel	22. Juvenile delinquency
9. Astronomy	23. Making friends
10. Other countries and their people	24. Etiquette
11. Indians	25. Television
12. Future careers	26. Sports
13. Music	27. Conservation
14. Photography	28. Dating

29. Negro-White question
30. Women in the armed forces
31. United Nations
32. U.S. Government
33. Volcanoes
34. Famous inventors
35. Good grooming

36. F.B.I.
37. Civil defense
38. Atomic energy
39. History of our city
40. Stamp collecting
41. Recreation in our city
42. Prehistoric animals

In addition to the use of direct questioning and the "I wonder" technique as means of developing a list of possible topics for study, the teacher should be alert to experiences that unexpectedly arouse interest and concern. A class period devoted to oral descriptions of books that pupils have enjoyed may identify an area in which a number show keen interest. For example, when Jim told about a book that dealt with archeological investigations in South America, some of the pupils were fascinated. As they discussed the things Jim told them, they asked many questions about the ancient Indian civilization that no one in the class could answer. The teacher, seeing their interest, suggested that the topic be placed on the *Waiting List,* in order that the class might consider it when new problems were selected. Such a *Waiting List,* posted in the room, is an excellent way to record topics that otherwise might be forgotten.

A trip to the Science Institute stimulated a desire for information about minerals in a group of tenth-grade boys. Examination of the teacher's collection of shells set another group into action. An unusual current happening reported in the newspaper frequently serves as a starter. A hurricane, a tornado, or a new satellite may arouse questions that pupils want answered. A scathing article on teen-age drivers can send a class on an extensive search for data on the controversial question of teenagers and their driving habits. A film, either classrom or commercial, is sometimes a springboard into a unit. *The Ten Commandments,* for example, started a group on a study of ancient Egyptian life.

Many of these experiences will occur while the class is still involved in solving problems started at an earlier date. Because these should be completed before new topics are selected, the *Waiting List* is a record of any special areas of interest that can be drawn upon at a later time.

A study of the topics suggested by any class will show a wide range of interest. In the ninth-grade list above, many deal strictly with personal concerns. A few pupils have moved into a consideration of other people. Still other topics are of much broader social significance. Over the years, the writer has observed that generally, in classes where there are no subject matter limits, ninth-graders tend to suggest and select personal interest areas. In the tenth grade there is a definite expansion to include relationships to other people. Eleventh-graders are much more concerned with social problems. The twelfth-graders revert to problems that deal with themselves but which relate to their future—jobs, marriage, handling money, and so forth.

Of course, the items as listed above are not problems, since they are neither "questions proposed for solution, questions propounded for academic discussion, nor perplexing questions or situations." They are topics about which pupils have questions to which they wish to find answers. At times problems are stated specifically, as illustrated by the following:

How is radar used to catch speeders?
How do jets operate?
Where are the Indians today?
What happens in juvenile court?

At the point of developing the list, however, the topical form is acceptable. Once pupils have selected a topic or area, they must, of course, state their specific problem clearly. Without such a statement, their efforts are likely to be scattered and aimless, lacking in unity and purpose.

The list was discussed by the class as a whole, many questions being asked about the different topics. What was meant by *civil defense?* by *myths and legends?* by *conservation?* by *Negro-White question?* What types of problems might be found in these? Would they be worth spending class time on? Was it likely that sufficient material could be found? What activities could be carried out in connection with them? The individuals who had suggested the areas, as well as other members of the class and the teacher, took part in the clarification. Reorganization of the list took place at this time also. Numbers 23, 24, and 35 were combined. Number 42 became a part of number 5. If number 4 was meant to be a study of the country and its people, it could be included under number 10. If, however, number 4 referred to the present relationships between Japan and other nations of the world, it would be better to let it stand alone. The resulting list was simpler and much more useable.

One problem area or more? Whether the entire class will study the same problem area, or whether five or six small groups will be formed, each working on different and possibly unrelated topics, is a decision that must be made before pupils make their choices. It is suggested that the teacher may make this decision at the time that a class is moving through this procedure for the first time. If the method is evaluated by the class and the teacher at the close of the unit, they will be guided in their procedure for the next unit.

There is much to be said for either technique. A single problem area lends solidarity to the unit and to the class, since all are working toward a common goal. It enables a class to delve into a greater number of aspects of the problem. It greatly increases the opportunities for sharing information and materials. On the other hand, it is often difficult to obtain sufficient material on a particular topic to accommodate a class of from thirty to thirty-five pupils. It is also often difficult to reach agreement on the choice of an area. The method used most often in selecting a single area is to make the decision by majority vote. At best there is a small opposing minority, but more frequently there is a large minority group whose members are disgruntled at being pushed into work on a topic in which they have little or no concern, after having been led to believe that their own problems were important.

Such a situation sometimes arises if a class has more boys than girls, or vice versa. Let us suppose that the boys are in the majority and have as their choice *hunting and fishing,* or perhaps *cars.* To the girls, these are usually not only unknown territory, but totally uninteresting. Yet if the class is to work on a single topic and the choice is to be made on the basis of a majority vote, the girls are likely to be forced into a situation that they cannot meet with any degree of satisfaction or success. If a single problem area is to be chosen, it is extremely important to work for selection by consensus rather than to use a quick majority vote technique.

Several points can be made in favor of organizing a number of small groups instead, each working on a different problem. It is unlikely that certain topics will be of concern to everyone in the class, boy-girl relations for example. In the eighth and ninth grades, many girls are eager to look at the problems arising from their growing interest in the opposite sex. But most of the boys, and some of the girls, are either completely uninterested or as yet unwilling to express that interest. However, if they are not forced to take part in a consideration of this problem, a year or so later, many of those who were violently opposed to the study of boy-girl problems will be clamoring to undertake it. It has now become important to them.

A further point that may be made in favor of the use of small groups working on different problems is that the entire procedure, from choice of a specific problem for the group, through planning, sharing of data, presentation, and evaluation is on a small enough scale to be clearly seen by the group members, and a feeling of responsibility develops on the part of each member to his group. The question that must be decided is whether it is of more value to insist that some pupils follow a problem in which they are not concerned in order that an entire class may work on a single problem, or to establish separate groups each of which will have the opportunity to work on a problem that has meaning to its members.

Method of selecting a number of problems. Let us again observe the class considered earlier in this chapter. The decision was made that all members of the class need not work on the same area, but that several different topics could be studied at the same time, each by a different group of pupils.

A further decision, made at the suggestion of the teacher, was that a topic must be selected by at least three pupils in order to be accepted. Unless a lower limit is placed on the number of pupils in a group, either through fear of working with others, or because of honest, intense interest in a particular area, some pupil is likely to refuse to work on any topic other than the one of his choice. If no one else in the class is concerned about this, he works alone and does not have the small group experience.

A pupil who has a very real interest in a topic that is of no concern to the rest of the class members must, however, not be lost sight of. He must be given an opportunity to develop this interest as well as to learn how to work with his classmates. He can, for example, be helped to see how his particular interest ties in with one or more of the areas selected by the class, or he can be helped to see how he may divide his time, working alone on his own problem part of the time and participating in the activities of a group part of the time.

There are several methods whereby pupils may indicate their choices of areas for study. As discussed in Chapter 3, it is important to use a method that will lead a pupil to select a topic that seems to have value for him instead of selecting one merely because his friends have chosen it. There should be enough other situations in which he may select his group on the basis of friendship so that he does not feel the necessity for selecting a problem for study in this way. One method is to ask each pupil to list the three or four topics that would be most satisfying to him, arranging them in order of preference. These are then collected, and the teacher or a committee organizes them into groups, placing each pupil in a group as near as possible to his first choice.

A second method is that used in the class we have been observing. The list of possible topics was on the chalkboard. Each pupil was asked to list on a sheet of paper the four areas that he felt would be of most value to him. The following directions were given by the teacher:

As I name a topic please raise your hand if this is one of those you have selected. You will raise your hand four times, once for each of your choices.

When we have finished we will cross off from our list any topic that has less than three votes, since it was decided earlier that a group can have no less than three people in it.

In this way a number of topics were eliminated at the end of the first round. Pupils were then asked to cut their lists to three choices and the process was repeated. The same procedure was then followed with two choices and finally with a single choice. Of the 42 original topics, 9 were listed by three or more pupils in the final count. These were:

Areas	Number of pupils
Space travel	3
Juvenile delinquency	3
Photography	4
Famous inventors	4
Hunting and fishing	5
Civil defense	3
Making friends	4
Dating	5
F.B.I.	4

It sometimes happens that one or two areas draw the attention of large numbers of pupils, such topics as *Hunting and fishing* or *Juvenile delinquency* having perhaps ten or twelve pupils selecting them. Although there is no particular number beyond which a group ceases to function well, one composed of ten or twelve pupils, inexperienced in group procedures, is not often highly successful. Teachers sometimes insist that a number of these pupils select other areas. For the writer it has always been more satisfactory to ask such a group to divide in half, each half working on a separate phase of the subject, or even perhaps duplicating the investigation being made by the other group.

Checking available resources. Before pupils formally organize their groups, they will do well to find out whether sufficient resource material is available for each of the areas that has been selected. Unless time is set aside for this, a group may find that it is involved in a topic for which there are no books or other resources available, or possibly that those at hand are far beyond their level of understanding. By the time this fact is recognized, it is not only too late to join another group, but the pupils are discouraged and not eager to select another topic. It seems wiser to make a survey of materials before the groups make detailed plans, so that, if necessary, pupils may select another topic to work on.

To make such a resource check, the class was divided into nine groups according to the choices made. Two days were spent locating books, pamphlets, and other sources in the room library, the school library, community and home libraries, and in looking into the possibility of obtaining films, filmstrips, recordings, and other illustrative aids. The sources were not read nor examined in detail, but only skimmed in order to see whether they dealt with the topics listed and were understandable.

A helpful approach to collecting this data is to initiate the class into the preparation of a *preliminary bibliography*. This is a list of all references a pupil can locate which, by title or brief skimming, *seem* to contain information that will be useful to him. It is a collection of possible sources of data to which he will later refer. Some of these references will prove to be helpful, others will be discarded since, on more careful scrutiny, the pupil finds they are not suited to his purposes.

Although it is not necessary to prepare a form on which such a bibliography can be recorded, pupils find it very helpful. Three separate sheets, one each for books, magazines, and audiovisual materials, with columns headed as in Figure 15 serve the purpose. In order to allow as much space as possible, headings may be placed along the length of the paper rather than across the narrow edge. The sheets, of a size to fit in the pupil's notebook, can be stapled together.

Under the heading, *Place Found,* the pupil records the place where the material is located, for example: school library,

PRELIMINARY BIBLIOGRAPHY BOOKS				Mark as Used X - good material 0 - not useful
Name of Book	Author	Place Found	Catalog Number	

MAGAZINE OR NEWSPAPER ARTICLES					Mark as Used X - good material 0 - not useful
Title of Article	Author	Magazine or Newspaper	Date	Place Found	

FILMS, FILMSTRIPS, RECORDINGS, MUSEUM MATERIALS					Mark as Used X - good material 0 - not useful
Title	Number	Company	Owned by School	To be Ordered	

Figure 15. A preliminary bibliography form.

Duffield branch library, home, Miss Janell's office. The column headed, *Mark as Used,* will be used later as the pupil reads the material. Here he indicates with an X or an O whether it has value to him in terms of his problem, or not. Unless some such indication is made, and references are thus checked off as they are used, pupils frequently lose time locating material they have already scrutinized.

The chief advantage in preparing such a bibliography previous to starting work on the problem is, of course, that it allows individuals or a group to see quickly whether there are sufficient reference materials available. A group may then know whether it is wise to continue on its selected topic or not.

Having indicated that resources are at hand, the bibliography continues to serve the group in many ways during later work on the problem. It widens the pupil's concept of sources of data, pushing him beyond the encyclopedia or a single book into periodicals, newspapers, films, recordings, and museum materials. He begins to sense that a school textbook, or even the school library, is not the limit of his source of information.

A second value, and one which pupils soon recognize, is that in the long run the bibliography is a time-saving device. For example, having listed all resources recorded in the card catalog, it is not necessary to return to the catalog each time another book is needed. The data necessary for finding the book has been recorded on the bibliography. The same point can be made relative to magazine articles. Repeated reference to the *Readers' Guide* takes a tremendous amount of time. Listing at one time all articles that may be pertinent is a much more satisfactory method. A third advantage in preparing a bibliography lies in the opportunity to order films, filmstrips, and recordings far enough ahead of time so that they may be available when needed.

In addition to these values, a bibliography serves as a stimulus to the intellectually able child to do a more complete and scholarly piece of work. A list of materials usually contains far more than the average pupil can cover in the amount of time available. Thus, the brighter boy or girl, being able to advance faster, and not having to pace himself by the output of his neighbor, can investigate a much larger number of the references he has listed on his bibliography. He does not lack for something to do.

Let us return now to the class we have been following. Having compiled their bibliographies, the nine groups took stock. Seven of these had found more than enough material. Two, however, had found so little on their chosen topics, *Space travel* and *The F.B.I.,* that the pupils concerned decided either to join other groups or to select new topics. Two joined the group on *Civil defense,* one joined the *Famous inventors* group, and one joined the *Photography* group. The other three, after checking to see that resources were adequate, formed a new group on *Aviation.*

Defining the problem. Up to this point, only the general topics or problem areas had been selected. Within each of these a specific problem must now be decided upon. The teacher briefed the class as follows: It would be necessary for the members of each group to reach an agreement on the particular problem it intended to solve. As a first step each recorder would make a list of all the questions that the members of the group wanted to ask relative to its selected topic. The time limit would be twenty-five minutes. Chairmen were urged to help everyone in the group to contribute his ideas.

Let us join the *Civil defense* group and see how this topic was transformed into a real problem.

The group of five appointed Bob as its chairman and Sue as its recorder. The discussion ran as follows:

BOB

Well, let's get started. I guess the first thing we have to do is to decide exactly what we want to work on, isn't it?

LINDA

I thought we had already decided that. Aren't we going to study *Civil defense?*

DENNIS

Sure, but how can we learn all about a topic as big as that in just a couple weeks? Seems to me we can only do part of it.

BOB

Yes, but what part?

DENNIS

I know what I'd like to find out. I'd like to know if foreign planes can be detected in time to give us a chance to get away.

JACK

I'd like to know how they can be detected. Who does it?

BOB

Sue, you're recorder. You'd better write all these questions down or we'll forget them.

The list at the end of the twenty-five minutes included the following questions:

1. Can foreign planes be detected in time to give us a chance to get away?

2. How can they be detected? Who does it?

3. What can you do if an H-bomb is dropped?

4. How many ships does the United States have?

5. How many planes does the United States have?

6. What can you do if you hear that there is going to be a tornado?

7. How can they tell that there is going to be a tornado in a certain part of the state?

8. Can a city really be evacuated in time if there should be an air attack?

9. What plans does our city have for evacuation?

10. Can an attack be launched from a man-made satellite?

11. How much of an atomic stockpile does Russia have?

12. Could we intercept an attack from a satellite?

13. How much damage would an H-bomb do? How do they know?

14. What happens to people who aren't killed?

15. What does civil defense have to do with floods?

16. What is meant by fall-out? Is it dangerous?

17. How does radar help? How does it work?

18. Who decides where pupils are to go during an air raid drill in school?

19. Are people in Russia anxious to come to the United States?

The second step in defining the problem was set by two questions that the teacher wrote on the chalkboard.

1. Do you have a number of questions that deal with the same or a similar part of your topic? What is the subject of these?
2. Do you have some questions that do not fit with these? Could these be dropped out?

Each group was asked to go over its list and decide how these two questions could be answered. The teacher moved from group to group helping pupils to clarify their thinking and offering suggestions if a group seemed to be having trouble. The *Civil defense* group, for example, was having difficulty, since two of its members maintained that the questions dealing with the effect of atomic attack had no connection with the means used to protect the citizens in case of attack. They wanted to drop these questions, whereas the other three members wanted them left on the list although they could not give a reason. The conversation between the teacher and the group was as follows:

TEACHER

Suppose that a boy falls from a boat into the river and when he is pulled out a few minutes later he has stopped breathing. The police are there. What does the policeman do at once?

DENNIS

He applies artificial respiration. Anyone who knows first aid would do that.

TEACHER

Why does he do that particular thing?

JACK

I know! We talked about that in swimming class. Because that's the only way to get the oxygen that he needs into his blood, until he can breathe by himself again. Mr. King says a person's heart keeps on beating for a little while after he stops breathing, but he has to have oxygen.

TEACHER

Is there any similarity between this and your difficulty today about the effect of the bomb on people?

A minute or so of silence, then:

BOB

Wait a minute. I get it. If you didn't know what happened to a person under water you wouldn't know how——

SUE

You wouldn't know what to do. And if you don't know what damage a bomb can do——

DENNIS

That's it. If the people working on civil defense didn't know the effect of a bomb, there would be no way to decide how to protect people.

At the end of fifteen minutes, recorders reported results to the class. The *Civil defense* group reported that it had two parts to its answer to the first question, but that these belonged together. There were eight questions that dealt directly with protection of people in case of an atomic attack, and three that had to do with the effect of a bombing. In response to the second question, four items could be left out, since they dealt with tornadoes and floods and the Russian people rather than atomic attack. Two others dealt with satellites, and, since little or no accurate information would be available on these, it was decided to leave them out as well. The group did not know what to do with three other questions that had been suggested but had decided that it would be good to wait with these and see whether they would fit in later.

Reports from the other groups showed the following: The *Juvenile delinquency* group found its main concern lay with the causes and remedies for delinquency. The *Photography* group was chiefly interested in home development of prints. The *Famous inventors* group discovered that they were not as interested in the inventors as in the inventions themselves, especially those that have been developed in the last fifteen years in the field of communication. Good camping techniques were the major concern of the *Hunting and fishing* group. How to make a good impression on people was the choice of the group on *Making friends*. The *Dating* group was concerned with how girls and boys should act on different kinds of dates. History of aviation was the major emphasis of the group on *Aviation*.

Thus each group had organized its questions so that it could see its specific problem area clearly. The final step was taken the following day when each group stated its problem in a question broad enough to cover the things they wanted to find out. As an example, the *Civil defense* group concluded that its problem could best be stated as follows: *What preparations are being made to protect citizens in case of an atomic attack?*

Method of selecting a single problem. If a single problem is to be studied by the entire class, the method of selection should emphasize value to the greatest number. As was indicated earlier, an effort should be made to reach as complete a consensus as possible, rather than to select a problem on the basis of majority choice.

The list of possible topics can be developed in the same manner as that described earlier in this chapter. It is, of course, necessary to eliminate from the list all areas that are of concern to only a few pupils. This can be done as indicated in the previous section, by voting four choices, then three, two, and one, in this way reducing the list to a small number that can then be examined in greater detail.

Another method that may be used is mathematically excellent but is likely to be disturbing to some pupils because they do not fully understand its operation. This is a weighting technique. Class members are asked to give a value of 3, 2, or 1 to every item on the list. A value of 3 indicates that the pupil feels the topic meets the criteria and is an excellent topic for study, 2 that it is of some worth, and 1 that it should not be considered at all. If this method is used it is helpful to prepare duplicated lists of the topics in order to save class time and to avoid confusion and errors in numbering. When pupils have finished weighting the items, the results are summarized. One pupil may be assigned to every seven or eight papers, with directions to record on a single sheet the weightings given to each topic on these papers. The values given to each are then added, and the total for each topic is recorded at the right-hand side of the page. Such a record for the first four items might appear as follows:

1. Radar $-$ 1, 1, 2, 1, 2, 1, 1, 1 $= 10$
2. Michigan $-$ 2, 1, 3, 1, 2, 2, 2, 2 $= 15$
3. Holidays $-$ 2, 1, 2, 3, 1, 2, 2, 2 $= 15$
4. Japan $-$ 3, 3, 3, 2, 1, 3, 3, 2 $= 20$

These summaries are then in turn totaled in order to determine which areas are of most concern to the entire class. Those having the highest weightings, perhaps seven or eight of them, should be considered in some detail before a final choice is made.

Let us suppose that the list from which a final single choice is to be made were the same list of nine developed on page 178, namely: *Space travel, Juvenile delinquency, Photography, Famous inventors, Hunting and fishing, Civil defense, Making friends, Dating,* and *F.B.I.* How can a wise choice made? The teacher's part in assisting pupils to come to agreement on a single topic lies in stimulating discussion on questions such as: What kinds of things could we find out in studying each of these? How are these topics related to our lives? Which best fits our criteria? What resource materials are available? What might be gained in each from interviews, field trips, or other such activities? If comparisons are made between the nine problem areas on the basis of answers to questions such as these, there is considerably more likelihood that the class members will reach agreement than there is if the discussion is only based on questions such as, "Which one is best?" or, "Which would you rather study?" Such questions are divisive, causing individuals or groups to battle for their own interests. Through the dicussions various topics are eliminated, the choice narrowing as time goes on. It may not be possible to reach complete agreement on a single area, although every effort should be made to do so, since the fewer the number of pupils who are "hold-outs," the more successful the unit will be. Although this procedure takes time, it is well spent, since, in addition to making a choice more satisfying to a greater number of pupils, it provides practice in the use of criteria in making decisions.

Having selected the topic, the procedure for defining the specific problem, or problems, within this area is similar to that followed by the small groups in the preceding section. In the case of defining an over-all class problem, however, the entire class is involved. The first step again is listing the questions pupils have in this topic area. The simplest method is to ask for questions from the floor, although it is not always a satisfactory way of drawing all pupils into the operation, nor of getting all possible questions. After the first flurry of suggestions has subsided, it is helpful to give a 3 by 5 inch index card to each pupil, asking each to jot down any questions not already listed. The list on the chalkboard serves to prime the pump, and the card gives everyone a chance to participate. This entire list can then be assembled and duplicated in order that each pupil may have a copy to use as a basis for organization, which is the next step.

The organization of the questions, too, must be on a class-wide basis. The same questions may be used as when small groups are organizing their material, namely:

1. Are there questions on this list that deal with the same or similar parts of the topic? What is the subject of these?

2. Are there some questions that do not fit with these? Could these be omitted?

A thorough discussion of these points should bring together questions bearing on the same phases of the subject. As an example, a class that had selected the area of *Juvenile delinquency* discovered that its questions fell into four categories: types of delinquency, causes, prevention, and treatment. From these the class decided to state its over-all problem as: *What can be done about juvenile delinquency in our city?* The sub-problems that served to divide the class into four working groups were:

1. What is meant by juvenile delinquency?

2. What are the causes of delinquency?

3. How can delinquency be prevented in our city?
4. What is being done to correct juvenile delinquency in our city?

Problems selected from predetermined areas

In classes in which the problem must be drawn from a series of areas that have been determined by the staff, the procedure is practically identical with that just described. The only difference lies in the fact that in this situation pupils do not develop their own initial list of possible areas for study, since they must accept the list prescribed by the staff and select from this. Accepting the limits of this list, the class may proceed on a pupil-teacher planned basis as described in the preceding section, selecting the topic within the prescribed areas that best fits their criteria, then defining a specific problem or problems.

Other schools assign particular areas, usually three or four, to a given grade level. These are studied one at a time, throughout the year. In this case pupil-teacher planning begins at the point at which pupils list the questions to which they would like to find answers relative to the assigned problem area. Here, too, the procedure may follow that described in the previous section.

Problems limited to specific course content

It is sometimes said that democratic procedures cannot be used in a subject-matter class such as history or literature. It is quite true, of course, that in these classes the degree of pupil-teacher planning is likely to be much more limited than in classes where no text is required, nor the specifics of the course prescribed. In a class in which classroom work must lie within the limits of the subject of a course, but in which a textbook is not required, pupil-teacher planning is possible to a relatively high degree. The same may be said for courses in which a textbook is standard equipment, but where there is no requirement as to how it is to be used. A teacher is seldom able, however, to achieve the level of democratic classroom living that is reached in some of the classes described in the previous pages, since most subject-matter courses are on a one-period time basis, whereas *core, general education,* and *basic living* classes usually cover a two or three period block of time. Thus, time pressure alone is a factor in reducing the amount of cooperative planning that is possible. If it is required that the class cover systematically a specified number of pages in a given textbook in a semester or year, little time is left to develop the skills of small group work, to do careful and consistent pupil-teacher planning of content or procedure, or to depart in other ways from the prescribed subject matter to consider pupils' problems and needs. It is even impossible to delve much below the surface of the subject matter of the text itself.

An even more important factor, however, is the goal concept of the teacher. If, in the eyes of the teacher, the sole purpose is to teach the facts concerning the subject matter of the course, it is unlikely that pupils will be given much part in planning the content and structure of their experiences. However, if the teacher recognizes that, however important facts may be, he also has an obligation to help his pupils learn how to live in a democratic society, he will involve them in the development of the classroom activities in such a way that the skills and techniques of democratic living have an opportunity to grow.

Naturally, some courses lend themselves to pupil-teacher planning more easily than others. Among these might be listed: *literature, civics, history, American problems, art,* some *science courses, health* or *hygiene, home and family living,* and *child care.*

If no textbook is required. Let us see how an eleventh-grade core class which was limited to the field of American history and in which no specific textbook is required developed on a pupil-teacher planned basis. The plans that can be made in such a situation, of course, depend considerably on the amount of reference material that can be made available. If there is no room library of maps and historical materials, one should be gradually built up. Since pupils are not required to buy a textbook, a fifty-cent or a dollar fee is frequently levied with which needed reference sources may be purchased. The teacher needs to acquaint himself with materials that can be obtained not only in the school and community libraries, but also in county and state libraries. He needs to know as well what is available through the audio-visual aids department of his own school or system, or of the state university, or the state department of public instruction, in order that he may give as much assistance as possible to his pupils.

In the eleventh-grade American history core class that will be described in the following pages, the teacher discussed with the pupils the degree to which the plans for the year would be developed jointly by the class members and himself, indicating that the subject-matter limits would be the field of American history. Pupils were free to purchase texts if they wished, although they would not be asked to do so. A one dollar fee would be required of each pupil in order to add new items to the reference material in the room library. Two major decisions would need to be made by the class and the teacher together: (1) the method to be used in studying American history throughout the coming year; and (2) the specific problems to be studied as the year progressed.

Through these statements pupils were made aware of the limits within which they might plan. If a teacher does not feel ready to tackle as much pupil-teacher planning as is indicated in the preceding paragraph, he should make clear the narrower limits within which pupils are free to operate. For example, he may feel that he is not ready to have pupils help plan the method of study, but is quite willing to have them assist in determining the problems to be studied. In this case, in order to avoid confusion, the method of study that the teacher has decided upon should be explained in order that class members may see the framework within which they are to be given choices.

Following the introductory explanation of the teacher, the American history class members were asked to think about the first decision that needed to be made, namely: What method could be used to study American history? They were asked to write descriptions of methods that they felt would be desirable. The teacher said to them:

Many of you have never participated in planning a semester's work. You have always followed the teacher's plan. But this is your chance to help find a way of working that you feel is best for all of us. You have usually read a textbook page by page and recited on the assignment in class. If you think this is the best way, do not hesitate to say so. If you can think of a better way, tell us about it.

The papers were to be brought to class the following day.

A few pupils, of course, had no ideas. Others had several. Many were duplicates. However, seven possible methods were suggested:

1. Free choice of topics anywhere in American history. Each pupil study a different problem.

2. Free choice of topics anywhere in American history. Small groups study different problems.

3. Everyone buy a textbook and study it one chapter at a time.

4. Divide American history into periods and study these in order, one period at a time. Small groups study different problems in the period.

5. Start with today's problems and trace them back to their beginnings.

6. Everyone read what took place between certain years, all using different books. A different group of pupils can lead discussion each week.

7. Groups select topics such as education, government, or industry and trace these from the beginning of this country to the present time.

The teacher then divided the class into random groups of six. Each group was asked to spend thirty minutes discussing the list of suggestions that had been made, considering the good and bad points of each in an effort to help each person decide which one seemed most desirable. The following day these were summarized, and the class discussed the ideas expressed by the different groups. The difficulties that would have to be overcome if various methods were used were discussed in detail, the teacher helping the pupils to look ahead as each method was considered.

The choice narrowed to: (1) free choice of topics anywhere in American history, with small groups studying different topics, and (2) dividing American history into periods, studying one period at a time in chronological order, and having small groups select different problems within the period. With more detailed discussion of these two possibilities, the first lost ground because pupils were afraid they would become too confused by the lack of order, since one group might be concerned with the Spanish-American War, while another might be studying the problems of colonial government. Almost complete consensus was reached in favor of the approach by periods.

Having made this decision, the question was raised as to what would constitute a period in history. The class felt that since they knew too little about the sequence of events, this decision should be made by the teacher. He accepted the assignment since he was well aware that the pupils were relatively unacquainted with American history, and for this reason were not well qualified to make such a decision at this time.

A similar situation arose when it was time to list topics that might be studied within the colonial period. He realized that pupils did not know what the possibilities were, and so could not develop a well-balanced list from which to choose. However, instead of taking the responsibility upon himself for developing such a list, he gave the class experience in methods of gaining an over-all view of a subject about which they knew little. He brought a number of films and filmstrips into the classroom that dealt with various phases of the period. Time was also spent in skimming books, both texts and those dealing specifically with the period. From these sources a list of possible topics was developed by the class. The technique was successful, and it was the procedure followed by the class prior to the study of each of the following historical periods.

From this point on, the procedure was little different from that described earlier. Criteria were established to serve as guide lines in selection. The suggested list of topics was discussed by the class, items were clarified, and the list was organized. Each pupil then listed the four areas in which he was most interested, and a poll was taken. Individual lists were reduced to three, then two, then one, a poll being taken each time. The class then moved into groups in accordance with the final choice each pupil had made, and a check was made on available resource material through the preparation of the bibliographies. This having been cleared, each group decided upon the specific problem on which it intended to work. These were as follows:

Group I:
  How were the different colonies settled?
Group II:
  How were the different colonies governed?
Group III:
  What was the home life of the colonists like?
Group IV:
  What relationship existed between the colonists and the Indians?
Group V:
  What kinds of work did the colonists do to support themselves?
Group VI:
  Who were the outstanding people of this period and what influence did they have on life in the colonies?

If a textbook is required. When a textbook is required for every pupil, there is a tendency on the part of many teachers to fail to give boys and girls an opportunity to look beyond it. The daily assignment is so much easier to cope with than the decision-making of pupil-teacher planned activities. The use of a textbook need not eliminate all pupil-teacher planning despite the fact that it often does. Let us look at a ninth-grade world history class as an example of what can be done when every pupil has a textbook and the teacher, although following the sequence of the text and using it as background material, feels free to move away from the usual pattern of page-by-page study and recitation. The section to be studied was entitled in the text: *The Civilization of Egypt Developed Along the Banks of the Nile.* The nineteen pages included two chapters: *Religion, Conquest, and Commerce Molded Egyptian Life:* and *Egyptians Built Foundations for Modern Life.*[5]

---

[5] Lester B. Rogers and Fay Adams and Walker Brown, *Story of Nations* (New York: Henry Holt and Company, 1956), pp. 20–38.

The teacher had prepared the room to serve as a stimulation and introduction to the study of ancient Egypt. On a colorful background were displayed pictures of places in Egypt, ancient Egyptian costumes, the pyramids, an Egyptian chariot, a funeral procession, a temple, and a map of the world with Egypt boldly outlined in color. Two small bulletin boards hung at the back of the room. The heading on one was *Then* and on the other was *Now*. The board labeled *Then* had pictures of a home in ancient Egypt, hieroglyphics, an Egyptian costume, a pyramid, ancient weapons, and a ship. The board labeled *Now* was empty with the exception of a large question mark in the center and sheets of colored paper that matched in size, shape, and position the pictures on the other board. Along the window ledges was displayed a collection of Egyptian artifacts and pictures borrowed from the city Children's Museum.

The teacher took the lead in introducing the study. She was obviously familiar with the articles in the exhibit, picking up several of them as she moved around the room and telling interesting facts about them. The geographical location of the country was pointed out on the map, and the pupils were drawn into a discussion of the place-relationship of Egypt to the lands they had already studied. The class was given time to look at the exhibit, and many pupils asked questions and made comments. A discussion of the bulletin boards marked *Then* and *Now* aroused a great deal of guessing, but no one in the room really knew how an Egyptian home looked today, how Egyptians dressed, nor what kind of weapons they used. They were fairly sure that the pyramids looked the same as they had centuries ago, and that ships must look something like our own.

The teacher then turned to the textbook, and with the pupils, skimmed the pages of the four chapters devoted to Egypt. The pictures were examined, the topic headings were read aloud, and from time to time the teacher commented on various points or told an interesting fact, and pupils also commented and asked questions.

The class was then divided into five random groups and assigned the task of listing topics that they felt would be good to work on. In doing this, they kept their textbooks at hand to help in recalling the many points that had been touched upon. Reports from the groups established the following list of possible problem areas:

1. Geography	9. Home life on farms
2. Pyramids	10. Egypt and the Bible
3. Egypt today	11. Schools of Egypt
4. The Nile River	12. Art of ancient Egypt
5. Science and inventions	13. Egyptian writing
6. Customs and manners	14. Egyptian wars and weapons
7. Religion	15. How Egypt was governed
8. Home life in cities	

These items were discussed, the list organized, and the selections made. Nine groups were set into operation, the following topics having been selected:

1. Geography	6. Art of ancient Egypt
2. Customs and manners	7. Egyptian wars and weapons
3. Religion	8. How Egypt was governed
4. Home life in cities and on farms	9. Egypt today
5. Education	

Each group decided upon its specific problem and set to work. In order to cover all units in the book that were required, a limit of four days was set in which to complete the collection of data for the solution of the problem. At the end of the four days, each group reported its findings to the class.

Conclusion

The selection of a problem for study on a pupil-teacher planned basis involves five major steps. Unless all of these are included each time new problems are selected, a teacher is likely to find the results less than satisfactory. The fulfillment of these five steps can be checked by asking oneself questions such as those listed below each step.

1. *A clarification of the limits of choice.*

   How far am I, the teacher, able and willing to carry out pupil-teacher planned procedures? What are the subject-matter limits? What are the procedural limits? Must I use a textbook? How much freedom in the use of a text do I have? Do the pupils understand these limits?

2. *Establishment of criteria for topic selection.*

   Did the pupils have a major part in establishing the criteria? Are the criteria developed for a previous problem still satisfactory? How can they be improved so that better choices will be made? Are they being used?

3. *Development of a list of possible problem areas.*

   Was every pupil involved in building the list? Is it representative of the pupils' concerns? Has every item that pupils feel to be important been included? Have the items been checked against the criteria? Were the suggested topics discussed by the class with respect to possible specific problems for study, and to opportunities for activities such as field trips, hand work, etc.? Has the list been organized so that topics that belong together have been placed under common headings?

4. *Selection of one or more problem areas.*

   Did the method of choice focus attention on the values of the problem areas? Were the available resources checked before final choices were made? If a single area was selected, was the decision reached by consensus rather than by majority vote?

5. *Definition of problem.*

   Were all group members involved in the process of stating the problem? Is the statement of the problem broad enough to cover the major items the group wants to know, but specific enough to limit the study to a particular part of the entire topic area?

6

Solving a Problem

LEARNING TO SOLVE GROUP PROBLEMS IS NOT EASY. It includes many tasks that are not a part of the usual classroom procedure, such as making detailed plans, using a wide variety of resources, taking notes, and sharing information with the members of one's group. It involves the development of attitudes and behaviors that do not lend themselves to quick solutions to problems. A pupil does not learn all these in a day, nor in a week, nor in a month. It takes time, and endless patience on the part of the teacher. But it can be done.

Scientific attitudes

Before approaching the specific activities in which pupils must engage in order to solve a problem, let us consider the general attitudes and behaviors that are basic to any type of research, whether this involves seeking an answer to a simple question or deals with the study of a highly complex situation. In educational literature, these attitudes and behaviors are frequently called *scientific attitudes* or *dispositions,* since they are typical of the approach made to problems by the scientist. They are, however, not only necessary for the solution of problems of science, but are the fundamental characteristics of clear thinking relative to problems in any field. Almost all lists of scientific attitudes contain the following items as characteristic of the person who approaches a problem critically.[1]

1. Has a lively curiosity about the world in which we live.

2. Believes that nothing happens without a cause.

3. Is unwilling to accept any statements as facts unless they are supported by sufficient proof.

4. Does not try to solve a problem in a careless or hasty way, but makes and carries through complete and careful plans for solving it.

5. Makes careful and accurate observations.

6. Weighs all evidence to decide whether it really relates to the matter under consideration.

7. Does not jump to a conclusion or base a conclusion upon one or a few observations, but seeks evidence as long as may be necessary in order to find a true answer to a problem.

8. Is willing to change an opinion or a conclusion if later evidence shows it to be wrong.

9. Respects other people's ideas, opinions, and ways of life.

10. Does not allow judgments to be influenced by personal likes and dislikes.

Pupils seldom develop such attitudes through direct teaching alone, since, like all attitudes, they are intangible, and are only accepted through experience that shows them to be valid. Direct teaching can be used, however, to provide an introduction to such attitudes and behaviors. For this purpose an eighth-grade teacher prepared a bulletin board display headed: *A Scientist Works Like This.* Each of the ten statements above was written, in letters large enough to be read across the room, on a separate sheet of paper. These were attached to the board, together with pictures of scientists at work. Across the bottom of the board was written: *What do these have to do with us?*

The opening response in the class discussion was, "We ought to know how scientists work because one of us might be a scientist some day." The closing statement several periods later was, "I guess everybody ought to try to do these things." The time be-

---

[1] Francis D. Curtis and John Urban, *Biology in Daily Life* (Boston: Ginn and Company, 1955), p. 571.

tween the two remarks had been devoted to a clarification of each of the statements listed on the bulletin board. Both teacher and pupils suggested simple, everyday examples that served to throw light on their meanings. At the conclusion of the discussion, the pupils were asked to copy the list of scientific attitudes into their notebooks in order that they might have them at hand for ready reference at later times.

The teacher then changed the bulletin board display heading to read: *We Have Agreed These Are Important.* The line at the bottom of the display read: *Which ones did you use today?* The display itself remained unchanged. This furnished material to refer to from time to time throughout the next few weeks, either for pupil self-evaluation, for class evaluation, or during discussions of daily class work. When the display was removed from the bulletin board, a copy of the ten scientific attitudes, on a large sheet of paper, was posted at the back of the room to serve as a reminder.

Another direct teaching device was used some weeks later. Each pupil was given a mimeographed copy of the statements listed below. The directions, printed at the top of the sheet, were as follows:

Which of these statements were made by persons who are learning to think critically? Mark such statements C.
Which were made by persons who are not learning to think critically? Mark such statements NC.

1. I don't think we have enough information to decide that.

2. That's the way it happened. Bill was to blame. I talked to a fellow who knew a man who was there.

3. I'm going to build a dog house. I guess I've got enough wood. I'll cut it and see how it turns out.

4. It was Joe's own fault that he had an accident. He should never have started his trip on a Friday.

5. As far as I can see from the things the principal and the policeman have told us and from the articles in the paper Jay is not to blame.

6. Everybody likes to have two reading days each week.

7. Let's not waste so much time. We know what's best without asking anyone else.

8. I'm not sure that I agree with you. Will you tell me more about your idea?

9. I'm going to build a book case. I've drawn a plan so that I'll be sure that it will fit between the windows.

10. No, I haven't read about it, but I know I'm right.

11. Mary can answer that better than I can. She studied about the City Council last term.

The teacher suggested that pupils refer to the list of scientific attitudes to help them make their decisions. The discussion that followed was based on reasons for these decisions. Before the period ended, pupils were asked to turn their papers over and complete the following:

As I look back over the last two weeks I think that I have been showing $\left\{\begin{array}{l} \text{scientific} \\ \text{unscientific} \end{array}\right\}$ attitudes in my work in class.

My reasons for saying this are: _____

Probably more important than such direct teaching is the behavior of the teacher in the day to day activities of the classroom, the discussions, group work, individual conferences, presentations, or business meetings. His own belief in the concepts stressed in the direct lessons must be evidenced by his actions. His consistent response to classroom problems with statements such as the following will serve as examples of the application of scientific attitudes, and will help pupils to become aware of them and to recognize their values:

1. What facts do we have that will help us make a decision?

2. I don't know the answer to your question, but I will see what I can find out about it.

3. I think I agree with you, Sue, but I would like to give it some more thought.

4. Is that your opinion, Fred, or have you reliable information on this?

5. Where can we get more information before we give Mr. Smith an answer?

6. Mary's idea is very different from Jill's. How can we test them to see what the results of each would be?

7. Are you sure that you saw everything just the way you have described it?

8. Why do you feel that would be the best thing to do?

9. What would have been the difference if we had taken our information from the pamphlet Gerry had rather than the book Joe brought in?

This is far more difficult than teaching "lessons" on attitudes. It is the scientific attitude in action, the translation of the attitude into behavior, and we are likely to miss many opportunities to demonstrate its value. However, without the daily expression of the teacher's belief in these attitudes as shown by his actions, the direct lesson will be worth little or nothing, for such concepts must be tested again and again before pupils will accept and practice them.

Acquainting pupils with such attitudes need not be pegged at any specific place in the year's work. Obviously it should be done early, certainly previous to beginning work on a major problem. The best place is probably in conjunction with an early, minor problem or immediately after the selection of the first major problem such as described in Chapter 5. The teacher's behavior should, of course, show evidence of his acceptance of these concepts from the first day of the semester, thus giving experience with them even before they are brought to pupils' attention. Let us turn now to the specific activities in which a group must engage in order to solve its problem.

Making a plan

Further observation of the class described in the previous chapter will illustrate the next steps that should be taken. Thus far the class had selected its problem areas; each group had defined its specific problem; availability of resource materials had been checked. As the period began, the chairman called the class to order and the secretary took the roll. The chairman then turned to the posted schedule of the day's work as it had been decided upon at the previous business meeting, and said:

Yesterday we decided how we wanted to state our problems. According to the schedule for today we will work in our groups and plan how we are going to solve them. Mr. Greene agreed to help us get started. He suggested that we not move into groups until after he has worked with us for a few minutes.

The teacher then directed class discussion toward making plans of action for solving the group problems. He compared this with the planning that is necessary in getting ready to go on a trip and said:

If you are going on a trip, you first decide where you are going. You also decide some of the places at which you want to stop along the way and the things you want to see. Certainly you need to know how you are going to get there and what sorts of things you need to take along. Solving a problem is much like taking a trip. It must be planned just as carefully or you won't reach a solution.

When he posed the question, "What sorts of things will each group have to decide before starting work on its problem?" the following ideas were expressed:

1. We have to decide what we want to find out.
2. We have to decide where to get information.
3. We have to decide how to divide the work so that it all gets done.

Mr. Greene agreed that these were the main parts of a well-constructed plan, pointing out to the pupils that they had already done parts of the first and second items, since they had already stated their problems and had checked some material at the time they were deciding whether there were sufficient resources available. He then gave to each pupil a mimeographed 8½ by 11 inch sheet of paper titled, *A Group Plan*. Six major headings were listed with an explanation following each, as follows:

I.   *Group membership*
Chairman—
Recorder—
Other members—
This is a record of the members of your group.

II.   *Statement of problem*
This is the final, over-all statement of your group problem. It is best to write this as a question.

III.   *Questions to be answered*
These are the questions that your group will need to answer in order to solve your problem. There will probably be many of them.

IV.   *Assignment of work*
This tells how your group plans to divide the work that needs to be done, in other words: For what is each person responsible?

V.   *Possible sources of information*
This is a list of every possible source of information that your group can find. Your preliminary bibliography is a good beginning on this.

VI.   *Special activities*
This includes any activities outside of reading which are undertaken by your group in connection with solving your problem, for example:

    a) bringing in a speaker
    b) taking a field trip
    c) making models, slides, graphs, charts etc.
    d) writing a radio script or play
    e) bringing in films, filmstrips, recordings
    f) making a recording

This was followed by two paragraphs:

A group plan is just what the words say: a plan made by a group. This means that every member of the group should take part in making it. When it is completed it should be a plan that the members have all agreed upon.

As you work on your problem, it may become necessary to change your plans. This should not be done unless the group agrees to the change. Be sure to record such changes on your own plan sheet and on the one you turn in to the teacher.

These points were discussed thoroughly and questions answered. Pupils were asked to keep these sheets in their notebooks in order to have them for later reference. Each group chairman was then given two copies of a mimeographed sheet titled, *Our Group Plan,* containing the same six headings as stated above, spaced on the front and reverse side of the sheet so that there was room for writing after each one. Upon completion, one of these was to be kept in the group record book and the other was to be given to the teacher. Mr. Greene reminded them that they had listed a number of questions at the time a group had selected its problem. This list could serve as a beginning to Item III. He also pointed out to them that there might not be enough room on the sheet for all their questions; in this case they could write them on a separate sheet of paper and staple this to the plan.

The groups required varying amounts of time to complete their plans, and varying amounts of assistance from the teacher. He moved from group to group raising questions, offering suggestions, and answering pupils' questions. Some groups were able to list many more questions than others, as well as many more sources of information, thus producing much more usable plans of work. An example of a well-developed plan was that made by the group interested in civil defense, which was reported in Chapter 5. The plan read as follows:

GROUP PLAN

I. *Group membership*
Chairman—Bob
Recorder—Sue
Other members—Jack, Linda, Dennis

II. *Statement of problem*
What preparations are being made to protect citizens in case of an atomic attack?

III. *Questions to be answered*
1. Can foreign planes be detected in time to give us a chance to get away?
2. How can they be detected? Who does it?
3. What could you do if an H-bomb were dropped?

4. How is our city organized for civil defense?
5. How is our state organized for civil defense?
6. How is our nation organized for civil defense?
7. Could our city be evacuated in time if there should be an attack?
8. What plans does our city have for evacuating the citizens?
9. How much damage would an atomic bomb do?
10. How can they tell how much damage an atomic bomb could do?
11. What happens to people who aren't killed?
12. What is meant by fall-out? Is it dangerous?
13. How does an atomic bomb work?
14. Who decides where pupils are to go during an air raid drill in school?
15. Does radar help? How does it work?
16. How can a citizen help in civil defense?
17. What do the bomb tests show?
18. What is atomic energy?
19. Does the state civil defense department tell the cities what to do?
20. If there were an air raid on our city would the state send help?
21. Would the state feed and clothe the people who had no homes?
22. Does the national government tell the states what to do?
23. Does the national government give money to the states for civil defense?
24. Who is in charge of our national civil defense?
25. Can an attack be launched from a man-made satellite?
26. Can a man-made satellite give protection?
27. Could we intercept an attack from a satellite?

IV. *Assignment of work*

Jack—How does an atomic bomb work? Questions 12, 13, 18.

Bob—How much damage would an atomic bomb do? Questions 9, 10, 11, 17.

Linda—What is our city doing to protect us in case of an air attack? Questions 3, 4, 7, 8, 14, 16.

Dennis—What is our state doing to protect us in case of an air attack? Questions 5, 19, 20, 21.

Sue—What is the national government doing to protect us in
     case of an air attack? Questions 6, 22, 23, 24.
Questions 1, 2, 15, 25, 26, and 27 do not exactly fit in our prob-
lem, but we all plan to watch for answers to them anyway.
V. *Possible sources of information*
Library books: public library
                school library
                room library
Civil defense offices: city
                       state
                       national
Films: Civil defense office
       Audio-visual department of our school
Newspapers and magazine articles
Mr. Hadley, the science teacher
The names of books, magazines, and films are on our bibliogra-
phies.
VI. *Special activities*
Show films to the class
Make a visit to the city civil defense office
Dennis can make charts or pictures for us, but we don't know
now what kind we need.

As can be seen by comparing the list of questions in the plan
with those listed at the time of problem selection,[2] many are the
same, some were dropped, and a number were added. It is sometimes difficult to get such a complete list rolling. A technique
that has been found helpful is to ask every pupil in the class to
write, each on a separate 3 by 5 inch index card, questions that he
would like to have answered in any of the areas being studied by
the different groups. These are then given to the groups. This
technique serves two purposes: (1) it gives each group additional
ideas for its list, and (2) involves every pupil in all problems
being studied in the class.

Item IV, the assignment of work, does not always lend itself to
an easy division of labor. Pupils frequently need help in fitting
the questions together so that each group member is assigned

---

2 See pages 183–184.

questions that deal with a clearly defined phase of the problem. Sometimes it seems wiser to a group to make no division of the work to be done. Each member agrees to study all aspects of the problem. Other groups will decide that some phases are to be studied by all members, whereas certain others are assigned to specific individuals. There is no one *best* method. It is to be hoped that, as a pupil works with different groups of boys and girls, he will experience all of them. The value of each is determined by the task that needs to be done.

For Item VI, special activities, pupils usually have few or no ideas at the time the plan is made. As the work progresses, however, they begin to see possibilities for such projects and to include these in their further planning.

How a plan is used. The completed plan has a number of uses. Especially in the initial stages of solving a problem it serves as a "handle" by means of which the members of a group can approach a difficult task. The questions help to break the problem into its parts, so that pupils may see more clearly where and how to make a beginning. It is also an aid in keeping the problem in focus, holding pupils on a reasonably direct road toward its solution. Without it, they too frequently tend to digress from its major aspects and lose themselves in unimportant details.

It further serves as a means of evaluating progress. By checking against the assignments they have set themselves, pupils are able to see how well they are progressing. Frequently such checking leads to improvement of the group plan, so that it becomes a more useful instrument. For example, new questions may arise or, as the result of the past week's work, it may have become clear to the group that certain others have no real bearing on the problem and should be dropped. Changes must, therefore, be made in the work assigned to some of the group members, or new activities must be planned.

Collecting data

Collecting the necessary data to solve a problem involves knowing where to go to get information, how to select from a large body of material facts that are pertinent to the problem, and how to record these so that they are in usable form. These three aspects of collecting data should not be considered as separate skills, but should be developed simultaneously.

Sources of data. Books are probably the most common source of data used in the classroom, although they are far from being the only source available. Certainly, however, they are nearest at hand. Since it is expected that pupils will not limit their search for information to one book, as wide an assortment as possible should be placed at the disposal of the class. If the room and school libraries are not equipped with sufficient materials dealing with the problems on which pupils are working, it is usually possible to obtain a fairly large supply from the public library or from county or state libraries.

An encyclopedia, at the reading level of the pupils is a must in the school library or, better yet, in the room library. Some pupils, however, tend to confine their reading to the encyclopedia alone, and need help in understanding how an encyclopedia can best be used. They may also need assistance in finding and using other types of reading material.

The use of the *Readers' Guide,* and such references as *World Almanac, Dictionary of American Biography, Dictionary of Social Studies,* and an *atlas,* will probably need to be taught and retaught. An introductory lesson on the *Readers' Guide* can easily be carried out by means of the opaque projector, using sample pages to show pupils how to find the information they are looking for, to understand the arrangement of sub-headings, and the abbreviations of magazine titles. Copies of individual references may be typed on paper, each on a single page to avoid confusion, inserted in the projector, and so studied in detail.

Later, when pupils are deep in the problem of finding material, a helpful reminder is a bulletin board display consisting of 9 by 11 inch sheets of construction paper, each naming and describing one of the many special reference books. An example of such a sheet would be:

Readers' Guide

Contains names of all articles that are published in magazines. Ask for it at the library desk.

Such a display might be headed: *Have you looked in these?* At the bottom, a wise teacher wrote: *If you need help in using these don't hesitate to ask for it.* A list of such references, together with annotations, may also be duplicated in order that each pupil may have a copy in his notebook to which he can refer.

Besides such books as have been suggested, films, filmstrips, and recordings constitute valuable sources of information. Some films will be helpful to the entire class; others will have value only to a small group. If the school has an audio-visual aids department, a list of audio-visual materials owned by the school should be obtained and posted where it is easily accessible to the pupils. The person in charge of the department can be invited to visit the class and explain the process by which pupils may order materials that are needed. Pupils usually need considerable assistance in learning to use a film or a recording as a source of data and to select and record the information that is pertinent to their problems. It is advisable, therefore, to set aside time to practice such skills, so that better use may be made of these sources.

Exhibit material—pictures, museum pieces, and collections of various sorts—also constitute sources of data that, as yet, too few secondary school teachers have learned to take advantage of. A glance into classrooms usually shows bare walls and bare bulletin boards. Sometimes displays serve only to beautify the room. Admirable as this purpose is, displays can also be made to serve as a major means of teaching. However, their use must be planned with care, and class time must be set aside for observation and study of what is exhibited, so that the potential value of these resources may be realized.

The arrangement of source material displays is sometimes planned and carried out by the teacher, and at other times by the pupils. A teacher frequently has pictures on file that would be of help to a class. Whether he arranges these himself or a committee of pupils does the work is usually a matter of convenience. Museum materials, or collections that have been borrowed, generally should not be handled by pupils and would, of course, be arranged for exhibition by the teacher. However, pupils, too, bring in a wide variety of articles such as charts, pictures, maps, models, and samples of substances being studied. These should be displayed as they come in if they are to serve as resources to the class. If possible, each group should be assigned a space for exhibiting its materials. If this is not possible, the available space can be allotted to groups on a rotation plan.

As in the case of films, pupils seldom know how to glean from exhibits, either of pictures or artifacts, the information that is before their eyes. They may enjoy seeing an exhibit of colonial kitchen utensils, yet see little value in it as a source of data. Dolls dressed as Puritans or Williamsburg belles ellicit no more than the remark, "Oh, aren't they cute!" from the girls, and not even a glance from the boys. With a little help, pupils can learn to use exhibits much as they would use books. Both interest and perception are involved in this process.

In order to assist an American history class in learning how to use objects as sources of data, the teacher brought three exhibits into the classroom at different times throughout the year. The first dealt with the American Indians. It included both pictures and artifacts and presented various types of weapons, utensils, food, and clothing, as well as models of a pueblo, a tepee, and a wigwam. These were spread out on tables so that they might easily be seen and handled.

In a brief introduction the teacher reminded the class that one of the scientific attitudes they had agreed to strive for was to be accurate in interpreting data of all kinds. This would, of course, include being accurate in observing things. This exhibit would give them an opportunity to see to what extent they were developing their ability to observe accurately. In groups of three, the pupils examined the exhibit. The only directions given them were to look at the exhibit carefully and to write down all the information they could collect from observing and handling the objects and from looking at the pictures. When they had finished they were to go to their seats. In less than fifteen minutes all thirty-five pupils were seated, the task presumably completed. The average number of statements collected by a group from the entire exhibit was six. With few exceptions, the items listed were derived from the pictures. In fact, any number were verbatim copies of the descriptive statements printed beneath the pictures, such as the third item in the sample list below:

1. Indians had ceremonial dances.
2. Indians did weaving.
3. The Hopi Indians lived, as they do today, on the high mesas of the Southwest.
4. Medicine men made sand paintings.
5. The Indians raised crops.

The teacher then discussed with the class various objects and pictures, and raised questions about them in an effort to help pupils see some of the facts revealed by the articles, such as the differences, as shown by the models and pictures, between a domed wigwam with its framework of poles covered with thatch and bark, a tepee with its conical shape formed by poles covered with hides, and rectangular clay brick pueblos. In the twenty remaining minutes of the period, fifteen additional facts were recorded on the chalkboard, as well as a list of questions to which no answers could be found in the exhibit, but which might serve as leads to further observation or investigation. Among these questions were the following:

1. Why did some tribes use wigwams, whereas others used tepees or pueblos?
2. What kinds of tools were used to make arrowheads?
3. Where did they get the colors to make a sand painting?
4. Do the Indians today still make sand paintings?
5. Why did some tribes make totem poles while others didn't?
6. What does it mean when it says that the Navahos were a nomadic tribe?

A second exhibit, brought in some weeks later, dealt with the colonial period in American history. This time it was suggested that groups not only record factual data discovered, but also list as many questions as came to mind and any words or names that would serve as leads for later investigation. Although the exhibit was smaller than the previous one, no one stopped until time was called at the end of thirty minutes. Each group had many facts, as well as a long list of questions, names, and words, that led to further study both in the library and the museum.

At a later time in the year, when a discussion had involved the Middle Ages, an exhibit dealing with this period was borrowed from the museum and the procedure was repeated. This time no one finished in less than thirty minutes, and fourteen of the thirty-five boys and girls were still working at the end of forty minutes, when the period closed. They were excited, had asked each other and the teacher dozens of questions, pointed out their discoveries to one another, and had so many leads for later study that they did not know how to use them all.

Special books on the subject of the exhibit can also be brought into the classroom from the library and placed with the artifacts and pictures as further assistance to the class. Pupils examining such source materials are shown in Figure 16. The exhibit need not be large, but the items should be selected carefully and be pertinent to the problems being studied.

Ability to see the facts shown in pictures may also be improved by detailed consideration of a half dozen or so that deal with a problem that is being studied. Shown through the opaque projector, pictures can be viewed by all at the same time. Questions such as the following assist pupils in learning to direct their attention to information-giving details:

1. Can you identify the people in this picture? How did you identify them?

2. What are they doing?

3. What are the objects on the table? What do these tell you about this period in history?

4. What do the people's clothes tell you?

Figure 16. Museum exhibits are sources of data.

5. What differences do you notice between the man on the right side of the picture and the one at the table?

6. What do their facial expressions tell you?

7. What can you tell about their political views from the posters on the walls?

8. What does the caption of the picture tell you?

Cartoons that appear on the editorial pages of daily newspapers also can be used to help boys and girls learn to interpret the pictures they see. The English teacher who asks his class to write a story about a given picture, using as many as possible of the details shown, is giving his pupils an opportunity to increase their ability to read pictures. Techniques such as those described above widen tremendously the range of possible sources from which pupils may gather information.

It is, of course, to be hoped that the school library maintains a good picture and clipping file. If it does not, room files can be developed without too much difficulty. As each new problem is studied, both teacher and pupils can be alert for pictures and clippings that deal with this topic. It is not long before a quite respectable and extremely helpful file has come into being. Metal filing cabinets are most satisfactory for storing such materials that should be sorted according to topics, and placed in labeled manila folders. Inexpensive cardboard file drawers are also available, which will keep the folders covered. Even cartons from the grocery store will serve the purpose. The important point is to have the pictures and clippings.

An enormous amount of inexpensive and even free material can be found if one knows where to look. Likely sources are various city, county, and state departments. Most school libraries have or can obtain copies of such books as the *Sources of Free and Inexpensive Educational Materials*,[3] which is helpful in procuring data on a wide range of subjects. A little initiative will cause the picture and clipping file to grow by leaps and bounds.

A further source of information is, of course, to be found in the so-called mass media, the radio, television, and public motion picture films. Since, obviously, programs on these are not planned with the problems of a class in mind, it is necessary to devise a system for keeping track of the daily programs so that any that might be helpful are not missed. A committee, either elected by the class or appointed by the chairman, may be assigned the task of listing all programs having any bearing on class problems.

---

[3] *Sources of Free and Inexpensive Educational Materials* (Chicago: Field Enterprises Inc., 1955).

Other less expensive references are:

Free and Inexpensive Learning Materials (Nashville, Tenn.: Division of Surveys and Field Services, George Peabody College for Teachers, 1957 ed.).

Gordon Salisbury and Robert Sheridan, *Catalog of Free Teaching Aids* (Riverside, California, P.O. Box 943).

These can be posted each day. In the selection of such a committee, some television and film "addicts" may well be included, not only because they are interested and informed, but also because the assignment may help them develop some discrimination.

The field trip, if properly used, is a valuable source of information. At times, an entire class may have need for such a trip; at other times, only a small group will need the special information a trip will provide. Generally a class field trip is taken on school time, but small groups, especially in older classes, can often make such trips on their own outside of school hours. However, whether it is an entire class or a small group, whether on school time or beyond it, careful preparation should be made for the trip in order that as much benefit as possible may be derived from it.

Pupils and teacher should have a clear concept of the purpose for which the trip is to be taken. It should never be just a "pleasant thing to do," or be considered a social event. Decisions relative to the place to be visited, time of departure and return, transportation arrangements, methods of keeping track of a large group, and courtesies involved in contacts with strangers should be made cooperatively by pupils and teacher. If at all possible, pictures and descriptive pamphlets should be obtained from the concern to be visited. This material should be studied before making the trip. Some companies will send a representative to the school before the trip to brief the pupils on what they will see. This helps to make the experience meaningful, and is by far the most helpful procedure.

During a trip, pupils can advantageously take notes to which they can refer on their return to school. A simple procedure is to cut 8½ by 11 inch paper into four equal parts, each approximately 4¼ by 5½ inches in size. Four of these sheets stapled together makes a small pad for each pupil. If a pupil's name is written at the top of each pad, roll can be taken at the time of departure by giving out the pads. Those left in hand have on them the names of pupils not present. It is also wise to carry six or seven extra pencils for the forgetful.

When making arrangements with the company to be visited, an effort should be made to have a half hour at the end of the trip assigned to a question-and-answer period. Pupils usually have many questions, and it is quite possible that the teacher may be unable to answer them. For this reason, an on-the-spot-session is extremely helpful. On return to school, at least a period should be devoted to a discussion of the trip and to summarizing the information collected and its relation to the problem the class is studying.

A seventh-grade class, as part of its study of our natural resources, decided to take a trip to a paper factory. A committee of four was elected to serve as *trip record keepers*. The members of the committee cut white wrapping paper into sheets 30 inches wide and a yard long. When completed, these were stapled together along one narrow edge to form a ten-page wall chart. A sturdy stick, 2 inches in width and 34 inches in length, was clamped to the stapled edge in order to give it body. Picture wire, fastened to each end of the stick, served as a means of hanging the set of sheets upon the wall so that all might see the record. Visibility was increased by writing with a brush pen.

The pages were prepared one at a time as the project progressed. The title page read:

Our Trip To the Paper Company

The second page, written after a class discussion relative to the purposes of the trip, contained the following:

Reasons for Taking the Trip

This is part of our unit on how we use our natural resources.
1. We went to see how paper is made from wood.
2. We want to see what the workers in a paper factory do.
3. We want to see what a factory looks like.

Page three was prepared after a representative of the paper company had spent a class period with the pupils. By means of an illustrated booklet, he had given them a preview of the activities they would observe at the factory. The page therefore read:

What We Expect to See

We studied the booklets from the company and Mr. Jackson told us we would see these things:
1. How the lumber is brought to the plant.
2. How the lumber is stored.
3. How the lumber is made into pulp.
4. How the pulp is made into sheets of paper.
5. How the paper is colored.
6. How the paper is cut into sizes for use.

The next six pages described the trip and were written after its completion. The contents were developed from the class discussion of what had been seen, and served as a summary of the information gathered by the pupils. This was recorded under the heading, *Things We Learned*.

The last page was devoted to an evaluation of the trip in terms of the purposes for which it had been taken. This, too, was the outgrowth of a class discussion. Page ten read:

Was the Trip Worth While?

Everyone in our class thinks we learned a great deal.
1. We understand now how paper is made from wood.
2. We learned what the workers do.
3. We learned what a paper factory looks like, but other kinds of factories would look different.
4. We learned how to plan a field trip. We are glad that we went.

In looking for sources of information, teachers too frequently overlook the use of people with special knowledge and ability. Representatives of various community agencies, city departments, political groups, churches and other special organizations are usually more than willing to lend a hand by coming into the classroom for an hour. Within any school faculty it is usually possible to find teachers who are well versed in special fields or who have special hobbies or interests. The most frequently over-

Figure 17. A parent as a resource person.

looked individuals, however, are the parents. Given an opportunity, they are usually glad to give assistance.

In one class, a father who was an outdoor enthusiast spent an evening with a group of five who wanted to know all about camping. A mother showed slides taken on a vacation trip to several national parks to a class studying this topic. A Ukrainian mother decorated Easter eggs in the classroom. A German father brought some of his wood carvings to class, as well as a piece in process of being carved. He explained the use of his tools, told about the type of wood needed, and showed the class how the actual carving was done. In Figure 17 we see a father who is a policeman answering the questions of a group of ninth-graders who were studying a problem in the area of juvenile delinquency.

Still another method of obtaining information from people,

particularly those who, for one reason or another, find it impossible to come to the classroom is to have the class select representatives to interview them. It is usually best to send two pupils for an interview, in order that each may give the other moral support. If this is the first time pupils have officially interviewed anyone, the procedure should be carefully planned with the class, or there can be a practice run by means of role-playing. Two phases of the interview need to be considered, making the appointment, and the interview itself.

A class that was working on the problems of recreation in a large city wished to have two representatives interview Mr. Jason, the community YMCA director. After discussing with the class how to make an appointment, the teacher changed pace and suggested that they try it out and see how it sounded.

TEACHER

Would someone like to take the part of Mr. Jason? (*A number of hands came up.*) All right Mike. You be Mr. Jason the first time. Who would like to call for the appointment? —— Ruth? Fine.

MIKE (*coming to the center of the room*)

If we are telephoning we shouldn't see each other.

RUTH

We could sit on opposite sides of the room and turn our backs to one another.

So it was arranged, and the two played their parts. The rest of the class jotted down their ideas of how it could be improved. When they were finished, hands were flying. All were eager to try it. Two more were selected and it was played through again with many changes. In the discussion that followed, the order of procedure was established as follows:

1. Tell who you are and where you are from.
2. Explain what the class is studying.
3. Tell the person that you would like to have an interview with him.
4. Tell him what you want help on.
5. Give him a choice of time but state your own limits, for ex-

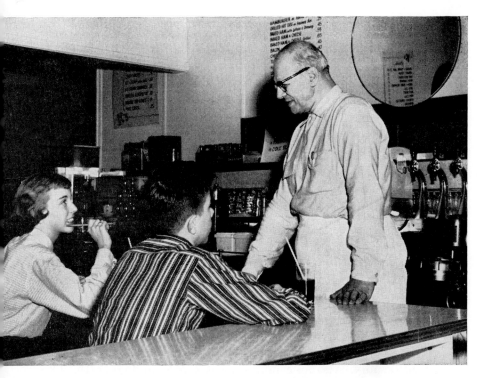

Figure 18. An interview with a member of the community.

ample: "I can come down any afternoon between three and five o'clock or on Saturday."

6. Thank him for the appointment.

A similar procedure was followed in planning the interview. The points to be observed were established as follows:

1. Be on time.
2. Plan your questions ahead of time.
3. Ask the most important questions. Don't waste the time of the person you are interviewing.
4. If there are two interviewers be sure that both take part. Divide the questions to be asked.
5. Take notes.
6. Thank the person interviewed for his time.

Pupils interviewing the owner of a shop in the vicinity of the school are shown in Figure 18.

Taking notes. A considerable part of the time devoted to a problem is spent in taking notes on information presumably helpful in reaching its solution. Frequently, however, pupils have difficulty in understanding and assimilating the ideas expressed by a writer and in recording these in their own words. To many, note-taking consists of copying passages, sometimes whole pages, into a notebook, without either being selective or stating the information in simpler terms. Thus, when an effort is made to use such data to solve the problem, confusion arises, since the pupil has no clear idea of the meaning of his notes and much of the material collected is irrelevant to the problem at hand.

There is, of course, no single correct form in which notes should be recorded. In teaching note-taking to a group of boys and girls, however, it is well to use a specific form, since this makes working with a whole class a much simpler procedure. The writer has found index cards, 3 by 5 inch size, to be most satisfactory. A sample note card is shown in Figure 19. This

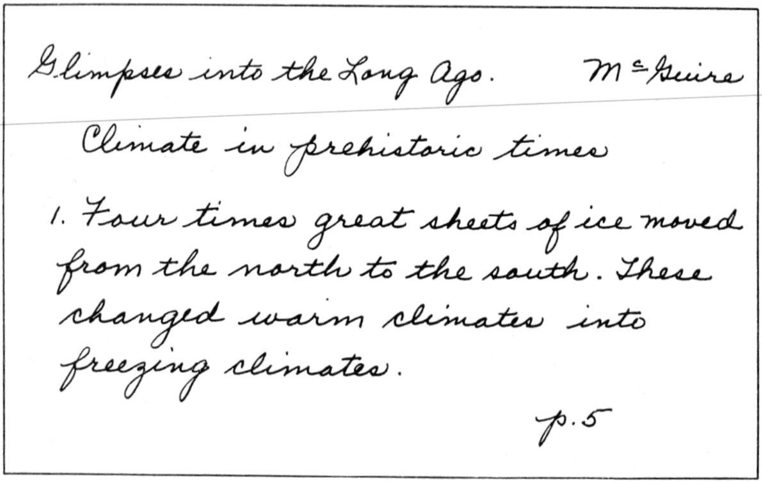

Glimpses into the Long Ago.   McGuire

Climate in prehistoric times

1. Four times great sheets of ice moved from the north to the south. These changed warm climates into freezing climates.

p. 5

Figure 19. Form for notes taken from books.

form may serve as a simple plan to follow in taking notes from books.

At the top of the card is recorded the name of the book and its author. Immediately below this are a few words which indicate the content of the note recorded on the card. At the end of the note is listed the page on which the note was found.

A similar form may be used in taking notes from periodicals or newspapers, as shown in Figure 20. The title of the article and its author are recorded at the top of the card. Below this is listed the name of the magazine or newspaper, together with the date of publication. The remainder of the card is completed in the same manner as when taking a note from a book.

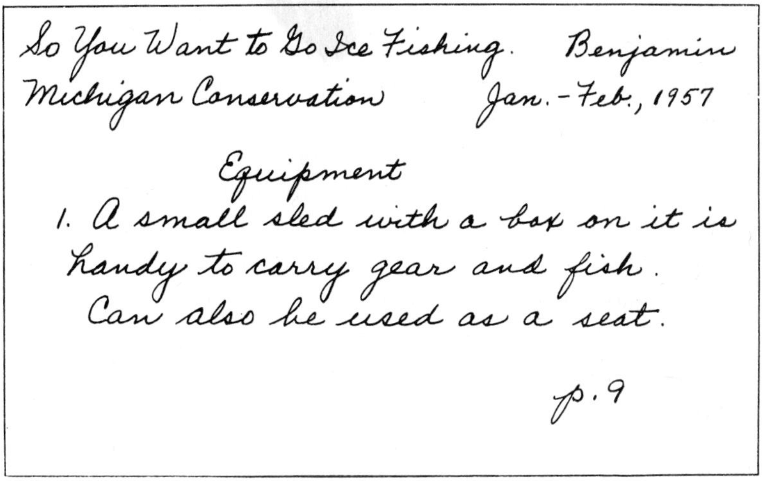

So You Want to Go Ice Fishing.   Benjamin
Michigan Conservation   Jan. - Feb., 1957

Equipment
1. A small sled with a box on it is
handy to carry gear and fish.
Can also be used as a seat.

p. 9

Figure 20. Form for notes taken from magazines.

In addition to discussing these with the class, it is helpful to give a mimeographed copy of such sample notes to each pupil to put into his notebook. In this way he will have a ready reference to use as it is needed at a later time. Together with such samples, it is good to duplicate the following points, which should be considered in the class lesson on taking notes:

POINTS TO WATCH IN RECORDING NOTES

1. Every card must have a complete heading.

2. If more than one note is placed on a card, these must deal with the same subject as the first note and must be from the same book. The number of the page from which note was taken must be recorded for each item.

3. The reverse side of the card is not used unless a few words will complete the sentence on the face of the card.

4. A note should not be continued from one card to another. Each card should be complete in itself.

5. If for some reason you want to remember the exact words of the author, put them in quotation marks. Usually, however, put notes in your own words.

It is not easy for pupils to learn good notes. They need a great deal of assistance, and the ner needs endless patience in teaching and reteaching. During the course of a unit, note cards should be called in several times, not for the purpose of grading, but in order to discover where the difficulties lie. Perhaps there are four or five pupils who are having trouble making their notes brief enough so that each can be contained on a single card. Others have abbreviated them to such an extent that they have no meaning. Perhaps another two or three have placed everything in quotation marks. If difficulties are noted in this way, pupils having similar troubles can be given assistance as a group.

If, as is likely to happen, many are having trouble deciding what is important to record and what should be omitted, it is time to work with the entire class for a period or two. The *Reader's Digest,* or some other magazine that is available in sufficient quantity so that each pupil may be supplied with a copy, is useful for this purpose. An article is selected, and then analyzed through class discussion, paragraph by paragraph, on the basis of questions such as the following:

What is the most important point in this paragraph? How can you tell that it is the most important?

Is there another important point in the paragraph?

What does the paragraph tell us that is not needed to make us understand the main points?

If no set of magazines is available, a series of paragraphs taken from an article may be typed on separate sheets of paper and shown through the opaque projector, or such a series can be duplicated in order that each pupil may have a copy. It is necessary to select material for such use with care. Textbooks and school magazines such as *Scholastic* are usually so condensed that almost every sentence is significant. Therefore, these will not serve the purpose.

Another means of pointing out errors in note-taking is to make copies of seven or eight pupil note cards that contain different kinds of mistakes and, also, with the opaque projector, show them to the class. The mistakes are located, and the boys and girls check their own cards for similar errors. Names of pupils should not be mentioned in connection with the cards shown.

Pupils should be urged to ask themselves the question, "Does this information help to solve the problem?" If the answer is *yes,* the note is worth writing down. If the answer is *no,* it should not be recorded. From time to time the group can well spend a period working in pairs, each member of the pair checking the other's information against this question. Learning to be selective when faced with a large body of data is not an easy task, and a teacher must recognize that such a skill is of slow growth. As boys and girls learn to take notes with greater ease, interest increases in gathering information. The library, of course, is used regularly, with other sources of data being used whenever possible. In class periods devoted to working on problems, a group of pupils can always be found around the library tables using the card catalog, the clipping file, books, and magazines, as indicated in Figure 21. Each is busy collecting data on his particular problem.

Sharing information. The fact that four or five individuals, having selected a common problem, do not truly constitute a group unless its members share their ideas, knowledge, and

Figure 21. Research in the library.

talents at *all stages* of solving its problem, is frequently overlooked. Strangely enough, it is overlooked even in many classrooms devoted to the use of democratic procedures.

It is not unusual to see pupils sharing ideas when defining
their problem and in planning for its solution. It is also not
uncommon to see them at a later time sharing ideas when developing plans for presenting material to the class. Between these
two stages, however, lies the relatively long stretch of time during
which pupils are gathering data. During this period, one seldom
sees a group of boys and girls pooling their information. They
tend to become strongly individualistic. The group has assigned
to each pupil a separate job for which he is responsible, and he
goes off by himself and does it. He loses track of what the other

226

members of his group are doing, and, consequently, the group often falls apart.

It is not surprising that this occurs most frequently during the data gathering period, for this is more like usual classroom procedure than any other phase of group problem solving. The school experiences of the majority of pupils involve an individual approach to studying. For many years they have heard: "Do your own work." "Don't ask your neighbor for help." "Don't look at your neighbor's paper." "Let your neighbor do his own work." The highest grades have gone to the person who had the most and best material; therefore, the wise course seemed to be to work hard but not to let others see what was being done.

When, however, a group of five or six pupils are attempting to solve a common problem, the situation is quite different. It is necessary that the members of a group come together frequently in order to maintain communication relative to their findings. Without this, the over-all problem is lost sight of, and each individual, engrossed in his own part of the task, forgets that the data being assembled by the other members of his group are as vital to the solution of the problem as his own.

The pupil's role during the fact gathering period must be a double one. He must carry out his individual responsibility of collecting as much material as possible on his assigned area *and* he must be a group member, sharing that information with his fellow members and gathering further information and understanding from them. He must be helped to see that he does not lose by sharing, but rather gains from the exchange. Specific periods of time should be built into the week's plan for such sharing, and assistance should be given in the establishment of techniques for carrying it out.

In a ninth-grade core class, the teacher had introduced the concept of sharing information, and, although the pupils were not very impressed with the idea, a period had reluctantly been scheduled for the class' first experience in this activity. Miss Barnes suggested that each group share the information of its members in whatever way seemed best to them. In order to plan future sharing-periods, the groups would later compare their methods and decide which had been helpful and which had not.

During the period, the teacher moved from group to group, saying little, but listening and watching reactions closely. There was little variety in the methods of the six groups. Three exchanged sets of notes and read them silently. In two groups, each member read all his notes aloud while the others listened. The sixth group was finished in ten minutes because each pupil merely told what he had read about, giving no factual data whatsoever.

The evaluation period was discouraging. No one had enjoyed the experience nor seen value in it. You couldn't read everyone's notes. There wasn't enough time. The handwriting was poor. People didn't listen to you when you read your notes aloud. It was boring. It was a waste of time.

All these reactions Miss Barnes had expected from her own observations. The problem was to find a way of doing it without having it be boring and a waste of time, a way that would give everyone a chance to be heard and that would be helpful to everyone. Through discussion the pupils reached agreement on the following points:

1. Reading each other's notes silently isn't a good method. It takes too long.

2. Having each person read all his notes aloud to the group isn't a good method. It takes too long.

3. You don't learn anything if each person just tells the group what he read about. Each person should tell some facts.

4. Each person should tell only the most important facts that he has found about the problem being studied.

5. Details should be given only when they are needed to understand the main points.

6. Everyone in the group should listen to everyone else.

Miss Barnes then raised the following question: "Suppose that Jerry is in your group. He makes a statement which you do not understand. In a sharing session, what should you do about this? Should you ask Jerry to explain his point or let it go? Which will

be of most help to all of you?" Although there was wide difference of opinion at first, the conclusion reached was that Jerry
should be asked to give an explanation, because the group members would learn more that way, and Jerry would see that this
point was not clear without a careful explanation. The class decided that this would be of help to Jerry later when he presented
his report to the class. As a result of this discussion a seventh item
was added to the list which read:

7. Questions should be asked if any point is not clear.

A further illustration was presented by the teacher. "Suppose
that Mary and Jane are members of a group of five people which
has had no sharing periods. When the group reports to the class,
a part of Mary's report deals with a point that Jane had described
a few minutes earlier. Their data, however, do not agree, Mary's
contradicting Jane's. Neither knew that the other had information on this point. What can they do about it?"

GUY

Nothing, anymore. It's too late.

MARIE

But if they had shared their information while they were taking notes,
they would have known about it.

MISS BARNES

What could they have done at that time?

GINNY

They could both have checked back to the books from which they
took their notes. Then they would have been sure which was correct.

ROB

Besides, when a group is giving reports it isn't a good idea to repeat
material. They would have been able to decide which one was to tell
about this point.

MISS BARNES

It sounds to me as though you are beginning to see some value in having sharing periods. Let's list some of the reasons for having them and
see if they are worth the time it takes to do the job.

REASONS FOR HAVING A SHARING PERIOD

1. It gives us a chance to ask each other questions.
2. We learn more facts about our problem than when each person works on it alone.
3. We can plan better when everybody knows what everyone else is working on.
4. People's questions help us to explain our material better when we give our reports to the class.
5. It keeps us from duplicating material that someone else in the group has studied.
6. We can see how the information fits together so that we can find a better answer to our problem.

Although the list above was not unanimously accepted, the class agreed to give sharing periods a fair trial. Throughout the following unit, the sharing period was set as the first ten minutes of each day on which note-taking was scheduled. At this time, each person told the most important facts he had collected since the last reporting session. Later in the year, when the class became accustomed to the sharing process and saw its value, it was decided to use one entire period out of four as the information-sharing time. Both methods were successful.

There are several techniques that are useful in helping pupils evaluate their own progress in sharing. One of the most satisfactory involves the use of the tape recorder. Each group in turn records one of its information-sharing periods. The tape is then played back, as shown in Figure 22, and the group makes an analysis of what has been said. A brief sample of such an analysis follows:

CARL

Let's see how we made out. You were first, Al.

(*Tape is played back and comments are made as it proceeds.*)

AL

Boy, I sure talked too much!

JEAN

Stop it a minute. I think you didn't need to tell all those little details.

Figure 22. Tape recorder play-back checks group's method of sharing data.

If you hadn't put those in, Nan would have had time to finish giving us her information.

AL

That's for sure!

(Playback is continued.)

CARL

That was a good question, Jean. I didn't understand that part either.

NAN

All three of us asked questions there. If we were all that interested the rest of the class will be too. Don't forget to tell them about that, Al.

A second technique that can be used to help pupils evaluate their sharing methods is, in a sense, quite similar to the one just described. One group, preferably a volunteer group, carries out its sharing period, with the remainder of the class serving as observers. At the close, the demonstration group is given the first chance to comment on its own procedure. The class then adds its observations.

Through sharing their information, the members of a group keep in close touch with one another and with the activities that are being carried on individually. Such a group stands little chance of disintegrating before the entire task is completed. Learning to share is actually another aspect of the development of group operational skills, which were discussed in Chapter 3. It is an application of these skills to a specific situation, and requires continuous attention to the points made in the earlier chapter. As pupils learn how to share information with one another, they learn more about how a group can function in solving its problem.

A criticism often made of group work is that it places too much emphasis on the group, neglects the individual, minimizes his opportunities to take responsibility, and that pupils thus trained are overly dependent upon one another. Group work in its true sense rather increases the responsibilties of the individual, since he is not only responsible to and for himself, but to and for his fellow group members. Not only must his own work be well done, but he must help make a success of a still larger job, the group job. Such responsibility toward one's peers should be learned, as well as responsibility toward a boss, who, in the schoolroom, is the teacher. The mutual criticism, as well as respect, that develops through the give and take of working in a group is far more effective than criticism or praise given by a teacher. A member of a group finds himself in all kinds of emergency situations in working with his fellows, and must develop ingenuity, foresight, and judgment to help meet these. He has a rare opportunity of becoming a truly responsible person.

Evaluation of progress

A record of achievement should be made regularly by each group as a means of evaluating progress toward the solution of its problem. In addition, such reports serve to identify difficulties and indicate to the teacher where special assistance is needed. The daily log, as described in Chapter 3, can be used for this purpose. In its simplest form, it includes only a paragraph describing the activities of the day. As indicated in the earlier reference, the addition of any questions that members of the group may have is most helpful in indicating to the teacher the kind of assistance needed by each group. A further extension of the log is the *daily activity record*. This includes a group evaluation as well as a space for comments. The group recorder is responsible for preparing the record. The contents of Items 2, 3, and 4, however, should be determined by the group as a whole. A sample, as recorded by a tenth-grade group, follows:

DAILY ACTIVITY RECORD

Problem: What is atomic energy and how is it developed and used?

Recorder: Ann B.   *Date:* December 8

1. *Activities of group today*
   a. *As a group:*
   We spent the first period in sharing our latest information. All of us had quite a lot of data except Mike. He only told us one fact.
   b. *As individuals:*
   The second period three of us went to the library to get more material. Mike and Ed checked clippings and pictures in the file. Jane had a conference with Miss Hunter.
2. *Questions your group would like to ask:*
   Which of the science teachers could help us most?
   If we wrote a letter to the Atomic Energy Museum at Oakridge, Tennessee, how would we address it?
3. *How satisfactory was group work today?*
   Good ———
   Fair ———
   Poor ———

4. *Comments:*
   We are a little mixed up right now. We do not understand some of the things we are reading.

Form sheets for this purpose may be duplicated, the recorder inserting a new one in the group notebook each day that the group works on its problem. The sheet for the day is easily accessible both to pupils and teacher if it is always inserted on top of the previous one.

Such activity records should be read by the teacher and returned to the group the following day. A brief comment written on the paper is sufficient to let pupils know that the record has been read. On the example above, the teacher might write the answers to the questions under Item 2, and he might jot down a promise to help the group with its difficulties.

A somewhat different progress sheet that can be used is a weekly report. It, too, should be duplicated. If both sides of the paper are used, the six questions may be spaced three to a side, thus giving adequate room for writing. This is somewhat different from the forms described so far, in that it asks for a record of progress in terms of the amount of material collected and the number of sources of data used, as well as the activities of the group members, their difficulties, and an evaluation of progress. Such a progress report from a ninth-grade class read as follows:

Group Progress Report

Topic: What happened to the Indian tribes in our country when the white man began to settle the land west of the Mississippi River?

Recorder: Leslie M.   *Date:* February 6

1. *From how many books or magazines have members of your group taken notes this week?*

Paul:	2 books, 1 magazine
Howard:	4 books, 4 magazines
Carol:	3 books
Lynn:	0 books, 5 magazines
Leslie:	3 books

   Our group used 8 different books and 6 different magazines.

2. *What have members of your group done this week towards solving your problem besides reading books and magazine articles?*

We saw a filmstrip on our topic. We got this from the visual-aids office and looked at it in there. We studied a map that showed where the various Indian tribles lived. We got this from the librarian.

3. *How much material has been collected by the members of your group this week?*

Paul: 11 cards of notes
Howard: 24 cards
Carol: 15 cards
Lynn: 6 cards
Leslie: 22 cards

4. *Has any member of your group worked on any special project this week?*

Howard and Paul have started to make a map like the one in the library, but it will be much larger.

Lynn is writing a play which will be part of our presentation.

5. *Did your group have any difficulties this week?*

There is so much information that we don't know how we can do all of it.

6. *How do the members of your group feel the work is progressing?*

We did much better than last week.

Group members:
Chairman: Carol
Recorder: Leslie
Other members: Lynn
                          Paul
                          Howard

An individual record of progress in collecting data that has proved to be very satisfactory is the *Research Record*. Each pupil keeps his own record up to date throughout the period of time needed to solve the problem. Each day he checks the references he has used, records the number of note cards made out from such research, and totals his amount of material in terms of the number of cards. There may be days when nothing is recorded, on others a great deal. A sample record is shown in Figure 23.

In using such reports, care must be taken that too much em-

	Date: Nov. 3-7					Date: Nov. 10-14					Date: Nov. 17-21					Date: Nov. 24-29				
	M	T	W	Th	F	M	T	W	Th	F	M	T	W	Th	F	M	T	W	Th	F
Atlas																				
Dictionary Am. Biography																				
Dictionary Social Studies																				
Encyclopedia					✓															
Fiction of period											✓	✓								
Film																				
Filmstrip																				
Information Please Almanac						✓					✓									
Interviews																	✓			
Lecture																✓				
Magazines	✓	✓																		
Map																				
Newspapers																				
Radio program																				
Recording																				
Reference books	✓						✓	✓	✓						✓	✓	✓			
Sent for material						✓														
Trip																				
T V program																				
World Almanac																				
Others – name below																				
Number of cards today:	4	3	0	0	5	4	0	7	2	4	0	1	5	0	7	1	5	0	0	6
Total note cards:	4	7	7	7	12	16	16	23	25	29	29	30	35	35	42	43	48	48	48	54

Figure 23. A *Research Record* for recording daily work.

phasis is not placed on the *amount* of material rather than on both the *amount* and *quality*. Without question, there should be sufficient material, but pupils must learn to be selective, so that the notes that are taken definitely help to solve the problem. They should be checked frequently for quality of information recorded. Let it be repeated, such frequent checking of note cards should not be for purposes of grading, but as a means of discovering pupils' difficulties.

Drawing conclusions from data

When note-taking has been completed, each group should spend a final session in reaching agreement on the conclusions that may be drawn from the data collected. Let us refer to the plan prepared by the group concerned with civil defense which was described earlier in this chapter.[4] The statement of the problem as it appeared on the plan was: *What preparations are being made to protect citizens in case of an atomic attack?* In their plan, the group had designated twenty-one questions that the members felt must be answered in order to reach a conclusion. Since these seemed to be the most important points to be considered in solving the problem, the final session of the group included a careful check to see that as many of these as possible had been answered. A review of the main facts concerning each served this purpose, the person to whom each question had been assigned being responsible for answering that question. Upon completion of the review, a written summary was prepared, which represented the conclusions of the group relative to the problem. The details would be given later in the oral presentation. If sharing information has been a regular part of group procedure, reaching a final conclusion is not difficult, since many misunderstandings and disagreements will have been ironed out long before the final session.

At the same time that such a check is being made against the original plan, a summary of the group's feeling of success in

---

4 See pages 205–207.

solving its problem should be recorded in response to such questions as the following.

How well did your group accomplish what it set out to do?
1. Did you accomplish everything that you had originally planned to do?
2. Did you fail to accomplish some things that you had originally planned to do? If so, what were these? Why were these not carried out?
3. Did you add to your original plans? If so, what was added?
4. Did you make other changes in your plans? If so, what were they?
5. Now that you have completed work on this problem, how do you feel about the results?
   Very pleased ——— ?
   Satisfied ——— ?
   Not satisfied ——— ?

Conclusion

Let us review briefly the steps to be taken in solving a group problem.

1. The problem must be clearly defined. It must be limited to an area small enough so that it can be satisfactorily investigated, but should be broad enough so that all members may have an active part in its solution.

2. A group plan is made which involves breaking down the problem into its parts, assigning the work that needs to be done to group members, listing possible sources of information, and indicating any special activities that should be carried out.

3. A preliminary bibliography of all possible sources of information is prepared by the group members. This includes every source that the pupils feel might yield helpful data.

4. The data are collected in note form.

5. Sharing of the data by the members of the group takes place at regular intervals. Further progress is planned in the light of such group sharing.

6. Through a consideration of all the data collected by the members, the group arrives at conclusions relative to its problem.

7. The group evaluates its success in solving the problem.

Solving a problem is an orderly procedure, one step following another. If additional help is needed in clarifying these various aspects of problem solving, there are a number of films that can be used as a basis for class study. Three of these are: *Using the Scientific Method; Find the Information;* and *The Importance of Making Notes.*[5]

---

[5] Coronet Films.

7

Reporting to the Class

QUESTIONS ARE SOMETIMES RAISED CONCERNING THE desirability of having groups report their findings to the class as a whole. It is generally agreed that, if the groups are working on different aspects of a common problem that has been accepted by the entire class, reports to the class are necessary in order that the data from all groups may be combined to solve the problem. It is argued, however, that when groups are working on separate problems that have little or no relationship to one another, it is enough that each group solves its problem, each member sharing the data he has assembled with the others in his group, without a group report being made to the class. The point is made that, since a group of pupils has selected a specific problem because of their concern with it rather than with any other, they should not be expected either to tell the class about it nor to listen to the reports of others. The feeling is that the value lies in the learning taking place in the group itself, and not in the sharing with people outside of the group.

This point of view may be questioned, although on the surface it appears logical. Certainly it cannot be denied that reporting merely for the sake of reporting, or reporting to earn a grade, is wholly unnecessary. However, group reporting, properly developed, can serve a number of purposes. It offers pupils an opportunity to check their ideas or solutions against a larger group of people, thus putting their ability to think critically to the test

240

by facing questions or criticisms. For the audience members, a similar testing takes place, since they frequently find themselves facing ideas that have not occurred to them before. Do they accept ideas too readily without asking for proof? In adding ideas to the discussion are their own statements accurate and can they be proven? Are they open-minded enough to consider more than one side of a question? The discussion following a group report presents opportunities for growth toward such scientific attitudes.

A further point to be considered in weighing the worth of group reports is the wide variety of problems to which the class members are exposed during the reporting sessions. These can serve to open doors to new areas that, perhaps, have previously not occurred to pupils. A new problem for study frequently arises out of the discussion following a group presentation. The report indicates as well the method of study used by a group. This often serves as a guide for later study by another group.

Perhaps more important than any of these is the nature of reporting. It is a wholly different process from fact-finding, for in the presentation much of the emphasis is on the use of art forms; creativity is its pattern. Thus, in addition to accurate and precise note-taking, pupils have the opportunity to use their imaginations to present the information that has been collected through a variety of media—music, art, handcraft, drama. Last, but not least, is the fact that reporting, used as a matter of course throughout the year, helps pupils develop a feeling of ease and poise when talking to a relatively large number of people. The arguments favor such reports, providing adequate techniques are developed. Let us, therefore, turn our attention to methods for making such reporting satisfying and valuable experiences for all members of the class.

When groups have completed the collection of their data and have reached conclusions relative to the solution of their problems, the Planning Committee should designate sufficient class time so that groups may make their preparations for reporting to the class. If this is the first time the class members have made oral presentations, considerably more time will be needed for preparation than later in the year. In this first attempt, pupils will probably need a great deal of help in developing interesting and varied methods of presenting their data. They must also decide the amount of class time each group will need to make its report. At this time, too, previous to the first presentation, a beginning should be made toward the establishment of criteria for good reporting.

Overcoming fear

The need for every child to develop the ability to communicate his ideas to other people should be obvious to anyone concerned with the education of boys and girls. Yet in many classes, it is not uncommon to find that a pupil seldom has an opportunity to express himself except in response to a direct question. Therefore, it is not surprising that pupils often panic as the time approaches for a first presentation of group reports. As work on the problem draws to a close, the question, "Do we have to give an oral report in front of the class?" is asked over and over again. Increasing restlessness and tension may be evident. The teacher must help pupils to feel that, although reporting is one phase of their work on the problem, it is not *the* most important part; that if, in spite of their best efforts, the presentation is not perfect, it is not a tragic failure. Pupils should feel that it is "safe" to make mistakes in this as well as in other class activities, and that the classroom is a place in which they may try again at a later time.

Actually this activity is an extension of the small-group sharing process discussed in Chapter 6, but for many pupils it is a much more difficult and painful experience to talk to thirty-five than to five or six of their classmates. The tensions resulting from fear of having to give a report before a class may be tremendous.

A ninth-grade teacher, realizing that he did not know exactly what it was that so disturbed his pupils at the thought of presenting their material orally, asked them to list those things that bothered them most whenever they had to present an oral report.

The composite list, of which the following are typical, contained thirty-two items, many of them reported by a majority of the members of the class.

1. I can't look at the class.
2. I can't stand still.
3. I can't remember what I want to say.
4. I don't know what to do with my hands.
5. I want to cry.
6. I can't keep my voice even.
7. I'm afraid people will laugh at me.
8. I can talk in a small group, but can't say the words to the whole class.

Since his pupils had been working on an individual rather than a group basis on this unit, the teacher gave each the choice of presenting his report to the entire class, to a small group, or not giving it orally this time at all. No pressure of any sort was exerted. The result was that fourteen chose class presentation, twenty chose small group presentation, and two did not report at all. An individual who chose to report to a small group selected the classmates to whom he would report. When presenting his data, the reporter and his group sat in a circle in order to make the task as easy as possible. Those who planned to report to the entire class were given help in the use of simple notes from which to speak. They were provided with a music stand, borrowed from the music department, on which to set their notes. The stand also served as a place to put their hands and a means of steadying themselves so that it was easier to stand quietly. The teacher taught them to look toward their audience by having them look just over the tops of the heads of the class members. This was so close to looking the audience "in the eye" that the pupils listening could not tell the difference, while the speakers were much less disturbed than when trying to look directly at their fellow class members. The pupils' self-evaluation responses showed great satisfaction with the results.

When it was time to present reports at the end of the second unit, the two boys who had not participated the first time offered to report to a small group. Nine of the twenty who had used small groups as audiences now reported to the entire class. A marked decrease in fear was indicated in the self-evaluation responses following the presentations. Oral reports had largely ceased to be nightmares.

Reporting creatively

Nothing is more deadly than listening to thirty-five pupils stand before a class, one at a time, and merely report the information each has collected. After the first half-dozen reports, a class tends to become restless and, as the days required to cover all reports drag on, pupils will pay little or no attention. If they are seated where they cannot be observed by the teacher, some will ignore the reports and work on home assignments for other classes, read books, write letters—anything to break the monotony. Others, while seemingly listening, are cheerfully daydreaming. Even the teacher becomes weary.

Such audience boredom can be prevented to a great extent by helping pupils to introduce variety into their methods of reporting. The information collected by a group can be presented in many different ways, limited only by the creative urge and ingenuity of its members and their feeling of security in the classroom. As was suggested earlier, it might well be argued that one of the reasons for such reporting is the opportunity that it offers for releasing the creativeness inherent in boys and girls.

Not many people claim to be creative. Yet, even a young child at play makes an automobile out of pieces of wood, builds a house out of his blocks, sings his own songs, squeezes a lion out of a chunk of clay, or draws a boat on a sheet of paper. Talent or no talent, he is endlessly creating something. The automobile may not look like an automobile to us, nor the lion like a lion, but that is wholly beside the point. As he plays, the porch railing becomes the railing on the bridge of a ship, and a cocked paper hat makes him a pirate with the ship's sails flapping in the wind above him. He makes up games and their rules. He and his neighborhood friends "put on" plays in a garage. The writer still has in her possession a dog-eared notebook in which are recorded the plans for ballet dances that were rehearsed in the backyard. And this in spite of the fact that she was anything but graceful. These activities may not reach adult cultural standards, but they are extremely satisfying to the child. These are his creations.

Yet this same child will probably grow up to be one of the adults who denies having creative ability. He will have lost the quickening excitement of making things himself. He will have lost the trick of letting his imagination run riot and having his hands follow his imagination, making something where nothing had been before. Creativeness for him will have become stereotyped—it will mean such things as painting a fine picture, writing a best seller, or designing clothes or cars.

It would seem that the classroom, not only in the elementary years, but far beyond, should furnish many opportunities for self-expression so that the thrill of creativeness is not lost, but becomes a part of everyday living. Yet most classroom work, being largely based on facts already recorded in books, does none of this. In a few schools throughout the country, the art class, in addition to its specialized job of giving direct instruction in art, serves as a center for helping pupils develop their ideas for expression in relation to the other subjects. A diorama is made that depicts a prehistoric scene, or a pictorial map of Mexico is developed. These are then taken into the other classroom. However, in most secondary schools, art classes are elective and are intended only for those interested in art. In general, they do not serve other classes. A few teachers of literature develop freedom on the part of pupils to express themselves dramatically, but in most schools dramatic creativity is left wholly in the hands of the teacher of drama or to a club devoted to the production of plays.

This leaves the creative development of most pupils in the hands of the regular classroom teachers, a thought that is frightening to many. It need not be, however, for the teacher's role in this situation is not that of the expert who knows all the answers. Rather he is the stimulator who sets the stage so that self-expression is an acceptable, respectable, and quite mature activity. He is the appreciator who admires what is being attempted. He is the encourager when something doesn't work. He is the helper insofar as he, himself, knows how to help, and when he doesn't, assists in getting help from those who are the experts— art, music, speech, drama and dance teachers, for example. Above everything else, he is an experimenter along with his pupils, willing to try his hand at activities that he has never tried before.

The writer has had a number of experiences that have taught her the value of participating in activities even though she had neither training nor skill in them. One of these occurred on a Friday afternoon when she had only fifteen pupils in her ninth-grade class, the remainder having been excused to take part in a field trip. For some days there had been half-hearted talk among the class members about illustrating their report material in some way, in order to make it more interesting. However, nothing had come of it. No one seemed to know where to start.

Having less than half the usual number in the room, it seemed to be a good time to see what could be done about this. The teacher provided paper of various types and colors, water-color paints and brushes, Scotch tape, crayons, pastels, clay, charcoal, magazines for pictures, scissors, paste, rulers, glass slides, and slide crayons. These were spread out on a table. She explained that she had overheard some of the remarks pupils had made about illustrating their reports and that it certainly had sounded like a good idea. Since no specific plans had been made for the day, she had brought the material spread out on the table thinking that some of them might like to start their illustrations. They were free to use any that they wished.

Nothing much happened during the first twenty minutes. Some took materials to their seats. A few half-heartedly tried out the charcoal and crayons. Several thumbed the magazines, while quite a number did not go near the material. All, however, watched one another furtively. If anyone caught his neighbor looking toward his paper, he quickly covered it with a hand. The remark "baby stuff" was heard in an undertone several times.

The teacher finally decided that nothing was going to happen this way. She said to the class, "This isn't easy to do, is it? Instead of trying to make something for the reports, let's all try our hand at working on the same subject. Maybe that way we will be able to see a lot of different things that could be done. This afternoon our football team is playing Clinton High School. None of us can go because it is out of town. Let's pretend we're there. Let's illustrate what's happening at the football game that we have to miss. If you were at the game right now what are some of the things you would be seeing? Don't tell me in words; make something that tells the story. I'm going to try it too."

With that the teacher turned away from them, picked up several large sheets of paper, Scotch tape, some paints and brushes, and a pair of scissors, sat down at a table by herself, and set to work. She hadn't the slightest idea of how to go about the job. But she finally cut four long strips of paper about three inches wide, fastened them together with tape, took her brush and crisscrossed the full length with brown paint. She set it up on the table so that it formed a large oval. She sat and looked at it because she didn't know what to do next.

Suddenly she discovered that a boy was standing back of her. "It's a fence, isn't it?" he said.

"Yes," she said, "it's the fence around the football field."

"It hasn't any posts. You'd better cut out posts and paste them on the fence every few inches," came another voice.

"That's right," said the teacher. "I didn't think of posts."

"I'll make 'em for you," said the first boy with a sigh.

"Fine. Then I can go ahead and make the bleachers." Suddenly the teacher caught her cue and played it. "But how in the world do I make those? They are like steps!"

Several more boys and girls had moved closer. "You fold the paper backwards and forwards—wait—I'll show you." And a girl was in the picture. "I'll make them for you." The teacher watched her make them. Then she tried it herself.

By that time fully three quarters of the group was ringed around the table.

"You have to have a field," said a new voice. "Do you know how to mark a field?"

The teacher shook her head and the boy laughed and said, "Where's some paper and a ruler? Want to help, Al? She doesn't know how a football field is marked."

"Joe and I can make a scoreboard for you."

"How about a ticket gate?" asked another.

"And a ticket taker."

"We haven't any players," said the teacher. "I suppose we could make them out of small pieces of cardboard, but they wouldn't have any faces."

"That doesn't matter—make half of them red and half of them blue for the two teams."

"I'll help you."

"Put numbers on them."

"Set them up so that they are in a position for a play."

"Yeah, near Clinton's goal posts."

"Goal posts. We need those. I'll make a set."

"Make a football."

And by the end of the double period the entire field was completed. Eleven out of the fifteen had participated in making some part of it. The other four had followed every move and offered advice.

"Wait till we show the kids what we made!" they said gleefully. Working with their hands with paper, paste, paint, and scissors was no longer a childish thing to do. They knew more about it than teacher did. She was *pretty* smart about the general idea, but she was not very smart at figuring out details; in fact, they were much better at it than she was. They were very satisfied, and so, by the way, was the teacher.

The following Monday the group told the story with relish to the rest of the class and showed the model with tremendous pride. Those who had not been present were a bit dubious about the whole thing at first, but the fun of telling how the teacher couldn't make steps and didn't know how to mark the field or a

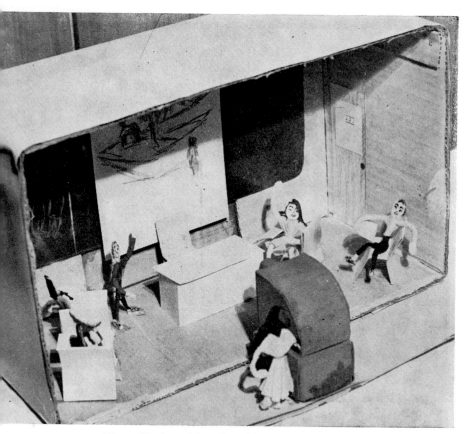

Figure 24. A model made to illustrate a report.

scoreboard was contagious, and they said they wished they had
been there to help.

That the day had been a real stimulant was shown by the fact
that five pupils had spent time over the week end working out
plans for their own illustrative material, and in the following
two weeks any number of the important points in the reports
were portrayed in one form or another.

There is a wide range of activities that a pupils may engage in
which give him an opportunity to express his feelings and understanding in his own fashion. It may be a small diorama made by
an individual pupil to illustrate some point in the presentation

249

Figure 25. The Westward Movement comes alive.

as in Figure 24, or it may be the product of an entire group. The activity often spills over into the after-school hours, with pupils cutting, sawing, painting, or sewing in the home of one of the members. Even parents sometimes help in these projects. Figure 25 shows a group presenting the story of America's movement to the West, with the stage setting entirely made by the pupils themselves.

For some the level of creativeness is much less pronounced than in others. To the boy or girl who has definite artistic ability, tracing a picture on a glass slide is not creative, but to the one who has no such special aptitude, tracing on the slide can be a thrilling experience. He has never done that before, and the very thought is creative, and exciting, and satisfying. The result war-

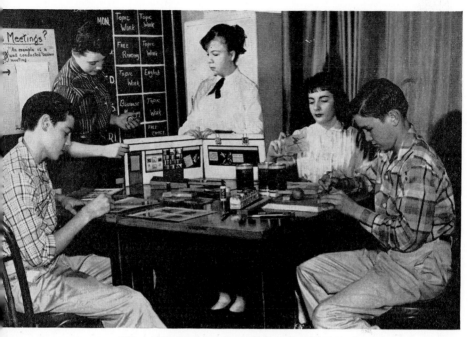

Figure 26. Creativeness at the work table.

rants as much commendation as the freehand mural of the young artist.

A table set aside for working on such projects keeps the materials assembled in one part of the room. It also gives the pupils who are working on them an opportunity to see what others are doing and to gather support as well as inspiration from them. In Figure 26 pupils are working with a number of media in preparation for their presentations. Pupils should be encouraged to engage in all types of expression. Clay modeling, soap and wood carving, map making, the fashioning of puppets, writing of music, dancing, writing of poetry, plays, and radio scripts should all be a part of the experience of boys and girls in the classroom.

Pantomime started an eighth-grade class, in which dramatizing in any form seemed almost impossible, on the road to creative oral expression. The first performance was given by the teacher, with the class guessing the sequence of activities represented. She pantomimed the baking of a cake, from putting on an apron to frosting the finished cake. At its conclusion, the pupils begged for another, and the teacher agreed on condition that some of the class members would assist her. The second performance involved two pupils and the teacher, with the teacher taking the part of a pupil coming to school with her mother to see the principal. A series of situations that might be enacted was then listed by a committee. Each was written on a slip of paper, and on the following day was drawn by eager volunteers for class performance. If more than one person was needed, the additional people were selected by the first individual to assist him. Simple situations such as the following were pantomimed:

1. Talking on the telephone with the family in the room.
2. Opening a locker and getting ready to go home from school.
3. Watching a football game when the home team misses a touchdown.

From pantomime the teacher led to verbal dramatization. A scene was selected by the pupils from a story that they had especially enjoyed reading. The class then divided into random groups of six, each group planning and presenting a short dramatization of the scene. Interest was so high in this procedure that it was repeated a number of times with other stories. Sometimes scripts were written and sometimes the performances were impromptu. Out of such activities developed the use of role-playing as a mean of gaining insight into classroom or home problems, as well as the use of dramatization in presenting group reports to the class.

The emotional reactions of an eleventh-grade class to an assignment by the teacher inadvertently opened the door to their creativeness. As a basis for a class discussion, the teacher made the assignment that each pupil was to bring to class an item that he felt was the most beautiful thing he owned. This might be anything, since no two people would necessarily consider the same thing beautiful. As the day on which these were to be brought to class drew near, the pupils' uneasiness became more

and more pronounced. There were many who said such things
as:

I can't bring what I think is most beautiful. My mother won't let
me.

Do we *have* to bring something?

I haven't anything beautiful.

I can't decide on what to bring.

I can't find the thing I want to bring.

There was even the hopeful one who said he couldn't bring his
if it rained. But the teacher held tight. She promised them that
she, too, would bring something.

And so the day arrived. Each pupil quickly slipped a box or
paper bag under his desk out of sight. That they were uneasy
and uncomfortable was obvious. But seats were swung into a circle and class was under way. In order to give her pupils support,
the teacher talked for a few minutes about how hard it had been
for her to decide what to bring. She said that she knew how they
felt about showing their things, because she felt hesitant about
showing them what she had brought. She said that she had finally
decided to bring four things, because each seemed beautiful to
her for a different reason. Then she opened her box.

The first item was a pure white pitcher with a raised pattern
of large tulips. She held it in her hand and ran her fingers along
the edge of the flowers and, cupping her hand, outlined the shape
of the pitcher. "Do you think it is beautiful?" she asked.

One said, "It's pretty."

Another said, "No, it's just a pitcher."

And still another said, "I like the flowers."

But one said, "It doesn't really matter what we think. It's
beautiful to you. I can tell by the way you move your hands on
it."

And the teacher said, "Yes, it is very beautiful to me. I like
to feel it. It even rests me to look at it." Then she passed the
pitcher to the boy sitting next to her, and it started on its way
around the circle, almost every individual running his hands over

it as the teacher had done. Here and there a face lit up and a smile came across the room.

The second object was a cherry-red ash tray with a dull black picture on it. The class liked it, and after much consideration decided that the teacher liked it because of the color. And they were right.

The third item brought a howl of laughter. It was a piece of white cloth about 2½ by 3½ inches in size, the edges pasted back over a piece of cardboard. On the cloth a figure of a child had been drawn in pencil and embroidered in color. The figure had only one arm, its shape more like a tennis racket than an arm, and the feet did not match. The stitches were big and crude and missed the outline in many places. When the laughter had died down, the teacher asked whether the little picture was beautiful and, of course, the response was, "No." "But," she said, "my mother always said that this was the most beautiful gift she had ever received in all her life. I made it for her for Christmas when I was five years old. I hid it all over the house and she kept finding it under chairs, under the bed, in books, everywhere. It was so dirty that she even washed and ironed it and put it back in its hiding place. And when I finished it and gave it to her, I thought it was a surprise. Now why do you suppose she thought it was so beautiful?"

Hands flew and they reached agreement quickly that it was beautiful to her because of the love that had gone into making it.

The fourth item was a flat, six-inch copper dish with a colorful enamel figure of a man against a gray enamel background. There were bad chips in the red enamel of the coat, and the background had obviously turned out poorly, for there was a streak of black in the wrong place. The teacher grinned and said, "I know it's chipped. I know that background is terrible. But it's perfectly beautiful to me because I made it. I call it my beautiful heartbreak, because I worked for days and days on it, each time trying something else and each time having it fail. I guess it's beautiful to me because it was my own idea and because so much of me went into it."

As the pupils handled the enamel dish, they would touch the chipped places and rueful smiles went toward the teacher. They understood.

During the time she had been showing her four items and expressing her own feelings about them, an interesting thing had been taking place here and there in the room. The bags and boxes were being quietly taken out of hiding and placed on top of desks. Pupils were ready to let others see what they had brought. It was "safe" now to let people see that you had feelings that you had never shown in class before. There were some who brought records; these were played on the record player that the teacher had in readiness. The selections amazed everyone. Who would guess that Jane would think such music was beautiful; or that big Bill would like classical music best! And when Edie said that the most beautiful thing she owned was a poem, she gave courage to Jean, who had also brought a poem. Rob, who didn't ever seem to care what he said or did, shyly read a prayer that he said he often repeated when "things get tough." Barbara brought a cup and saucer that was beautiful to her because her grandmother, who was no longer living, gave it to her. Walter said he thought his ring was the second most beautiful thing he had, and he had brought it because he couldn't bring the most beautiful. When pressed to tell his first choice, he hesitated, then straightened up, and said quietly, "It's my mother." And nobody laughed at anyone.

Many things developed from this experience, such as the decision to set aside a period every two weeks for listening to music brought by different pupils. But above all there developed a feeling of freedom to try new things. Several showed the class poetry they had written. Others, who had never admitted that they liked to write, wrote scripts for their group reports. Presentations were more alive and exciting and dramatic. Pupils were no longer afraid of being laughed at, for they had developed a wonderful respect for one another. Members of a class showing one another what they had brought to school as the most beautiful thing they owned are shown in Figure 27.

Figure 27. The most beautiful thing I own.

Further assistance in developing ideas for creative expression relative to the problems on which pupils are working may be given through a bulletin board display illustrating by pictures and actual objects as many different types of activities as possible. An exhibit of the workmanship of a previous class serves the same purpose. Pupils should also be encouraged to seek assistance from teachers who have special abilities. Perhaps the art, music, dance, or craft teachers can be induced to spend some time with the class. Again, the help of parents should not be overlooked, for among them may be some who have special abilities.

The products of such creative attempts may not be exceptional, and although pupils should be urged to do the best job they possibly can, the goal is not a perfect product, but the development of the creative urge itself, and the personal satisfaction that comes from such expression.

Establishing criteria

Unless pupils have had previous experience in group reporting, they are seldom able to establish a highly satisfactory list of criteria for good group presentation until they have participated in, and watched others take part in, such reporting of group data. They are usually able to see the importance of only one or two items, such as the desirability of making the report interesting, the need for individual group members to speak clearly, or perhaps the importance of looking at the audience while speaking. However, even such meager bits serve as a beginning and should form an initial criteria list.

The ideal time to establish a more complete and satisfactory list is at the conclusion of the first group reports. Having just experienced such reporting, pupils are now much more aware of the characteristics of a good presentation than they were earlier. A list developed by a tenth-grade class at this time was as follows:

Criteria for a Good Group Presentation

1. There should be evidence that it is a presentation of the whole group.

2. It should be well organized.

3. The members of the group should know their information well enough so that they can *tell* it to the audience, not read it from notes or a paper.

4. The material should be presented in an interesting way.

5. All members of the group should present sufficient information so that the audience fully understands it.

6. Individuals should:
    a. speak clearly, and loud enough to be heard.
    b. look at the audience.

7. Members of the group should use good English.

8. If possible they should have material to illustrate their reports.

Planning the presentation

Pupils can be on the lookout for ideas for presentation throughout their work on the unit. The illustrative materials they prepare, for example, may serve as a center around which they weave their plans. A group studying conservation of natural resources in its state prepared a series of 3 by 4 inch glass slides in color. Out of this grew the plan for the presentation. The five group members played the roles of conservation officers, each responsible for seeing that the people of the state were aware of the work of the conservation department in his respective field. They presented a series of "television broadcasts," during which they used the pictures they had "taken" to illustrate their points. The slides were shown by means of the slide projector, and the television show was complete with introductory music and commercial. Needless to say, the audience gave the group full attention.

A ninth-grade group studying city housing problems constructed a table-sized model of an ideal housing arrangement, as well as a large number of charts. At the close of the unit they found themselves unable to reach a decision relative to the problem they had undertaken. Their data were excellent, but they could not agree as to what the information added up to. They finally decided to present it to the class members, asking them to help in arriving at a decision. A bulletin board display of the charts was prepared. When presenting their data, they moved a table to a position in front of the display and placed the model on the table. The audience was asked to sit in a circle, in order that all might see to best advantage. Throughout the presentation, group members made frequent references to the charts and to the model, pointing out important aspects of the problem. The audience, involved in helping to find a solution, was definitely not bored.

A map was needed by a group studying the early explorers in order to compare the routes taken by the different ships. None large enough was immediately available; so one member drew and painted a huge map of the world. On this the group plotted the course of each explorer. When it was time to plan the presentation, it was quite obvious that the map should be the focal point of all the reports. Figure 28 shows this group presenting its data to the class.

A group working in the area of the armed services placed three tables end to end and seated itself along one side of these facing

Figure 28. A presentation results from group planning.

the audience. A sign placed in front of each indicated the branch for which he was the "expert." Attached to the chalkboard above their heads was a sign reading, *You Ask Us.* The audience asked questions, and the panel answered them. When questioning began to slow down, each member of the group added any information that had not been touched upon.

A senior class had completed a unit on careers. This had not been developed on a group basis, since each individual had studied a different area. The class decided not to ask each person to present a complete report. The desks were moved into a circle, each pupil hanging a sign over the front of his desk indicating the areas he had investigated. A sample sign read as follows:

NANCY ANDREWS

Doctor's Secretarial Assistant
Nurse
Occupational Therapist

259

The chairman called for questions. Any pupil might ask any other boy or girl questions relative to the careers indicated on his sign. To the amazement of the teacher, the questioning did not begin to lose fire until the fourth class-period. At that time, any person having interesting information that had not been asked for had an opportunity to present it.

A study of the community by a tenth-grade class resulted in the preparation of a mimeographed twenty-page booklet entitled, *Community Journal.* A copy was presented to each member of the class.

A group of four girls studying the Revolutionary War prepared a painting on the reverse side of a 4 by 4 foot piece of oilcloth. A square in the center showed a map of the colonies. The four corners were soldiers in uniform. Along each of the four sides was a panel containing an illustrated map of one of the campaigns of the war. As the battles were described, the painting was turned to the campaign being discussed. It might be good to add that only one of the four girls was artistically talented. She outlined the content of the painting, and the other three did the color work.

Space men, in helmets, ear phones, and yards of wire equipment, flew into a class with much engine sputtering on a ship composed of four schoolroom desks to see what the social customs of earth teen-agers were like. A series of skits was enacted, illustrating correct and incorrect dating behavior. These were discussed in detail by the space men before they took off. The class exploded into laughter as they came in and went out, but that they had missed nothing was obvious from the discussion that followed.

A group of six boys wrote the script for a "You Are There" program dealing with the battle of Bunker Hill, rehearsed it under the direction of one of their number who was much interested in dramatics, and presented it, sound effects and all, over the public address system. At its conclusion the class asked that it be repeated. The first part of the script read as follows:

BATTLE OF BUNKER HILL

VOICE (*slowly*)

June 17, 1775. The Battle of Bunker Hill—You are there!

(*Fade*)

QUINCY

This is John Quincy in New York. We have just received a report from Boston that a group of the colonial militia, which has been besieging Boston, has infiltrated onto the Charlestown Peninsula in an attempt to fortify Bunker Hill. It must be pointed out that, if the colonists succeed in their attempt, they will have complete control over shipping in Boston Harbor. The hill is situated on the Charlestown Peninsula overlooking both Boston and the harbor. If a cannon could be set upon the hill, you could well imagine the devastating effect of their fire on the British ships in the harbor. Just one moment please! I have just received a bulletin from your Boston station that they have dispatched two men to Bunker Hill. We now take you to Boston.

(*Fade out—up. Background of heavy guns firing*)

HENRY

This is George Henry in the British encampment at the foot of Breed's Hill. The sound of the guns you hear are the British warships anchored in the Boston Harbor. They have been shelling the colonial redoubt since they discovered the fortifications this morning. Apparently the surprise move by the colonists has completely bewildered the British high command. The British camp is in a state of high excitement as it awaits the decision of the chiefs of staff, who are meeting now with General Gage in his hut. Soldiers here about me are cleaning their rifles and generally readying themselves for a battle which, in the opinion of the British, is inevitable. To the left of me the British are setting up a number of their heavy field pieces. While I was coming to the British camp, I saw that people were standing on the roofs of their houses and taking advantage of almost every bit of high ground, waiting and watching for a battle which everyone expects. Ladies and gentlemen, I see that Colonel McGovern is coming our way. He has just come out of the headquarters of General Gage. Just one moment Colonel, I would like to ask you some questions.

(*Background of guns and voices*)

MC GOVERN (*broad English accent*)

Yes, what is it?

HENRY

Sir, is the conference over?

MC GOVERN

Yes, that is correct.

HENRY

Sir, do you know what plan of action General Gage intends to take?

MC GOVERN

He plans to storm the hill in a direct frontal attack immediately.

HENRY

Why a direct frontal attack?

MC GOVERN

Some of the staff proposed other plans of action. But it is General Gage's opinion that the colonists cannot withstand a concentrated frontal attack. Now if you will excuse me sir ——

Presentations such as these necessitate a considerable amount of group planning. Pupils will, of course, look ahead to their presentation throughout the time they are working to solve their problem. However, detailed planning is done at the close of the information-gathering period, with special time scheduled for this. An outline of the procedure a group plans to follow, including the assignments of work, and order of participation, should be prepared by the recorder and filed in the group notebook.

To check readiness for reporting, questions such as these are helpful:

Is Your Group Ready to Present Its Material?

1. Has your group reached agreement on a method of reporting?

2. Does every member know exactly what he is to do in the presentation of your material to the class?

3. Does every member know his material well enough so that he can present it to the class without reading it?

4. Has your group rehearsed its presentation?

5. How much time does your group need to make its presentation?

6. What is the date on which your group will make its presentation?

A participating audience

Even when groups have prepared excellent presentations, the length of time required for five or six of them often wears heavily on a class. Pupils begin to lose the thread of the reports; they become restless. As teachers, our usual reaction to such behavior is emphasis on the importance of sitting still and listening. In all probability, in one way or another, we can insure the sitting still, but enforcing listening is another matter. The mere reminder is not enough to achieve the desired result. All teachers have had experience with the class that looks attentive but hears not a word that is being said.

A more satisfactory method of insuring attention involves audience participation. Some group presentations have built-in devices for holding the attention of an audience. The group that was unable to reach a conclusion to its problem asked the class members to consider its data carefully and help in reaching a decision. The *You Ask Us* group threw the burden of activity into the lap of the audience when it announced that the group members would answer any questions the audience might have relative to the armed services. The mimeographed booklet on the community that was presented to each class member held interest and attention. A group of boys reporting on the effect of machines on the modern world announced at the beginning of the presentation that they had prepared a quiz, which would be given at the conclusion of the report, boys competing against girls. Needless to say attention was at a high level.

All presentations do not, however, have such natural interest-catchers, nor are all groups clever enough to build them into the structure of the reporting session. Therefore, it behooves the teacher to develop some method of involving the pupil audience in the day's proceedings, for unless the class has heard the reports and learned something from them much of the value is lost. The most usual technique is to require pupils to take notes as the reports are being given. It has always seemed to the writer that there is limited value in this procedure. Without question, it

helps to keep pupils from doing other things. It does not, however, involve a pupil in thinking about the information he is
hearing. He is much too busy writing as fast as he can and trying
to catch up with the material he has missed. Especially for
younger pupils, the notes have little meaning when they are completed, nor do they serve to stimulate discussion at the conclusion
of the presentation. The questions asked by the audience in this
situation usually deal with some name, place, or date that the
individuals were unable to catch in the scramble to record the
information and which they want repeated for their notes.

A method that has proven to be of much value is the use of the
form shown in Figure 29. The heading and column lines are duplicated, preferably on legal length paper in order to give sufficient space for writing.

During the presentation of a group report, class members jot
down items under any of the three headings. At times, an individual has a number of questions but can add nothing to the information given in the report. At other times, he has much to add
and few or no questions. The amount of material recorded in the
last column is sometimes quite extensive, but varies from one
individual to another, as well as from one problem to another.
True, pupils are, in a sense, taking notes. It is not, however, an
attempt to record everything that is being said, but is a means of
stimulating *thinking about* what is being said. The discussion
following the use of such a device is alive. The questions deal
with such things as clarification of points made, further information, sources of data, or perhaps with the extension of a point
made. The pupils sometimes catch a weak spot in the reasoning
of the person reporting, and, whenever possible, contribute their
own knowledge, or opinions, or doubts to the discussion.

Such a form can advantageously be developed by the class. In
its original form the teacher had used the following headings:

Questions
Points not clear
Things I learned

```
                    AUDIENCE PARTICIPATION

Name_____    Date _____

| Persons reporting | Questions I want to ask | Points I can add | Things I want to remember |
|---|---|---|---|
|   |   |   |   |
```

Figure 29. An audience participation form stimulates thinking.

The first change came as the result of a pupil-teacher discussion concerning its use. The first and second headings were felt to be overlapping. At this time the second was omitted. After using this form for some time, the class members felt that space should be provided for jotting down items that they would like to tell about that came to mind as the report was in progress. At that time the heading, *Points I can add,* was inserted. In a discussion concerning the use of such a form with a later class, the heading, *Things I learned,* was changed to, *Things I want to remember,* because the former made them feel that they must record everything, and thus they had little time to work with the other columns.

Class discussion following presentation. Although it requires additional time, each group presentation should be followed by a period, sometimes two, spent in discussing the information presented. It is largely through such discussions that pupils recognize the relationship of the data to their own lives and experiences and extend their thinking to other similar problems. To a considerable extent this has already taken place for the members of the reporting group, since, in the course of working together, they have frequently shared their ideas relative to the problem. The other class members, however, quite possibly are coming in contact with this information for the first time. They should have opportunity to investigate its meaning and implications.

The audience participation form described above serves well as a springboard for such a discussion. The questions and comments may turn the thinking of the class in a variety of directions, and the teacher must be alert to utilize any leads that arise. Out of the discussion may develop an activity of some sort as did the discussion in a twelfth-grade class following a report on teen-age city recreational facilities. In the course of this discussion, the question was raised a number of times as to the possibilities for recreation for adults. There was expressed the not unusual teen-age feeling that there was little of interest for adults to do or see; in fact, being seniors, they were looking ahead a bit dolefully.

As the result of a discussion of this feeling, the class decided to investigate the question of what there was to see and do in their city that would be of interest to adults. They decided to make a direct study of this through trips to places of their own choosing and on their own time. A pupil could take the trip alone, with a friend, with a group from the class, or with his family. An agreement was made to visit four places in the course of the fall semester.

If a trip had been unusually interesting, a brief oral report was made to the class and, in addition, in order to keep a record of the places visited, a report was made on a 4 by 6 inch card. An example of such a record follows:

Name ___Joann Clark___

Place visited ___Lecture by the governor___

Date ___October 10___

The lecture was on the topic of the politician and his Christian activities. The governor is very good at expressing his views. He gave interesting information as to how his Christian background fitted in with his political background. His lecture was very worth while and I enjoyed it immensely. There were mostly adults present.

A committee assumed the job of checking the newspapers each day and cutting out notices of lectures, concerts, plays, outstanding films, exhibits, and unusual entertainment. These were clipped to a bulletin board in the classroom. The activity was so succesful that it was continued through the spring semester and included an all-class trip to the Cranbrook Institute of Science. By June, a total of sixty-seven different places had been visited, and the class felt that it had only skimmed the surface. They no longer had any doubt concerning the number of interesting things that adults could do or see.

Another activity that was the outgrowth of a class discussion following a group report on photography was the production of a movie by a group of seven. This was carried out wholly on their own time, with most of the scenes laid in and around the homes of the pupils. The script was written by one member and revised with the help of the group. The scenes, lighting, recording of voices, and filming were planned in detail. Let us admit that *The Pearl of the Pacific* will never make Hollywood, but their experiences in the months spent in the adventure were something that none of the participants will ever forget.

A major responsibility of the teacher during a discussion period is to assist pupils in relating the data presented to other problems. It is not enough that boys and girls understand the facts reported by the group. They must be given opportunities to apply these to other areas. During the time that groups are collecting data, the teacher should be looking ahead to the discussion period. He is well aware of the type of information his pupils are collecting. Part of his planning should include the preparation of a number of questions for each presentation that can be used to stimulate thinking beyond the mere acceptance of the reported data. Questions similar to the following, but fitting the particular problems being studied in the class, of course, are helpful in developing a worthwhile discussion.

1. How does the information presented by this group relate to the major foreign problem detailed in this week's news?

2. Does this information have anything to do with the school problem discussed at the last assembly?

3. Does this information help us to understand the situation described in the book we have been reading?

4. What similarities do you see between the situation described by this group and the situation in our city today?

5. What differences do you see between the situation described by this group and the situation in our city today?

6. Do you think these discoveries will have any influence on the future?

7. Can you think of a similar situation in another country? At another time in our history? In our country today?

8. What effect do you think this will have on the people living on farms? In cities?

Frequently a discussion following a presentation is the ground from which a new problem evolves. A group had been deeply

interested in a study of early American Indians, and the report
to the class had been well done. In the course of the discussion
that followed, a pupil asked a question about the Indians today.
The reporting group could not help the questioner, nor could
anyone else in the class. The teacher answered the question, then
spent a few minutes describing his own experiences with the
Indians of upper Michigan. Suddenly a boy's voice said, "Say,
that would be a good topic to put on our *Waiting list.*" There
was quick agreement with this, but a moment later another boy
said, "No, let's not put it on the list to do later. Let's do it now."
And so, after more careful consideration, a second unit was born.

If, however, the class had held to its original descision, the
problem area, *Indians today,* would have been added to a growing list of possible areas for later study. Without such a list,
maintained throughout the year, many excellent suggestions are
forgotten.

The teacher's attitude toward the reporting periods and his
actions during the time that a presentation is in progress have
much to do with the degree of success achieved by the group and
with the attention and feeling of satisfaction of the class as a
whole. The teacher who looks bored, who corrects papers, who
participates only to urge haste, or to criticize, does little to make
this a stimulating experience. If, however, he shows his interest
in the reports by giving the group his close attention, if he participates in using the audience sheet and is active in the discussion that follows, if he admits from time to time that he has
learned something he had not known before, he will help tremendously in making the reporting time an important and significant
period.

Evaluation of presentation

Upon completion of a group report, evaluation in some form
should take place. This should include evaluation of the activity
of the group, of each individual, and of the value of the problem
studied.

Evaluation of group. Evaluating a group is difficult for pupils, since they are relatively unaccustomed to considering a number of people as a unit. If, however, working together is considered an essential element of democratic procedure, it is necessary that pupils develop the ability to look at a whole as well as the ability to consider each individual.

A simple group self-evaluation, to be filled out by each member following the presentation, is as follows:

MY GROUP'S PRESENTATION

1. I was $\begin{cases} \text{pleased} \\ \text{satisfied} \\ \text{dissatisfied} \end{cases}$ with the way our group presented its material.

_____

2. I think that the best things we did were: _____

_____

_____

3. I think the reporting of our group would have been much better if we: _____

_____

In addition to the appraisal by its own members, a group can learn much from a similar evaluation made by the pupils who served as an audience when the report was presented.

AUDIENCE EVALUATION OF PRESENTATION

1. I $\begin{cases} \text{enjoyed} \\ \text{did not enjoy} \end{cases}$ the presentation. _____

2. I think the best things the group did were: _____

_____

_____

3. I think the group's presentation would have been much better if:

_____

_____

Such evaluations should give consideration to the criteria for good group presentation that were established earlier by the class, although it is not necessary that each item on the list be referred to. If these points are written on the chalkboard, they will serve as a guide.

When all group presentations have been made, time should be scheduled by the Planning Committee, during which the groups assemble to consider the evaluations that have been written both by their own members and by the members of the audience. Each group first examines the evaluations of its own members. They are compared and, through a discussion of the points made by the individual members, a composite group self-evaluation is arrived at.

Each group then considers the evaluations written by the audience, and comparisons are made between these and the group's own evaluation. By means of such comparisons, many ideas for improvement of future presentations are developed.

A more detailed group evaluation is the use of a questionnaire based on the criteria list. Such a questionnaire might read:

EVALUATION OF THE PRESENTATION BY A GROUP MEMBER

1. Was the presentation of your group well organized?
2. Was your whole group well prepared?
3. Did you feel that the presentation held the interest of the audience? How could you tell?
4. Did your group present enough information so that the audience could understand everything?
5. Did your group use enough visual aids?
6. How would you evaluate your group's presentation? Excellent _____? Good _____? Fair _____? Poor _____? Unsatisfactory _____?

A similar questionnaire would, of course, be filled out by the members of the audience.

EVALUATION OF THE PRESENTATION BY THE AUDIENCE

1. Was the presentation well organized?
2. Was the whole group well prepared? How could you tell?
3. Did you find the presentation interesting?
4. Did the group present enough information so that you could understand everything?

5. Did the group make good use of visual aids?
6. How would you evaluate the presentation? Excellent _____?
Good _____? Fair _____? Poor _____? Unsatisfactory _____?

Too frequently this type of question, however, is answered with a brief *yes* or *no*. Although this serves well to indicate whether or not the presentation was received with satisfaction by the listening class members, it is of little value in improving the quality of reporting, since a *yes* or *no* response gives no indication of the specific points that were considered good and that were felt to be poor. The series of questions that will be described in the following pages provides a simple and somewhat more helpful approach. An examination of the results of using this with a ninth-grade class will indicate its usefulness.

A group of six boys and girls had completed its presentation of data relative to the problem, *How has the community within which our school stands changed during the last fifty years?* The discussion following this had been concluded and pupils had filled out evaluation sheets, the audience using one form and the reporting group using another. The two sets had been collected and set aside to be used later. When all groups had completed their reports, time was scheduled for examination of the evaluation sheets. Each group met separately.

During the first part of the period, the members of the group compared the evaluations that they themselves had made. An example of these as written by a member of the group that had studied the history of the community is as follows:

EVALUATION OF GROUP BY GROUP MEMBERS

Topic title: How has the community within which our school stands changed during the last fifty years?

1. *What things did you think were especially good in your group presentation?*
   I think that our pictures of the old farmhouses and stores and our old maps were good. Bringing in Mr. Danell to tell about his boyhood was good too.
2. *What could have been improved?*

We had too much information about the early part and about today and not enough about the time half way between then and now.

3. *Did you enjoy presenting it to the class? Why or why not?*
   Yes, I did, because everyone was so interested.

4. *Do you feel that your group worked well together in planning and preparing this presentation?*
   I think we planned together fine but we only rehearsed part of it and we didn't decide when to show the pictures. It mixed things up a little.

5. *How would you evaluate the presentation of your group? Excellent? Good? Fair? Poor? Unsatisfactory?*
   I think it was mostly good or even a little better. In some places though it was only fair.

Name: Pat Shields

The comparison of the evaluation sheets of the six members of the group brought various self-criticisms to light, as well as quite a number of things with which they were well pleased. A summary of the items on which they agreed was prepared by the recorder under each point on the evaluation sheet. This was used for comparison with the evaluations made by the audience.

As can be expected in any audience, the evaluations ranged from thorough enjoyment of the presentation to strong criticism. The majority, however, indicated definite approval. A sample audience evaluation is as follows:

EVALUATION OF GROUP BY AUDIENCE

Topic title: How has the community within which our school stands changed during the last fifty years?

1. *What things did you think were especially good in this presentation?*
   They all spoke loud enough so that you could hear everything they said. Bringing Mr. Danell in was very good. I liked the quiz at the end. I liked the way Walt introduced the topic. They had a great deal of information.

2. *What could have been improved?*

They could have divided their time more equally. They should have shown the pictures right when they were telling about those things and not all together at the end.

3. *Did you enjoy the presentation? Why or why not?*
   Yes. I enjoyed it more than any report this semester because it was something I had often wondered about.

4. *As you watched this group report did it seem to you that the members had planned well together? Explain your answer.*
   Yes and no. They had their material in order but sometimes they didn't seem sure what was to come next. But you could tell they had planned the quiz together because it went off so smooth.

5. *How would you evaluate this presentation? Excellent? Good? Fair? Poor? Unsatisfactory?*
   I think it was good.

From the responses to questions such as these, groups can draw conclusions relative to the degree of their success in presenting their material. Pupils learn where their strengths and their weaknesses lie. They learn that certain methods of reporting are successful, whereas others are not satisfactory. They also learn that some methods require special planning. For example, the use of either a tape recorder or the public address system as a vehicle for a presentation is not a success unless rehearsed repeatedly before either making the recording or tuning in the audience on the public address system. They discover that unless this has been done, the result is usually rejected by the audience. They learn that visual aids are helpful but do not replace solid information, that unless they know their material well and have sufficient information they cannot answer questions that are asked by the audience. A group discovers that an audience is well aware of careless planning, and can see the weak spots quickly. Such discoveries lead to improved reporting.

Individual evaluation. Although the emphasis has been on the evaluation of the group, the individual's part in the presentation should not be lost sight of. He should make an evaluation of his own performance. When first attempting this it can be quite simple, following the form described earlier in this chapter.

My Part In My Group's Presentation

1. I was $\begin{cases} \text{pleased} \\ \text{satisfied} \\ \text{dissatisfied} \end{cases}$ with the way I presented my material.

_____

2. I think that the best things I did were: _____

_____

_____

3. I think that my reporting would have been much better if I: _____

_____

_____

Later a somewhat more detailed form may be used.

My Part In My Group's Presentation

1. What things did you think were especially good in your presentation?

2. What could you have improved?

3. Did you enjoy presenting it to the class? Why or why not?

4. Do you think that you contributed as much as you could toward presenting a good group report? Explain your answer.

5. Was there something that you found difficult to do?

6. How would you evaluate your own part of the presentation? Excellent? Good? Fair? Poor? Unsatisfactory?

Such self-evaluations should be filed in the pupils' personal files. At the time of preparing another presentation these serve well as means of reviewing strong points and weaknesses. Item 5 should guide the teacher in giving individual assistance.

Any evaluation sheet described in this section does not take much time to fill out, at most ten minutes at the conclusion of a group report. They are then laid aside until all have completed their reports. At this time, each group examines its evaluations. The comparison made by a group of the evaluations written by its own members and the further comparison of this composite evaluation with audience appraisals will, in all probability, take two class periods, or between sixty and eighty minutes.

Evaluation of problem studied. When all presentations have been made and evaluations analyzed, a final period should be spent in a consideration of how wise the members of the class feel they were in the selection of their problems. This is not a question of whether pupils enjoyed the work, but whether the problems were worth the time that has been spent in solving them. It will be recalled that, previous to the selection of a problem area, a list of criteria was established by the class, which was used as a basis for making choices. The discussion following the completion of the problems should focus attention on the degree to which these problems fulfilled the promise they held at the beginning. Using the sample list of criteria presented in Chapter 5, questions such as the following should be considered:

1. In what ways has studying this problem helped us to understand the world in which we live?
2. In what ways has it helped us to understand ourselves better?
3. In what ways has it helped us to increase our understanding of adult life and its problems?
4. In what ways has it helped us to understand the connection between life in the past, our present life, and life in the future?
5. Was the problem broad enough so that everyone in the group could take a part in it?
6. Was it small enough so that it could be completed?
7. Were there sufficient materials available?
8. In solving the problem, were there opportunities for activities that helped us to achieve our class goals?

A consideration of the worth of the completed problems to the individuals studying them helps to summarize the values gained from the present study or, in case a poor choice has been made despite the use of the criteria at the time of selection, to recognize its lack of value. It is a means by which pupils can learn to measure value for themselves, instead of accepting without question the value judgments of the teacher. Such pupil evaluations of problems studied is a step toward more careful and thoughtful selection of later problems.

Conclusion

Group reporting can and should be a high point in the solution of the problem, a culminating activity. Whether it is such or not depends upon the answers to questions such as these:

1. *Is the social climate of the room of such a nature that pupils feel free to attempt new activities?*

> Is there a warm pupil-teacher relationship? Do pupils feel free to express their feelings and ideas? Is the teacher interested in their activities and willing to help whenever he is needed?
>
> Is there a friendly pupil-pupil relationship? Is there evidence that pupils are interested in one another and in their activities? Are pupils aware that presenting a group report is a learning situation and that for all of them mistakes are inevitable but not tragic? Is it "safe" to try out a new method of presenting material?

2. *To what degree is creativeness fostered?*
> Are materials at hand with which to work?
>
> Is appreciation shown for the "copy" work of the inartistic as well as for the original drawing of the talented?
>
> Does the teacher encourage and assist in the development of new ideas? Does he experiment with new techniques along with his pupils? Does he obtain specialized assistance when it is needed?

3. *Are the criteria for a good presentation developed with the class?*
4. *Is sufficient time devoted to planning the presentation?*
5. *Is the audience actively involved in the presentation?*
6. *Is opportunity given for discussion following the presentation?*

8

Relationship with Parents

IF PARENTS UNDERSTAND WHAT IS GOING ON IN THE school their children attend, they can usually be counted on to cooperate, and the results are generally beneficial. However, although the truth of this proposition is well recognized, many schools pay little more than lip service to it. If asked about their programs for providing such understanding, teachers or principals usually say, "Oh yes, we have open-house each year during American Education Week," or perhaps, "We have designed a special auditorium program to demonstrate some of the activities of the school," or "We have a very active and helpful Parent-Teacher Association." In addition to these, especially for parents of elementary children, there may be child study groups composed of parents who are interested in finding out more about the growth and development of their children. In many elementary schools, mothers of children in each grade take turns serving as room mothers.

Yet, in spite of these commendable practices, in relatively few places, especially on the secondary level, have efforts been made to bring parents into close contact with the immediate activities taking place in the classroom. Too often it happens that the only time a parent meets his child's teachers during his years in junior and senior high school is on such occasions as the child is in difficulty and the parent is sent for. Even then he may not meet the teachers, but only the counselor or principal. The parent is un-

278

happy or angry as the case may be, the child is in trouble, and faculty members are complaining. Such a situation can hardly serve as a basis for building the friendly and understanding relationship that should exist between a child, his teachers, and his parents.

The most common reason given by teachers for making no effort to become acquainted with parents is lack of time. And let us not minimize this reason. It is quite true that a teacher who has five or six classes a day cannot possibly visit every home nor have a school conference with each parent. Another reason commonly given is that parents do not want to come to school. True, many of them do not, and, of course, some of them cannot come for one reason or another. But many would come if they were invited. And, after all, there are many other ways of helping parents keep in touch with classroom activities that teachers could use to advantage.

The real reason probably lies deeper, and is to be found in the more or less unconscious feeling of the teacher that establishing relationships with parents is really not the teacher's concern. The primary objective is to teach a certain subject matter content— to cover the course. The result is that there is too little concern for the pupil as an individual, as a member of a social group such as the class, much less for the pupil as a member of a family, or as a person influenced by and influencing his home and community. Where such an attitude prevails, no effort is made to bridge the gap between parents and the classroom, since it seems to have little to do with furthering the goal set for the class, namely, the acquisition of a specific body of knowledge.

However, in a classroom dedicated to helping pupils develop their capabilities in a democratically functioning group, contact with parents is a necessity by virtue of the purpose for which the class has been established. Over and above whatever factual information is prescribed, this purpose involves helping boys and girls to learn to think and work with other people in solving common problems. To achieve this goal it is essential that the teacher understand each child as completely as possible. This he cannot do without family contact, without a satisfying child-teacher-parent working relationship. Without it, he cannot help a pupil fully realize the success of which he is capable.

Reversing the coin, parents need to know the experiences their children are having in school. By its very nature a democratically functioning class is different from other classes, different in purpose and in procedures. Parents who understand these differences and the reasons for them can be a help to a child, whereas those who do not understand frequently undermine his security in the class situation. This, in turn, can become a destructive factor in the operation of the class as a whole. The wise teacher will make every effort to bring understanding to the parents of his pupils.

Indirect contact

Probably the most usual contact between teacher and parents is of the hit-and-miss, indirect variety, the informal and unplanned conversation with a pupil about his family and his home. Although this approach is not completely satisfactory, if teachers will take full advantage of it, they will find that it can often be quite helpful. Examples of such indirect contacts follow.

PUPIL

My father thinks it's a good idea for our class to build our own book shelves.

TEACHER

I'm glad to hear that, Joe. He's a builder, isn't he? Would you ask him what kind of wood would be best for us to buy?

PUPIL

My father said he would drive some of us to the picnic grounds if we needed him.

TEACHER

Wonderful! Will you thank him for us, Bill? We'll let him know our plans later when they are completed and we see how many are going.

PUPIL

I told my mother the story you told us about the cookies you baked that weren't any good. She said that you probably didn't beat them long enough. She said she would write out her recipe for you.

TEACHER

I would like that very much, Judy. Maybe then I will know exactly what to do. Will you thank her for me?

PUPIL

You like red, don't you, Miss Mathews. My mother does too.

TEACHER

Yes, I like the color, red, very much. I often choose a dress with something red on it.

TONY

My mother says that life in Italy is different than it is here.

TEACHER

I guess it must be, Tony. Would you ask her to tell you some ways in which it is different? Then you could tell us. We'd like to know.

Such conversations are spontaneous and in all probability are not carried on with every pupil. Some are just bits of friendly talk, but some can be used to good advantage if the teacher is quick enough to see their possibilities. For example, Joe's father might be willing to help the boys build the shelves or perhaps to meet with them to develop the plans. Bill's father may be willing not only to transport pupils to the picnic, but to stay and help with the baseball game. And there is just the possibility that Tony's mother might be willing to come to school and tell the class about Italy herself, if she is invited.

Another method of establishing indirect contact with parents is to assign pupils the task of discussing with their parents a question that is being discussed in class. For example, at the time the class is considering the meaning of democracy, the teacher might say:

When you go home tonight ask your father and mother what the word *democracy* means to them. See whether your ideas agree with their's or not. We will talk about this tomorrow.

The following day there will be many statements starting with the words, "My father thinks——," or, "My mother thinks——."

If the teacher takes time to check a day or so later, he will find that many parents have asked their children, "What did your class decide is the meaning of democracy?"

A teacher should, of course, be cautious in disagreeing too directly with parents' opinions. If any cannot be accepted completely, the statement may be met with, "Yes, that is certainly part of it," or "Let's think about this idea and talk about it later." When it has become one of many ideas, it tends to lose its identification with any particular person.

Parents and the curriculum

Any change from curricular practices with which parents are familiar is likely to be suspect, and most certainly a teacher-pupil planned class is such a change. In most schools, little or no effort is made to help parents understand the reasons for the new procedures, nor the implications of these changes for the well-being of their children. And the idea of involving them in the planning is rarely considered.

In a few schools, however, curricular programs are developed with the help of parents. The *Combined Studies Program,* which grew out of work done in the New School[1] in the Evanston Township High School,[2] is the result of recognition by the school of the role of parents in solving school problems. The program, dedicated to preparing high-school age boys and girls for democratic living, has been developed with the active assistance of parents.

The major parent body is the Combined Studies Parent Council, which is composed of all parents of pupils in the program. This group meets with the department chairman for the purpose of assisting in interpreting and planning the program. It sponsors a rummage sale to buy needed equipment, and plans a yearly family dinner and class-parent group meetings. A smaller group,

---

[1] Charles M. MacConnell, Ernest O. Melby, Christian O. Arndt, and Leslee J. Bishop, *New Schools for a New Culture* (New York: Harper & Brothers, Publishers, 1953), pp. 95–110.

[2] Evanston Township High School, Evanston, Illinois.

the Planning Committee, meets regularly to "think through" and find solutions to the problems faced in any of the above activities.

In addition, several mothers from each class are designated by the council to serve as room mothers. They serve in any capacity in activities for which adults are needed, for example, in assisting at parties or on field trips. The room mothers, together with the council officers, constitute the Executive Committee.

Another example of parent participation is the preparation by a committee of a questionnaire that is sent to the parents of all pupils in combined studies classes for the purpose of evaluating the program from the viewpoint of the parent. Still another committee is active in the preparation of publications describing the program. Thus, parents are not only informed by the school as to its activities, but are active in evaluating the experiences their children are having and in developing the curriculum to meet the needs of the pupils involved.

Typical of the requests for evaluation is the following letter:

PARENT EVALUATION

Pupil _____   Date _____

From time to time we have made changes in the Combined Studies Program on the basis of our experience and on the suggestions of parents and pupils. Therefore, your comments, brief or lengthy, are studied carefully. To help us plan for next year will you please return this page in the addressed envelope.

Will you please comment on the characteristics of the program which contribute to the development of the skills and attitudes you wish your child to acquire. What are you eager to have us continue doing?

What suggestions do you have for changes?

_____
Parent Signature

If parents were initially involved in the decisions relative to the establishment of democratically functioning classes, there still remains, year after year, the need to induct the parents of the successive classes into the program. Plans must be made and

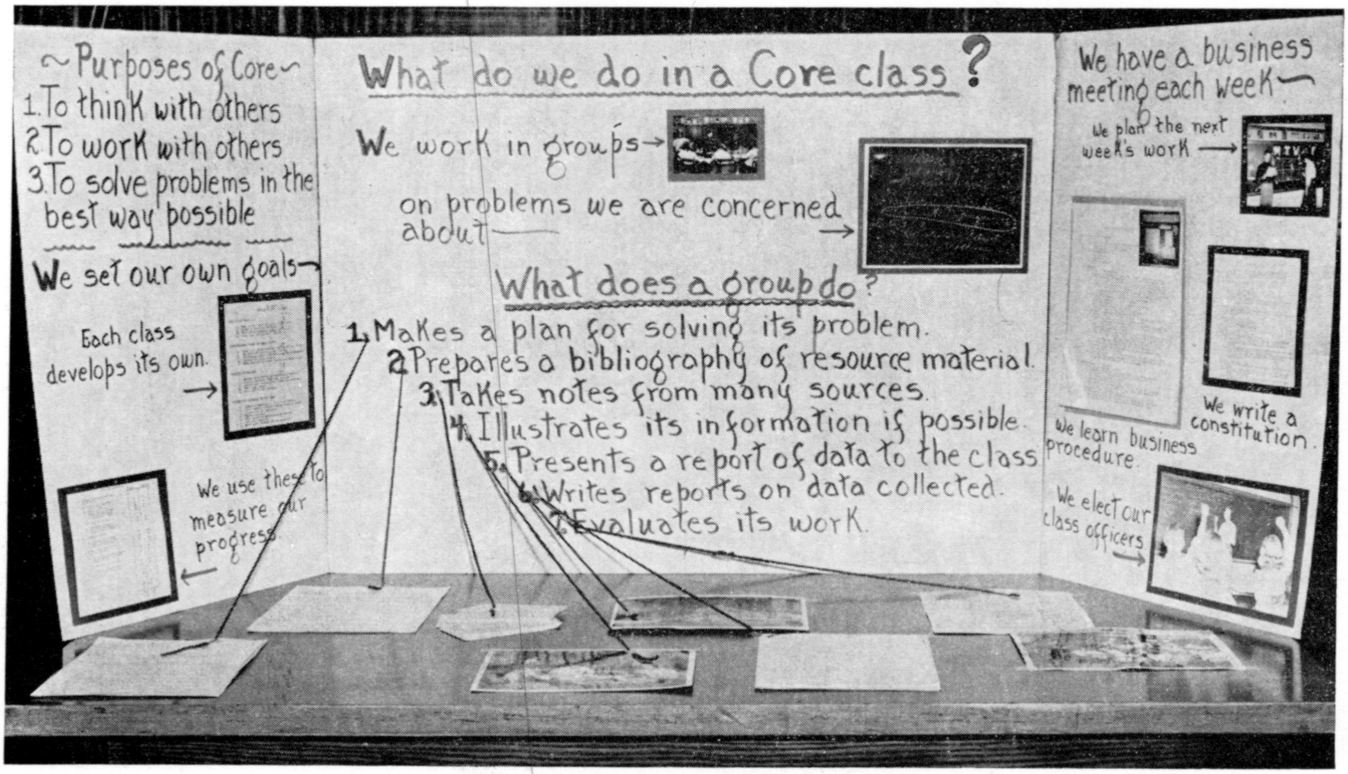

Figure 30. An exhibit for parents.

carried through for keeping them in touch with what is going on and for providing opportunities for them to ask questions and express opinions. Effective communication between the class and the parents must be established and maintained.

In a number of secondary schools, the parents of pupils who expect to attend the school the following semester are invited to come to an evening program to help acquaint them with the school—the building, the curricular and extracurricular offerings, the faculty, and the administration. Requirements for graduation, school regulations, and organization are explained. In one school, a film that shows a wide variety of the school activities is a usual part of the evening's program. Rooms throughout the building are open, and teachers are available to describe activities taking place in them.

Since the school has a core program, rooms in which these classes are held are open too, with core teachers on hand to answer questions and to clarify the purposes of the program. An exhibit is prepared, as shown in Figure 30, which gives parents an over-all view of the core procedures, and each parent is given a mimeographed sheet containing a description of core activities and summarizing its purposes. The teachers feel that this evening provides extremely valuable contacts with the parents in the community.

In the same school, early in the first semester, the parents of the beginning ninth-grade core pupils are invited to attend the *Ninth-Grade Core Parent Night*. Invitations read as follows:

DEAR MR. AND MRS. EDWARDS,

This semester your child is a 9B student at Edwin Denby High School. Among other things he has probably told you that he is in a core class. Since he may be a bit confused as yet, and not able to give you a clear picture of what we are trying to do in this course, we would like very much to have an opportunity to explain it to you.

On the evening of Tuesday, October 14, we are inviting the parents of the boys and girls in the 9B core classes to come to Denby. At this time we will explain what the purposes of the core classes are and how they operate. We will show the Denby core filmstrip, "A Core Curriculum Class in Action." You will have an opportunity to meet your child's core teacher. There will be time set aside during which you may ask any questions you have relative to the core program. Refreshments will be served. The meeting will be held in Room 202 and will start at 7:30 P.M.

If you have younger children who cannot be left at home, please feel free to bring them. We will have older core pupils to care for them here at school during the evening.

Won't you try to come? We would like to have as many parents as possible understand the experiences these children are having.

Yours sincerely,

— —

Please fill out and return this section to your child's core teacher in order that we may know how many plan to attend.

I will
   will not be present.

Parent's signature:

_____

Name of Pupil:

_____

Every effort is made to make parents feel welcome. Knowing ahead of time who is planning to attend, the teachers prepare name tags, each selecting a different color and shape in order to distinguish one class from another. The names are written large enough to be seen at a distance. As the parents come in the door, these tags are pinned on them by upper-class core pupils who assist wherever they are needed throughout the evening. Until the program starts, the teachers move about the room greeting the parents, the colored name tags helping them to identify quickly parents of their own pupils.

The first part of the meeting is given over to showing and discussing the filmstrip, *A Core Curriculum Class in Action*,[3] which was made in the school some years earlier. Parents learn about

_____

[3] Audio-Visual Utilization Center, Wayne State University, Detroit.

the history of core development both in the school itself and in the country as a whole, its underlying philosophy and purposes, and some of the procedures that are followed.

The group then divides, each teacher meeting the parents of his pupils in his own classroom, thus giving them an opportunity to see the room in which their child works and to meet his teacher in a group small enough so that there is some possibility of becoming acquainted with the teacher and with other parents. Simple refreshments are served, and the remainder of the evening is devoted to the questions parents wish to ask, to a discussion of the problems they raise, and to a description of the activities carried on to date by this particular class. Generally there is little opportunity for direct consideration of the problems of any particular child, although there is no doubt that a teacher learns many things about his pupils that he has not known before, from the reactions of parents in the discussion period as well as from the few minutes of individual conversation he has with each one. Frequently, too, a parent follows such a meeting with a request for a conference, in order to consider the specific difficulties of the child, or the difficulties the parents may be having with him. Through this relatively simple procedure, a feeling of trust and security is built up in both parent and teacher that provides for mutual understanding and simplifies future contacts. The meetings are always exciting and challenging and, although the teachers go home weary at the end of the long evening, they would not give up Parent Night.

For those parents who, for one reason or another, were not present at the evening meeting it is a good idea to prepare a mimeographed sheet containing the major points touched on at the meeting. This might include a brief history of the movement toward democratically functioning classes, the purposes for which such classes have been established in this particular school, a short outline of procedures followed, and a series of questions usually asked by parents, together with their answers. The questions asked, as well as their answers, will vary in differ-

ent schools. Answers to such questions as the following might
be included:

1. How are children selected for this class?
2. Is credit given for this course?
3. Can a child go on to college having had this course?
4. How long does the child stay with the same teacher?
5. What happens at the end of the year?
6. Do other schools in the city have this type of class?
7. Will the child have difficulty in other classes because of this
   course?
8. What do they learn in this class?

If an evening meeting is not feasible, invitations might be
issued to mothers to come during the class period. This is quite
possible in double-period classes. Such a meeting will probably
be of a different nature, since both pupils and parents will be
present, whereas the evening meeting does not include the pupils of the classes involved. A description of one such meeting,
written by a pupil as a part of the history of a year in a ninth-
grade core class,[4] is a follows:

On Thursday, February 18, we held Open-House for our mothers
from 2 to 4 o'clock in the afternoon. Seventeen mothers came.

After we were settled, Frank Adano called the class together and we
presented a sample business meeting. Then Miss Wells summarized
core and its work in a very interesting talk. Graphs were drawn on the
blackboard to help describe just what had been accomplished. After
Miss Wells had finished, she asked if any mothers had any questions.
Some did and were given the information they desired. Caroline Henderson gave a short talk on the *Core Council* and on *What Core Is.*
Then Richard Hande talked on the *Work of Core,* and lastly Barbara
Watson talked on *What Core Means to Me.* After the talks, Florence
Craft and Doris Borg served refreshments of ice cream and cookies
and candy mints. Our tea table was decorated with a bouquet of
spring flowers and our color scheme was red, white, and blue. When
the bell rang at the end of the tenth hour, no one left for home but
stayed and talked and finished their refreshments. Everyone had a
good time.

---

[4] *This Way to Democracy,* Appendix.

Advanced classes that have had several years' experience in democratic procedures frequently hold an evening parent meeting toward the end of the school year. Such a meeting provides the occasion for a kind of progress report. It is planned by pupils and teacher together and is geared to give parents as clear a picture as possible of the experiences the pupils have had during the year and what they feel they have gained from these experiences. Sometimes it is decided to invite someone from outside the group, such as a representative of the admissions office of a neighboring college to discuss the question of admission to college of pupils who have gone through a core program, or perhaps a representative of the personnel staff of a local business concern to discuss the requirements for success in the business field in relation to the present experiences of the pupils. Generally, however, the program is presented entirely by the class.

The program for one such parent meeting, given by an eleventh-grade class, was as follows:

ELEVENTH GRADE PARENT NIGHT

Welcome to Parents . . . . Russell Carter
How Our Class Operates . . . . Nancy Woodson
Topics and Problems We Have Studied . . . Carol Johnson
Books We Have Read . . . . Phyllis Demarr
Trips We Have Taken . . . . Allen Smith
Our Social Events . . . . John Leland
Explanation of Our Exhibits . . . . Jane Hobbs
Problems We Have Faced This Year . . . . . Jack Shepard

Panel—Our Feelings about Core This Year
   Elizabeth Pelski
   Bill Edwards
   Jean Meyers
   Frank Hill
   Tony Rocco
The panel will also answer questions parents may wish to ask.

Refreshments

An exhibit was prepared by a committee and included samples of written work done by various members of the class, creative projects such as charts, graphs, dioramas, slides, and models, and a series of enlarged photographs showing pupils at work in the classroom, on field trips, and at parties. The secretary's daily record book was a part of the display as well as a copy of the class constitution and the class goals.

In addition, the teacher assembled as many books and pamphlets as he could locate that dealt with the subject of core in the school curriculum. These were made available to the parents for home reading. A mimeographed, annotated list of these was given to each parent in order that selections might be made later and requests sent to school by way of the pupils. Although all parents did not make such requests, many did, and it was felt to be desirable to have reference materials available, if for no other reason than to show that the idea of core was not merely a local matter.

A variety of other methods of informing parents of class activities may be used to advantage. The introductory sheet prepared for pupils as a part of their orientation to the democratic class, which was described in Chapter 2, can be used to introduce parents to the program long before a parent night can be organized. Pupils may either be asked to take this sheet home and show it to their parents, or a companion sheet may be prepared, which is addressed to the parents rather than to the pupils but containing similar information.

An annual mimeographed newspaper covering the activities of all classes involved in a core program was prepared in one school in an attempt to give parents a broad view of core experiences and procedures over a year's time. The articles were written by representatives of the various classes who served as reporters on the activities taking place in their own classes. An upper-class group took the responsibility for assembling the material, proofreading the contributions, determining the paper's format, and mimeographing the entire collection of articles. The first article in one of the issues indicates the purpose of the paper as follows:

An Open Letter to Parents

This core newspaper is primarily for you. It was published by the students in order to give you greater insight into the core program in which they have been participating.

You have had various opportunities to observe some of the procedures of core, and, no doubt, your son or daughter has told you of some of his core experiences, but we hope, through this paper, to give you more complete knowledge of the many phases of core work.

We believe that this newspaper will be interesting and valuable to you, and we hope that it will help you to become more familiar with the core program.

When you have finished reading the newspaper, will you please fill out the questionnaire which is attached and have it returned to your child's class.

The headings to various pages and their contents were:

Meet the Teachers

The year's professional activities of each core teacher were reported on this page. Conferences attended, as well as trips taken, new additions to families, and awards won, were recorded.

How We——

This included such things as selecting problems, beginning work on problems, gathering information, taking notes, presenting material to the class.

Democratic Procedure

How a class sets its goals, carries out its business meetings, and makes its weekly plans were described under this heading.

Classroom Activities

Such things as outstanding topic presentations, stimulating discussions, films that had been unusually helpful, and problems that had been studied in the different classes were reported here.

Senior Activities

This page was devoted entirely to the activities of the seniors—a unit on careers, a dinner planned, prepared, and served by a committee for the class at the home of the teacher, scrapbook exchange with a group of Navajo Indian children.

Class Officers

This described how officers were elected and what their duties were, as well as the names of officers in the various classes.

We Visited——

The field trips taken by the various classes throughout the year were recorded under this heading, for example, trips to Greenfield Village, *The Detroit Times* newspaper printing plant, and Cranbrook Institute of Science.

Have You Heard——

Here were reported activities of individual members of the core classes in sports and clubs. The seniors who received scholarships and pupils who received awards of any nature or who were elected to school class offices were listed.

Core Fun

This included reports of class parties, an all-core party, Christmas carolling, bowling contests, and splash parties.

Core Speaks

Interviews with former core pupils were recorded under this heading, as well as the opinions on core of present pupils.

Dots and Dashes
Odds and Ends

These two pages contained miscellaneous articles of interest to parents—new books that had been purchased for room libraries, a report on 9B Parent Night, visitors to the core classes, a conference for core teachers attended by three pupils, and a number of items that the staff could not bear to leave out but could not place anywhere else.

The last page was a questionnaire to be filled out by the parents and returned to the class teacher. The questions asked were the following:

How Do You Feel About This Paper?

Did you enjoy reading it?

Should this paper be continued? Why?

Do you have any suggestions for improvement of this paper?

What did you find most interesting?

What did you find least interesting?

What things, if any, would you like to see included in this paper that were not included?

A paper such as this may well be developed on a single-class basis as well as on a program-wide project. In this case, there is assurance that parents will be interested in all parts of the paper, since all of it pertains to their child and his class. A sample of such a class paper, originally duplicated in booklet form, is included in the appendix. Under the title, *This Way to Democracy*, a class of ninth-graders recorded the year's events. Their pride knew no bounds, and the teacher could rest assured that every parent read every word.

Parents as resource people

Parents can often give assistance in the classroom and are usually more than willing to do so, but their help is seldom asked for. Teachers feel, too frequently, that only the school can promote knowledge and understanding in boys and girls. Yet, parents often are well informed in areas about which a teacher knows little or nothing. Welcomed into the classroom, parents can share their experiences with pupils and teacher, and serve as invaluable resource persons. They may have special hobbies or talents, knowledge of which would serve to broaden pupils' academic, social, or emotional horizons. As a parent becomes a participating member of a class for an hour or two, he, too, learns many things—how a class of this type operates, the kinds of experiences his child and his classmates are having, the relationship of his child to his peer group and to his teacher, some of the problems the teacher and pupils face each day. The experience is frequently a revelation to both teacher and parent.

In a few schools, an effort is made on a school-wide basis to discover at the beginning of the school year the types of activities in which parents are willing to participate. For this purpose a checklist is sent home, the parent checking those activities for which he is willing to give assistance. The cards are then filed in the main office according to items checked. This furnishes a valuable resource file for use as occasions arise in which help is needed. When such a checklist is sent home, a statement should, of course, be included to the effect that the number of parents called on for help will depend largely upon the activities that are undertaken as the year proceeds, and that, even though everyone may not be needed, their willingness to assist is much appreciated.

A similar technique may well be used in the classroom. When class work is based to any extent upon the interests and concerns of the pupils, the range of problems touched upon can at times be alarmingly wide. It is necessary to tap every possible resource, not just those available within the school walls. The following letter served to locate the possible sources of assistance within the ranks of parents of pupils in a tenth-grade class.

DEAR MR. AND MRS. WILSON,

Jack is in my tenth-grade core class and, although I have not had an opportunity to meet you as yet, I am hoping that it will not be too long before we have a chance to become acquainted.

But I am not going to wait until we meet to ask for your help. As you know, in a core class a great many questions arise and activities take place that ordinarily do not arise in other classes. There are times when I do not know where to find as much help as my pupils need. The thought has occurred to me that among the parents of my thirty-six tenth-grade boys and girls there must be any number who have had experiences and have participated in activities about which I know little or nothing. There must be parents with special abilities, hobbies, or knowledge who would be willing to share these with us for an hour or two if we needed them.

Would you be willing to help in any of the following activities?

1. Help chaperon a class party or picnic? _____
2. Assist on a field trip by:
   a. Helping to furnish transportation? _____
   b. Or going with us on the trip if we go by bus? _____
3. Come to class and tell about an interesting trip you have taken? _____ If so, where was the trip taken? _____

_____

4. Show films or slides taken on a trip? _____ If so, where was the trip taken? _____

5. Are you interested in special activities or hobbies that you could tell us about or demonstrate, such as any of the crafts, music, dancing, weaving, or any other special interests? _____ If so, what are these?

_____

_____

6. Do you have any articles from foreign countries which would help boys and girls understand the people of these countries better? _____If so, what articles from what countries? _____

_____

Would you be willing to loan them to us for a few days? _____
Would you be willing to bring them to class and tell us about them?

_____

7. There must be many things that I have not mentioned. Is there any other help that you could give us? _____

_____

You will understand, I am sure, that we will not need everything at one time. May we keep this sheet on file and call on you as the need arises?

Yours sincerely,

Or, later in the semester when the class members have selected their problems, a letter such as the following may be sent home.

DEAR MR. AND MRS. RICHARDS,

At the present time in our class there are small groups of boys and girls, each of which is working on one of the following problems:

a. How are commercial motion pictures made?

b. How does our national government operate?

c. What are some of the legends of our country and how did they arise?

d. How did prehistoric man live?

e. What countries are members of the United Nations and how do they work together to solve their problems?

Do you have any material that would be of help to them, such as pictures, books, pamphlets, illustrative material of any sort? If so, would you be willing to loan them to us for a few days? Or could you come to school and tell us about them?

Yours sincerely,

The response is often amazing and not only is valuable and unusual material obtained for class use, but parents become aware of the problems being studied by their children and the experiences they are having in order to solve them. Whether they come to school or not, whether they furnish material or not, a closer relationship has been established between parent and classroom.

Class visitation

Another method that has been used to bring parents and schoolroom together is to invite parents to visit the class in groups of three or four. Usually, of course, only mothers are able to come during school hours. However, fathers are sometimes at home and are frequently quite willing to come. Such visitation days may be spaced at perhaps three-week intervals. Let us say that every third Thursday is a visiting day. During the preceding week a note of invitation is sent to the parents whose turn it is to be asked to come. The letter might read as follows:

DEAR MR. AND MRS. MEADER,

Jane has probably told you that our basic living class is making an effort to have all of the parents come to school and visit this class at some time during the year in order that you may know and understand what we are doing. We plan to do this by inviting groups of three or four parents every three weeks.

On Thursday of next week, November 8, we are hoping that you will be able to spend the time from 9:20 A.M. to 11:05 A.M. with us in room 230. We are also asking Mr. and Mrs. Eldon and Mr. and Mrs. Jalik to come the same day.

We are not planning a special program but would like to have you see a regular day in our class.

Yours sincerely,

If the plans for the over-all program of visitation have been made, as they should be, by pupils and teacher together, the letter may be composed by a committee. The same committee may be responsible for writing the invitations to the parents every three weeks. If there are small children in a family who cannot be left at home, arrangements might be made for one or two girls in the class to take care of them during the parents' visit. Coloring books, crayons, a few story books, or a toy work wonders.

Another committee might prepare a copy of the day's schedule of activities for each parent, including a short paragraph welcoming them. Thus each visitor will know what is taking place and what to expect during his stay in the room. Still another committee may be selected to greet the parents at the door, introduce them to the class and teacher, and seat them.

The activities carried out on such a day should involve the usual, everyday work in the classroom. If it is time to make a bibliography, this is the order of the day. If a discussion is needed, then this is scheduled. Perhaps the only thing to be avoided is a reading period, for this is a silent, individual task and would be of little value to observe. Such an activity can easily be scheduled for another day.

Home visits

Home visits are probably considered by most teachers to be a difficult method of bringing parents and classroom in touch with each other, difficult not only because of the time element, but because of the fear of not knowing what to say. Yet, in many instances a visit to a pupil's home is the most rewarding experience a teacher can have and, strangely enough, once the ice has been broken, there is more than enough to talk about.

Home visits may, of course, be made for a number of reasons. The most usual one is to talk with parents concerning some particular problem relating to the child—he is not doing well in your class, or he does not get along with his classmates, or he seems to be listless and lacking in energy. For any problem of this nature, a visit to the home can often be the key to understanding.

It is always wise to make an appointment, for no mother enjoys being caught with her hair in pin curls and perhaps down on her knees scrubbing the kitchen floor. With a disadvantage of this sort the meeting is not likely to get off to an especially good start. It is equally important to let the pupil know that you plan to visit his home if you wish to maintain his confidence and respect. Withholding the fact that you are going to visit his parents seems to him to be dishonest and unfair, and is likely to make him suspicious of your motives.

Some of the most satisfactory visits, however, are not the result of difficult situations in the classroom, but have as their purpose the establishment of friendly relations between the parents, the child, and the teacher. Because there is no particular problem, none of the participants fears the visit. If good rapport has been established between teacher and pupils, it is quite possible to draw class members into a program of visitation in which the teacher plans to visit every home sometime during the year. To make this really work, he must show that he is eager to get to know each pupil's family—not in order to "tell" what Joe does in school, but just to become acquainted. It is, of course, expected that the child will be present at the time of such a visit.

A class in which one would least expect to find enthusiasm for a program of this nature was a ninth-grade group of behavior-problem boys. Yet the teacher had made his visits such pleasant experiences for the boys and their families that there was intense rivalry for them. When he asked, "Who am I scheduled to visit this week?" a boy shouted, "Me!" and another said, "Me too. It's about time." Still another asked, "Mr. James, are you sure you're coming to my house on the fifteenth?"

The visits were on an invitational basis and were scheduled as the invitations were issued by the boys and their families. Mr. James and his wife called on each family, and he said, "I wouldn't miss it for the world."

A similar approach can be made by means of a letter to each family reading somewhat as follows:

DEAR MR. AND MRS. DUNCAN,

Jim is in my tenth-grade core class and since I will be his teacher all this year I would like very much to have an opportunity to become acquainted with you. I am hoping to spend an hour or two with the family of each of my core pupils before the semester is over. Would you perhaps have an evening free sometime soon when it would be convenient for you to have me spend a little while with you and Jim in your home? I am looking forward to meeting you.

Yours sincerely,

Such letters should, of course, not be sent out without drawing the class into the program and should certainly not be attempted until good working relations have been established between teacher and pupils.

Before making a visit to a pupil's home or having a conference with a parent, a quick review of all available data on file relative to the family is of invaluable assistance. The pupil's autobiography, written earlier in the year, often gives information concerning the relationship of the child to other members of his family; the record of the family pattern gives a picture of the ages of brothers and sisters as well as indicating which live at home and which are away; and the work data specify the type of work done by the members of the family. Any one of these can serve as a lead to friendly conversation and make parents feel that the teacher is interested in them.

Perhaps the most valuable aid a teacher can take with him is a clear mental picture of at least one thing the child who is to be visited does well. Sometimes it is difficult to identify even one, but there must be something. He is courteous to others (even though he can't read beyond the sixth-year level). He puts forth a tremendous amount of effort (although you know that he hates teachers). He takes an active and helpful part in small groups (but finds it impossible to talk in a large group). The illustrations he has made are excellent (even though he upsets the class with his wisecracks). This home visit is to establish a friendly relationship with the family, and there is everything to be gained and nothing to be lost in recognizing the child's good points.

There is time later for discussing his problems. A record should be made, of course, of each home visit, the data being added to that already accumulated for each pupil.

For interviews designed for collecting systematic information from parents, Taba[5] suggests six questions as the means of acquiring as much information as possible.

1. Opening
   "How do you feel _____ is doing?"
2. Aspirations and goals
   "What plans do you and your husband have for _____ ?" or, "What are your hopes for _____ ? What are your husband's hopes?"
3. Association with other children
   "How do you arrange for _____ 's friends?" or "How do you try to select your children's friends?"
4. Neighborhoods
   "You know this neighborhood better than I do. Are there opportunities that you would like your child to have?" or, "How do you like this neighborhood?" or, "Do you think this is a good neighborhood for boys and girls?"
5. Worries and pleasures
   "What gives you most pleasure about your child? What worries you most about _____ ?" or, "What are some of _____'s best qualities and habits?" and, "What do you think are _____'s worst faults, faults we may not see at school?"
6. Closing the interview
   "Is there anything you would like the school to do for you?" "What suggestions do you have for _____ 's program here?"

Reporting progress to parents

In most secondary schools, a pupil's progress is reported to his parents by means of report cards sent home at regular intervals throughout the year. The most common method used to indicate

---

5 Hilda Taba, Elizabeth Hall Brady, John T. Robinson, and William E. Vickery, *Diagnosing Human Relations Needs* (Washington: American Council on Education, 1951), pp. 36–39.

success or failure is the use of a four- or five-letter rating system. Such letter ratings indicate little more than the position of the pupil relative to his peers in the class or to certain arbitrary standards, and are not very informative; yet this is the most usual method employed and is the system within which a large majority of teachers must operate.

However, even when it is required that letter grades be used, it is possible to extend the report sent home so that not only may parents see the basis for such a rating, but also that pupils, through self-evaluation, may participate in the determination of their own marks. Such a method was developed in a tenth-grade class as an outgrowth of a class discussion concerning what had been accomplished in the six-week period since the last card marking. As different activities were mentioned they were listed on the chalkboard. At the end of the period the list read as follows:

We had business meetings.
We chose problems to work on.
We made plans to solve our problems.
We made bibliographies.
We took notes.
We read books on our problems.
We kept a Research Record every day.
We planned our presentations.
We illustrated our reports in different ways.
We read books for pleasure.
We worked in groups.
We had class discussions.
We made newspaper clipping scrapbooks.
We took the Mooney Problem Checklist questionnaire.
We read current news articles.
We made a list of things we wonder about.
We helped plan each week's work.

From this list a committee of pupils and the teacher constructed a form on which all activities were recorded in somewhat greater detail than on the list. These were mimeographed and each pupil filled one out. In blank spaces following each item a pupil indicated his own participation in the activity. For a number of activities, he was asked to evaluate his work in them and, after considering all his contributions, he was asked to give an over-all evaluation of his work during the six-week period. In order to have reasonable assurance that these had been seen by parents, a short questionnaire was appended that parents were asked to fill in and return to the teacher by way of the child. The completed form was as follows:

A Record of Six Weeks in Our Core Class

Pupil _____ Date _____

During the six weeks since the last card marking our class has carried out many different activities. We selected new problems for study and have been working on these in small groups. The problems are:

1. How does our national government operate?
2. How is a motion picture made?
3. How are people with mental diseases taken care of?
4. How and where does the wildlife in Michigan live?
5. How are Greek myths and American legends alike and different?
6. What were prehistoric times like?

The problem I chose to work on is: _____

_____

My group has _____ members in it.

The part I agreed to do in order to solve our problem was: _____

_____

_____

I have carried out this job: well _____ ; fairly well _____ ; not very well _____ .

The next thing we did was to make bibliographies of all the material that we could find on our problems, such as books, films, and magazines. On my bibliography I listed _____ books, _____ magazines, and _____ films.

Then we began to do research. We did this by taking notes as we read the material we had listed on our bibliographies. I took notes from the following materials:

_____ Author: _____
_____ Author: _____
_____ Author: _____
_____ Author: _____
_____ Author: _____
_____ Author: _____

We recorded our notes on 3 by 5 inch index cards. I have _____ cards of notes. I have/have not handed them in. A sample of my notes looks like this:

Miss Harden marked my note cards as follows:

Quality _____

Form   _____

We kept daily Research Records to keep track of how much work we did each day. My record shows that I took notes on _____ days out of _____ . I did/did not turn my Research Record in on time.

We have finished taking notes and each group is now planning how to present its material to the class. So far my group's plan is: _____

_____

My part in this is: _____

_____

We are also trying to figure out ways to illustrate our information. So far my group's plan is: _____

_____

_____

_____

I expect to take part in this by: _____

_____

We have also had opportunities to read books for pleasure. The class decided that everyone should read at least one book every card marking period. When we finish a book, we write a short review of it on our Reading Record. I have read and recorded _____ books during the last six weeks. The names of these are: _____

_____

We have learned more about writing. Some of the things I wrote about were: _____

_____

Every Friday we have a business meeting. Our class officers conduct the meeting. We have a Planning Committee to plan the next week's work, a Social Committee to plan any social events for our class, and a Scholastic Planning Committee to plan how best to use the *Scholastic Magazine*. Last week's plan looked like this:

Period	Monday	Tuesday	Wednesday	Thursday	Friday
1					
2					

The Social Committee is planning a Christmas party.
My job each Friday is: _____

_____

I have carried out this job: well _____ ; fairly well _____ ; not very well _____ .

We made news-clipping scrapbooks in order to see what problems were being discussed in the daily papers. I did/did not hand one in.

We made lists of things we have heard, or seen, or read in the last few weeks which we did not understand. I did/did not hand in a list.

We have had many class discussions. I take part in these: always
_____ ; often _____ ; sometimes _____ ; seldom _____ ;
never _____ .

We have read and discussed many articles from the *Scholastic Magazine.*

We answered a questionnaire called the *Mooney Problem Checklist.*

We had a picture taken of the whole class.

One of the things it is necessary for each of us to learn to do is to use class time to advantage and keep at work. I feel that I do this: always _____ ; often _____ ; sometimes _____ ; seldom _____ ;
never _____ .

Another thing we must learn to do is to handle ourselves well with class officers and with the people around us, in other words, to develop good self control. I feel that I do this: well _____ ; fairly well _____ ; not very well _____ .

Considering all these activities I feel that my grade for these six weeks should be _____ because: _____

_____   _____

_____

— —

PLEASE HAVE YOUR CHILD RETURN THIS SECTION

1. Is this type of report helpful to you? _____
2. Would you like to have a report like this every six weeks? _____
3. Have you any questions you would like to ask? If so, write them in the space below.

_____

_____

_____

_____
Signature of parent

This report was sent home by way of the pupil on the same day as the official report card. Parents' reactions were so highly favorable that the technique was repeated throughout the year. Many questions were asked by parents and answered by the teacher. A number of requests for personal conferences were received, as well as a great many phone calls. A device such as this may be used at card-marking time as described above, or, developed at any time during the semester, it may be used as a means of informing parents of current activities. It might be added that it also serves to summarize accomplishments for the pupils themselves.

Another method of making letter ratings more meaningful to parents, as well as giving them insight into the objectives of the class, is based on the use of the list of goals set by the class at the beginning of a year. The list is duplicated with three columns at the right-hand side of the page. One column is used for recording the pupil's judgments, the second for the teacher's, and the third for agreements reached through a conference. Numbers are substituted for letters: 5, 4, 3, 2, and 1, a 5 representing the highest rating, and a 1 representing the lowest. Achievement in each item on the goal list is marked by the pupil; the values are totaled; then they are divided by the number of items, thus averaging them. This final number is translated into a letter grade.

The teacher then takes the sheet, covers the pupil's marks, and places his judgments in the second column. A comparison of the two columns shows any differences. When the sheets are returned to the class members, either pupil or teacher may ask for a conference. The purpose of such a conference is not to give the teacher an opportunity to tell the pupil that he is wrong, but to reach mutual understanding and to arrive at agreement if at all possible. The pupil explains his reasons for his evaluation and the teacher does the same. Sometimes it is the pupil who sees that he was wrong, but just as often it is the teacher, and at times the conference shows that both were wrong in their judgments.

In the example shown below, the evaluation sheet was entitled, *Progress Toward Class Goals*. The differences between the judgments of the boy and the teacher with respect to his achievement led the teacher to ask for a conference.

PROGRESS TOWARD CLASS GOALS

Name: Larry Anderson   Date: Nov. 2

	Pupil	Teacher	Conference
I. *Working in groups*			
1. Be responsible for my share of the work.	4	3	4
2. Stick to the work that needs to be done.	3	3	
3. Share information and materials with other members.	4	2	4
II. *Class discussions*			
1. Take active part.	2	2	
2. Be quiet while others are talking.	4	4	
3. Listen to other people's ideas.	4	?	3
4. Be friendly.	4	4	
III. *Working on problems*			
1. Collect information from many sources.	4	4	
2. Select best material that fits the problems.	4	4	
3. Collect enough material to solve the problems.	4	4	
4. Be able to use the card catalog.	3	3	
5. Be able to use the *Readers' Guide*.	2	2	
6. Write notes in own words.	3	3	
IV. *Reporting to the class*			
1. Organize material so that it is smooth.	3	3	
2. Give reports without reading notes or paper.	4	4	
3. Speak clearly.	4	4	
4. Use good English.	4	4	
5. Illustrate the material.	1	4	3
Total points	61		62
Average	3⁷⁄₁₈		3⁸⁄₁₈
Key: 5 = A, 4 = B, 3 = C, 2 = D, 1 = E	C+		C+

307

The conference with Larry was as follows:

TEACHER

Have you had time enough to look at your evaluation sheet, Larry?

LARRY

Yes. In some things your marks are different from mine, Miss Burns. Sometimes yours are lower and sometimes they're higher.

TEACHER

That's right. Let's see what each of us had in mind when we made these evaluations. Maybe we're not as far apart as it looks on paper. There are probably important things that I failed to consider and perhaps there are things that you missed. Where should we start?

LARRY

I guess it doesn't matter.

TEACHER

How about starting with the one where we are farthest apart, Item IV —5, illustrating your material when you presented your report? I thought you did a fine job of that with your sketches, but you apparently thought you did very poorly.

LARRY

But those were only on the chalkboard. They weren't on paper and handed in. I didn't think those should count at all.

TEACHER

But they illustrated what you were talking about. They helped us to understand your data, didn't they?

LARRY

Sure. But I guess I thought something like that wasn't an illustration —— But—well—they weren't worth a 4 because there wasn't any reason why I couldn't have made them on charts and in colors. They would have been much better. The ones on the board were just rough sketches, just average—a 3 maybe. I can do better than that next time.

TEACHER

All right. I'll settle for a 3. I think too you could do much better, but the chalk drawings were surely worth a 3 rather than a 1. Now let's look at some of the others. There are two points in the first section, Items 1 and 3, on which we didn't agree.

LARRY

Well, I don't understand why you think I'm not doing very well there. I take part in the group discussion every day. I tell the group what I've found out. I think I do pretty well in that. That's why I gave myself a 4.

TEACHER

Do you mean in your small work group?

LARRY

Yes. I take part every day. You can ask the people in my group whether I do or not. I really do it.

TEACHER

No, I don't have to do that. You would know that yourself. But in class discussions you seldom take part unless you are asked a direct question. You have shown that you realize this by giving yourself a mark of 2 in Item II—1, which deals with taking an active part in class discussions. Have you any idea why you take part in the small group but almost never when the whole class is having a discussion?

LARRY

I guess I'm not as scared when there are only five people to talk to. I used to be afraid even with them—the first few days. But now it works fine. I don't even think about it.

TEACHER

Maybe I haven't really watched you in a small group. I've thought of you as you are in a class discussion. Now that I think about it, you were pretty active in that group each time I sat in with you people, but when I marked your chart I was seeing you in the big group. That makes sense. Let's change my 2 to match your 4. And that would make it necessary to change my 3 to a 4 in Item I—1 because I felt that your lack of participation was a lack of taking enough responsibility.

LARRY

What does the question mark mean in Item 3 under *Class Discussions?*

TEACHER

I couldn't see how I could measure how well you listened to other people's ideas. You seldom respond to them so I can't tell whether you have even heard them. Is the mark of 4 accurate?

LARRY

Well, yes and no. Sometimes I listen and sometimes I don't. I guess a 4 is pretty high. A 3 would be more like it.

TEACHER

Are you sure this change should be made?

LARRY

Yes, I know it should.

And so the conference ended with give and take on both sides. Larry now understood that Miss Burns wanted to be fair with him and that she trusted him to be honest. Miss Burns, in turn, realized that she had not been seeing all that was taking place in the classroom and had a better understanding of one of Larry's problems. The fact that the final average remained almost identical is immaterial. Larry had looked at himself from many angles and had analyzed his weaknesses and strengths. These were not lost in an over-all mark but rather they had been combined, and he had seen how one related to another.

If no agreement can be reached between teacher and pupil, it is wiser to accept the pupil's evaluation than to insist that the teacher knows best. A plan should be made, however, for an evaluation conference every week or two during the period between the present and the next home-reporting date. To many boys and girls, self-evaluation is a new and difficult experience and they need help and practice in looking at themselves and their activities. Breaking a six-week period between card-marking dates into shorter units of time helps develop skill in self-evaluation, since it is not so difficult to look back over one or two weeks as it is over six.

Such teacher-pupil conferences may be carried out in class while the rest of the class members are busy with their regular classroom work. One or two, of course, may require out of class time. Throughout the year, as pupils become more adept at self-evaluation, the number of conferences required diminishes.

The evaluation sheet, including pupil evaluations, teacher evaluations, and agreements reached through a conference, may be sent home at the same time as the official report card. Through the self-evaluation and the pupil-teacher conference the pupil is able to discuss with his parents his own achievement in detail. The parents are able to see exactly what aspects of their child's growth have been considered in determining the card mark and to what degree he is succeeding in achieving each of the various goals of the class. A brief explanation of the evaluation sheet should be stapled to it. Space should be allowed for questions from parents and a line on which father or mother may place his signature. This page, detached from the evaluation sheet, should be returned to the classroom teacher.

A method of reporting progress directly to parents is the parent-teacher conference. Although found most frequently in elementary schools, increasing numbers of secondary schools are using the conference method, either as a replacement of the report card, or in conjunction with it. A secondary school that has developed this procedure over a number of years is Holt High School[6], a seventh- through twelfth-grade school. The results show that, on an average eighty per cent of the parents come to school to participate in the conferences.[7]

Two opportunities for conferences are given in a year, the first at the end of the first nine weeks of the fall semester, and the second at the end of the first nine weeks of the spring semester. Two afternoons and one evening are devoted to conferences, school being dismissed at noon in order to make all teachers available.

Parents are notified of the time of conferences by means of a letter similar to the following:

DEAR PARENTS:
Parent-Teacher conferences are to be held this Spring on April 4, 5, and 9.

The conferences will be held in the gymnasium as in other years. We would like you to try to attend according to the following schedule in order to avoid having too many parents at any one time. Those with last names A—F will try to arrive between 12:30 and 2:30 on Thursday, April 4; G—L between 2:30 and 4:30 on Thursday, April 4; M—R between 12:30 and 2:30 on Friday, April 5; and S—Z between 2:30 and 4:30 on Friday, April 5.

---

6 Holt High School, Holt, Michigan.
7 In the Holt elementary school, over 95 per cent of the parents participate.

For those parents who can't possibly attend the afternoon conferences, there will be an evening conference on Tuesday, April 9, from 7:30 to 9:00.

The evaluation sheets on students, which you pick up before entering the gymnasium, will not be available, except at the conferences, until after April 9.

Last fall we had an 86 per cent attendance at our Parent and Teacher Conferences. We on the faculty are sold on the conferences. They are tiring and trying for us, as they are for many of you, but they certainly are of invaluable assistance.

We hope to set another new record in attendance. See you at the conferences.

Sincerely yours,

Previous to the day of the conferences, each subject-matter teacher fills out the form shown below for each pupil in his classes.

Student _____

Grade _____ Subject _____

Home Room Teacher _____

Marking period _____

To the Parent:

This report is designed to center the parent and teacher conference upon a few specific items. The teacher has circled the items that apply to this student.

We wish to point out that the teacher cannot observe each and every student well enough to comment in the specific area of each of these items.

We, as teachers, will welcome your observations of the student in any of these areas and, especially, in areas where we have not commented.

Individual Behavior

Courteous to others .... a

Follows directions .... b

Uses time well c

Maturity above age group ... d

Discourteous to others .... e

Careless or destructive with
   property .... f

Inattentive .... g

Wastes time .... h

Maturity below age group i

Behavior in the Group

Participates in group activities a

Assumes his responsibility for
   success of the group .... b

Disrupts group activities c

Does not participate in group
   activities .... d

*Attitudes Toward the Class
Work*

Accepts responsibility .... a

Work is very commendable .. b

Teacher _____

* If this is circled, look upon the other side of this paper for further comments.

Academic grade: A B C D E

Works up to capacity c
Shirks responsibility .... d
Work is seldom handed in
  promptly .... e

Other Comments

Has trouble reading the material .... a
Has not demonstrated ability
  to do the work .... b
Poor attendance record c
Work seems to be handicapped
  by outside activities .... d

The academic grade is indicated in the lower left-hand corner. Any items in the right-hand column that apply to the individual under consideration are checked. These forms are then sent to the homeroom teacher, who staples together the subject-matter reports for each pupil and prepares for each a composite record that is kept in the pupil's personal file. The reports are then alphabetized by grades.

The conferences are held in the gymnasium. Chairs, one for each teacher,[8] are arranged in rows and spaced so that there is sufficient room between them to give a semblance of privacy. Each teacher's name, printed on a card in letters large enough to be seen at a distance, is fastened to the back of his chair. Next to each chair is a second chair for parents.

At the entrance to the gymnasium the parent registers and is given the reports for his child. He examines these and decides with which of his child's teachers he wishes to confer. It may be that he wishes to talk to only one. On the other hand, he may want to see all of them.[9] He locates the teacher by means of the name cards and waits his turn. Conferences generally are relatively brief, but with the aid of the report forms no time is lost. To help make the conference a pleasant experience, coffee

---

[8] Holt has a staff of 30 teachers.

[9] Approximately 60 per cent of all possible teacher contacts are made by the participating parents.

and cookies are served in the cafeteria for both parents and teachers.

Reports that are not called for are later sent to the home. Any of these parents are, of course, free to come to school at a later time if they wish to confer with teachers.

Thus, once each semester reports of progress are given directly to parents. For the final grade at the end of each semester, a report card with letter grades, A, B, C, D, or E in each subject, is sent home and no conferences are called for. It is felt that two each year are sufficient to bring parents and teachers to increasingly better mutual understanding.

Conclusion

The methods described in this chapter will, of course, not all be used with any single class. The choice will depend upon such things as the nature of the class, the extent to which it is an accepted part of the school's operational pattern to establish friendly teacher-parent relationships, and the experience a teacher has had in such activities. If this is a first attempt, a relatively simple procedure might be used, such as the development with the pupils of a record of the activities that have been carried out in the class. Or the mothers might be invited to a program held in the classroom during the class period. During a second semester a further approach can be made.

It is good to obtain administrative approval for any procedures that differ from those traditionally used in a school, in order that no difficulties or misunderstandings may arise. This is especially important in the area of school-community relations. The principal should be aware of what is taking place in his school and, with his support, the teacher will gain security and courage.

As was stated earlier in the chapter, the establishment of a good teacher-pupil-parent relationship is an important aspect of any class. For the success of a democratically functioning class, however, it is an imperative.

9

Emphasizing the Basic Skills

THE MAJOR PURPOSE OF THIS BOOK HAS BEEN TO describe methods of developing the attitudes and skills of democratic living—the skills of interpersonal and intergroup relationships, those which are classified under group processes, including the leadership function and participation in problem solving. This major purpose is made explicit here and elsewhere lest those who are critical of democratic methods and fear that anti-intellectualism is being glorified may be concerned when only one chapter out of ten is devoted to the academic essentials. The reader is reminded that what has been described relates primarily to classes designated as core, common learnings, general education, basic living, or unified studies, though it may not always have been specifically so designated. Although many of the methods can and should be used with other subjects, their application to such courses as mathematics, science, and languages has not been elaborated here. Since it has been implicit throughout that these are being taught, it seems only necessary to make explicit some of the methods that can be incorporated into the freer type of classroom organization described as relating to the communication skills—reading, writing, spelling, and oral discourse, instruction in which is usually brought together in the school subject of English. This will be followed by a brief summary of the social skills developed in learning to perform what Havighurst has termed the pupil's developmental tasks.

English, as a school subject, developed from the earlier English grammar, which in turn had superseded Latin grammar as a subject of emphasis in the secondary school curriculum. In later years, it has become a kind of miscellany including instruction in reading, writing, speaking, and the study of selected English and American classics, all generally taught with a grammatical undertone. The fact that traditional Latin grammar is not adapted to the vagaries of English usage has been emphasized by the linguists. There are many, however, who affirm that systematic instruction in formal grammar is what is needed, when what they actually mean is that children should be taught to speak and write standard English. In a well-developed program of the kind here described, continuing attention is given to this objective, and the means to attaining it are many, including direct instruction in rules and in language forms, whichever proves to be the most effective.

Reading

There can be no question concerning the importance of helping pupils develop proficiency in reading. There can be no question either concerning opportunities to use and improve the reading ability of boys and girls in a democratically functioning class. It is a skill used daily through reading from a wide variety of sources in order to find data to solve problems, as well as through frequent reading for enjoyment.

Research reading. As an example of a class in which no single textbook is used and in which the problems have grown out of the pupils' expressed concerns and interests, we can refer to the group described in Chapter 6. The problem selected was: *What preparations are being made to protect citizens in case of an atomic attack?* In its plan of work, this group listed the following as possible sources of information:

Library books: public library
               school library
               room library
Civil defense offices: city
                 state
                 national
Films: civil defense office
       audio-visual department of our school
Newspapers and magazines
Mr. Hadley, the science teacher

A mere glance at this plan shows that a considerable amount of reading will be necessary—books from the libraries, newspapers and magazines, materials from the civil defense offices, and without doubt Mr. Hadley will produce resources that must be read. In addition, the teacher will bring in as much source material as possible. "But," says the critic, "all pupils will not read all that material."

No, of course not. But they know what they are looking for, and they know they will be expected, not only by the teacher but also by their group, to do their part. The teacher's problem will not be to arouse interest in what comes next in the textbook, but to help pupils individually to develop the skills in which they are deficient, in order that they may solve the problem they have selected. The amount read by each member of the group will depend, as it does in any class, on his ability to read, his interest in the problem, the amount of time he has available outside of school, and on his study habits, as well as on his personal feeling of comfort and satisfaction in both his school and home life. It depends, too, upon his past educational experiences. Some pupils find the transition from teacher-directed study to self-directed study very difficult. As a consequence, they tend at first to read less than might normally be expected of them.

Since, however, most democratically operating classes are on a multiple-period basis, meeting anywhere from two to four periods each day, the teacher is aware of many of these factors, since he is far better acquainted with his pupils than is the teacher whose class meets only one period each day. If a part of each week is used for working on the research problem during class time, he can identify and assist pupils with faulty study habits, or those who, despite a class lesson on the *Readers' Guide,* still do not understand how to find magazine articles. By such observation or by reviewing pupils' Research Records[1] he can discover at a glance which ones are limiting their reading to one type of material, the encyclopedia, for example. From the record he can also see how little or how much is being read in the course of a week. He may discover that the boy who is reading little or nothing, and is the class behavior problem during research periods, is one who has never had to decide what to read but has always been told precisely what pages to study. It is often wise to do exactly this at the beginning, first making specific assignments, then giving him a choice of two sources, and, as his insecurity subsides, assisting him to find what he needs himself.

It is especially important that the reading level of each individual be determined. If recent data are not available in the school records, a reading test should be given to the entire class that will indicate where each pupil stands with respect to vocabulary, reading rate, and comprehension. Such a test may be repeated at the end of the year in order to measure growth in reading skills.

For those pupils who have reading deficiencies, the teacher should make every effort to obtain material that is at the level of their comprehension. This is not always easy to do, of course, since much of it, especially in a problem such as the one dealing with protection from atomic attack, is on an adult level. It is sometimes necessary, therefore, to work with a group when it is in the planning stage, in order to help in allocating to the slow reader that part of the problem which he is most likely to be able to handle. The pupil with high reading ability should, of

---

[1] See Chapter 6, p. 236.

course, be urged to take on the more difficult phases and to seek source materials on his own level of achievement.

Reading for enjoyment. In addition to research reading, another type of reading usually becomes a part of the week's program. This is reading for enjoyment and is sometimes called "free reading," because it is a period of time during which pupils select books of interest to them from the room library or the school library and read during the class period. These books are, of course, often taken home as well. The critic quickly raises a question at this point. "Are these books the classics which every pupil should read?"

This is, of course, an interesting question, because no one knows with certainty what classics every pupil should read—if there are any. One can hardly argue that those read "when I was in school" should necessarily be on the list. The traditional selections have been changed from time to time, and the original basis for selection seems to have been lost in obscurity. Many of the books that should be made available in the room library and the school library would properly be placed in the category of classics. However, many others would be claimed just as good reading for teen-agers, chosen from the lists prepared by city and state departments of instruction, and librarians who have made a study of juvenile literature. Many of the classics that are on the shelves, but that are not required reading, will be read and enjoyed without the pupils becoming aware that they "ought" to read them.

The educational objective of such a program is, of course, to encourage pupils to read in order to improve their reading, and to develop enjoyment in reading. In such a situation, which offers opportunity for guidance by the teacher, it is possible to assist a child to do a number of things:

1. To find books that are interesting to him.
2. To widen his field of interest by introducing him to new books.
3. To find books at his own level of reading ability.
4. To move from the short story to full-length books.

5. To raise his choice of reading to a more mature level, which for some would include the "classics."

It is recognized that the process of forcing pupils to read and study selected literary works sometimes opens their eyes to riches they had not realized existed. But it is equally certain that the same process has often killed what interest other pupils may have had. Is it not better to adapt, insofar as possible, to the wide differences in reading ability and literary development that are found in any class, and not discourage reading, but instead to open up for all those vistas which encourage further exploration?

To do this it is, of course, important that the teacher know the reactions of each pupil toward reading. Does he enjoy it? How many books of his own choice has he read during the past month? What kinds of books does he like? What are the names of the four last books he read? Does he like short stories? What magazines does he like? What magazines are taken regularly at home? How many books are in his home? With such data at hand, as well as a knowledge of his ability to read, a teacher is well equipped to start pupils on a reading program and to make the reading periods both profitable and enjoyable.

A full-fledged room library does not spring up over night. It can, however, be made to grow steadily over the years. As stated in an earlier chapter, the simplest method of obtaining funds is the assessment of a small fee, such as fifty cents per pupil each semester. When no textbook is required, this fee might be raised to one dollar. If, in addition, a school can appropriate a sum to start the library, so much the better. Many teen-age novels may be obtained in paper-backed editions, and, although these do not last as long as hard cover copies, many more of them may be purchased with a given amount of money. Furthermore, probably as the result of the influence of paper-backed novels in the corner drugstore, pupils will often read these when they refuse to touch their counterparts in what seems to them the larger, hard-cover editions.

A wide variety of books should be included in the room library, both fiction and non-fiction. These should be at many different levels of difficulty, for the poor reader must be able to find satisfying material and so must the pupil with very advanced reading ability. Topics that are selected frequently by pupils serve as partial guides in the selection of the non-fiction reference books to be purchased. In addition to these it is most helpful to have a set of encyclopedia, an atlas, a *World Almanac,* and dictionaries. It is also a good idea to include subscriptions to a number of magazines that will appeal to young people.[2]

Pupils should be free at all times to use books from the school library instead of, or in addition to, those in the room library. It is an excellent variation to borrow a large number of books from the school library and bring them into the classroom to supplement the room collection. Librarians are sometimes opposed to the development of room libraries, feeling that pupils are being limited to too small an assortment of books and that they will not make use of the school library facilities. However, where room libraries are properly used they are not limiting factors, but serve as an introduction to the much wider possibilities of the large library. Instead of using the school library less, pupils from such classes have been found to use the school and public libraries more than the average pupils.

In a double-period eleventh-grade core class working on pupil-selected problems in the field of American history, 29 out of a class of 32 used the school library as a source of material in a semester's time. In the same class, 28 out of 32 had gone to the public library for material at least once during the semester. This was in addition to their use of a fairly comprehensive room library of history books. A check on a comparable traditional American history class, using a textbook, showed that 6 out of a class of 28 had used the school library and 7 had used the public library during the semester.

If it is not possible to provide a room library, frequent use

---

2 Among those that serve a class well are: *Newsweek, U.S. News & World Report, Look, Life, Reader's Digest, Nature Magazine,* and *National Geographic.* For older classes *The Atlantic, Harper's,* and *Cavalcade* are good.

should be made of the school library. Especially at first, arrangements should be made for the entire class to go into the library in order that the teacher, who knows the particular problems of his boys and girls, may, with the assistance of the school librarian, help them to find books that are of interest to them. This means, of course, that the teacher must be fairly familiar with the books on the library shelves.

Methods of Stimulating reading. In every classroom some pupils quickly make their choice of books, settle down, and read. Others make no move toward the book shelves, apparently thinking that the longer they wait, the less time it will be necessary for them to hold a book. However, there are always some who go quite willingly to the shelves but cannot make up their minds which books to read. A pupil in this group often spends most of the period picking up one book after another, thumbing it, and placing it back on the shelf. He is not happy about the situation, but he doesn't know what to do about it.

Such pupils can apparently make no connection between the title and the probable contents of a book, even with the help of pictures. They cannot decide whether they will enjoy it or not. For the boy or girl to whom reading is not too great a pleasure anyway, this inability to guess whether it is an interesting book or not is extremely frustrating. And to many a teacher such indecision is equally frustrating. So he may say, not without a note of exasperation, "Just pick out a book and read it!" In some classes it is even true that, having taken a book that he finds he doesn't like, a pupil cannot return to the shelf and exchange it for another. There is hardly a more certain way of spoiling an otherwise good reading program.

Selecting a book is often a difficult problem even for an adult who thoroughly enjoys reading. But in a book shop the adult can at least read the synopsis on the book jacket and obtain a reasonable picture of the contents. In a schoolroom, the book jackets are usually removed, because they become torn and ragged within a few days. So there remains only the title, chapter titles that may or may not be helpful, and possibly a picture or two to give clues as to the contents. In a room library, there is no reason why the jacket synopsis cannot be cut from its surrounding material and pasted on the inside of the cover. The objection that teachers most often make to this procedure is that pupils copy from this in writing book reports. The question might well be raised as to whether books are only being read in order to write book reports. It would seem wiser to give pupils this help in selecting books and to find other methods of checking on the amount read.

The *Cumulative Reading Record,* published by the National Council of Teachers of English, is excellent for this purpose. For each book read, the record provides a 1¾ inch space in which to record a brief synopsis of the story, and a letter code for indicating how well the book was liked, and what was liked and disliked about it. A record of this sort allows the teacher to see at a glance the type of book a pupil is reading and the number he has read over a period of time.

In addition to recording the books each pupil had read on such a reading record, a ninth-grade class kept a chart of all books that were read. As a new book was read, the pupil listed it in a column at the left-hand side of a large sheet of ¼-inch cross-section paper. In a second column, the book was identified as to contents, for example, as *adventure, mystery, sports, animals,* and so forth. This was followed by a small gummed circle, either green, blue, or red. A green circle indicated that the reader had found the book very interesting, a blue circle that it was fair, a red circle that he had found it not interesting. No book could be recorded unless it had been read completely. As other pupils read the same book, each added his own colored circle. Thus the reactions of an ever-increasing list of readers were indicated. The book record was referred to by class members throughout the year and it became a rather dog-eared and disreputable looking sheet long before the end, but it never lost its usefulness.

Another class took time once a month to divide into pairs, each pupil describing to the other the book or books he had enjoyed most. The members of still another class reported orally on their favorite books, "selling" the books to their classmates, the measure of success being in terms of how many pupils read the book by the end of the semester.

In an effort to draw a group of non-readers into the reading circle, an eighth-grade class spent considerable time reading short stories and dramatizing them. The class was divided into small groups. Each group read a different story, selected the most outstanding incident, and prepared a dramatization. For this the non-readers were willing to read, and the average and good readers stretched themselves toward a good production.

A college-bound group of seven pupils in a twelfth-grade core class selected as its unit of study, *Some of the classics.* They spent the better part of the year reading and discussing among themselves books that were far above the level both of reading and understanding of most of their classmates. In the course of the year they asked for the assistance of the head of the English department as well as that of various English teachers and the drama teacher. It was an exciting experience for all of them.[3]

In any reading program it is necessary to start with such reading as pupils can handle successfully—even if it is only comic books. A show of shock or ridicule at such a situation is likely to close the door to any opportunity to work successfully toward improvement. For the good reader who is marking time on reading below his maturity level, the same warning holds. The motion forward is gradual and, unless it brings success and enjoyment to the pupil, he will not achieve the degree of proficiency in reading of which he is capable, nor will he obtain from the course what he has a right to expect.

Writing

"In my class each pupil must write a theme each week," says the critic. "Yours don't do this!"

---

[3] The following were read by one member of this group, and several others were not far behind: *Divine Comedy, War and Peace, Anna Karenina, Promises Men Live By, Thou Israel, The Mature Mind, The Masque of the Red Death, The Purloined Letter, The Tell-Tale Heart, Tales of a Wayside Inn, Hamlet, Julius Caesar.*

This may be an effective method of developing skill in writing when more judgment is used in selecting topics than in Stephen Corey's famous case of the poor scholar who had to write on "What a Daffodil Thinks of Spring." But there are ways to develop writing skills without resorting to a weekly exercise. The writing in the kind of program described in these pages is for a purpose, it is meaningful to pupils, and it is frequent. Let us look at the various activities in which pupils in such classes participate in order to estimate the amount of writing practice each one will have.

Relative to solving problems. While working on the solution to a problem, the members of the several groups have many writing experiences. The first of these comes in preparing a group plan of action. Suggestions are made orally and are written down by the recorder, whose copy is modified by the group members. As a result, it says what they want it to say. It is not at all unusual for one pupil to ask, "But is that what we mean?" or for another to object, "That sentence isn't clear. A week from now we won't know what we mean by it." Attention to clarity of expression continues, for when a plan is completed a copy is given to the teacher, who checks it for completeness, clarity, spelling, and organization and returns it to the group, where it is reviewed and corrected. Further attention to completeness and clarity comes as the result of difficulties of individual members in fulfilling their obligations. "But the plan didn't really say I was to do that. If the group wanted me to look that up we should have put it in words that said it exactly." Another time more care is taken in developing the wording of the group plan. And finally, at the time of evaluation of the finished product, the group checks its completed job against the plan. Among the evaluation statements will be some like these:

We didn't do the fourth part because we couldn't remember what we meant by it.

Jim did not do one of the things assigned to him because we wrote it down wrong and he didn't understand it.

Such realization of the importance of definiteness of expression leads to a kind of self-criticism that can well be expected to transfer to other situations.

Note taking itself is practice in writing, and one in which every pupil participates. If notes are taken on 3 by 5 inch index cards and a pupil is taught to make each card complete in itself,[4] it becomes necessary that he condense the material that he reads and put it into his own words. This must be a clear statement or its significance will be lost in a few days. He must know the meanings of words in the reference material or he cannot explain it in his own words. Thus, note taking involves reading, understanding, and clear writing. Since pupils frequently take fifty or sixty cards of notes on a problem, this constitutes a considerable amount of practice in the skill of writing.

At the completion of the oral presentation to the class, each pupil in the group is usually expected to write a report covering his findings on that phase of the problem on which he worked. In preparation for this report, the pupils learn to make outlines from their notes, which serve as a basis for the written report. The cards are organized according to the major points indicated by the subject headings on their note cards. These major points become the main divisions of the outline. Under each are listed all sub-points. Thus, a workable outline is developed from the pupil's own material.

A further step that is most helpful is the preparation of a rough draft of the written report, which is based on the outline the pupil has made. On this he can make corrections, changes, or additions. If these are brought into class, a number of things can be done with them that will be of assistance in writing a more satisfactory final draft. For example, pupils may have failed to mention their own reactions to what they have found, or any of their own experiences that relate to it. The first papers are likely to be rather dull citations from the sources, lacking in interest and originality. This deficiency can be identified by the pupils themselves by having them reread their first drafts and underline their

---

4 See p. 224.

own contributions to the paper. If this is the first written report, there will usually be little or nothing to underline, since, for many, such additions are a wholly new idea.

Time should then be taken to help pupils understand how they can make such reports their own. One method of doing this is to ask each child to read his own first page silently. Ask him to write the answers, on an extra sheet of paper, to the following questions:

What do you agree with on this page? Why?
What do you disagree with? Why?
What experiences have you had which support or refute the data you have obtained?
Have you heard other people talk about this? What did they say?

Using one or two papers as examples, the teacher can show how the answers to such questions may be worked smoothly into the body of the report. Everyone then attempts to do a similar thing with his own paper. With the teacher moving from desk to desk giving assistance wherever it is needed, pupils begin to see how they can combine their own knowledge and reactions with the words and ideas of others.

As a means of helping boys and girls become aware of their errors in writing, a class period can be spent in exchanging rough-draft papers. Each pupil checks the paper he has at hand for spelling, punctuation, capital letters, paragraphing, and grammar. He also indicates whether the opening and closing paragraphs seem to be satisfactory. All mistakes are certainly not caught by the reader. Learning to identify errors is necessarily gradual. But the experience of reading the papers of others tends to develop the ability to perceive errors and the habit of being critical, so that pupils prepare their own copy more carefully and become more alert to note their own mistakes. The final draft naturally has fewer mistakes as a consequence of this exchange.

Pupils can learn very early to prepare a simple bibliography of the materials they use in assembling their data. In the early secondary grades, it is sufficient to record the name of the book and the author, or, in the case of a magazine article, the name of the article, the author, the magazine, and the date. By the eleventh grade, however, complete data should be recorded in correct bibliographical form. Eleventh-graders should also know how and what to footnote, although in the younger classes this need not be over-emphasized.

Another kind of writing is also introduced. This is creative writing, which emphasizes self-expression as well as correctness. In many classes this is a very popular activity. Sometimes it is decided to have a *Writing Committee,* which selects topics from which class members may choose. In other classes, the game element can be introduced as a kind of challenge. Each pupil writes the name of a possible subject on a slip of paper and three of these are drawn from a hat, any one of which may be selected as a subject for writing. One such drawing produced such an unlikely array of topics as: an apple tree, a lump of sugar, and a hat with feathers. At other times, the class may give itself a greater challenge: to incorporate all three items into a story. With this kind of approach, one can almost see the imaginations of the pupils working, and when a combination such as a black umbrella, a spider web, and a black cat turns up, fabulous mystery stories spring into being. Another scheme, though certainly not a new one, is to read an exciting short story aloud to the point of climax, each member of the class then finishing it as he thinks best.

It is no doubt obvious that such assignments can go flat if they are made with an "Now today I want you to write about ——" attitude. But if generally accepted techniques of good teaching are employed, such procedures provide the opportunities for creativity that are needed—not creativity with a long face, and an ever serious air, but the kind that is fun and even exciting.

Meeting difficulties in writing. Pupils' written work should usually be corrected by the teacher and returned to the pupil. The word "usually" is used because there are some types of written expression which it seems wiser not to disturb with corrections or rewriting. Such, for example, are the autobiography and any personal file material, such as: *Myself as I See Myself,* or *Changes in Me Since September.* Pupils should know before writing these papers that, although they should write in their best form, they will not be graded beyond checking that the papers are in their files. Freed from the red-pencil and mark threat, pupils usually express themselves more openly concerning their lives and their thoughts.

Other written assignments, however, should be corrected and returned to the pupils. A teacher will find it helpful if, while correcting a set of papers he prepares a check-list to assist him in seeing the kinds of errors his pupils are making. There will be such items as: punctuation, capital letters, incomplete sentences, possessives, appositives, agreement of subject and verb, paragraphing, lack of clarity, spelling, and so forth. On this sheet he checks each error made, thus showing where the major difficulties lie.

An example of such a sheet is shown in Figure 31. Each vertical line represents an error. The errors made by one pupil are separated from those made by another by a short horizontal line. Wherever an unusual number of errors of one type is made by a pupil, a star and a number is placed on the record that refers to the name key at the bottom of the page. Thus, the record indicates both the errors that are being made repeatedly by an individual, and those that are being made by many pupils in the class.

The sample record was made by the teacher as the papers were read; therefore the items are not alphabetized, nor in any special order. It is possible, of course, to prepare forms for such recording of errors that would include all possible types in alphabetical order. But the data stand out just as clearly on a hand-written page.

Such a check-list serves as a basis for attacking the problems that are widespread in any one class and makes it unnecessary to spend time on matters with which pupils are already familiar and in which they make relatively few errors. But what is done

9B Error List		
Type of error	Number of errors	Number of pupils
Paragraphing — I-I-I-II-I-I-I-I-I-I	11	10
Tense — IIII-I-I	6	3
Plurals — II-I-I-I-I-I-I-II	10	8
Words in series — II-I-I-I-II-II-I-I-III	14	9
Sentences run together — III-卌-[#2 卌 III]-IIII-III-I-I-II-III-卌-II-II-II-III-I-III	48	16
Clarity — I-I-I-I-II-I-I-I	9	8
Punctuation — II-I-II-I-III-I-[#3 卌 卌]-III-III-I-I-I-III-II-卌	39	15
Possessives — II-II-I-I-III-II-I-I-II-I	16	10
Capital letters — [#1 卌 IIII]-II-II-I-II-卌-I-III-II-II	29	10
Dividing words at syllables — II-I-I	4	3
Abbreviations — I-I-I-II	5	4
Incomplete sentences — I-I-I-II-III-I	9	6
Appositives — III-I	4	2
Contractions — I-II-III	6	3
Quotation marks — II	2	1
#1 — Barbara #2 — Elizabeth #3 — Bill		

Figure 31. A record of errors in written composition.

about the corrections is the important thing. How are the pupils to learn from their mistakes?

A simple and helpful approach to the correction of an error characteristic of many pupils can be made through the use of the opaque projector, using examples taken directly from the pupils' papers. Sentences or paragraphs can be typed or written on cards or sheets of paper and inserted in the machine. The class members identify such errors as they are aware of in the projected excerpts, and the teacher assists in locating those that are not recognized. The grammatical reasons for the corrections, if any, are brought out, discussed, and either written or oral practice may be given in the standard usage. Many errors, of course, are idiomatic in nature, for which there is no more valid reason than that "we don't say or write it that way." Pupils also search their own papers for similar errors and make the corrections. There should, of course, be ample opportunity for them to ask questions.

At times the teacher works with small groups of pupils who have a common problem, paragraphing for example. At other times, an individual has difficulty with a phase of writing that is peculiar to him alone. He is given assistance without involving other pupils, as can be seen in Figure 32.

Written work such as research reports, current events reviews, film reviews, or other papers of this nature should be considered from two points of view—the form, or correctness of the writing, and the content. It has always seemed helpful to the writer to indicate to a pupil where he stands in both of these by assigning a separate grade to each of them, as well as indicating his errors in both phases of his writing in the body of the paper. It is quite possible that his writing is excellent but the content is weak. On the other hand, a pupil who has difficulty in writing may include a great deal of information and show evidence of clear thinking. Pupils should become increasingly aware of the fact that both content and form are important in writing.

The correcting of a paper should not be only a means of indicating errors. There can be nothing more disheartening to a pupil than page after page of red marks, each shouting more loudly than the last of errors. In almost every paper there are good points to be noted—a fine first sentence, capital letters all in place, neatness, an interesting or well-written paragraph, or improvement in sentence structure or spelling. Such notations

Figure 32. Help for the individual with special problems.

should be generously included, perhaps in a few sentences at the end, or in the margins. A pat on the back often goes much farther than criticism.

All papers written by a pupil should be filed in a folder to which he has access at any time. Before writing a major paper it is good to have boys and girls look at their previous products in order to remind themselves of earlier errors and to avoid similar ones in the present paper. Such a file of each pupil's work also serves to help both pupil and teacher to estimate progress.

In what other ways do pupils have opportunity to develop skill in writing? Many write letters requesting materials to be used in their study of problems. Others prepare dramatizations or radio scripts as a means of presenting data to the class. All write evaluations of various activities—of a group presentation, a business meeting, a field trip, a film, a discussion of a film or of the week's activities. Records are kept of daily class activities and of group activities. Requests are written to people whose help the class would like to have. Thank-you notes are written. In all such situations the writing must be the best of which the pupils are capable. All of them are learning situations.

Spelling

In a class in which there are no prescribed units of work, there is probably no prescribed list of words that pupils must be able to spell. But correct spelling is a part of good writing and so cannot, and should not, be ignored. There are a number of means by which pupils' spelling may be improved, ways that are more effective than the traditional spelling lesson. There should, of course, be continuous emphasis on accurate spelling whenever words are written—in note taking, on the chalkboard, in letters, in the recorder's minutes, in project reports, and in creative writing. Quite early in the term, preferably immediately following the return of the first corrected papers, time should be set aside to help each pupil start his own word list, which will be added to throughout the year. Such a list may be kept in his notebook where it will be at hand at all times. It includes those words, now correctly spelled, that he has previously misspelled. For some words, such as *receive* and *believe,* it helps to have pupils underline the difficult spots. A pupil-pupil check on these words can be made from time to time, pupils exchanging their lists in pairs and taking a written "test" of their ability to spell the words on their own lists as pronounced by their mates.

The room should have as part of its equipment a number of dictionaries, in order that class members may have assistance at hand at all times. Also, if possible, each pupil should carry, as part of his daily classroom supplies, a small pocket edition of a standard dictionary.

Interest in spelling is often increased by methods of word study that look toward increasing pupil vocabularies. A tenth-grade class developed a very effective method that grew out of the interest of some of its members in learning new words. It was decided by the class that, during the weeks spent on research, each member of a group would be responsible for acquainting all others in the group with any new words discovered. When the group made its presentation to the class, a summary list of important new words that would be used in the oral reports was duplicated, a copy being given to each class member. Opposite each word was its definition. Each group held itself responsible for knowing the pronunciation and meaning of any word used in the oral presentation. The interest in words became intense, and the pupils almost made a hobby of their activity, treating new words as carefully and fondly as a stamp collector might handle a new stamp.

Oral communication

There is much more opportunity for oral communication in a democratically functioning classroom than in the traditional class. Some of this is highly informal, for example, the friendly, casual talk before and after class, or the gay chatter at social events. Some is much more structured, as in a business meeting, or in a group's presentation of data to the class. In between these are many activities that involve communication between pupils —the give and take of ideas within small groups, class discussions following the showing of a film, or the periods set aside for discussion of class problems or of topics that pupils are eager to talk about.

The major purpose of presenting many opportunities for oral expression, either informal or formal, is to develop the pupil's ability to talk to and with individuals or a group with poise and ease, and to express his ideas clearly, so that he is understood.

In the traditional classroom, the pupil's recitation is often stilted, partly because of stage fright and partly because he knows that what he says will be judged critically by the teacher. On the other hand, some progressive teachers who are in the *"laissez-faire"* rather than the "democratic" category are inclined to think that pupil chatter in itself is educative. The latter has its place, of course, as a process of developing friendly relations and group acceptance. In an earlier chapter, the importance of establishing a classroom climate within which pupils feel secure and at ease was discussed. Without this feeling of safety, free and open discussion cannot take place. But communication cannot stop here if pupils are to learn. By far the largest percentage of class discussion should relate to problems in the process of being solved or questions that are under consideration, and facts must be presented that bear on these problems and questions. Perhaps the most important point of all is that any question considered should deal with an area in which pupils feel some real concern. The techniques elaborated in this volume contribute directly to this objective and can be used to bring such topics into the open for consideration. If class discussions in general are not functioning well, if only a small number of pupils participate, a teacher will do well to ask himself the following questions. Are the pupils hesitant about expressing themselves because of a fear of being laughed at by their peers, or of saying things that will not be approved by the teacher? Are the discussion questions poorly chosen and of no real interest or concern to the pupils?

A film, for example, that is to be used as a springboard for discussion must be selected with care. It must be one that raises real questions or presents situations that stimulate pupil thinking. It should be previewed, and when brought into class should be introduced in such a manner that the thinking of the pupils has a common starting point.

In a tenth-grade class, some rather distinct cleavages were apparent between three groups of pupils, each of which had been in a different class the year before. Each group held firmly to the idea that its method of operation had been the only right one. No group would give an inch, and life in the classroom was fast edging toward an explosion. The teacher decided to use the film, *Boundary Lines*,[5] as a possible lead to discussion of the class problem.

---

5 McGraw-Hill Book Company, Text-Film Dept.

There are a number of "boundary lines" that could be con sidered as the result of witnessing this film—lines between races or religious groups, or political groups, or nationality groups, or age groups, or the lines between the three groups in the class. The teacher gave no indication, however, of the fact that he hoped to lead the discussion toward consideration of the class difficulty. It was far too touchy a subject to bring into the open in this manner and the teacher felt sure that no discussion would result if it were mentioned at this point.

He introduced the film by saying that the picture was a kind of abstract production, not using actual people at all, and that he thought the class would enjoy figuring out its meaning. He explained that it dealt with the imaginary lines that people in the world draw between themselves, for example, the line many people draw between the yellow race and the white. He asked them to list, as they watched the picture, the many boundary lines that can come between people, and to try to determine the results of these in the world.

There was plenty to talk about, for the film proved decidedly stimulating. In the discussion, none of the three class groups was threatened, since the problem was seemingly about the world outside of the classroom. Gradually the teacher turned the discussion toward the school. Were there lines between groups in the school? Yes, of course. There were those with cars and those without, those who worked after school and those who didn't, those of one social group and those of another. They saw and expressed quite frankly the effects of these "boundary lines." When the teacher finally moved into the area of the classroom itself, the class was ready to talk about its own problem. And talk they did! For three days of two periods each! But they managed to look at, and to break, their own boundary lines. Almost every pupil in the class participated in the discussion, because it had meaning for him. Many other lines were broken during those three days—lines of fear of saying what they thought, and fear that their ideas weren't as good as someone else's. It was of such vital importance that no one could afford to miss a chance to say what he thought.

Some classes are eager for discussions and set aside a day every week or two for this purpose. An eleventh-grade class developed a list of topics, each pupil turning in the titles of one or more subjects that he felt would be good for class discussion. The pupils felt that there were many things that they would very much like to spend a period or two on, but would not want to work on as a regular, full-length unit. Some of these, however, later became areas for concentrated study, the discussion having opened doors so that pupils saw their possibilities. The completed list contained fifty-four subjects, a few of which were as follows:

Teen-age drivers vs. adult drivers
City council decisions
Effect of expressways on the city
The place of the United States in the United Nations
Meaning of the symbols around the school building
Negro-White problems
Military service

The class soon found that discussions were being based almost entirely on opinion, and that it was very difficult to draw any accurate conclusions from them, since factual data were lacking. A change was then made in the approach to the discussion period. The topic to be considered was selected by class vote at a business meeting at least five days before the discussion was to be held. A committee of four was appointed by the chairman, the members of which were responsible for collecting a reasonable amount of accurate data on the subject chosen. The four also served as leaders in the class discussion. A different committee was in charge each time. The method proved to be highly satisfactory.

The use of current happenings can also serve as a basis for classroom discussion. A method used in a ninth-grade class served a number of purposes in addition to giving pupils something worth-while to talk about. A current events discussion was scheduled one day every two weeks and, instead of using the usual classroom papers or magazines devoted to current events, the class decided to select topics for discussion from the daily newspapers. One section of the class selected the area of national happenings, one chose city affairs, another state affairs, and another foreign events. It was agreed that articles selected should generally not include murders, robberies, or events of a purely sensational nature.

Each pupil selected an article that he felt was important, cut it out of the newspaper, and pasted it on a sheet of paper. Next to it he wrote a review of the article in his own words. He was responsible for being able to talk about the article in class and for helping to lead the discussion about it. Thus, practice in reading, writing, and discussion were involved in the procedure, as well as what was perhaps more important, the development of interest in public affairs.

The weekly business meeting is another opportunity for active verbal participation. The plan of work for the following week is determined; committee reports are made, discussed, and acted upon; plans for social events or field trips are worked out both by committees and by the class as a whole. The activities carried on in a business meeting require precise wording. The social committee that reports that it "guesses about fifty cents" will cover the cost of transportation is soon set back on its heels. Is it fifty cents or isn't it? The individual who says, "I make a motion that we vote," soon sees that this only leads to voting to vote, which is not what he intended. He begins to learn to say what he means, for example, "I make a motion that we use the film."

A tenth-grade class, in establishing rules covering the election of officers, decided that the maximum number of nominations that could be made for any office would be six. It then proceeded to say that the nominations could not be closed until the maximum number had been made. In the following election, all went well until nominations were being made for secretary. Only three people were nominated. No more nominations were forthcoming, yet the rule stated that the list could not be closed until there were six. The class was upset, because they had meant that the nominations could not be closed until the maximum number of six had been made *unless there were no more nominations.* This experience taught them to watch the effect of words on actual situations. Nothing was pushed through hurriedly after that. Someone always said, "Let's wait a minute. Does it cover every situation?" or, "Does it say what we mean?"

Quite frequently a class problem serves as a stimulus for discussion, giving pupils an opportunity to develop ability to express their ideas to one another in an everyday situation, one that has meaning and importance to every boy and girl in the class. There is frequently more active participation in such a discussion than in any other kind. Through such experiences pupils increase their ability to communicate rationally with their fellows. An example of discussion relative to such a problem follows.

It was the second week of school when Jack came to Miss Goddard, teacher of the eleventh-grade core class, and asked whether it would be possible for him to become a member of the class. He had had only a semester's core work in the ninth grade and then had moved out of the city, thus having had no further experience in core. Now he was back and was eager to be a member of a core class. The teacher was dubious, since it was against the department's policy to accept a pupil in an upper grade unless he had had a full year's core experience in the ninth grade. On the other hand, in talking with him, she felt that Jack could well be an asset to the class.

She hesitated, however, to make the decision. As far as possible she had always asked her class to help in making decisions that affected them. She knew that the boy was known to at least some of the members of the group. When the class met in business meeting the following day she told them of the situation, and of her own inability to reach a decision without their help. The following is a record of the discussion as well as Miss Goddard could reconstruct it from her notes.

NAN

I think we should accept him. As I remember him I think he's all right.

JOHN

He certainly would be a help to us. He isn't the kind of fellow who sits back and says nothing.

KATHY

I don't know him, but do you suppose he's changed any from what he was like in the ninth grade?

DENNIS

Of course he's changed some. We've certainly changed, haven't we? We don't even think the same as we did then.

JIM

Sure. He probably *has* changed some and we would be taking a big chance having him in here.

RALPH

We're taking a chance! How about *him?* Seems to me he's taking a big chance too. He's thinking of those of us that he knew as being just the same as we were in the ninth grade, and we're not.

BILL

You're right. We're not the same. We've moved a long way ahead this last year and we want to keep on moving ahead, not be stopped by someone who hasn't lived through things with us.

NORINE

But, Bill, we'll probably stop anyway, and even fall backwards, just the way we did last year. But we saw last year that we could always move ahead again and each time we went ahead a little farther than we had reached the time before. I don't think having Jack come in will make any difference.

BILL

Well, I do.

MARGARET

It seems to me that taking him in *may* set us back, but, like Norine said, we'll move still farther ahead because we've learned to accept a strange person. That's important in life, isn't it?

GARY

Why?

JOE

Don't be silly. When we get on a job, we'd better know how to get along with new people or we aren't going to be worth much.

HELEN

I agree with Marge and Joe.

GARY

I don't.

BILL

Every time we start to do something we'll have to take time to explain it to him. He'll be new to everything. That's a waste of time.

TEACHER

Is there a way around this part of the problem?

KATHY

Of course there is. The Ways and Means Committee can take time right at the beginning to explain to him how we are organized and how we do things.

LARRY

Or maybe the class officers could do it.

BILL

And then what? He'll want to change things.

LARRY

I don't see that that is necessarily true. But so what? He may be good and *our* ideas may not look as wonderful as we thought they were. But isn't it a good thing to look at new ideas?

PETE

It won't hurt us, that's sure. But I don't think he'll try to take over the way Bill thinks he will.

BILL

He will, don't worry. I've seen his kind. Didn't John say he isn't the kind to sit back and say nothing?

PETE

Bill, did you know Jack when he was here before?

BILL

No, and I don't want to.

MARY

Bill, you have no right to make that kind of a statement. You've just built him up in your mind as a certain kind of person whom you don't like and he probably isn't like that at all. You aren't even giving him a chance.

SAM

Miss Goddard, if it doesn't work, can we get rid of him?

TEACHER

What do you think?

SAM

Well, it doesn't seem to me we ought to get stuck with him if we shouldn't like him.

TEACHER

If the class decides it doesn't like *you,* should we ask *you* to leave?

SAM

Well . . . well . . . no.

TERRY

But that's different, Miss Goddard. Sam belongs, but Jack's an outsider.

MARGARET

But our class represents a democracy. We don't just throw people out because we don't like them. We have to learn how to get along with them.

FRANK

Marge is right. In our country we don't say it's just for us. We let other people come in and learn our ways and take part in things. Why shouldn't we do it in our class?

BETTY

That's right. And I've found out too that there are a lot of people I think I'm not going to like, but after I've worked with them a while I change my mind. When I get to know them, I find they are O.K. and I like them. It seems to me we ought to be willing to give Jack a chance.

MARGARET

I think this could be like an experiment to us. We can try ourselves out and see how honestly democratic we are. It would be like a test of ourselves.

DENNIS

I think you've got something. It's a way to prove things to ourselves.

TEACHER

What things do you think this would prove?

NAN

I think it would prove how well we've learned to get along with people—not just us—but new people.

MARY

I think it would prove—well—that we could face up to a hard problem.

JOE

Maybe it would show us whether we were strong enough to take in another person without following him blindly and without making him follow us blindly. I mean it would test how well we could accept new ideas and how well we could help him see what we've been thinking.

RALPH

Marge said this could be like an experiment. I don't like the idea of an experiment. I think it would be an experience, and a good one for us to have.

JOHN

If we ask him to come in we can't ever blame him for things that go wrong with our class.

TEACHER

Who would we blame?

JOHN

Us. All of us. Because one person can't throw a class unless it lets him do it.

TERRY

Well, I was opposed to having him come in, but I'm willing to go along with it if the class thinks it will work.

JIM

I guess the arguments in favor of having him come in are better than the ones for keeping him out.

BILL

Mark my words, it's dangerous, but if everyone else says O.K. who am I to hold up the business?

It was decided by the class that a three-quarters majority would constitute agreement. Secret, unsigned ballots were made out. The result was twenty-six in favor of accepting Jack into the class and five opposed.

You will perhaps be interested to know that Jack became a very happy and active member of the class. He was accepted graciously by most members when he entered, and little by little made friends with his classmates. Although no open discussion was ever held concerning the results of their decision, as the months went by many pupils expressed to the teacher their satisfaction at having him in the group. Even Bill eventually admitted that he had been wrong in his estimate of the new member.

Correcting grammatical errors in speech. Helping pupils become aware of their errors in speech and to correct their faulty habits of expressing themselves orally is far more difficult than correcting mistakes in writing. On the written page it is not a face to face correction, it does not carry a critical tone of voice, and, above all it does not stop the flow of ideas, since on the written page the ideas have already been expressed. The color that rises in a pupil's face when he is corrected as he makes a mistake in speech, and the halting words that follow, tell what is happening. And yet, someway, he must be helped to improve.

To initiate an attack on the major grammatical errors being made, one teacher made a list of those he heard in class over a period of several days such as:

Him and me went skating.
They ain't got no television.
Bill he went out.
My father learned me how to do it.

The errors were discussed, reasons for their inaccuracy explained, and the list, together with the corrections, posted on the bulletin board. The class then watched for similar errors, taking a few minutes each day to check the mistakes made during the period. The list grew by leaps and bounds and, being a very human individual, the teacher was found in error several times too.

One rule was strictly adhered to: No one interrupted another to correct his mistake while he was speaking. In the later discussion period it might be said that Jim used a double negative and the sentence be repeated, but Jim was not stopped at the moment of the error. Although improvement might be slower this way, the teacher and class felt that a pupil should express his ideas without interruption.

Pupils became more careful of their use of words and little by little became aware of many of their own slips of tongue, frequently correcting their own errors. Care was taken to keep this activity on a good-humored basis, without making pupils feel guilty when mistakes were made. No checks were placed against them in the class-book for errors, nor did they receive unfriendly criticism from either teacher or classmates. This technique was followed throughout the semester and the class worked enthusiastically for improvement.

In another class, a committee, membership in which rotated each week, watched for errors, and, during a designated class period, wrote these on the board for consideration. In still another class, pupils worked in pairs, each trying to catch the errors made by his partner as the usual class activities were in progress. The pairing was changed frequently in order to avoid a situation in which a pupil was paired permanently with one who seldom recognized a mistake, or one whose personality was such that, despite all efforts to smooth the edges, having him catch an error was an unpleasant experience for the one who made it.

Sometimes the only way to convince a pupil that he makes serious grammatical errors is to make a tape recording of a report that he presents to the class and play it back for him so that he may hear himself. Neither cutting the tape nor playing it back should be done in front of the class unless it is done for all, or at least a large number, of the class members. If this is to be done for only one or two pupils, the reports can be repeated at other times away from the class. Such a recording is often a great surprise to a pupil and serves as an incentive toward some degree of improvement.

Although no specific evaluation techniques were employed, any more than they are in the traditional classroom, it seems reasonable to conclude that the recognition of errors and the desire to correct them that such techniques develop is of definite advantage.

Social skills

It doesn't help much if a pupil has learned how to write or how to speak correctly but, when he faces a practical situation, doesn't know what to say or when to say it. As has been indicated earlier in this chapter, in the informal kind of class organization here described, the everyday situations that are met in the classroom are used to provide instruction in the writing and speaking skills. Such situations must, however, be recognized and dealt with appropriately both from the standpoint of academic skills and of social skills.

Although it may be argued that the social amenities should be learned at home, the fact is that many homes do not provide this instruction, and when they do, it is often not the kind that is helpful in a group of thirty or thirty-five young people. The havoc that is sometimes wrought at children's birthday parties bears ample testimony to the need for supplementary instruction.

Then too, from another angle, employers sometimes complain that young employees are often competent enough on the job, but they do not have the "attitude" or "personality" that is needed. When analyzed, this often means that these young people simply do not seem to know how to meet people, fellow employees or prospective customers, and relate to them successfully. If they do not know, it means that they have probably had no opportunity to learn; they have not had experiences in which they practiced these important skills.

No one seems to question the propriety of a teacher saying to a pupil, "You must apologize at once or go to the principal's office," or to a class, "I was ashamed of the way you behaved when Mr. X spoke to us," or even to bring stronger sanctions to bear when pupils "talk back" or are guilty of "insubordination." Whether such undesirable pupil behavior should be classified as lack of "manners," or something more fundamental, it is certain that basic patterns of social response develop as a consequence of school as well as home experiences, and that instruction and practice is often more effective in developing desirable behavior than punishment. Some of the classroom situations that provide opportunities for such instruction and practice will be briefly described in the following pages.

Guests in the classroom. On many occasions the class has visitors. They may be from other schools or from other cities. Parents from time to time spend an hour in the classroom. Or perhaps a fellow teacher has agreed to serve as a resource person, or it may be a supervisor, or an administrator of the school. Some have been invited and some have not. But all must be taken care of graciously while they are in the classroom.

The most frequent visitor is a resource person from whom help has been requested. The invitation to such a person may, of course, be extended by the teacher, but the occasion provides excellent opportunity to help pupils learn how to make such requests themselves, either in writing or orally. If it is decided that a letter is to be written, class time should be taken to develop a general understanding of what such a letter should contain, and its proper form. The writing itself may be done by the small group that is asking for help, or by the social chairman with one or two to assist him if the resource person is to serve the entire class. If the invitation is to be given orally, a list can be quickly developed of the points to include in making such a request. The wording can often advantageously be tried out in class sociodrama style.

Taking care of the guest on his arrival is equally important, whether he is a resource person, a parent, or a casual visitor who may wish to see what the class is doing. In some classes there is a *Guest Committee,* membership on which rotates from week to week in order to provide experience for as many pupils as possible. In other classes the chairman and assistant chairman serve as the welcoming group.

When a guest arrives, it is frequently the teacher who must take the first step. This is especially true if the visitor is a stranger, perhaps brought to the room by a member of the administration. But he must be very sure that if a Guest Committee has the responsibility for taking care of visitors, that this group is not by-passed. He should immediately introduce the guest to the committee and step back. The introduction of the guest to the class should be made by a member of the committee and, of course, the seating of the visitor should be the committee's responsibility. A member of this group should also be ready to explain to him the current activities of the class, so that he is not in the dark as to what is taking place. If no such committee exists, the visitor should be introduced to the class chairman, who, in turn, introduces him to the class. In this situation, a class officer, perhaps the assistant chairman, should be responsible for explaining the activities to the visitor.

If a particular group has invited someone into the room to give assistance to its members, it is quite likely that these pupils will feel responsible for handling the necessary introductions. In this case, the situation would involve, in addition, personal introductions of the group members to the resource person.

Progress in learning to make introductions properly and with ease depends to a considerable degree upon the class room atmosphere that has been developed. If a pupil feels that, although it is better to do it correctly, it is not a disgrace if, in the excitement of the moment, he introduces Miss Durand to Bill Knight instead of Bill Knight to Miss Durand, he will be willing to try again.

If, in addition, time is given in class to the problem of introductions, they will gradually cease to be so difficult. A tenth-grade class, after an experience of stumbling over the introductions of a group of visitors and class members, assigned to a committee of four the task of collecting all information possible on the subject. This was reported and discussed thoroughly in class. Then a mimeographed paper was prepared containing a series of names in pairs. Space was left after each pair, and pupils wrote the words they would use to introduce the people in each pair to one another.

Miss Jones and Mr. Smith
Miss Jones and Mrs. Brown
Mrs. Wills (age 70) and Mrs. Mathews (age 25)
Mary White (age 15) and Ruth Thiele (age 16)
Jim Jarand (age 17) and Fred Mentz (age 16)
Jim Jarand and Mary White
Mary White and your mother
Mary White and your father
Fred Mentz and your mother
Fred Mentz and your father
Miss Jones and Mary White

This, of course, was followed by a discussion of the different situations as well as many that were not included in the list.

A practice session was held in a ninth-grade class. Thirty cardboard signs were prepared by a committee, each bearing a name and an age. Half of them were male and half female names. These were spread out reverse side up, male names on one side of the desk, female names on the other. Three pupils at a time came to the desk. Two of them drew cards, girls drawing from the female pack, and boys from the male. These were held up for the third pupil to see and he made the introduction in terms of the information on the cards, the class checking his accuracy. After each introduction, the cards were replaced and the stack was reshuffled, thus making a large number of combinations possible. This was an exciting activity and certainly one in which pupils learned to adjust quickly to different situations.

The need for saying *thank-you* graciously arises whenever a resource person gives assistance to a class, or perhaps when a parent loans materials to a group. It may be that a verbal *thank-you* as the person is leaving is sufficient. But if there has been any special assistance in terms of time and materials, a note should be written. Such a letter should not be sent until it is in good form, words are correctly spelled, and the message is well stated.

Interviews. Since pupils frequently go to people outside of the classroom for assistance in collecting data concerning the problem on which they are working, care should be taken that they know how to conduct these interviews in as orderly and courteous a manner as possible. The use of sociodrama in relation to planning satisfactory methods of interviewing was discussed in Chapter 6. The important points in requesting an interview, introducing oneself to the person being interviewed, asking for the desired information, and a courteous thank-you, can all be acted out. Proper dress for such an interview should also be discussed. Ability to handle these aspects of interviewing may well be considered as important as the data obtained from the interview.

Social events. Parties, hikes, picnics, and skating parties may seem to be outside of the realm of classroom consideration. However, in classes such as have been described in the preceding pages, where there is a feeling of friendship and belonging between the class members, it is not at all unusual for pupils to want an extension of these classroom satisfactions into out-of-class time. There is, in fact, a need for such activities, for a party can serve many purposes that are sought in vain in the classroom.

It is often at a party during which the teacher takes an active part in the games and fun that he really becomes accepted by the class. And only at a party or similar event can a teacher discover the social maturity of his pupils. How do they handle themselves with respect to their peers when general school controls are off? It is sometimes quite a shock to a teacher to see how little he really knows about his pupils.

There is Gail, for example, who is so quiet in class, apparently so shy and withdrawn that she seems to be making no friends at all. But here you see that she is an outstanding dancer and a number of the boys are dogging her footsteps.

And there is Marilyn, who is always helpful in small groups and has excellent suggestions in business meetings and in class discussions.

But she is lost in the fast, non-academic tempo of a party. She sits by herself most of the evening, finding it difficult to join in the fun.

The boys are not as ready as the girls for the social side of group life. In class they seem willing to work with the girls, but here many of them pull away into a corner by themselves rather than take part in the activities.

Then there is Mary, who does fair work, but never impressed her teacher with her ability to solve a problem. But here someone was needed to assemble the refreshments, plan a way to distribute the dishes, silver, and food, and organize a committee so that the job would be well done, and it was Mary who did it, and very effectively.

Probably the most important value of a party lies in the fact that friendships are cemented during an afternoon or evening of fun and laughter, and, as a result, the class is a far more cohesive group than before.

In today's sophisticated world, where many very young teenagers have already experienced social events of a kind in which an earlier generation had no part until they were much older, a party is not always easy to plan. So often the only suggestions for activities are food, which does not lose its appeal in any generation, and a record player and records in order that they may dance. Yet most parties of tenth-graders or younger children fall to pieces if this is all that is planned. Many do not dance. Boys, by and large, will not ask the girls to dance. So we find groups on the sidelines having no fun at all, or, if some of them are having fun, it is totally apart from the rest of the guests.

For a first social activity it has always seemed to the writer that it is best to have a classroom party. In this way one can be assured that almost every pupil will be present, the time available will not be long enough for boredom, and there will be no problem of transportation, which is often a major consideration. The party should be carefully planned, a social committee taking the lead in arranging activities and determining what refreshments are possible. However, this group should not "run" the party. Committees of volunteers should be set up for the many jobs that have to be done—buying paper plates and napkins, ordering food, setting up the refreshment table, serving the food, making preparations for the different games, moving the furniture, and, of course, for clean-up.

The activities should fit the classroom. Team games, many of which can be played with pupils seated, are excellent, such as the gloves-and-gum-in-the-bag game, in which sticks of gum and a clean pair of cotton gloves are placed in a paper bag. Each member of the team must put on the gloves, find a stick of gum in the bag, unwrap it, put it into his mouth, and put the wrapper and gloves back in the bag before passing it on to the next person. For each game the teams should be changed in order that pupils have an opportunity to be with a large number of their classmates. Care must be taken that there is no lag between games. It is a good idea for the teacher to have an idea or two for extra games up his sleeve. They may be needed.

Most teen-agers will respond to a games party and have a wonderful time, but many hate to plan games because they are afraid of appearing childish. If a classroom party can be made a huge success, later parties, of whatever variety they may be, will be easier to plan, because pupils will now be willing to do more than bring a record player.

A class party should be evaluated the next day by the class members, though this will not usually take very long. Were they satisfied with the party? Did they have fun? Was it well planned? Were all jobs well taken care of? What can be done better next time? A brief class discussion will serve the purpose.

When there is pressure for a party outside of school, in a pupil's home, for example, it is necessary to discuss with the class the differences between a room party and a home party and what would be expected of them as guests in a home. A tenth-grade class listed the following items as things that would have to be done in a home:

1. Everyone would have to be introduced to the parents.
2. You would have to take good care of things in the house.
3. Everything would have to be left in good order. For example, all

dishes would have to be washed, rubbish placed in containers, and furniture put back in place.

4. You can't tear around a person's home.

5. Everyone should talk to the parents during the evening.

6. The hostess should be thanked when you leave.

7. A thank-you letter would have to be written for the class after the party.

The teacher added four rules that she said they would have to be willing to abide by if it was to be a class party, and if she was to be responsible for the group for the evening. There was to be no smoking, no drinking, no sitting in cars, no loitering outside of the house. Although these would affect very few in the tenth grade, she felt that these points should be clear and a decision for or against a home party should be made with these in mind. The seven points listed by the pupils, plus the four stated by the teacher, served as a guide line for many enjoyable parties in the years these boys and girls were together, a number of which were held in the teacher's home.

There are many social niceties that disturb boys and girls. One that has always amused the writer has been their aversion to using guest towels placed in the lavatory for their use. Anything else was used—a handkerchief, a slip, toilet tissue, a family towel, but *not* the small guest towels. Even after explaining their use, the result was still zero. The situation was not conquered until a paper towel was found that had a picture of fish swimming across, and the words:

> Little fishes are all wet;
> They haven't used a towel, I'll bet.

That did it. They used them.

Parent night. There are many other events that give opportunities for developing social sensitivity and so increase pupils' social skill. A program that a class presents for the parents, for example, must be more than a fine program. There are invitations to be planned and written. A welcoming speech must be prepared. The content of this can be planned by the class even though it will probably be written by one individual and presented by one. On the appointed afternoon or evening, each pupil has the responsibility for seeing to it that his parents meet his classmates, their parents, and the teacher. To make it easier, name tags can be made ahead of time and given to parents as they arrive. These are of great assistance when, in the confusion of making an introduction correctly, a boy or girl forgets a name.

With some groups it is even good to discuss ahead of time possible topics of "small talk" that they can use in talking to parents during the time refreshments are being served, as well as before and after the program. Because such a program is usually presented in the classroom, and because the pupils know each other so well, there is a feeling of warmth and friendliness that makes it much easier for them to carry out the social amenities than with a large and strange group of people.

Christmas carols. At Christmas time, too, there are often special activities that call for a knowledge of what to say and do. Each year the oldest core class in one school sings Christmas carols in a convalescent home. This has become a traditional event, each class adding a bit to the ideas of past groups. There is a Santa Claus or a Miss Christmas Carol, and there are candle bearers. The pupils bring a huge basket of oranges and a basket of home-baked cookies and soft candies that have been put in individual cellophane bags and tied with red ribbons, and a small, gaily wrapped gift for each patient. These are given out personally to each one.

The singing is not always wonderful, but as they walk through the Home, girls in dark skirts, white blouses, and big red bows, and boys in dark trousers, white shirts, and green bows, tiny bells jingling as they walk, they are youth personified and are welcomed from bed to bed as they sing their way through the rooms. Such a group is shown in Figure 33.

In this situation, too, boys and girls learn how to handle themselves socially. The request for permission to visit must be made. Gifts that will be fitting for such patients must be found, and, of course, there is the question of what to say to the patients. Most

Figure 33. Christmas carols.

pupils have never been in a convalescent home and have probably given little thought to the aged. In fact, it is necessary to spend some time in preparing them for what they will see, in order to cushion their emotions and give them understanding. It is a moving experience to see a big, strong, seventeen-year old boy shyly move out of line as the group is leaving a room and bend over a tiny, tired old man and shake hands with him and wish him a Merry Christmas. Others follow his example and later, as he stands near you he says, "I'm *glad* I came. I'm *glad* I could wish him a Merry Christmas. It felt good."

One year three little old ladies followed the class from room to room. But, as the group climbed the stairs to the second floor, they fell behind. They couldn't keep up. But the teacher, watching from below, saw three boys turn back and come downstairs again. Each tucked a little old lady's arm through his and slowly they all mounted the stairs together, satisfaction and pride written on all six faces.

Another class may turn to a different activity, deciding to bring food and toys to an unfortunate family. The delivery of these will probably be made by a committee of pupils. The entire class, however, helps in deciding what is best to say to the people who come to the door, how to present the gift graciously, and how to take leave.

Class study of social behavior. One of the problems for serious study most frequently selected by teen-age pupils deals with questions of social behavior. Such questions as what to do on different kinds of dates, how to order a meal properly in a public dining room, what to talk about when with a person you do not know very well, how to take care of a guest in your home, these and many more are of real concern to many young people. It may well be that adults often misjudge juvenile rudeness, thoughtlessness, and even downright misbehavior, and that the difficulty really lies in the fact that the young person just didn't know what to say or do in a complex social situation.

Out of a unit centering around such problems may develop any number of activities in which pupils can try out their newfound knowledge. In one class, a group of seven attended a concert and a play in order to see how adults conducted themselves in such situations, as well as to try their own wings. In another class, it was decided that the class would go out to dinner together to a good, but not too expensive, public dining room. Out of the class of thirty-two, nineteen attended. This brought to light questions concerning the proper use of knife, fork, and spoon, correct handling of a napkin, manner of addressing the waitress, tipping, care of coats, and the special attention the boys would give to the girls. This illustration reveals that the pupils were not from the socially élite families, but many of our young people are not. For them such a party provides the opportunity to learn some of the social graces that their upper-class peers have acquired in other ways.

In a senior class, the members asked permission to give a

dinner—which eventually became a Sunday night supper—in the teacher's home. A committee of five girls acted as hostesses, prepared the meal, set the tables, welcomed the guests, and served the meal. At its conclusion, everyone sat on the floor around the fireplace in the living room and talked it over—a strange new experience for many of them. It was counted as a huge success by the class. As one boy said long afterward, "Every time I take a girl out to dinner and I hold her chair for her, I think of our dinner. Holding chairs and things like that never seemed important until then."

Consideration for others. In a class of boys and girls, together for several hours each day, and in some cases over a period of years, there are many occasions on which they can show special consideration for one another. It only takes a minute to sing *Happy Birthday to You,* but it gives a warm feeling of belonging to a boy or girl to know his birthday is remembered. And it provides a little of the ceremony for which people seem to have a real need and which is too often lacking in our hurried lives. So far as the mechanics are concerned, a list of birthdays in the back of the secretary's book provides a simple reminder.

A card, signed by everyone in the class, sent to a member who is ill, not only gives pleasure to the absent member, but teaches all who signed it that this is what one does for friends who are ill. A sheet of wrapping paper on which each pupil writes a message or draws a cartoon is also a gay greeting. Or perhaps a half hour can be taken in class to write letters, which are bundled up into a pack and delivered to the missing classmate. If the pupil's absence is extended and visitors are welcomed, it may be suggested that class members visit him.

A member of a senior core class dropped out of school and joined the armed services. A letter soon came that told of his loneliness and it was decided that each week two different class members would write to him. True, they sometimes slipped and failed to write, but for months letters were sent in order that he might know that he still belonged to the group and was not forgotten. His letters, in turn, were always eagerly awaited and upon arrival were read aloud to the entire class.

There is another type of occasion that adolescents should be helped to meet, for it is one that, although not a happy one, they can expect to face many times in their lives. What should one do when death occurs in the family of a friend? Let us suppose it is the death of the mother of a class member. Pupils are usually very sympathetic at such a time. They are anxious to know what they can do. If it is a school where children have allowances or if they are old enough to be earning money, some will want to send flowers. Others may wish, instead, to send a Mass card, with which they are familiar through their religious training. And some may think both should be sent.

The teacher must take the initiative here and help the class see the limits both of the situation itself and of general good taste. If the person was a Protestant, a Mass card is not in order, which is a new thought to some teen-agers. And if the person was of Catholic faith, possibly there are among the class members some who would not wish to send a Mass card. All these points must be weighed before a decision is made. The question of the total amount of money to be used must be considered as well. In their eagerness to express their sympathy, pupils sometimes fail to examine this point. One of the writer's most difficult tasks on one such occasion, was to help a class to see that a levy of a dollar per pupil, making a total of thirty-five dollars, was completely out of line as an amount for a class to spend on flowers, that it would seem to others to be ostentatious, or in their own language, would seem to be "showing-off." Their generosity had out-run good judgment and good taste.

There is another aspect of the funeral problem that must be met. It is so easy for the teacher to say, "I'm sure that all of us who can possibly do so will go to the funeral home and express our sympathy to Jane." And it is so hard for teen-agers to do. They usually do not know what to do when they get there, nor what to say. And so they stay away. They need help in finding simple words to express their sympathy and they need to know what to do if, for example, the family is Catholic and they are of another religion, or if they, themselves, are Catholic and the family is of another religion. Not knowing whether to kneel at the casket, for example, when others attending are doing so can make one quite uncomfortable. A frank explanation will clear up such matters. If it is possible for the teacher to go with some who are hesitant, it is a very kind and helpful act.

Perhaps the most outstanding evidence of pupils' growth in consideration for others can be seen in their attitude toward any classmate less fortunate than themselves—the girl who stutters, the boy with a hearing aid who also needs to watch the speaker's lips, the one with a low reading ability, or the one who is not normal either in ability to think or to handle himself physically, or possibly the one who is awkward as the result of polio. The members of a class that has any handicapped pupil must be helped to see that they have a very real part in making his life worth-while.

Perhaps on a day when he is absent or when a legitimate reason can be found for sending him to another part of the building, the teacher can, so to speak, lay the cards on the table, at least those which the pupils will understand and which it is ethical to disclose. Adolescents are usually sympathetic and helpful if they understand a situation.

For example, there was Diane, a member of a ninth-grade core class. She had been ill and in bed most of her life. Now, for the first time, she was able to be in school almost every day. She was brilliant, read everything she could lay her hands on, could out-think and out-talk most of her classmates. She had more ideas than any three of them put together. Needless to say, she was a "spoiled" child, her parents understandably having given in to her on most things through the long, difficult years. So in the classroom, too, she wanted her own way and frequently was sharp-spoken and too persistent. But more than anything in the world she wanted friends, which was something she had been unable to have previously. The pupils did not know her background and judged her solely by her quick tongue and her too powerful drive toward getting her own way. They did not like her and showed it.

On a day that she was absent, the teacher told the class of Diane's long years of illness and of what it meant to her to be able to come to school. Through this discussion of the situation the pupils were helped to see for themselves why Diane was sharp and strong-willed. They were helped, too, to see why she did not know how to make friends, and that perhaps for a while they would have to make efforts toward a friendship they did not feel. They saw clearly and honestly, however, that she had an endless store of ideas. These they needed. At the end of the discussion their conclusions were well summed up by one boy's remark, "I guess we could sure try giving her friendliness when she gives us so many good ideas."

Several months later, the problem was discussed further, and the conclusion was drawn that, as they became more friendly toward Diane, she became happier and much less sharp. A number also admitted that they were no longer merely pretending friendliness. They truly liked her now. At the end of the year, complaining had droppd to a minimum, for Diane had also learned to give in when necessary, and as she learned that her classmates liked her, she no longer felt the need to push her own ideas to the fore. She learned that there were others who could contribute good ideas. So eventually, in their friendship, all learned that it is necessary to both give and take in order to live peaceably together.

Conclusion

As can be seen in the preceding pages, the fundamental skills of reading, writing, spelling, and speaking are not neglected in the democratic classroom. They are a part of every classroom activity, and for their development the teacher uses techniques that are accepted teaching procedures. Because of the pupils' interest in the problems they have elected to work on, and their participation in the activities that they, themselves, have planned, here is unusual opportunity for growth in these basic skills. Pupils see the need for reading, for writing, and for speaking, and because of this they put forth a surprising amount of effort toward improvement.

The development of the social skills is also an integral part of life in a democratic classroom. Although the process of developing such skills in several sample situations has been spelled out at some length, it is readily seen that, in general, it is not particularly time consuming, certainly not in comparison with the importance of these skills for young people. It should be recognized that most of them involve not only the development of the social skills, but of communication skills as well. They are part and parcel of the individual's participation in learning, problem solving, and skilled action—these are appropriate for the school to cultivate.

10

Retrospection

THE MEMBERS OF CLASSES THAT HAVE BEEN TO-
gether in a class for three or four years have a strong feeling of
belonging together. This is obvious from the number of reunions
that are held, which for some groups continue for many years,
with husbands, wives, and children included as marriages occur.
In a ten-month period following the graduation of a class that
had been together for three years, the teacher heard from 23 of
the 26 members, 20 of these contacts being personal visits and
the rest by letter or telephone. The question that never fails to
be asked is, "What are the others doing?"

The feelings of these young people relative to their experiences
are often expressed, but because of the time and difficulties involved, no effort has been made to carry out an over-all follow-up
study. For one class, however, which had experienced democratic
procedures in a core class in grades nine through twelve, and
which was having its second reunion at the teacher's home, arrangements were made to have the members discuss their reactions to their experiences in response to questions raised by Dr.
Theodore Rice of Wayne State University.

The material reported in this chapter cannot, of course, be
considered as an evaluation of democratic procedures or as an
evaluation of core. It is the result of interviewing one available
class. That these responses have value we cannot doubt, but

Figure 34. Three years after graduation.

we must recognize that responses from other classes, even those having the same teacher, might well be different.

The interview took place nearly three years after graduation, with 13 out of 19 class members attending. Five were in their third year in college and the others were working. Arrangements were made to have the discussion recorded on a tape, and a teacher[1] was asked to record it in shorthand. In order to assist the interviewer, a name plate was prepared for each person, which he placed on the table in front of him. The teacher of the class was not present during the major part of the discussion period. A picture of this group is shown in Figure 34.

As in all discussions in which people feel free to express their opinions, the conversation often moved so fast that the subject of discussion sometimes changed before everything had been said. At a later time it might be referred to again in a context in which the remark did not fit. The writer has taken the liberty of putting together all statements dealing with a common topic, as well as including comments that were made after the official interview was ended. These comments, each marked with an

---

[1] Jenine Kemp of Condon Junior High School, Detroit.

asterisk, were made during the reunion party and were not recorded on the tape. In a few places words have been added that in no sense change the meaning of the comment, but clarify it for the reader. The preliminary give and take of getting acquainted with the interviewer and the recorder, as well as the interviewer's efforts to set the group at ease, have not been included.[2]

The discussion has been assembled under the following headings: (1) What was the first semester like? (2) What brought about improvement? (3) What experiences are remembered? (4) Who should have core experience? (5) What should be changed? (6) What is the value of core? In addition to the brief glimpse these young people give of their core experiences as they look back to them, the writer has followed each section of dialogue with information that will serve to give the reader a better understanding of what took place in the days the class was in operation, as well as some implications that may be drawn from the discussion. It is hoped that this will assist the practicing teacher, or teacher in training, to anticipate some of the experiences and problems that he is likely to encounter in guiding a core class.

What was the first semester like?

INTERVIEWER

Do you remember about the first days you were in core? What was it like at first? Did the teacher tell you what it was all about? Did you spend a lot of time trying to find out?

SEVERAL

We were in three different classes in the ninth grade. It was in the tenth grade that this group came together.

INTERVIEWER

Did you like it at the beginning? How did the teacher try to help you?

JIM[3]

In our ninth-grade class there were a few boys who had heard about

---

[2] The original transcription has been included in the Appendix.

[3] Since fictitious names are used in this description, the names do not match the names shown on the name plates in Figure 34.

core from other sources and they definitely wanted out right away. So they got out. I think we started with a prejudice against it. Everybody wondered what core was about. I remember it took us quite a while before we started on the first project, but Miss Wells helped us out and explained what it was all about.

FRANCES

The general opinion of kids in regular English classes in the ninth grade was, "Are you too dumb?" or, "Do you think you are special?" or, "Do you think you are going to get out of some work?"

WALTER

You were more or less put in the class and some resented it.

JIM

Other students asked how we were chosen for it and was it hard to get into. I think that confused me.

DAN

The first day I was in core I come out and somebody said, "Where are your books? Aren't you getting any books for English and history? That's a kind of dumb class." And the first day in school that kind of gets you. I wondered about it and my folks wondered, too.

INTERVIEWER

Do you remember anything about the classroom that struck you as different from other classrooms? What was the atmosphere as compared to that in other rooms?

SCOTT

More friendly.

GINNY

There were plants, drapes at the windows . . .

RUTH

Brighter.

ELLEN

It had more things in it than other rooms. There were pictures on the wall and the bulletin boards had exhibits on them.

U. V.[4]

Pictures.

WALTER

Lots of color.

---

4 Unidentified voice.

JIM

It was easier. Some people were able to get away with things and it was easier than in a regular English class. Some people did that—not all of them.

DAN

We had some kids who didn't want to work. And we had topics on the board like hot-rods, hunting, and things like that. If you wanted to learn English or history or something like that, it wasn't any good. Of course you get lots of writing.

INTERVIEWER

Would you agree with the statement then that the atmosphere was more informal, brighter somebody said, and that there were more things in the room? Bulletin boards . . .

U. V.

Yes, bulletin boards.

SEVERAL

Frances did the boards in the tenth grade.

INTERVIEWER

And did you let her because she was so good? Frances, did you do all the boards or did somebody help you?

FRANCES

Betty helped.

WALTER

I helped, too.

DICK

We all helped once.

FRANCES

We used to have a picture painted on the blackboard around the schedule for the week.

MARGE

Don't you remember? It was a fall scene.

INTERVIEWER

Well now, I don't know whether you want to talk about this. Maybe you don't. Questions like these: How did the teacher make her way with you? How did you become acquainted with each other? Did she make an effort to get you acquainted with her?

JEAN

When we came together in the tenth grade, she had a party here in her home on Hallowe'en, and a Christmas party. Miss Wells always opened her home to us. For the most part it was done right here. Everybody showed up at the parties. The first one was in October, so that was close to the time we came together.

INTERVIEWER

How did you get acquainted with her? Let's turn that around. How did she get acquainted with you? Did she try?

FRANCES

She tried awfully hard.

U. V.

You can't stay unfriendly with her.

MARGE

She made name tags for us like these we have tonight. And we used to go down and sit in her office and talk to her.

FRANCES

That must have been for conferences.

*BETTY

We always felt welcome in her office.

WALTER

When we first came together we told the class where we were from, and what our interests were.

JIM

I remember that we told our life story in class.

GINNY

We didn't get up and report it.

WALTER

Miss Wells sat in with the class, in the middle of the class.

INTERVIEWER

How do you mean?

WALTER

If we sat in a circle, she sat in with us, like one of us.

INTERVIEWER

Did you ever write autobiographies?

RUTH

I think we did.

INTERVIEWER

Critics might say some teachers try to find out things they have no business asking about.

JEAN

Pupils don't have to tell her if it's none of her business.

FRANCES

You can't really feel that way with Miss Wells.

INTERVIEWER

Do you feel that it was helpful to you to have her find out things about you? You were pretty successful. You don't have any scars.

DAN

She didn't go that far.

MARGE

One time she had trouble with Sue—but it was only to help her. She had trouble at home and Miss Wells tried to help her.

JIM

It was something anyone would do who had an interest in the girl. But that wasn't in front of the class.

*GINNY

She helped lots of us and nobody knew about it. I know she helped me several times.

The aspects of the beginning of their core experiences that these young people remembered some six years later included their initial feelings of confusion, the appearance of the room and its relaxed atmosphere, the feeling that it was "easy," working together on the bulletin boards, the beginning of group unity, and the teacher's guidance efforts.

The fact that initially these pupils were so confused is not as surprising as appears at first glance. There were so many things that threatened their security. The course that they had expected to be English and social studies was called core, a strange name with no meaning at this point. The teacher said they need not purchase textbooks, and for most of them a class for which one did not need a textbook was almost unheard of. The teacher also said something about the members of the class helping to select the topics to be studied, but that made little or no sense either, for teachers had always told them what to study. These things that they could not understand nor explain to others made them feel "different" from pupils in other classes, and this is hard on teen-age boys and girls.

The confusion expressed by the pupils in the interview should make us realize that the teacher has an obligation to help pupils see as clearly as possible, and as soon as possible, what the course is about, what its purposes are, how it will be conducted, and how it fits into the curriculum. This part of the orientation work is of vital importance in order to minimize the insecurity so clearly pointed out in this discussion.

It is also obvious from the comments made by these young people that sufficient accurate information about the course had not gone out to people outside of the program. Most of the pupils, themselves, had heard nothing about it before entering the class, although one or two had heard things that made them want to drop the class. This would seem to indicate that consistent efforts should be made to clarify the program to other pupils in the school, to faculty members, to parents, and to the community. True, in a school of 4,200 pupils, which was the size of the one attended by these boys and girls, such a campaign is not easy to conduct. But insofar as possible, through the school newspaper, the teachers' bulletin, a teachers' meeting, a parent-teacher meeting, a letter to parents, and even the community newspaper, information should be brought to those who are not directly involved in the program, but, because of their contact with core pupils, have need to understand it.

Other persons who should be made aware of what takes place in such classes are the upper-grade teachers in schools that send their pupils to the junior high school or the senior high school in question. These teachers should have sufficient knowledge of this type of class to give reliable and unbiased answers to pupils looking ahead to the new school and to the possibility of being in a core class, or, in other communities, a basic living class, a unified class, or perhaps a common learnings class.

In response to the interviewer's question concerning the differences that the pupils had noticed between the core class and other classes, the statement was made that it was easier, and that "some people were able to get away with things." In what does this feeling have its origin and what can be done about it? It is not difficult to see why pupils might feel that the work is easy in the first few weeks. The first activities deal with orientation—getting to know one another and the teacher, becoming familiar with the school, and being initiated into the techniques of group work and class discussion, all of which are necessary for later operation. Generally, however, there are few specific study assignments, since the major part of the activities are carried out in the classroom. This is quite different from daily assignments in a textbook, where the individual can see, *and say,* that the class has studied from page 1 to page 40 in the first two weeks.

That pupils sometimes feel that they are not learning anything in the early weeks is implied in the question that is from time to time asked: "When are we going to start work?" It is not clear to them that they have already started to work.

Perhaps this gives a clue as to what needs to be done. If pupils feel they are not learning anything, there are two obvious possible explanations. The first is that they really *are not* learning anything, that the activities have no meaning to them. The second possibility is that they are unable to identify the things learned; therefore, they are unable to verbalize them, and so it *seems* as though they have accomplished nothing. The latter is the more likely. A technique that has proved effective is to keep a record either on the chalkboard or on a large chart of all the activities carried out by the class during the first few weeks. Under each are recorded the things that the pupils feel they have learned from them. This is kept up to date by a five- or ten-minute review of the day's activities at the end of each class period. The list grows fast, and the pupils are astonished at how much has been accomplished. Such a technique focuses attention on the learning that has been taking place, and helps a pupil to have an answer for the question parents often ask: "What did you learn today?"

With some classes it is good to assign specific tasks rather regularly during the early weeks in order to maintain the pupils' feeling of accomplishment in the manner to which they are accustomed—a written report of their tour through the school, a review of the get-acquainted interview in story form, directions written to other newcomers telling them how to use the library. They are familiar with such assignments, duly handed in and corrected. These constitute "school work."

The less formal climate of the democratic classroom is often misinterpreted by pupils to whom this is a new experience. The teacher can usually identify those who have come from a school in which there was rigid discipline and teacher control. These are the ones who, after a day or two, seemingly explode. For a time they are likely to be the class disturbers, and the ones who do no work. Until they have tried their wings against this relaxed classroom atmosphere and, with the help of the teacher and their classmates, have discovered that democracy is not license and chaos, they can be problems.

For these people it is especially important, as indicated in Chapter 2, that the approach to pupil-teacher planning be relatively slow. Several units, such as the orientation and democratic living units, should be carried out according to the teacher's plan and under the teacher's direction, with only minor questions being decided by the class. These units form a bridge from complete teacher direction to pupil-teacher planning. As the pupils are able to accept greater responsibility, they are, of course, given the opportunity to take an ever larger part in planning class activities.

A point that is both interesting and important to note is the effect of the present greater maturity of the young people being interviewed on their judgment of the value of areas suggested for study in the ninth grade. Such topics as hot-rods and hunting now seem to them to be unacceptable as subjects to be selected for study in a classroom, but at the time they were in the ninth-grade class, some six years earlier, these had been important. True, they would not be selected by everyone, but at that time, as pupils in the class, they saw no reason why they could not be on the list. The fact that such topics are rejected now that these people are older indicates that the interests and concerns of young people change, a fact that certainly none of us would deny. It helps us to understand, too, why we, as adults, are frequently upset by the choice of topics made by teen-agers. We, like the young people interviewed, have forgotten what was of real concern at another age level.

The importance of efforts to develop group unity, a feeling of belonging together, can be clearly seen in the fact that so many of the activities carried out to achieve this were remembered. The bulletin boards on which various class members worked, the parties, the name tags, pupil get-acquainted interviews, being able to talk freely to the teacher, the fact that she was a part of the class group, and that she tried to give help whenever it was needed, all would indicate that these were important steps in welding the class into a whole. That the room itself helped in building an atmosphere conductive to group friendliness is implied in their recollections of the plants, the drapes, the pictures on the wall, the bright colors, and the bulletin boards with exhibits. Good pupil-pupil and pupil-teacher relationships do not develop without planning situations in which there will be opportunity for such growth, as well as utilizing as completely as possible those occasions for friendly contact that arise in the classroom every day. The setting in which these take place is equally important.

What brought about improvement?

INTERVIEWER

Something you said earlier raises a question. Was the atmosphere so informal that people could get away with things and not take any responsibility?

DAN

I didn't mean this class. That was in the ninth grade.

BETTY

I think that was in the beginning. We were just in high school and kids thought they were getting away with something.

*GINNY

Only a few kept on trying that.

*MARION

It was much better by the end of the ninth, but not as good as in the tenth grade and later.

INTERVIEWER

What do you suppose happened that made it different after the ninth grade?

DAN

I think the caliber of the student picked for the tenth-grade core was better. The ones who didn't care were weeded out.

INTERVIEWER

Can you think of someone who might have been weeded out but who turned out to be a pretty swell person?

BETTY

Jean. (*Everyone laughed, including* JEAN.)

FRANCES

At the end of the ninth grade there was a choice given as to whether you would stay in or get out.

U. V.

I think it was the caliber of the students they had later. Because they wanted to learn.

BETTY

The class got to be a real interest and so we began to put more into it.

INTERVIEWER

Did you get so that you put more into it as the years went by? You've made it sound as though if anybody wanted to get away with anything in core, he could do it. But you are not ready to buy that, are you? Did you learn some group controls?

*JEAN

In the ninth grade I think a big part of the trouble was that we really didn't understand and didn't really know how to do things without the teacher ordering us to do it.

FRANCES

I think that partly you grow out of it, too. If you have any interest in school at all you would be wasting your time. We had double periods and you don't just waste away two periods. You want to do something if for no other reason than from sheer boredom.

INTERVIEWER

Was there anything about the class itself that would make a person get to work?

BETTY

The kids who didn't do any work weren't liked too well by those who worked and everyone told them about it and they were sort of looked down on. It wasn't so much the teacher who told them. The pupils told them.

MARGE

If another group was working real hard and your group wasn't, then your group wasn't going to be up to the others.

*DAN

You pushed the ones who weren't working if you thought your group wasn't doing as well as the others.

INTERVIEWER

This was a kind of social pressure from the class itself, wasn't it.

FRANCES

The group was very close, too—the members of the class, I mean. I think that had a lot to do with it.

INTERVIEWER

I wonder what happened? Did you ever take a look at the groups to see how they were working?

WALTER

Self-evaluation.

JIM

We used to do self-evaluation and group evaluation. You had your evaluation sheets, too, and you marked yourself. If you knew it would be a lie, you wouldn't say you had done "B" work if you hadn't in gathering information and in group work.

BETTY

You could get by. But then you had an evaluation and you marked yourself and you had a guilty conscience. So after we had evaluated ourselves everyone tried to do better. You didn't want to get by with so much and you did more because you didn't feel like saying you deserved a "B" if you had earned a "C."

INTERVIEWER

You weren't kidding anyone but yourself.

GINNY

In our evaluations of our oral reports, the class would say something about our diction, how we had presented our topics, our posture, whether our English was poor and everything.

INTERVIEWER

You mean the class evaluated your report?

GINNY

Yes. They would tell us what they thought of it. It was fun.

INTERVIEWER

Do any of you have any unhappy rememberances of that?

BETTY

I don't think it bothered anyone because of the fact that we had always worked together.

JIM

Sue was sensitive to it. She used to resent it sometimes.

MARGE

But that was her personality.

INTERVIEWER

She was defensive?

GINNY

Yes, but everyone criticized everyone else so it didn't make any difference.

FRANCES

We didn't feel they were doing it to be brutal. It was more of a help.

WALTER

It was constructive criticism more than anything else.

*DICK

We evaluated our reports, too, and we knew if they weren't good.

FRANCES

Another thing—in our speech Miss Wells would correct us if we used poor English grammar.

INTERVIEWER

So she was at work all right.

DAN

A lot in core depends on the person.

JIM

Core depends on the person.

DAN

. . . what you put into it and what you want to get out of it.

As was indicated in the first section of the interview, as well as in this, the group felt that at the beginning there had been a decided tendency to try to "get away" with as little work as possible in the core class. It had seemed "easy," and not much effort had been put forth. It was also pointed out, however, that this attitude did not persist with most pupils, a few continuing to do this throughout the ninth grade, but that from the tenth grade on such behavior had largely disappeared.

The discussion in this section of the interview indicates that a class's acceptance of the responsibilities of operating on a democratic basis is gradual. If these boys and girls could actually look back and see themselves as they moved through the years they were together, they would realize that in ability to function democratically they had moved forward and fallen back time without number. It was not a steady march ahead. But with each falling back they learned something that helped them to move forward again. This should give food for thought to those who are disturbed when a class cannot handle itself in too satisfactory a manner by the end of a semester. Growth in the skills of democratic living is gradual; in fact it is probably never fully achieved, for, as each new situation arises, there is always more to be learned.

A point might be made, however, which is apparent to a teacher, but would not be recognized by pupils. Almost every ninth-grade class, no matter what the subject, has some members who try to see how far they can go without working. In a core class, however, such behavior is more obvious than in a traditional class. The shirker has no textbook to hide behind, and there is little of the question and answer type of activity in which his lack of work only comes to light if he cannot answer when he is called upon. It is clear at all times that he is doing nothing— he takes no part in making class decisions, nor does he contribute information toward the solution of a group problem. He sits through a business meeting with no participation. In the informal atmosphere of a core class he may often be found chatting instead of working. His more ambitious classmates are very aware of what he is doing and, as indicated in the interview, resent his lack of cooperation.

In response to the interviewer's question concerning the causes for the improvement that took place in the class, the following were set forth: (1) higher caliber of pupil in the tenth-grade core class; (2) increased interest; (3) social pressure; (4) self-evaluation as well as evaluation by the class. The teacher would agree with all these except the first. Although it is true that those who did not like the class had dropped out at the end of the ninth grade, this had little effect on the range of ability, reading levels, for example, running from the fifth grade through the eleventh.

The statement was made that pupils who didn't do any work weren't liked too well and that everyone told them about it and they were sort of looked down on. Certainly it is true that an individual who persistently avoided work was not welcomed with open arms when he joined a group. It is true, too, that, when an individual's failure to work affected the productivity of a group, the other members "pushed" him, as Dan said. His responsibility was pointed out to him. However, although the group members' disgust at his failure to cooperate showed plainly, the statement that such a person wasn't liked too well and that he was looked down on is an overstatement of fact. He did not become an outcast in the class, an isolate sociometrically speaking, for, as Frances has indicated, the class was a closely knit unit. It was this closeness that made it possible for a group to exert social pressure on the one who shirked his responsibilities and it was the closeness that made him feel the pressure and respond to it.

It is interesting to note the importance placed on evaluating one's own progress. This was an area in which the teacher initially met strenuous resistence in this class. Many pupils felt that this was in no way their job. The teacher should be the one to "give" grades for any work done. But as they moved from evaluation of such simple things as their participation in a class discussion to the more complex aspects of group life, resistance died out and self-evaluation came to be recognized as an important aspect of core class activities.

Reference was made in the interview to their consciences as being the means of keeping them from giving themselves higher grades than they had earned. It is necessary to add that their consciences were of minor assistance at the beginning. At first it seemed to some to be a marvelous opportunity to obtain a good rating with little effort. Only after experience with the process of evaluation in many different situations were reliable criteria established for accurate self-evaluation. The pupils had to learn *how* to evaluate themselves and to see evaluation in the light of their own growth toward the goals that the class had established. Gradually there developed pride in achievement rather than pride in a mark.

Evaluation of an activity such as a group report by the class was, as has been indicated, usually done in a constructive manner, and was generally well accepted. As illustrated by the case of Sue, however, such evaluations by a pupil's peers must be watched carefully. The teacher must be alert for unnecessary criticism, for the sharp tone of voice, or for words that have even a faint sarcastic tinge. At the beginning, it is often good to have the class watch only for the good points in presentations or reports. The teacher may then add general statements on points that ought to be corrected. The habit of watching for things to commend thus becomes established before pupils begin to make adverse criticisms.

What experiences are remembered?

INTERVIEWER

Some critics say that people in core can do anything they want to as far as the projects they choose to work on are concerned. Is this true?

JIM

I think so.

GINNY

No, not any individual.

JIM

You can do anything you want to a certain extent.

BETTY

It depended on how many people you could get to do what you wanted to do. You would suggest the subject you wanted to study to the chairman and he would put it on the board. But the class might vote it down.

DAN

You put the suggestions on the board. They were then open for discussion. We cut the list down by voting.

DICK

We divided them into groups first and then took each group and eliminated those we thought wouldn't work out.

INTERVIEWER

How could you tell they wouldn't work out?

BETTY

We had a set of rules, a basis for judging.

MARGE

Was it interesting, would it help us, was it useful . . . ? When we got the list down to a certain number we held them up to these criteria.

*ELLEN

Was it something we hadn't studied before?

INTERVIEWER

So you had some kind of rules to go by in deciding.

GINNY

Yes.

INTERVIEWER

Would it have been the subject wanted by the best talkers?

JIM

No, I don't think so. I think everyone had a statement to make when it came to choosing topics.

INTERVIEWER

Could you tell who was going to work on what?

GINNY

In the beginning I think you could. The fellows wanted to study . . .

BETTY

. . . something like hot rods. At first the fellows were working in groups and the girls were in groups, but after a while they started mixing up. Then you began to get more variety.

INTERVIEWER

Can you remember anything you thought especially good? Some high points and some that were really low?

MARION

I can't remember.

JIM

I remember studying about Admiral Byrd. I think it was in the ninth grade—his book, *Alone*—and I did other research on that. I remember I thought it was a good topic. That was by myself. I had some illustrations, too. I remember I had some pictures and used the opaque projector.

INTERVIEWER

Do you suppose you remember the individual assignments better?

BETTY

It was easier to do group reports. You didn't have to worry about getting up in front of the class alone and having everyone looking at you. We had a real good one on ancient Egypt.

JIM

We had something about manners.

JEAN

The creative project . . .

*FRANCES

Our group studied prehistoric life.

BETTY

I remember one we did one time. Was it in the twelfth grade when we did the one about what jobs we were going into? That was a doozy!

INTERVIEWER

What was doozy about it?

DAN

It took a lot of work.

U. V.

It took about a year.[5]

INTERVIEWER

Did it mean anything to you? Was this something you folks figured out that you wanted to do.

RUTH

No, it was required.

JIM

We had to write about three possible careers we would like to go into: interview people, find out about the jobs, do some research.

INTERVIEWER

Was that vocation unit any good? This careers study, did it help?

WALTER

For some it did.

JIM

It was right along with what I'm doing now. I was interested in the things I had in my report for about a year before I wrote the report. But it did help me.

*ELLEN

It helped me make up my mind.

*SCOTT

It pushed me into choosing between two kinds of work.

*DICK

It made me stop dreaming.

INTERVIEWER

Do you think you remember things that were required of you more than things you decided you wanted to do?

---

5 Actually, work on this unit lasted from October through December.

CAROL

You mean required by the teacher?

SEVERAL

No.

DAN

As far as requirements in class are concerned, we always handed in notes, reports, and things like that. They were always written up and handed in.

INTERVIEWER

Have you got any of them now?

JIM

I used one of mine recently for a speech class. I was making a speech and I had to look up some material and remembered I had made a similar report in core. So I got it out and it helped me a lot.

FRANCES

Another thing that I remember was that when we were studying manners we had a dinner down here in this room with waitresses and everything. We were studying manners and etiquette.

INTERVIEWER

What year was that?

FRANCES

That was in the twelfth grade, too.

INTERVIEWER

Did it do you any good?

SEVERAL

Oh, yes!

MARGE

The fellows pulled the chairs out for us and everything.

DICK

We left tips and everything.

FRANCES

We cooked dinner upstairs.

MARGE

Hot dogs with bacon around them!

WALTER

I remember I had quite a case of indigestion afterwards!

JIM

That was good though.

(*Much laughter throughout the discussion of the supper.*)

INTERVIEWER

Somebody mentioned creative projects.

GINNY

The reason we did it was because it seemed that everybody was getting mixed up. We couldn't settle on anything. We didn't want to take a regular topic. Everyone in the class was arguing with each other. Miss Wells suggested getting into groups—to do something which represented what we did in core. Each group took a phase of core. One was the way people presented topics. We put ours in a hat box . . .

MARGE

Our group went around and took pictures. Some made models of groups working together, and a business meeting, and showing different things we were doing.

GINNY

Pipe cleaner figures of people who participated in reporting a topic—the way they presented it.

WALTER

It represented the whole core program. We made stuff out of cardboard.

FRANCES

Wasn't that something Miss Wells tried with us when we just got together? Wasn't that when we first combined classes?

RUTH

No, it was after everyone knew each other.

JIM

No. But it wasn't in the twelfth grade because Jeff made a model of the opaque projector and he wasn't in our twelfth-grade class. That *was* in the tenth grade.

GINNY

We did this because everybody was always working in the same groups. Everyone knew everyone in his group. We drew names to see if we could work with different people.

INTERVIEWER

They were forming cliques?

FRANCES

Our class had been formed from parts of three ninth-grade classes. We were getting into cliques.

INTERVIEWER

Did it work?

FRANCES

Oh, yes. We worked better after that. We had a closer union.

INTERVIEWER

At least it was an ice-breaker for your class. I get the idea that you used the creative project especially as a way to get acquainted.

JIM

After we used it that way we made other things later on to illustrate our projects.

RUTH

Yes, we did use it afterward.

DAN

I gave a report on my trip from Scotland and made a model of clay to show my trip across the Atlantic. I think that was later on.

WALTER

I remember that.

MARGE

We had a parent night later and used some of our creative projects to illustrate how we did things in core—like the pictures and a lot of the others.

INTERVIEWER

Any other unit that you remember?

U. V.

The core newspaper.

MARGE

It was mainly for the parents.

SCOTT

All core classes contributed articles. Had reporters.

RUTH

There were pictures.

*WALTER

Frances drew the cover design.

*JIM

We were the oldest core class and so we were in charge of it.

*DAN

It was a good paper.

*MARGE

We cut all the stencils . . .

*GINNY

And corrected errors in articles . . .

*FRANCES

The staff met here in this room several evenings.

INTERVIEWER

Was this for all classes?

U. V.

Yes, for all grades.

JIM

Navajo Indians. That was from Miss Wells's trip. When she was in Arizona she went to some Indian school and the kids made a recording or something.

WALTER

When she was away she brought back a tape recording from the Navajo school in Arizona. They sang and talked to us.

JIM

We thought we would reply to them. So we made a tape and talked and told them what our school was like.

JEAN

We took pictures.

FRANCES

In a scrapbook we put things about Detroit and our class. Miss Wells told us how little they had in their homes—so much different from ours, and we told them what our homes were like.

INTERVIEWER

Can you remember anything you learned from the Navajo tape? Do you suppose they learned anything from your tape?

DAN

No, we were the ones who learned things.

WALTER

I don't know if you remember about the differences in ages. A few kids about fourteen years were still in the fourth grade due to lack of education.

MARGE

They have several classes in one big room. Older students with the younger ones—lack of teachers.

INTERVIEWER

Would you say American education for Indians is like or equal to that of regular high school students?

DICK

Not equal where it's a regular Indian village. That was a reservation.

JIM

Another thing we did was carol at the home for the aged at Christmas. Miss Wells took the group to carol.

JEAN

On Grand Boulevard.

WALTER

She always took the twelfth grade but didn't have one that year, so we went. We were the closest to the twelfth, so she let us do it and so we did it for two years.

MARGE

When we went carolling we took little bags of candy that we made up like baskets.

*GINNY

We took oranges. A big basket of them.

*MARION

We had candles lighted.

INTERVIEWER

Can you remember anything that just left you cold? Something you did as an individual or group that was just a dismal flop?

SCOTT

I didn't like the creative one.

DAN

The thing I thought was a flop was music appreciation. We set aside a day . . .

FRANCES

I don't think we were ready for it.

BETTY

The day everyone brought something that was supposed to be the most beautiful thing he had. Everybody sat around and no one took it seriously, just laughed.

INTERVIEWER

Was it because you were embarrassed?

MARGE

You were sort of baring your soul.

DAN

I thought the reason it was a flop was because I, myself, spent about five minutes preparing that project that day and maybe others did too. Made it a last minute thing. That might have been part of the trouble.

INTERVIEWER

Did you learn anything from that kind of lesson?

JIM

I listened to the various items and that was about it.

BETTY

Most did it because they had to do something. No one took it seriously. Scott said his wallet. Walter's was a picture of his mother. Someone brought a record. Ruth a ring.

*FRANCES

Walter didn't bring his mother's picture. He showed a ring.

SCOTT

What did you bring?

MARGE

I brought a poem.

*FRANCES

I brought a poem, too.

INTERVIEWER

How do you happen to remember these things?

GINNY

It was so different.

INTERVIEWER

Now let's see. Field trips . . .

SCOTT

I'll always remember Greenfield Village.

DAN

Pushing Scott around in a wheelchair.

MARION

Cranbrook.

INTERVIEWER

How did you decide on field trips? What did they relate to? Were they picnics or picked in terms of things to study? You mentioned Greenfield Village and Cranbrook. Did the teacher pick those for you?

WALTER

Everybody made suggestions and we picked one from the list.

SCOTT

We discussed them.

BETTY

Did we ever complete the one we were going to do relating to religions? We were going to visit different churches. We didn't ever do that.

FRANCES

Didn't we take some trips that related to our topics?

MARGE

When we did that project on Egypt we went to the Art Institute. And we set up those individual field trips just to broaden our outlook.

DAN

We went to Greenfield Village. That interested me.

DICK

Didn't what Marge said have something to do with culture?

MARGE

Yes, we had a certain number of places to go during the semester. We were to go as a group or by yourself. It started about Detroit. We were saying that there . . .

DICK

There are a lot of things in Detroit we normally don't see until visitors come into town and ask about them. We were going to see these things.

GINNY

Then we reported on these trips.

MARGE

We kept a list on the bulletin board of plays, shows, ballets, concerts, things we could go to see.

JIM

There was a TV program about church—something about church service—that we wanted to see, so we had a television set brought into the room to see it.

WALTER

Wasn't it an Easter service?

The four units remembered best were: (1) manners; (2) the creative project; (3) the core newspaper; (4) jobs. Field trips might be added to these four, although they were not study units. The Navajo Indian project was not a unit that involved study, but was an activity that the class carried out over a period of several weeks in its spare time. The visit to the convalescent home took a week and a half to prepare for, in addition to time outside of school. There are two elements common to all of these. They were all units in which everyone had some part, and they all involved activities that were different from ordinary research procedures.

The fact that everyone had a part in them made each, of course, a much bigger affair than if only a small group had been responsible for it. The teacher tends to believe, however, that the thing that made them remembered more than other units were the activities connected with them. With the unit on manners, a Sunday night supper was planned, prepared, and carried out by members of the class; for the creative project, there was the novelty of making things with one's hands; for the newspaper, there were meetings outside of school, frequent contact with other classes, cutting the stencils, and mimeographing and assembling pages into the finished paper; for the job unit, there were unusual tests to be taken, people to interview, and finding things out about oneself; and for the field trips, there was the fun of going to many different places. In the Navajo Indian project, everyone participated in preparing the tape recording and had a hand in getting the scrapbook ready. Carolling at the convalescent home required rehearsals, the assembling of bags of cookies and candy, and above all, there was the carolling itself. The teacher also feels that these are remembered because all were highly motivated, even the job unit, which Betty says was a "doozy." Although not pupil-selected, this unit was of vital concern to each one at this time, since all were getting ready to move either into college or into a job.

Some of these units have been described in other parts of this book.[6] Having read the pupils' comments, it might prove interesting to turn back and read the teacher's descriptions developed from her notes written at the time the units were completed.

The activity that was considered to have been the most dismal failure was a one-day experience rather than a long-term research unit. Each pupil was asked to bring to class that item which he counted as his most beautiful possession. The teacher's description, which is the exact opposite to that of the class members, should be read again at this time.[7] In the interview it was described as a flop, as something that no one took seriously, about which everybody laughed. If these descriptions are accurate, one would hardly expect the experience to be remembered so clearly. Yet, despite the fact that it was completed in one class period of less than two clock hours, there were vivid recollections of what was brought by different individuals.

When leaving on the evening of the interview, two people, in wholly separate statements, rejected the impression given in the interview, although at the time they said nothing. One said, "I didn't say anything, but I liked the most beautiful possession project because I had never realized that other people felt the way I did. I brought a prayer and so did Diane." The other said, "We *didn't* laugh about the most beautiful thing. It wasn't funny. It was wonderful and we didn't laugh."

---

6 Unit on manners: See pages 356–357.
  The creative project: See pages 75–77.
  The core newspaper: See pages 290–292.
  Field Trips: See pages 266–267.
7 See pages 252–255.

Two days later another called on the telephone and, after talking a bit said, "I don't think most people really felt like they said about the most beautiful project. I know I didn't. I liked it and always remembered it."

This experience had obviously touched them deeply and, although at the time that they were in class together every day and were a closely knit group it was "safe" to admit their emotions, it was no longer possible to do so in public; so the experience had to be rejected.

Perhaps the most important point that is indicated to us by the descriptions given in this part of the interview is, as has been stated above, the value of activities other than book work in conjunction with a unit. These may be highly creative presentations, the preparation of a series of slides or a movie, field trips to gather more information or to illustrate some phase of a problem, the preparation of a magazine for the class, or any of dozens of other projects. They highlight the work that is being carried on as words alone can never do. Even the day's experience with the objects the pupils considered beautiful would not have been so clearly remembered if the items had only been talked about instead of bringing the actual articles into the classroom.

Who should have core experience?

INTERVIEWER

Well, is there something we have overlooked? Who should have been in core and who should not have been in core? Would you be able to recognize somebody who ought not to be in core?

BETTY

If you could point out someone who should not be in core, actually, that is the one who should be. The person who is rebelling against this type of learning is the one who needs to be in core because he needs more help, because that one is going to have trouble later on.

MARGE

It can't work miracles. I don't think core could solve the problem for those people, but it could give them a helping hand. In other classes you just throw them in with everyone else. They get special help in core.

JEAN

Shouldn't core be for special people? Those who are having trouble?

WALTER

Don't you remember the time Jeff made the projector and a lot of us admired it and it made him feel good and more willing to work? If all in the class were like Jeff, how many would go up to him like that?

MARGE

In the rest of their lives they're not going to be in special groups. They have to work with people who aren't special people too.

FRANCES

If you had only people of that type, you would feel as though core was a dumping ground.

*DAN

I don't think they should be all the smart ones or all the ones who can't do anything. They should be mixed the way we were.

*WALTER

I think everyone should have core and lots of it.

*JEAN

But if it helps the slow ones, then it should be for them.

*MARGE

But it helps everyone, only in different ways.

In some schools core is considered as a class for the slow learner. The difficulties involved in making such a class a true core, however, are tremendous, although it is possible to use many of the techniques that have been described. The slow learner finds it very difficult to deal with the abstract concepts of democracy. An understanding of group roles, for example, is almost impossible to develop, much less to put into operation. In a class that has a cross section of ability, although the concept may remain vague for the less able, there is leadership among the brighter, and the techniques of group operation are learned from their example.

Ideas are at a premium in a group composed only of pupils of below-average ability. This, of course, forces pupil-teacher planning onto a very low plane, since the ideas must come more often from the teacher than from the pupils. Planning of any kind lacks the spark that sets an activity into motion. Presentations, for example, are dull and plodding, for there is lack of imaginative ability. In a heterogeneous group, however, the ideas of the brighter pupils serve as guides to the others and frequently they not only follow, but through contact with such ideas, some up with some of their own.

Strangely enough, a class of all high ability pupils presents problems as well. These pupils often reject any deviation from the traditional textbook method of operation and strictly academic subject matter. They frequently resent the need for cooperation when working in groups, for their pattern of learning has been highly individualistic and competitive. Self-evaluation is scorned for they conceive this to be wholly the teacher's job. The time that is needed to settle a question democratically irks such a group, and they imply that if the teacher would just say what he wants they could move ahead. Thus the problems involved in helping a class composed of all high ability pupils to understand and use democratic procedures are as great as in a class of all low ability. It is just that the problems are different.

The reactions of the young people to the question, "Who should be in core and who should not be?" as expressed in the interview, are good. Betty stated it as follows: "If you could point out someone who should not be in core, actually, that is the one who should be. The person who is rebelling against this type of learning is the one who needs to be in core because he needs more help, because that one is going to have trouble later on."

A class operated on democratic principles is an experience needed by all pupils, whatever their ability. Boys and girls less capable than others are yet going to grow into men and women who need to know as much as they can absorb of how to function in a democratic society, of how to be good citizens, and those with superior ability need exactly the same thing. These, however, should absorb a great deal more than their less able fellows.

As adults, both groups will come in contact with people of all levels of ability. They will not be isolated. Each will need to know how to work with the other in the solving of common problems.

For this they need the practice that a heterogeneous, democratically functioning class can give them. A homogeneously grouped class (if there is such a thing) gives only limited experience. As Dan said in the interview, "I don't think they should be all the smart ones or all the ones who can't do anything. They should be mixed the way we were."

What should be changed?

INTERVIEWER

If you had youngsters going to school, would you like them to have core experience?

JIM

Right after you get in core, for a year it's not so good, until you get organized. So if you put our youngsters in core after it was rolling, it would be okay.

GINNY

You waste a lot of time getting organized. It would be better if you didn't have to spend all that time getting organized.

BETTY

But that helps you to learn to organize.

INTERVIEWER

You said that if you could get your youngsters in core after it gets rolling that would be all right. Would you say that first year was hard work?

MARGE

You have to learn how to make it roll, to get it organized.

WALTER

I don't see how you could do it any other way.

JIM

When you think about it, maybe that was one of the best parts of core. Maybe we're talking that first year down too much. Maybe that was where we learned more about core than anywhere else.

GINNY

I don't think it's necessary to have core for four years.

INTERVIEWER

How would you know when you were through with it?

*JEAN

When you're going out to meet the public. I think it should be the last two years.

MARGE

But when you are coming from a grade school to high school, although Denby is bigger than most high schools, going into any high school is quite a jump. Core helps you to make that change. So I think it's important in the first two years, too.

INTERVIEWER

So, if we could cut out the awkwardness in the first two years . . .

GINNY

There's too much planning all at once.

FRANCES

I think it's a matter of making too many decisions, too.

GINNY

You just can't do it because everything is coming at you all at once. First you have to set up your goals. Then set up criteria. You start so many things and you don't know where you are going or what you're doing them for.

DAN

If you could have it along with English and history, then core would just be a matter of learning to get along.

GINNY

I know you can, but you don't choose history to study in core. It's because you don't want to do it. If someone made you do it, you would study it, and I think you should have history in high school.

INTERVIEWER

What would you lose?

FRANCES

If you had straight English and history class combined with core, you would lose something, because core isn't English and history.

GINNY

I think core should be a separate class.

INTERVIEWER

As you reminisce a bit about it, did you find yourself dreading to go to core sometimes?

GINNY

I was always anxious to go to core.

JEAN

I was too.

FRANCES

Yes, I was too.

MARGE

It was a relief to get away from running into a class and opening your books and getting ready for a test.

INTERVIEWER

Now let's see. Was it important to have a two period class or should it be cut down to one?

WALTER

Two periods are important because sometimes you'd just get started and the bell would ring.

*JEAN

We only had one period in the twelfth grade and it wasn't enough. It should be two.

*SCOTT

You couldn't collect enough notes in one period to make it worthwhile.

*DICK

Just getting to the library makes a big hole in one hour.

The major point made in this part of the interview was that the first year of core was difficult and seemed to the pupils to be a waste of time. They felt that too much time was taken to organize and get under way, that there was too much planning all at once, and that there were too many decisions to be made. An analysis of these comments would seem to imply that core teachers should watch class reactions carefully during this time. The meaning of democratic process, class organization, establishing class goals, and learning to work in groups are all time consuming operations and, more especially, are largely on a verbal level. There is little action involved.

Too frequently a class moves through long periods of discussion in order to make decisions. The length of such discussions should be determined by the length of time that a class remains actively involved in the question. An inactive group, or one that, after a time, allows two or three pupils to carry the discussion for them will reach no satisfying conclusions. The wise teacher makes provision for a change of pace and turns to other activities for a while, realizing that the adolescent's span of attention is often not as long as he thinks it is. Of late years, the writer has learned to introduce the first unit for research much earlier than she did years ago, and to hold back for a time such an activity as setting class goals. Research involves going to the library, taking notes, preparing a presentation, all of which are quite different from a class discussion. Emphasis on the details of group process, such as defining group roles, also can be held back. This has helped immensely.

However, Jim points out the importance of this first year's activities when he says, "When you think about it, maybe that was one of the best parts of core. Maybe we're talking that first year down too much. Maybe that was where we learned more about core than anywhere else." This is true, for this is the year in which the basic structure of democratic techniques is learned. Without this, later growth cannot take place. Because this is so, a teacher cannot omit these essentials. They should, however, be planned carefully so that one does not follow immediately after the other.

The question that is raised relative to having a core class in addition to the classes it usually replaces, in this case history and English, or of combining the two with core, is difficult to answer. Where a combination of the two subjects, in the form of a unified studies class, is attempted, the emphasis is usually so heavily on the subject matter that the democratic processes are largely lost sight of. If the subject matter in a course of study must be covered, there is little time for anything else, and relatively little opportunity is given for pupil-teacher planning within the area of the two subjects.

And in today's crowded schools there is little extra time or room space for another class such as core to be added to the curriculum. A choice must be made and, in the school from which the pupils being interviewed graduated, the course replaced English and history, although eleventh-grade core problems were limited to American history, and English was never lost sight of, as was indicated in Chapter 9.

Opinions differed concerning the length of time pupils should remain in core. One felt the last two years of high school would be best, another said the first two years, and a third thought it should be a four-year experience as this class had had it.

As has been said before, growth in ability to function consistently in a democratic fashion is slow. A year's experience is only a good start. This is not always apparent to teachers who have their classes for only one year, for many groups learn the major surface techniques in that time. It remains for the teachers who keep the same groups over a period of two, three, and even four years to see the root system of these surface techniques begin to grow, so that democratic action is no longer conformity to a superficial pattern but is a belief and a faith.

What is the value of core?

INTERVIEWER

Has core had any influence on your life since you are out of high school? Has it helped you in any way?

WALTER

The problems we worked on—the teamwork involved. I noticed that as I got out. I'm in the accounting field and it has helped me in working with the other accountants. When you're working on those core problems it's like the factories I go to and you have a product you want to put out. You have to have all your work ready to do it.

JIM

I think you could apply this to any situation, but you could get it anyway. I learned some of that where I work in a butcher shop.

INTERVIEWER

You mean you could have gotten it without core.

WALTER

But not as easy. And it would be harder for someone to get up and talk before someone.

DAN

Core helps you. In my college speech class I find I am able to get up in front of the class much more easily than some of the members who didn't have core. I never got so scared or worried. I was always more relaxed. But the other students always were so scared and fumbling around.

GINNY

I think it helps me on my job. I work with a lot of difficult people. I'm a dental assistant. People who come to our office don't want to be there in the first place and core helps me in knowing how to work with them.

INTERVIEWER

What about problem solving? You haven't had any problems since you left high school, have you?

EVERYONE

Oh, no!

MARGE

I think choosing what you wanted to study in core helped me. You learn to weigh things. I think it has helped me since I've been out of high school.

JIM

In my history of religion class the instructor gave us 118 topics to choose from for a term paper. From weighing topics in core I was able to choose my topic faster. Another student came up to me and was all upset. He hadn't chosen a topic yet. Of course I don't know whether that was just a lack of time or what.

MARGE

A lot of college students get confused in choosing topics for term papers. And they don't know how to start them. The techniques are the same as in core although the papers are longer than those required in core—taking notes and all that.

*SCOTT

Another thing is that core students ask questions in college classes when they don't understand or when they want to know something. I think they learned in core that when you want to know something you ask and find out.

*FRANCES

Core students are way out ahead in knowing how to find materials in the library, to do research, I mean. We're used to it.

*MARGE

And in note taking. Lots of students have trouble with that because they have never taken notes.

INTERVIEWER

I heard you say something about Miss Wells being away a year. What happened during the time she was away?

JEAN

We had regular English and American history.

BETTY

I think that was a test in itself.

SEVERAL

It was!

GINNY

We rebelled at first. Here was someone telling us, "We're going to do this or that today."

INTERVIEWER

Why was that? Wouldn't it have been a relief to have someone tell you what to do?

SEVERAL

Oh no, not at that stage of the game.

FRANCES

I think we were afraid to go into the regular English class but we found we did better than we thought we would once we were in it.

JIM

When we started English in college and were taking a required English course, I remember telling the professor that I had never had regular English. He wanted to know what I had had and when I said core, he said, "Oh, that." But we did well in English and were as capable as other students. Some who had had four years of English failed in the university.

INTERVIEWER

There is one more question I would like to ask you. How did you explain core to your parents? Were they interested?

JIM

I know my folks were.

GINNY

When you try to describe core to anyone, it's very hard to get it across because you don't have a textbook. You can't say you are using a certain book and tell how you use it. Then you say we use several books and we each take a project. When you've finished trying to explain it, people are more confused than ever.

INTERVIEWER

Did any of you develop a way in which to explain it?

FRANCES

The way I tried to explain it was that we didn't actually work with a teacher as boss of the classroom. It was a more democratic way of studying. We had most of the same things that pupils our age studied, but we decided what we were going to study instead of having the iron hand of the teacher over us, and having her tell us we were going to do such and such, to take a book home and read so many pages.

INTERVIEWER

Did your parents ask what you learned, or what you did? Was it easy to answer that? Which was the hardest one?

SEVERAL

What did you learn today?

FRANCES

I don't think you could so much say what you did or what you learned, but it showed.

INTERVIEWER

Some of the things you learned became a part of you?

FRANCES

More as a matter of your own personality—leadership, this business of making decisions, knowing what you wanted to do and doing it.

Since the interview was not intended to be an evaluation of the success of core, no more emphasis was given to the question of the influence of core on the lives of these former pupils than to the other questions that were asked. That these people were satisfied is obvious, although the college students were more articulate than those who were working.

The college students felt that core helped them in learning to make choices, in knowing how to approach a problem and do research on it, in taking notes, and in talking before a group or in asking questions in class. As Scott said, "When you want to know something you ask and find out." This would seem to be a basic concept in an approach to the problems of life, whether in college or on a job.

The non-college people indicated that doing a job is similar to working out a class problem, and that core training had been of assistance in facing problems at work. It was also pointed out that core had helped them in learning how to get along with people.

Explaining core to people who have had no contact with it is never easy as the responses in the interview show. Nor is it easy to express in words exactly what has been learned. We are accustomed to measuring learning in terms of retention of factual subject content. Although this is a part of core learning, and can be measured, there are also the intangible elements involved in the skills and techniques of democratic living, which form a major part of what it is hoped will be achieved through core experiences. How does one measure precisely how much insight an individual has acquired in the area of thinking and working with others? How does one measure ability in problem solving and in attainment of scientific attitudes and dispositions? How does one measure such things as ability to take responsibility or to have respect for minority opinion?

How can *growth* in these areas be measured? Surely not by paper-and-pencil tests, but actually only by the behavior of the individual as he meets his own life problems. Frances pointed this out when she said, "I don't think you could so much say what you did or what you learned, but it showed." She then went on to say, "More as a matter of your own personality—leadership, this business of making decisions, knowing what you wanted to do and doing it."

Much that pupils have experienced in a democratically functioning class is only fully understood years later. Time without number former pupils have said, "Now I understand the value of our business meetings," or, "Now I understand why we spent so much time on learning to work in groups. On my job I have to work closely with three other fellows and now I see the meaning of the things I learned." Or perhaps it's the young man with a six-year-old daughter, who says, "I've joined the Parent-Teachers Association in my daughter's school. I remembered that if we wanted to get something done in core we had to take an active part."

VALUES FOR DEMOCRATIC LIVING

The actual measure of achievement in the intangible areas of interpersonal relationships and problem solving lies in the lives of the pupils after they have left core far behind and are facing their problems on their own. This is where the only real evaluation can take place, and it is beyond the power of the teacher to follow.

As the result, however, of many years of experimenting with democratic teaching techniques and from close association with the boys and girls in her classes both before and after graduation, the writer has formed a number of strong convictions relative to the values they have derived from their experiences in core.

Sense of personal worth

Perhaps the foremost of these values is *a growing sense of the personal worth of every human being.* This involves two things, understanding and acceptance of self, and understanding and acceptance of others. The young person who does not have a sense of his own personal worth, accepting himself honestly for the person he is, will have difficulty understanding and accepting others.

In a core class such understanding of self has an opportunity to develop. Self-appraisal in a great variety of situations is a common occurrence, for example, in group work, in discussions, in presentations, in reactions to films dealing with teen-age problems. These serve as bases both for class discussion and for teacher conferences, which help the pupil to see himself as he really is, to identify his strong points and to recognize his weaknesses as well. In such a class, he also has an opportunity to discover and investigate his own interests and concerns, and to contribute from these according to his ability to the activities of the class. Finding his own contributions acceptable, he is increasingly willing to accept those of his classmates.

As he becomes more aware of his own problems and of his abilities, he becomes more sensitive to those of other people, recognizing that all people have problems and also have abilities, quite possibly different from his own, that are worthy of his attention. This need no longer arouse a jealous twinge, for he is beginning to sense his own potentialities. As his understanding of himself increases, he is able to accept himself as a person, and with this comes greater ability to understand and accept others.

Communicating with others

A second value that the writer is convinced develops from the experiences in a democratic classroom is the *ability to communicate with others,* especially in the area of oral communication. To a large extent this is a natural outgrowth of the pupil's acceptance of himself and of others discussed above. As long as he is insecure, does not feel that what he has to say is worth anything, and as long as he fears or mistrusts the reactions of his peers, he is unlikely to express what he really thinks. But as both he and his classmates gain confidence in themselves, there is increased exchange of ideas in both class and small group discussions.

Along with a pupil's growth in ability to express himself comes a recognition of the need to *listen critically* to what others are saying, and to respond in terms of what he has heard. Such thoughtful participation is a vital part of democratic living. This is especially true in a world in which we are continually being bombarded with the ideas of others through the media of radio, television, and visual advertising.

Solving problems

A third value derived from the experiences a pupil has in classes such as those described in the preceding chapters is the growing *ability to face and solve problems*. He practices the techniques of problem solving in many different situations and learns to apply these, not only to his academic problems, but to those of a personal nature as well. He learns to identify the problem, to plan how it may be solved, to collect information from a wide variety of sources, to organize such data, and to reach a tentative conclusion. He learns that jumping to conclusions is often costly, that few problems can be solved without careful planning, and he is increasingly careful about accepting as facts statements that are not supported by proof. He is developing a scientific attitude.

Some time ago the writer was unexpectedly out of school for several weeks, leaving no plans for a substitute. The eleventh-grade class faced the problem of a substitute who knew nothing about core, as well as what to do about proceeding in class work at a time when a unit had just been completed and no new project was under way. Their first decision was to ask the substitute to let them go ahead on their own. She complied and sat quietly on the sidelines, somewhat abashed at the turn of events. The class then proceeded to identify new areas for study, to make choices, and to move into small groups. Plans were made to solve the problems, groups went to work collecting data, conclusions were reached, and planning for group presentations was carried out. On the day the teacher returned, the first group presented its material to the class. These pupils had had two and one half years of experience in core and were ready and able to face a major problem.

Working with others

A fourth value to be derived from a democratic class is obvious in an analysis of the experience just described, namely, *self-direction* in conjunction with *ability to work cooperatively with others*. The class could not move forward unless individual members worked together toward the common purpose. Neither could it make progress unless each individual member accepted the responsibility for carrying out a specific aspect of the work.

Over the years, a pupil discovers that when anyone fails to take his personal responsibilities seriously, the entire group suffers. He also learns that when an individual ceases to work *with* the members of his group, his own work suffers, since he misses the contributions made by his fellows. He gradually sees that responsibility for himself and responsibility to the group go hand in hand, and he learns to direct his own actions as well as to work with others.

Through his activities in many different groups he also discovers what is needed to make a group progress, the various roles that must be played. Through self-analysis he recognizes the roles he, himself, plays, and the effect of these on a group. At times he sees himself in a supporting role and at times in a leadership role, and gradually he recognizes that both are of vital importance.

Faith in democracy

With the development of these four, (1) a sense of the personal worth of every human being, (2) ability to communicate with others, (3) ability to face and solve problems, (4) self-direction and ability to work cooperatively with others, comes a fifth and major value, namely, an *understanding of the meaning of democracy.*

Democracy ceases to mean freedom to do as you please, and it becomes more than a series of words: government-of-the-people-by-the-people-for-the-people. The words are gradually translated into the practical experiences of sharing power and sharing respect with those who are in the classroom. They are translated into activity that looks toward the good of the group as well as of the individual. The boy or girl who has had experience in the operation of a democratic class has come to realize that not only are there special *rights* for him in a democracy, but that in order to achieve these rights he must accept his *responsibilities.* The classroom has given him practice in these important aspects of life in a democracy on a level which he can understand and in which he can take an active part.

As a teacher faces a group of boys and girls in his classroom, he knows that he will not be able to see the ultimate successes and failures of the pupils in front of him. But if he has faith and belief in democracy as a way of life that we do not want to surrender, he will see the time spent with these pupils in a democratically functioning classroom as an opportunity for helping them to lay strong foundations for such democratic living—in their homes, on their jobs, and in their every relationship to their fellow man. What better training can we give young people for the maintenance of our democratic freedoms in a world that today would gladly destroy them?

Bibliography

Alberty, Harold, *Reorganizing the High School Curriculum,* revised. New York: The Macmillan Company, 1953.

Association for Supervision and Curriculum Development, *Creating a Good Environment for Learning,* 1954 Yearbook. Washington, D.C.: The National Education Association, 1954.

————, *Fostering Mental Health in Our Schools,* 1950 Yearbook. Washington, D.C.: The National Education Association, 1950.

————, *Guidance in the Curriculum,* 1955 Yearbook. Washington, D.C.: The National Education Association, 1955.

————, *Preparation of Core Teachers for Secondary Schools.* Washington, D.C.: The National Education Association, 1955.

Benne, Kenneth D., and Bozidar Muntyan, *Human Relations in Curriculum Change.* New York: The Dryden Press, 1951.

————, and Paul Sheats, "Functional Roles of Group Members," *The Journal of Social Issues,* 4:2:42–47, Spring, 1948.

Bladensburg Junior High School, *A Core Program in a Junior High School Curriculum,* filmstrip and recorded script. Upper Marlboro, Maryland: Board of Education of Prince George's County.

Board of Education of the City of New York, "Practices in Experimental Core Classes," *Curriculum Bulletin,* 1953, 54 Series No. 8, 1954.

Bogardus, E. S., "A Social Distance Scale," *Sociology and Social Research,* Vol. 17, 1933, pp. 265–271.

Bossing, Nelson L., *Principles of Secondary Education,* 2nd ed. Englewood Cliffs, N.J.: Prentice-Hall, Inc., 1955.

————, "What is the Trend Toward Core Curriculum in the Senior High School?" *Bulletin of National Association of Secondary School Principals.* 4D:360–363, April, 1956.

Bush, Robert Nelson, *The Teacher-Pupil Relationship.* Englewood Cliffs, N.J.: Prentice-Hall, Inc., 1954.

Cantor, Nathaniel, *Dynamics of Learning.* Buffalo, N.Y.: Foster & Stewart, 1947.

Cunningham, Ruth, and associates, *Understanding Group Behavior of Boys and Girls.* New York: Teachers College, Columbia University, 1951.

Defining Democracy, 16mm sound film. Wilmette, Illinois: Encyclopedia Britannica Films.

Educational Policies Commission, *Education for All American Youth: A Further Look*. Washington, D.C.: National Education Association, 1952.

———, *Learning the Ways of Democracy*. Washington, D.C.: National Education Association, 1940.

———, *Purposes of Education in American Democracy*. Washington, D.C.: National Education Association, 1938.

Evaluation Committee, *Pupil Self-Evaluation in the Classroom*. Detroit: Metropolitan Detroit Bureau of School Studies, 1957.

Faunce, Roland C., and Nelson L. Bossing, *Developing the Core Curriculum*, 2nd ed. Englewood Cliffs, N.J.: Prentice-Hall, Inc., 1958.

Havighurst, Robert J., *Developmental Tasks and Education*. New York: Longmans, Green, and Company, 1950.

Jennings, Helen Hall and associates, *Sociometry in Group Relations*. Washington, D.C.: American Council on Education, 1948.

Jersild, Arthur T., *In Search of Self*. New York: Teachers College, Columbia University, 1952.

———, *Psychology of Adolescence*. New York: The Macmillan Company, 1957.

Kelly, Earl C., *Education for What Is Real*. New York: Harper & Brothers, Publishers, 1947.

———, *The Workshop Way of Learning*. New York: Harper & Brothers, Publishers, 1951.

———, and Marie I. Rasey, *Education and the Nature of Man*. New York: Harper & Brothers, Publishers, 1952.

Lane, Howard, and Mary Beauchamp, *Human Relations in Teaching*. Englewood Cliffs, N.J.: Prentice-Hall, Inc., 1956.

Lurry, Lucile L., and Elsie J. Alberty, *Developing a High School Core Program*. New York: The Macmillan Company, 1957.

MacConnell, Charles, Ernest O. Melby, C. O. Arndt, and Leslee Bishop, *New Schools for a New Culture,* revised. New York: Harper & Brothers, Publishers, 1953.

Mickelson, John, "What Does Research Say About the Effectiveness of the Core Curriculum?" *The School Review,* 65:2, Summer, 1957.

Miel, Alice, and others, *Cooperative Procedures in Learning*. New York: Bureau of Publications, Teachers College, Columbia University, 1952.

Moreno, J. L., and Helen H. Jennings, "Sociometric Control Studies of Grouping and Regrouping," *Sociometry Monographs,* No. 7. Beacon House, 1947, pp. 20–29.

Noar, Gertrude, *Freedom to Live and Learn*. Philadelphia: The Franklin Publishing Company, 1948.

———, *The Junior High School—Today and Tomorrow*. Englewood Cliffs, N.J.: Prentice-Hall, Inc., 1953.

Parish, Louise, and Yvonne Waskin, *Teacher-Pupil Planning for Better Classroom Learning*. New York: Harper & Brothers, Publishers, 1958.

Practicing Democracy in the Classroom, 16mm sound film. Wilmette, Illinois: Encyclopedia Britannica Films.

Redl, Fritz, and William W. Wattenberg, *Mental Hygiene in Teaching*. New York: Harcourt, Brace and Company, 1951.

Stratemeyer, Florence H., Hamden L. Forkner, and Margaret G. McKim, *Developing a Curriculum for Modern Living*. New York: Teachers College, Columbia University, 1957.

Taba, Hilda, Elizabeth Hall Brady, John T. Robinson, and William E. Vickery, *Diagnosing Human Relations Needs*. Washington, D.C.: American Council on Education, 1951.

The Staff of the Division on Child Development and Teacher Personnel, *Helping Teachers Understand Children*. Washington, D.C.: American Council on Education, 1945.

Toops, Myrtle, *Working in the Core Program in Burris Laboratory School*. Muncie, Indiana: Ball State Teachers College, 1955.

We Plan Together, 16mm sound film. New York: Teachers College, Columbia University, 1949.

Wiles, Kimball, *Teaching for Better Schools*. Englewood Cliffs, N.J.: Prentice-Hall, Inc., 1952.

Wittenberg, Rudolph M., *So You Want to Help People*. New York: Association Press, 1947.

Wright, Grace S., *Core Curriculum in Public High Schools: An Inquiry into Practices,* 1949. Bulletin 1950, No. 5. Washington, D.C.: U.S. Office of Education.

————, *Core Curriculum Development Problems and Practices,* Bulletin 1952, No. 5. Washington, D.C.: U.S. Office of Education.

————, *The Core Program Abstracts of Unpublished Research: 1946–1955.* Washington, D.C.: U.S. Office of Education, 1956.

————, *Block-time Classes and the Core Program in the Junior High School,* 1958. Bulletin 1958, No. 6. Washington, D.C.: U.S. Office of Education.

Zapf, Rosalind, *A Core Curriculum Class in Action,* filmstrip. Detroit: Audio-Visual Utilization Center, Wayne State University.

Class Constitution

We, the members of the 11th grade core class in room 220, the fifth and sixth hours, have compiled and accepted the following as the constitution by which we shall be governed during our class periods through the school year.

ARTICLE I Executive Department

Section I Presidential Duties
   a. Calls class to order.
   b. Shall act as moderator in discussions.
   c. Announces work to class.
   d. Appoints any further officials (non-elective) when needed.
   e. Calls rows to get books on free reading days.

Section II Vice Presidential Duties
   a. Assists President any time called upon to do so.
   b. Takes over presidential duties in the event of said officer's absence.

Section III Secretarial Duties
   a. Takes attendance every day.
   b. Has minutes ready daily in case it is necessary to refer back to previous activities.
   c. Writes all letters for the class.
   d. Reads minutes of previous business meeting at weekly business session.

Section IV Council's Duties
   a. Writes class Constitution.
   b. Records amendments when necessary.
   c. When writing Constitution has power to decide on obscure points without bringing them before class.

411

    d. Explains any obscure points in Constitution to members or teacher.

    e. All amendments to Constitution must be brought before the Council.

    f. Sees to welfare of class as whole.

    g. This body shall meet every Monday and after said meeting shall bring important issues to attention of the class during its following business meeting.

Section V Librarian's Duties

    a. Keeps books in core library neat and in correct order at all times.

    b. Is responsible for care of books during all free reading days during school term and shall make sure that library books are not taken from room without permission.

    c. In case of absence of librarian, assistant librarian shall take over that person's duties.

    d. Takes care of history books, sees that they are kept in order and that no one takes books out of the room without having first signed a slip containing the following information: person's name, date, title of book, and author.

Section VI Social Committee

    a. Arranges social events with approval of the teacher and the class.

Section VII Treasurer's Duties

    a. Shall collect any money from class when needed.

    b. Shall keep accounts.

    c. Makes sure that everyone who is going to attend an event contributes.

    d. Shall do all class buying.

    e. Can ask President to appoint assistant if necessary during planning of social events.

ARTICLE II Legislative Department

Section I All laws for the purpose of operating this class are made by the Board of Education, the principal, our class, and the Council as in order of their importance.

    a. The teacher is considered as a member of our class but has authority to make a ruling when the class does not meet a situation adequately.

b. No law can be passed by anyone which interferes with a law passed by any higher authority.

Section II Laws by Which Our Class Operates

    a. All members of this class are to be in this room when the bell rings at the beginning of the period.

    b. After the bell rings, members of this class are to be at their assigned places ready for the official business at hand.

    c. No work is to be done in this classroom by members of this group for purposes other than the progress or benefit of this class.

    d. Members of this class are to follow and obey their class officers.

    e. There is to be no undue sarcasm or prejudice expressed by members or officers of this class.

ARTICLE III Amendments

As new problems arise, this Constitution may be amended in order to produce a smoother, more efficiently run class.

Section I Procedure for Making an Amendment

    a. Ideas may originate from any eligible source (members of this class or the teacher).

    b. Ideas may be given to members of the Council at any time.

    c. Council members should keep a record of the name of the member who presents the item to the Secretary.

    d. The Council shall study all cases, and shall present pros and cons of the item to the class during our weekly business meeting.

    e. A class vote is taken, and if two thirds or more of this class vote for either approval or denial, the case is completed.

    f. If the vote is divided, the class shall review their views concerning the matter. After these are considered, a second vote is then taken.

    g. When any item is accepted by the class the Council adds it to this Constitution as an amendment.

ARTICLE IV Repealment of Laws

Section I Laws made by the Council and class may only be repealed when careful consideration shows that it hinders the progress of the class.

    a. Repealment may only be obtained by at least an 80% majority of votes against the law in question.

b. Any law or amendment made contrary to a ruling of a higher authority is automatically repealed.

ARTICLE V Elective Department

Section I All committees already selected are to be held in office until the end of the semester.

a. If a member of this class notices that any person on a committee is unsatisfactory he may report to the Council who will bring it before the class.

b. A two thirds majority is needed to remove a committee member. If the motion is carried the officer is withdrawn from office.

Section II The election of officers is to be held every seven weeks starting September 8.

This Way to Democracy[1]

by

THE BOYS AND GIRLS OF NINTH-GRADE CORE

Edwin Denby High School

Detroit, Michigan

Preface

Our aim in writing this book is to explain just what a core class is and to help other people understand our purposes and methods. We have tried to cover everything that has happened during our year in core which would interest and be of importance to the readers. But in a book as small as this, it is next to impossible to include everything that has happened. We sincerely hope that when you finish reading this book, you will have gained enough knowledge on the subject so you will understand core and how our class is run.

Who Are We?

We are the members of a ninth-grade core class in Denby High School, Detroit, Michigan. Our first meeting was almost a year ago and most of us were utter strangers. We had come from different grade schools all over this district. Some of these were the Arthur, Finney, Jackson Intermediate, Robinson and even some schools outside of the state. We have now been in this class for one year, two hours each day. We have enjoyed being together and feel very close to our fellow members.

---

[1] *This Way to Democracy* originally appeared in mimeographed form as a 6 by 8½ inch booklet. One was presented to each member of the class.

Chapter I

What Is Core?

We Define It

Core is a small sample of the world at large. It helps to make us better citizens; it helps to develop our sense of responsibility to a large group of people whom we are bound to meet in our everyday life. It is a class in which we learn to respect others' opinions and to get along well with others.

The things learned in core are such as these:

1. How to work together for the good of the class.
2. How to think critically and carefully.
3. How to face our problems instead of running away from them.
4. How to solve our problems when we meet them.
5. How to gather all information possible on certain topics and how to put it together.
6. How to communicate ideas, in oral and in written form.
7. How to measure our growth toward maturity.

These are things that can be used anywhere, at any time, and in any situation that may arise in our future life.

Chapter II

A Baffling Mystery Confronts Us

We Are Confused

To show how confused we were when we first entered the core class we are including the records of three members of the class, one of whom entered class at the end of the first term when we were already well under way.

A Core Class

Already confused by Denby, I felt more so when our English and history teacher explained to us that this class was not what we expected. It was a core class in which we were not going to use any special textbook nor were we going to study English and history. I hadn't the slightest idea of what she was trying to get across to us.

Then I began to think that this was a class for incompetent people and that we would have Miss Wells to humor us for a year. I commenced to worry because up to then I had not considered myself as feebleminded. When I got home I tried to explain what was already badly muddled to me, to my parents. My mother and dad thought that this must be a lazy man's class and wondered if it would count in credits towards college. It took me quite some time before I really began to understand what core was all about.

What Did I Get Into?

I stepped into Room 217 rather nonchalantly, coming into what I thought was a history and English class, two very boring subjects as far as I was concerned. No sooner did the bell ring than the teacher introduced herself and began to tell us what kind of class we were in. Much to my surprise it wasn't history and English but something called core. Core, what a queer name, and what a queer class I thought. Did it mean we were human guinea pigs for some professors or was it to help us? I didn't know. The first week of school passed and I was still as much in a fog as before. Then we started to train our thoughts. Were we going to just discuss things two periods a day all year? Oh! such a mess! What did I get into? Slowly I began to get the idea of what core was trying to do for me, but it took quite a while.

Much to My Amazement!

My first impression of core was one of bewilderment, and admiration. I was bewildered at first because it was so different from any of my other classes. I was very mixed up the first day of school because I entered the last of the semester and the pupils were very busy with all their work, and so I had to get along as well as I could. When I entered I was seated at a table with four other students instead of at a desk by myself. The class was brought to order as a club meeting would be, then we discussed problems that came up. After that we had our daily work, which was always interesting.

I admired the students and the work they did. I thought it was wonderful and wanted very much to be one of them and try to accomplish some of the work they were doing. It was not long before they made me feel like one of them.

I did accomplish some of their arts, especially one, which was speaking my ideas before the class, but I would not have done so well if it had not been for the help of the others who are now my very best friends.

CHAPTER III

Our Core Room

Arrangement of Our Room

Our core room is arranged to suit our needs. It contains six tables placed around the sides of the room and two rows of chairs in the center. The teacher's desk is at the front of the room. One side of the room has windows looking out on the playground. The opposite side has a three section cupboard with glass doors in which we keep our core library books. Beneath it are drawers where we store our work projects. On the right side of this is a bulletin board, at the present time showing pictures of the leaders in the world. On the left is a bulletin board with our Book List on it.

In the back we have colorful maps of the world fastened on the blackboard. There is also a bookcase with a set of encyclopedia on the shelves. On top of this is a movable bulletin board with pictures made by our class. Above this is a narrow bulletin board along the top of the blackboard. Students decorate this. Two lovely snow scenes mounted in picture frames hang below this. At either end of the front blackboard is a space ruled off in which we record our weekly plans. Above are work projects done by students. Our room is arranged sensibly and we enjoy it very much.

CHAPTER IV

On Your Mark, Get Set, Go!

Our Introduction to Denby

At the beginning of our first term of core, we spent several weeks following an "orientation program" planned by the teacher. As we were new in the school we did not know where anything was, so this was a great help. Our teacher asked the school nurse to come in and tell us all about her work in our school, to tell us where her office was, and the days and hours we could see her if we needed her.

The editor of our school paper also accepted an invitation to visit us. He told us all about the *Log*, our school paper, how it is prepared and printed. He explained how often it is published and how much it would cost us for a term's subscription.

One of the student librarians then came in and told us all about our school library. She explained such things as how to take out books, and when the library was open. The class then went down to the library and the librarian showed us all around and explained how to use all of the material. When that was over we knew a lot more about our library than we had before.

After two weeks of visiting about our new building and listening to people tell us about the school, we began to feel a bit more at home in Denby.

We Discuss Democracy

Following our orientation program we spent several weeks discussing democracy in the world. We considered such questions as what countries have democracy, what countries do not have democracy. We did some research in the school library on certain sub-topics of democracy and we discussed these in class. Then we approached the problem of whether democracy could be worked out successfully in a classroom. The class brought up many objections and agreements. We finally came to the decision that we could run the core class as a democratic class.

Then we felt that we had to have an organization or a plan by which to run our own class. We worked this out by having every pupil write out his or her idea of the type of organization needed. We then divided into small groups to discuss our plans and to have the members of each group exchange ideas until they, as a group, had a plan which they felt to be good. These were then reported to the entire class for further consideration. We then chose the plan of organization which best suited our needs. This will be described in the next section.

Election of Officers

At the beginning of each term our class elected officers. We elected a President, Vice-President, Secretary, Treasurer, Clerk, Hostess and General Substitute. In electing our officers we put the nominations for each office on the board and then discussed the qualifications needed for each position. This was followed by the election. The person who received the most votes was elected for each office. This method was used for electing all of our officers.

The duties of the officers are as follows: The President asks for the attention of the class at the beginning of the class periods, asks for the minutes, and the attendance. He also takes care of any business which has to be discussed by the class.

The Vice-President and the President alternate each week and when the President is absent the Vice-President is able to take his place.

The Secretary writes the minutes for the class and is responsible for reading them before the class the following day. Sometimes the General Substitute reads the minutes to vary the program. The minutes are then corrected and accepted by the class.

The Treasurer collects and keeps an account of any money collected.

The Clerk takes attendance.

When there are visitors the Hostess gives them chairs and explains the work so that they understand what we are doing.

The General Substitute takes the responsibilities of any officer during his absence.

CHAPTER V

This Is the Way We
Run Our Class

How Our Core Class Is Run

To you that line would probably mean that our core class is run by the teacher, but it is not. No, we have elected officers to lead our class. Oh, now do not think that our teacher has nothing to do with us, because she has. She helps and guides us whenever we need help and guidance. Our core class is often called a "democratic class" because everything we would like to do, or that we have to do, is discussed by the class and then voted on to see whether it is worth while, what good it will do us, and whether we approve of it.

Every day our class is opened by the President, who calls the class to order. He then asks the Secretary to read the minutes. After this the class corrects the minutes, and a motion is put on the floor to pass the minutes as read and corrected. The Clerk takes the attendance and the President asks if there is any business to be taken up. If there is we discuss the topic that is brought up. For example: one day we may discuss the organization of a baseball team, another day we may discuss our marking system, both of which take much time. The business meeting is then adjourned, and the teacher takes over the class. Some of the students prepare our bulletin board, while others may go to the library to work on topics or read books.

Every week the President and Vice-President get together and choose a committee to work out a schedule for the following week. The schedule they make then goes on the blackboard and tells us what we will do the week following.

So you see our core class is not just an ordinary class.

Our Weekly Scheme

During the first semester, our class planned our work as it came along but we found it did not work out well because we were always leaving something out.

While visiting a core class in Evanston, Illinois, our teacher noticed that they made a weekly plan. They put it on the blackboard and in this manner the class could tell at a glance what the week held in store for them. In that way they included the things that would otherwise have been omitted. At the beginning of the second semester a member suggested that we follow their example which was approved by the class.

The President chooses a group of students each week to make the plan. The class corrects it and it is then written on the blackboard. A special space is set aside on the blackboard, which is used for recording our weekly plan. One week it looked like this:

CORE II

Monday	Scholastic Test	and	Discussion of Scholastic Articles
Tuesday	Creative Writing	and	Work on Topics
Wednesday	Report: Caroline	and	Work on Topics
Thursday	Book Work		
Friday	Free Reading Library		

Our First Adventure in Topics

"Topics! What on earth are those? I'm not prepared for this kind of work!" This was but one of the many remarks the teacher was confronted with.

Before the members of our class selected their topics a list of suggestions was put on the board to help us. This list was made up of suggestions made by the boys and girls and the teacher. From this list the area of work was selected which was of most interest. The members of the class then divided into groups, with each group selecting a part of the work on which they were most anxious to work. When the groups were organized they went to work collecting their material.

"Teacher, someone made a mistake! I have a topic but no one told me where I could get any material on this!"

At last we were on our own and we had to struggle for ourselves. Material must be collected from every possible source by ourselves. No one was there to place the material in our hands. We had no textbook. It was our responsibility.

We now have learned extremely well how to get material from the school library and the public libraries. Some of the students went down to the main public library to search even deeper into the mystery of our topics. A lot of the pupils sent away for information on their topics. Our teacher often brings in any books, material, or clippings she happens to find that will help us.

Our topics, we discovered, were both interesting and educational with fascinating titles such as "Youth Movements," "Communism," "Democracy," "The Orient," and many more.

Core has taught us to work and think for ourselves successfully. It has enabled us to work in a truly democratic way. With the help of our teacher and our fellow students, we succeeded in gathering satisfactory information about our problems.

We Join Hands with Other Core Classes

The Core Council is a body composed of two representatives from each core class in the school. The group has as officers a Chairman and a Secretary. The Chairman calls the meeting to order and asks the Secretary to read the minutes. The minutes are read, corrected, and passed by the council members.

The attendance is taken and if a representative has an absence record of 3 against his name a new representative must be chosen from his class. Then the business is continued. Such things come before the council as: (1) How to keep the rooms clean and attractive; (2) What bulletin board space may be used by each class; (3) How to develop respect toward officers in a class; (4) How to make the members of the core classes feel that they are not alone in their problems of core.

The council helps to solve the problems of the classes and to make plans to keep further problems from arising. It acts as a steering body. The council is a new organization in Denby.

One of the biggest problems that the council has faced is the problem of whether to have all eight core teachers present at the meetings or to only have two. This problem is still bothering us. We hope to settle this and many others satisfactorily for the benefit of the classes.

A Week in Review

Monday, October 28.

The class was called to order by the Acting Chairman. For our business discussion today, we considered the problems of electing our class officers. This discussion proved to be of help to most of us. We discussed the qualifications for the various offices during both class periods. It would have lasted longer if the class had not been disturbed by the bell at the end of the tenth hour.

Tuesday, October 29.

The meeting was opened when the Acting Chairman called the class to order. We discussed what officers were needed to carry on our business. We discussed and voted on whether we should have the following: a president, a vice-president, a secretary, a clerk, a hostess, and a general substitute. During the tenth hour we voted for our class officers.

The meeting was adjourned at the tenth hour bell.

Wednesday, October 30.

With the help of Miss Wells the new officers conducted the class for the first time.

We then discussed what topics would be interesting and valuable for study.

The tenth hour we voted on what topics we would like, and it was unanimously accepted that we have as our main topic 'Special Interests."

The tenth hour bell concluded the meeting.

Thursday, October 31.

The President called the class to order, the Secretary then read the minutes, and the Clerk took the attendance. Both reports were accepted as read. Some of the pupils went to the Forum meeting at which the Negro-White integration problem was discussed. The remainder of the class worked in the room and in the library on their topics.

During the tenth hour some of the pupils remained at the Forum meeting. The pupils who were left went to the library to find some information that would help them further with their topics. The bell ended our class period.

Friday, November 1.

We had our news events today, which proved to be of interest to all of the class. After discussing the news, the entire class went to the library as it was our library day.

The class was ended for the day when the tenth hour bell rang.

Imparting Wisdom

After the pupils have chosen problems to work on they decide on a certain length of time in which the reports must be finished. Before a person starts work on his problem he prepares a plan or outline of what material he can find on his topic.

He then spends days and often weeks collecting information on his subject. After a time all this material is put together and made ready for a report.

When all is ready he presents his work to the class. Sometimes it is in the form of an oral report, sometimes a play, or perhaps a scrapbook. The report is judged by the class on such things as the speaking ability of the person, the way he holds the attention of the class, how well he is prepared, how well he has organized his material, and how thoroughly he has covered his subject. This is to help him see how he can improve his work and do an even better job another time. After all this is finished, the pupil is ready to start on another problem.

Action on All Fronts

Since we do not really study history in core we thought it would help us to learn about some up to date happenings in the world about us.

Three ideas for doing this were in the spotlight.

No. 1—general discussion with the President in charge.

No. 2—a small group to take charge of a discussion of happenings on various fronts.

No. 3—a different person to lead the discussion each week.

We had a long discussion as to which was best. Number 1 was decided upon but we discovered later that our system did not work out because too often everyone was not prepared to join in the discussion.

There were many topics of interest. Outstanding events concerning the state or the nation were considered as they came into the limelight.

Our present way of handling news events is to have a short test taken from our *Scholastic* magazine every Monday. The *Scholastic* contains the outstanding happenings during the week throughout the nation. Lately we have chosen students to prepare the test instead of the teacher. The test is followed by a discussion led by volunteer members of the class. We have found this method of giving the news helpful to us in understanding our present situation in the world.

CHAPTER VI

We Have Bookworms

Too

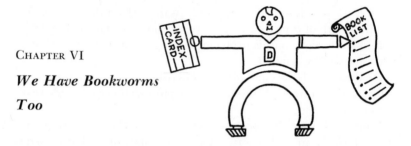

Bookworms' Special Cupboard

We have at last found a cure for those pesky bookworms, which have somehow managed to get into our classroom.

Oh my no, not traps, but a library in our classroom, with books ranging on every subject from stuffy history books to very interesting fiction books.

How do we get our assortment of books? At the beginning of every semester we all wonder why our pockets are fifty cents lighter than we expected. Then we recall that we have each turned that amount in for the purpose of buying new books for our core library. It is a slow process to build up a good library, but in some way the number of books seems to increase and our noses go deeper into the collection of books each semester.

How do we organize them? The non-fiction books are arranged according to the Dewey Decimal System. The fiction books are placed alphabetically according to authors on the shelves.

Bookworms please note: Drop around sometime and see our shelves of books of which we are so proud.

Read It and List It

There is a group in our core class that we call our bookworms. These people read books constantly. All the books they read are recorded on a list. This list consists of the name of the book and next to the name of the book we have a series of little colored dot stickers to indicate the interest in the book, for example a blue dot means that it is an excellent book, a red dot shows that it is a good book, a green dot means fair, and an orange dot means that it was poor and has not been enjoyed at all.

Every person who reads a book reports it to the small, but energetic, group that keeps the list up to date. If one of our bookworms wants a good book he refers to the book list and selects a book that is shown to be popular according to the number of little dots, preferably blue or red dots, pasted after it.

We Read for Our Topics

Reading for our topics has had many advantages. We learned how to use the library and while looking for information we found not only what we were looking for, but also interesting material which will be useful to us at all times. There are many sources to which we can turn for material for our topics. Some of these are encyclopedia, newspapers, magazines, and reference books.

One fine Saturday noon some of the members of the class took a trip across the city to the main public library with our teacher. There we learned much about a large library and spent the afternoon looking for more information for our topics.

We really enjoy reading for our topics because of the information we acquire, and we also learn how to use this information.

CHAPTER VII

Danger—Proceed at Your Own Risk

Marking Report Cards

Strange as it may seem, we mark our own report cards. To you it probably seems that we have an opportunity to always get good marks. This is not the case, because we try to mark ourselves as honestly as we can. We use the following method. The class chooses areas in which we will try to improve through our work in core. Both semesters our class has selected as the two main areas (1) citizenship, (2) achievement in work. Then, under these areas, we list points to be considered.

CITIZENSHIP GOALS

1. Self-Control
2. Get along well with others
3. Help solve any problem I or the class may have
4. Courtesy to all members of the group
5. Carry out that for which I am responsible
6. Pay attention at all times
7. Help others whenever I can
8. Consider both sides of every problem
9. Give in gracefully when I am wrong

ACHIEVEMENT IN WORK

1. Take an active part in the work of small groups
2. Take an active part in the general class work
3. Select problems that are of interest, importance and value to me
4. Keep at work until it is finished
5. Gather all the material possible within the time limit
6. Work steadily at my project during work periods
7. Work on my topic or project outside of class
8. Completed work is well done
9. Participation in Scholastic work:

    a. Reading of magazine
    b. Success in tests
    c. Participation in discussions

When report card marking rolls around we record in the squares after each point on our goal sheets the number which best describes where we stand. The following is an example:

CITIZENSHIP			5 – excellent
	Pupil	*Teacher*	4 – above average
Self-Control . . .	4	3	3 – average
Courtesy	3	3	2 – below average
			1 – very poor

In the first column we mark our opinion. If I were above average in responsibility and only average in courtesy I would mark myself as above. After I have continued down the column I would average the numbers. If my average was 4, I would look on the column below to find my mark:

$$5 - A$$
$$4 - B$$
$$3 - C$$
$$2 - D$$
$$1 - E$$

That means my mark would be a B. I put this mark on my goal sheet. The teacher then goes through all of the records, writing her opinion in the next column. If she thinks I am only average in both Self-Control and Courtesy she would mark as in the sample. Unless her marks vary much from mine, she will not change my final mark. But if her marks would differ widely, she would hold a conference with me to see how I had marked myself, and she would explain her marking. Between us, we would decide on the best evaluation.

It may sound confusing but it is comparatively simple and has turned out to be successful.

CHAPTER VIII

Detour to Fun

Talent on Parade

The radio play was one of our many achievements, and this was one of the most interesting.

Joan, who is a member of a drama class, noticed a play in our *Scholastic* magazine called, "The Snow Goose." She brought it to class and raised the question as to whether we wanted to try to produce the play. We did. So we had tryouts with Joan directing. She had the boys and girls who were interested each read a part of the play to us so that we could judge who was best for each part.

The preparations for the play are not complete as yet, but they are still continuing and we hope to hear the finished play over the public address system in our room soon.

Discussing World Affairs

Our introduction to the Forum was accidental. On October 8, we found ourselves locked out of our classroom because the door knob had disappeared, and we were invited into the room across the hall where the Forum was meeting. The purpose of the Forum is to discuss problems that are before the world today. It is a student organization and is largely attended by upperclassmen. We were surprised by the warm welcome we received as freshmen. That being our first visit, there was very little discussion among the audience and very few questions. We then automatically became members of the Forum, which meets every Thursday, the 9th and 10th hours.

The next week, Miss Wells asked for volunteers to attend the Forum meeting for the next two periods. They discussed "The Integration Problem." Since then, we have been going quite regularly. Some of the topics that have been discussed are Inflation, Russia, and The Student Council. We enjoy this opportunity to work with some of the older students.

Using Our Imaginations

One day in January Miss Wells broached the subject of creative writing to us. There were many groans and few approvals, but this was one of the few times she told us to do something so we tried our hand at it.

Our first subject was supplied by Miss Wells in the form of pictures of winter scenes. We were to choose any one we wished and follow our imagination to write a story, a poem, an essay, or an ode, whichever our fancy was best suited for. When it neared the end of the period we stopped, and a few boys and girls rather reluctantly read their stories out loud and we were surprised at the thoughts some of the group had expressed. There were some who really had talent for this sort of thing.

We discussed the subject the next day and we arrived at the conclusion that we did get some benefit out of it in the sense that we were having experience at using our imagination and expressing our thoughts on paper. We decided we would use different methods to start our imaginations working. Some that were planned were as follows: taking a walk, listening to music, and looking at pictures. The second time we did it in what we thought was a very original way. We darkened the room and Miss Wells stood in front of the class and in the silent, black room struck a match, holding it aloft until it flickered and died out. Then we wrote down what we had been thinking while the match had flamed.

When Miss Wells read some of these to the class she did not tell us who wrote them. This made it much more interesting. This was done quite a while after the first time and there were many more approvals.

The following are examples of our attempts at creative writing.

FREEDOM OF WORSHIP

The soft, melancholy music of a church organ played endlessly on as a dim yellow light lit the faces of people as they prayed in silent meditation.

An elderly woman lifted her head long enough to gaze upon a service flag and then once more bowed her head in solemn prayer. Heartbreaking throbs pulsed through the quiet, peaceful church as she thought of her little boy over in free America, fighting to preserve what he loved, "freedom of worship."

A Night in Hungary

It is night in Hungary, and we are walking slowly through the deserted streets. We see a faint glimmer of light coming from behind some heavy black curtains. If the sentry were to see this light it would mean almost certain death for the occupants of the house. We cautiously go to the door, knock a signal—three short taps and one long. The door opens quickly and we enter, for in the corner is a secret radio picking up a short wave broadcast from England. The Russians do not like this and anyone caught listening to a secret radio will be shot immediately! It is well after midnight and the small group sits about the radio listening intently. Suddenly at a distance can be heard the footsteps of the guard making his rounds. Swiftly the radio is concealed in the fireplace. The lights are put out, and the night is quiet except for the sound of the soldier's footsteps coming closer and closer. Suddenly he stops at the door. Our hearts are pounding as he tries it. But as he finds it closed he proceeds on his way.

Nature's Creatures

The woods were alive with tiny creatures. Mother hare was sunning herself and three babies while father hare kept watch for enemies. The sun, just risen, was nature's alarm clock for her woodland creatures. The crows, five in number, were admiring the three hare children with much cawing and flapping of wings. Then came the naughty blue jay who sent them flying away in haste. He had no praise, just his loud harsh call that echoed through the woods.

Scurrying up and down the sides of sombre pines were the thick-furred squirrels, teasing, praising, and announcing everybody's business to all who would listen.

Down by the lake a flotilla of wild baby ducks were venturing for the first time onto the quiet surface of the water. Occasionally one would be upset by the ripples coming from the warm south wind. Their parents watched them carefully, uttering sounds of encouragement as they faltered.

Deeper in the woods the bigger creatures were enjoying this day of spring. The spotted fawns leaped nimbly around their more serious parents whose loving brown eyes follow their every move.

Waltzing down a tiny path to the lake came a beautiful animal, whose luxurious fur was ruffled by the wind. Behind came three miniature replicas of the leader. With dainty steps, and heads held high they defied all enemies. The blue jay flew above and came floating down to rest on a bush near the four. The white fur on their backs bristled and the blue jay left in a hurry. The skunks proceeded daintily on their way.

The Honor Roll

Much to our amazement and delight we have discovered that we have a very talented class.

Ellen Wendt, Ruth Jones, Helen Constantine, Betty Hoffman, and Irene Janette, participated in the Christmas Concert, and we were very proud to hear them sing.

Irene might be called the all-around girl, because we later discovered she also belongs to the Home Economics Club, which is one of our school's many clubs, and also works with the Junior Counselors, who help other students who are behind in their work.

Our school orchestra is one of our greatest prides and we were very pleased when we found that Betty Hoffman and Ruth Jones played the piano, making two more students to be added to our Honor Roll.

Frank Adano came stalking into the room one day with a large letter D on his sweater. He won it playing basketball.

Walter Kerr comes to our rescue during air raid drills. He is a member of the Bomb Squad, whose duty it is to protect the school and its students by disposing of incendiary bombs and helping to evacuate the school in case it should be badly hit.

Barbara Watson, Frank Adano, Caroline Henderson, and Ann Arnau participated in the Projection Club by assisting teachers in running the movie machine when it is needed.

We believe we have every right to be proud of our class. Before entering core, we were just plain students, and now we have become singers, players, authors, athletes, actors, and air raid assistants. Core has helped us to become all of these and in our future perhaps we will be able to thank core for our success.

CHAPTER IX

Social Interlude

Holiday Spirit

One of our biggest social events came at Christmas, when we held our Christmas party. The preparations for the party were made by small groups of students selected by the class.

When the day arrived for the party, the room was decorated with Christmas pictures and the furniture was arranged so that we could play games and dance. One of the games we played was as follows: Each person wrote a question on one piece of paper and an answer to it on another. These were then collected and mixed up so that each person had a question and answer that didn't belong together. Then each person read the question and answer he held. This provided amusement for quite some time. After that we played more games and danced.

Some days before the party we had drawn names for an exchange of small Christmas gifts. These were brought in and placed in a big, beautifully decorated box. Frank played postman and delivered the red and green wrapped bundles. There were many "oh's" and "ah's" and we enjoyed it. Then the refreshments of pop, cookies and all kinds of candy were served. We ate and ate and ate!! We all had a very good time and want another party before the end of the year.

Social Welcome

On Thursday, February 18, we held Open House for our mothers from 2 to 4 o'clock in the afternoon. Seventeen mothers came.

After we were settled Frank Adano called the class together and we presented a sample business meeting. Then Miss Wells summarized core and its work in a very interesting talk. Graphs were drawn on the blackboard to help describe just what we had accomplished. After Miss Wells had finished, she asked if any mothers had any questions.

Some did and were given the information they desired. Caroline Henderson gave a short talk on the "Core Council," and "What Core Is." Then Richard Hande talked on the "Work of Core" and lastly Barbara Watson talked on "What Core Means to Me." After the talks Florence Craft and Doris Borg served refreshments of ice cream and cookies and candy mints. Our tea table was decorated with a bouquet of spring flowers and our color scheme was red, white, and blue. When the bell rang at the end of the tenth hour, no one left for home, but stayed and talked and finished their refreshments. Everyone had a good time.

Through the Halls of Denby High

The second semester our class thought it would be nice to lend a helping hand and show some of the 9B's around our school. So we sent an invitation to the 9B core class in the next room, asking them if they would not like to have us show them around. They accepted gladly. Then we got together in groups of two and drew names to find out whom we would take. It also took a day to list the important places in the building to show them.

On the appointed day, we went next door in pairs and each person was introduced. Then we started out on our tour through the building. When we came back to our room, we brought our guests in and introduced them to Miss Wells. Miss Wells then explained some things about core and also asked Barbara and Caroline to tell what they thought about core. After that we went around and got acquainted with everyone.

CHAPTER X

Something to Remember Us By

Our Book

One day we were struck with the brilliant idea of writing a history of our year in core. We discussed this, the class giving their comments and suggestions. Through this book we hoped to bring you closer to the aims of core, to help you understand the work that is done in core, and to show you some of the things accomplished in our class.

The staff chose officers and they are as follows:

Editor .... CAROLINE HENDERSON
Assistant Editor .... LARRY SHAEFFER
Feature Editor .... MADGE HOLLIS
Arranging Editor .... MARIE WILLETT
Publishing Editor .... BARBARA WATSON
Copy Editor .... LILLIAN ROSS
Illustrating .... FRANK ADANO

There were many others on the staff besides the editor in each department. This group of staff members has worked hard to make the book a success. All the chapter headings were suggested by different members of the class and were put on the board and voted on by the class. Several ideas for the title page were presented to the class for their opinion. The cover was decided upon in the same way. To meet the deadline the staff officers stayed after school to complete the book.

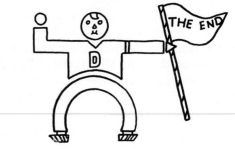

CHAPTER XI

Summing It Up

Our Conclusions

Our final conclusions are much different from our first impressions, because we have learned what core is. It is a class where we learn to work with other people, a class where we learn to live in a democracy. Core has done much for us. We have learned how to use the library because we needed it for work on our topics. Most of us have overcome our fear of speaking in front of a group, because we have had to do it when we discussed our problems. Core has also improved our manner of speaking. We have learned to consider both sides of any problem and we have learned to think for ourselves. We feel that we really have accomplished things in our year in core.

Interview of Former Core Pupils

The following is a complete transcription of an informal discussion of the recollections of thirteen former pupils of Denby High School, Detroit, concerning their four years' experience in a core program. The discussion took place in the home of Miss Wells, their former core teacher.

The interviewer[1] opened the session by commenting on the various aspects of core experience these young people might have had in their four years of high school. He asked them to name whatever came to mind at the moment as they thought back to their core class. Since the tape recorder failed to pick up this brief introduction, the record starts at the following point.

INTERVIEWER

Creative projects, since that was one you mentioned . . . Then we will go from that to the business meeting.

GINNY

The reason we did it was because it seemed that everybody was getting mixed up. We couldn't settle on anything. We didn't want to take a regular topic. The whole class was arguing with each other. We had a creative project on the board but no one knew what to do. Miss Wells suggested getting into groups—to do something which represented what we did in core. Each group took a different phase of core. One was the way in which people presented topics. We put it in a hat box . . .

MARGE

We went around and took pictures. Some made models of groups working together, business meetings, showing different things we were doing.

---

[1] Dr. Theodore Rice, Wayne State University, Detroit.

GINNY

Pipe cleaner figures of people who participated in this topic—the way they presented it . . .

WALTER

It represented the whole core program. We made stuff out of cardboard.

INTERVIEWER . .

Was this pretty easy, do you remember?

U.V.[2]

While Miss Wells was away.

U.V.

No, after she came back.

FRANCES

Wasn't it something Miss Wells tried on us when we just got together? Wasn't that when we first combined classes?

RUTH

No, it was after everyone knew each other.

JIM

No. It wasn't in the twelfth grade because Jeff made a model of the opaque projector. That *was* in the tenth grade.

GINNY

We did this because first of all everybody was going into the same group. Everybody knew everyone in the group. We drew names to see if we could work with different people.

INTERVIEWER

They were making cliques?

FRANCES

Three classes were broken up. We were getting into cliques. I think we thought it was our idea to get into this project; but after . . .

INTERVIEWER

Did it work?

FRANCES

Oh, yes. We worked together better after that. We had a closer union.

INTERVIEWER

At least it was an ice-breaker for this group. I get the idea that you used the creative project especially as a way to get acquainted.

---

[2] Unidentified voice.

JIM

After we used it that way we used it later on to illustrate a project.

RUTH

Yes, we did use it afterward.

MARGE

We had a parents' night after that and used some of the things to show them what we did in core—like the pictures and a lot of things.

DAN

I gave a report on my trip from Scotland and made a model of clay to show my trip across the Atlantic. I think that was later on.

WALTER

I remember that.

INTERVIEWER

Do you remember about the start of core? What was core like at first? Did the teacher tell you what it was all about? Did you spend a lot of time trying to find out?

SEVERAL

We were in three different classes.

INTERVIEWER

Did you like it? How did the teachers start out? How did the teacher try to help you?

JIM (*Names four different teachers in core.*)

In our class there were a few boys who had heard about it from other sources and you see you were just put into the core class and these definitely wanted out right away. So they got out. Everyone wondered what core was all about. I think we started with a prejudice against it. I remember it took us quite a while before we started on the first project but Miss Wells helped us out and explained what it was all about.

INTERVIEWER

Do you remember anything about the classroom that struck you as different from other classrooms? What was the atmosphere as compared to other rooms?

WALTER

Outside of bringing the class together . . .

SCOTT

More friendly.

GINNY

There were plants, curtains on the windows . . .

RUTH

Brighter.

JIM

It was easier. Some people were able to get away with things easier than in regular English class. Some people—not all of them.

INTERVIEWER

Do you mean the atmosphere was so informal that people did not have any responsibility?

DAN

Not this class here. That was before. I think the caliber of students picked up for the final core class . . . weeded out . . .

INTERVIEWER

Can you think of someone who might have been weeded out but who turned out to be a pretty swell person?

GINNY

Jean.

(*Everyone laughed, including* JEAN.)

INTERVIEWER

What do you suppose happened that made it different later?

U.V.

I think it was the caliber of the students they had later. Because they wanted to learn.

FRANCES

At one point there was a choice given as to whether you would stay in or get out.

INTERVIEWER

What about your class? Didn't you pick names or something like that?

MARGE

You were more or less put in it and some resented it.

DAN

You get some kids who don't want to work and we had projects on the board like hot-rods, hunting, and things like that. If you want to learn some English and history or something like that, it wasn't any good. Of course you get lots of writing.

MARGE

Don't you remember? It was a fall scene.

INTERVIEWER

I don't know that the tape recorder will sort us out. I think it's better to do that because you stimulate each other. As I hear you describing that room it is a room that is so informal that people can get away with things.

BETTY

I think that was more in the early years. You were just in high school, less responsibility, you thought you were getting away with something and so you did. At first I think it was more as a means of getting away. It got to be an interest so we began to put more into it.

INTERVIEWER

Did you get so you put more into it as years went on? I am interested because it sounds like if anyone wanted to get away with anything he could. But you are not ready to buy that, are you? Did you learn some group controls?

FRANCES

I think you could grow out of it because if you had any interest in school at all you would be wasting your time. We would have double periods and you just don't waste away two periods. If for nothing else just out of sheer boredom you would want to do something.

INTERVIEWER

Was there anything about the class itself that would make a person slow down?

BETTY

The kids who didn't do any work were looked down on by those who worked and everyone told them about it and they weren't liked as well. It wasn't so much the teacher who told them. The pupils told them.

INTERVIEWER

This is a kind of social pressure from the class itself.

FRANCES

The group was very close, too. I think that had a lot to do with it.

INTERVIEWER

Let's see whether there is something else in this bunch of notes that relates to this. Could you tell who was going to work on what?

FRANCES

The general opinion of kids in the regular English class in the n
grade was, "Were you too dumb?" or "Did you think you were spe
or going to get out of some work?"

JIM

How were we chosen? Is it hard to get in? I think that could confu
you.

DAN

The first day I was in core I came out and sombody said, the othe
students would ask, "Where are your books? Aren't you getting any
books for English and history? That's a kind of dumb class." And the
first day you're in school it kind of gets you. I wondered about it and
my folks wondered, too.

INTERVIEWER

Let's make a note about this question: How did you get into core?
Would you agree with the statement then, that the atmosphere was
more informal, brighter, somebody said, and that there were more
things in the room? Bulletin boards . . .

U.V.

Yes, bulletin boards.

U.V.

Pictures.

WALTER

Lots of color.

U.V.

Frances did the boards.

INTERVIEWER

And you let her because she was so good? Frances, did you do all the
boards or did somebody help you?

FRANCES

Betty helped, too.

WALTER

I helped, too.

DICK

We all helped once.

FRANCES

We used to have a picture around the schedule.

U.V.

In the beginning I think you could. The fellows wanted to study . . .

BETTY

. . . something like hot-rods. At first the fellows were working in groups and the girls were in another group, but after a while they started mixing up. Then you began to get more of a variety.

INTERVIEWER

I wonder what happened? Did you ever take a look at the groups to see how they were working?

WALTER

Self-evaluation.

JIM

We used to do self-evaluation and group evaluation.

DAN

I think another thing we used to worry about, too, if this group wasn't doing work and you were doing work, you wondered what was going on. You knew it would spoil the class. You thought if they were going to get away with it you were going to try to get away with it.

MARGE

If another group is working real hard, then your group isn't going to be up to the others. It reaches a state of balance, if you think your group isn't doing as well as the other group.

DAN

You marked yourself and had your evaluation sheets. If you knew you would be lying, you wouldn't say you had done "B" work if you hadn't in gathering information and in group work.

INTERVIEWER

You weren't kidding anyone but yourself.

DAN

A lot depends on the person.

JIM

Core depends on the person.

DAN

What you put into it and what you want to get out of it.

INTERVIEWER

Well, I was saying that you can anticipate what people want to work on. Can you remember anything you thought especially good? Some high points and some that were really low?

MARION

1 can't remember.

JIM

I remember reading about Admiral Byrd. I think it was in the ninth grade—his book, *Alone*—and I did other research on that. I remember I thought it was a good topic. That was by myself. I had some illustrations, too. I remember I had some pictures or something and used the opaque projector.

DAN

I think it was for our final exam—individual reports. The only one I can remember was my own.

INTERVIEWER

Do you suppose you remember the individual assignments better?

BETTY

It was easier to do group reports. You didn't have to worry about getting up in front of the class and having everyone looking at you. We had a real good one on ancient Egypt.

JIM

We had something about manners.

BETTY

I remember one we did one time. Was it in the twelfth grade when we did the one about what jobs we were going into? That was a doozy!

INTERVIEWER

What was a doozy about it?

DAN

It took a lot of work.

U.V.

It took about a year.

INTERVIEWER

Did it mean anything to you? Was this something you folks figured out that you wanted to do?

U.V.

No, it was required.

JIM

We had to write about three possible careers we would like to go into: interview people, find out about them, do some research.

INTERVIEWER

Do you think you remember things that were required of you more than things you decided you wanted to do?

MARGE

You mean required by the teacher?

SEVERAL

No.

DAN

As far as requirements in class are concerned, we always had to hand in notes, reports and things like that. They were always written up and handed in.

INTERVIEWER

Have you got any of them now?

JIM

I used one of mine recently for a speech class. I was making a speech and I had to look up some material and remembered I had made a similar report in core. So I got it and it helped me a lot. I remember that.

INTERVIEWER

Was that vocation unit any good? You had already made your decisions, had you? This careers' study, did it help?

WALTER

For some it did.

JIM

It was right along with what I'm doing. I know everything I had in my report I was interested in for about a year before I wrote the report. But it did help me.

INTERVIEWER

Can you remember anything that just left you cold? Something you did as an individual or group that was just a dismal flop?

SCOTT

The pipe cleaner one.

DAN

The thing I thought was a flop was music appreciation. We set aside a day . . .

FRANCES

I don't think we were ready for it.

BETTY

The day that everyone brought something that was supposed to be the most beautiful thing he had. Everybody sat around and no one took it seriously, just laughed.

INTERVIEWER

Was it because you were embarrassed?

MARGE

You were sort of baring your soul.

DAN

I thought the reason it was a flop was because I myself spent about five minutes preparing that project that day and maybe others did too. Made it a last minute thing. That might have been part of the trouble.

INTERVIEWER

Did you learn anything from that kind of lesson?

JIM

I listened to the various items and that was about it.

BETTY

Most did it because they had to do something. No one took it seriously. Scott said his wallet; Walter's was a picture of his mother. Someone brought his record. Ruth a ring.

U.V.

What did you bring?

U.V.

I brought a poem.

INTERVIEWER

How do you happen to remember these things?

GINNY

It was so different.

INTERVIEWER

Business meetings. Did you learn anything from those things?

DICK

Democratic procedures.

JIM

The thing I got mad about was the planning committee. The planning was always left up to certain individuals in class. Instead of having an all-out discussion about what we were going to have during the week they just put it on the board and it was accepted just like that. And that was that.

WALTER

We voted to have a planning committee and didn't we change the planning committee every so often? What did we plan for?

FRANCES

We had a day for movies, reports, a business meeting . . .

BETTY

There were just a certain number of things that we could do so what was the point of going out into the hall. You knew you had to do certain things. We always looked forward to movie day.

INTERVIEWER

That reminds me of a core class I had in Evanston. They had set up a schedule. The class had a series of reports and after each report I commented. This threw them off their timetable and the chairman said to me, "If you're going to make comments on the reports after they're read, shouldn't we put you in the schedule too?"

You don't remember any real issues in the business meetings?

DAN

Sometimes the issue was raised more than any other, when you were getting pressed for time for your report and maybe a business meeting, or movie, or something was put in and you thought you should have more time for group work—in other words, have three days for group work—that's when we would get into arguments.

JIM

I remember when I was chairman banging away with the little old mallet. I remember I got some dirty looks.

(Much laughter.)

INTERVIEWER

Can you remember what the issues were?

BETTY

Some were far behind and needed more time. Others were up and wanted to go ahead. Some weren't progressing.

INTERVIEWER

Now, let's see. Field trips . . .

SCOTT

I'll always remember Greenfield Village.

DAN

Pushing Scott around in a wheel chair.

MARION

Cranbrook.

INTERVIEWER

How did you decide on field trips? What did they relate to? Were they picnics or to be picked in terms of things for study? You mentioned Greenfield Village and Cranbrook. How did you get out on those trips? Did the teacher pick those for you?

SEVERAL

Everybody made suggestions and we picked one from the list.

SCOTT

We discussed them.

INTERVIEWER

Did you go anywhere you wanted to?

BETTY

Did we ever complete the one we were going to do relating to religion? We were going to visit different churches.

INTERVIEWER

You have that yet to do?

FRANCES

Didn't we take some trips that related to our topics?

JIM

Different groups took trips that fit their topics.

MARGE

When we did that project on Egypt we went to the Art Institute. We set up those individual field trips just to broaden our outlook.

DAN

We went to Greenfield Village. That interested me.

DICK

Wasn't that something to do with culture?

INTERVIEWER

How did that come about?

MARGE

Yes, we had a certain number of places to go during the semester. We were supposed to go to a certain number during the term as a group or by yourself. It started about Detroit. We were saying that there . . .

DICK

There are a lot of things in Detroit normally we don't see until visitors come into town and ask about them. We were going to do these things.

GINNY

Then we reported on these trips.

MARGE

We kept a list on the board of plays, shows, ballets, concerts, things we were going to see.

JIM

There was a TV thing about church or something about church service we wanted to see so we got a TV to see it.

WALTER

Wasn't it an Easter service?

INTERVIEWER

Some critics say that people in core can do anything they want to as far as field trips and projects are concerned. Is this true?

JIM

I think so.

GINNY

No, not any individual.

JIM

You can do anything you want to a certain extent.

BETTY

It depended on how many people you could get to do what you wanted to do. Maybe the subject you wanted to study you would suggest to the chairman and he would put it on the board and it might be voted down.

DAN

You put so many suggestions on the board. They were then open for discussion. We broke them down into a certain amount after one vote.

DICK

We divided them into groups first and then took each group and eliminated some we thought wouldn't work out.

INTERVIEWER

How could you tell they wouldn't work out?

BETTY

We had a set of rules, a basis.

MARGE

Was it interesting, would it help, was it useful . . . ? When we could get them down to a certain number we held them up to this criteria.

INTERVIEWER

So you had some kind of rules you had to decide on.

GINNY

Yes.

INTERVIEWER

Would it have been the subject of the best talkers? You said that the business meeting was often run by about the same people.

JIM

No, I don't think so. I think everybody had a statement to make when it came to choosing the suggestions.

INTERVIEWER

Well now, I don't know whether you want to talk about this. Maybe you don't. Questions like these: How the teacher made her way with you. How you became acquainted with each other. Did she make an effort to get you acquainted with her?

ELLEN

She had a party here in her home on Hallowe'en, and a Christmas party. Miss Wells always opened her home to us. For the most part it was done right here. Everyone showed up at the parties. That was in October so that was real close to the time we got together.

JIM

There was this Home for the Aged where Miss Wells's mother passed away and where Miss Wells took the group to carol.

JEAN

On Grand Boulevard.

WALTER

She always took the twelfth grade but didn't have one that year so we went down. We were the closest to the twelfth so she decided to let us do it and so we did it for two years.

FRANCES

Another thing I remember was when we were studying manners we had a dinner down here with waitresses and everything. We were studying manners and etiquette.

INTERVIEWER

What year was that?

FRANCES

That was in the twelfth grade, too.

INTERVIEWER

Did it do you any good?

SEVERAL

Oh yes!

FRANCES

The fellows pulled the chairs out for us and everything.

INTERVIEWER

Could you trust them?

DICK

We left tips and everything.

FRANCES

We cooked dinner upstairs.

MARGE

Hot dogs with bacon around them!

WALTER

I remember I had quite a case of indigestion afterward.

JIM

That was good though.

(Much laughter throughout the discussion of the supper.)

INTERVIEWER

How did you get acquainted with her? Let me turn that around. How did she get acquainted with you. Did she try? How did she?

FRANCES

She tried awfully hard.

U.V.

You can't stay unfriendly with her.

MARGE

She made our names like these. We used to go down and sit in her office.

WALTER

When we just got together we told where we were from, our interests . . .

JIM

Didn't we have to go to her office for something?

FRANCES

That must have been for conferences.

ELLEN

You were doing some typing for her.

INTERVIEWER

Did you ever write autobiographies or anything?

U.V.

I think we did something.

JIM

We did what Walter says—gave a life story in class.

GINNY

We didn't get up and report it.

WALTER

Miss Wells sat in with the class, in the middle of the class.

INTERVIEWER

How do you mean?

WALTER

If we sat in a circle, she sat in with us, like one of us.

INTERVIEWER

Critics might say some teachers try to find out things they have no business trying to find out.

JEAN

They don't have to tell you if it's none of your business.

FRANCES

You can't really feel that way with Miss Wells.

INTERVIEWER

What she did find out did you feel was helpful to you? You were pretty successful. You don't have any scars.

DAN

She didn't go that far.

MARGE

One time with Sue . . . but only to help her. One girl had some trouble at home and Miss Wells tried to help her.

JIM

It was something anyone would do who had an interest in the girl, but that wasn't in front of the class.

INTERVIEWER

I don't know how much more you want to talk about but you mentioned the Old Folks' Home. Was there any other community service? Then we want to talk about these parents.

MARGE

When we went carolling we took little bags of candy we made up like baskets.

JIM

We took a basket . . . Navajo . . . That was from Miss Wells's trip. When Miss Wells was in Arizona she went to some school, and I guess the kids made a recording or something.

WALTER

When she was away for the Ford Foundation she brought back a tape recording from the Navajo school in Arizona. She was away for the whole year. They sang and talked to us. It was a tape recording of the Navajo school in Arizona.

JIM

We thought we would reply to them. So we talked and told them what our school was like.

JEAN

We took pictures . . .

U.V.

Core newspaper . . .

MARGE

It was mainly for the parents.

GINNY

We had reports from every class. Had reporters.

SEVERAL

All core classes contributed articles. There were pictures.

INTERVIEWER

Was this for all core classes? Can you remember anything you learned from the Navajo tape? Do you suppose they learned anything from your tape?

U.V.

Yes, for all classes.

U.V.

No. We did.

FRANCES

In a scrapbook we included things about Detroit and our class. Miss Wells told us how little they had in their homes—so much different from ours, and we told them what our homes were like.

WALTER

I don't know if you remember about the differences in age. A few kids about fourteen years still in the fourth grade due to lack of education.

MARGE

They have several classes in one big room. Older students with the younger ones—lack of teachers.

INTERVIEWER

Would you say American education for Indians is like or equal to that of regular high school students?

U.V.

Not where it's a regular Indian village. That was a reservation.

INTERVIEWER

Maybe there is some discrimination there. Now this parent business. When you tried to explain to your parents, were they interested?

JIM

I know my folks were.

GINNY

When you try to describe core to anyone it's very hard to get it across because you don't have a book. You don't have anything to say about using this book and we do this. Then you say we use several books and we each take a project. By the time you try to explain it, they're more confused than ever.

INTERVIEWER

Did any of you develop a way in which to explain it?

FRANCES

The way I tried to describe it was that we didn't actually work with a teacher as boss of the classroom. It was a more democratic way of studying. We had the same things that other students studied our same ages, but we decided what we were going to study instead of having the iron hand of the teacher tell us we were going to do such and such, to take a book home and read so many pages.

INTERVIEWER

I think we might let that one stand. Is there anything that has happened in your life since then . . . what might there be about how to manage a group and make them do what you want them to do?

JIM

Core in a way is similar to the basic ideas of every classroom. What you learn in core in some ways you learn in other classes besides core.

WALTER

Topics—teamwork involved. I noticed that as I got out. I'm in the accounting field and it has helped me in working with the other accountants. When you're working on these topics it's like the factories I go to and you have a product you want to put out; and you have got to have all your work to do it.

JIM

I think you could apply this to any situation, but you could get it anyway. Like I work in a butcher store.

INTERVIEWER

You mean you could have gotten it without core.

WALTER

But not as easy. And it would be harder for someone to get up and talk before someone.

DAN

Core helps you. In speech class I find I am able to get up in front of the class much more easily than some of the members who didn't have core. I never got so scared or worried. I was always more relaxed. But the other students always were so scared and fumbling around.

GINNY

In organizing people—I think it helps to organize people. I think it helps me in my job. I work with a lot of difficult people. I'm a dental assistant. People who come to my office don't want to be there in the first place and I think it helps me with them.

INTERVIEWER

What about problem solving? You haven't had any problems since you finished high school have you?

EVERYONE

Oh, no!

MARGE

Well, in choosing topics and things like that in core you choose what you want to study. I think it helped. You can weigh things. I think it has helped me since I've been out.

JIM

In the history of religion class he gave us 118 topics to choose from for a term paper. With core and weighing other topics before, I was able to choose a topic faster. Another student came up to me and hadn't chosen a topic yet. Of course I don't know whether that was just a lack of time or what.

MARGE

A lot of them get confused choosing topics for term papers. And they don't know how to start them. The techniques are the same although papers are more than those required for core—taking notes and all that.

INTERVIEWER

That's all right if you are in school. Any other evidence of follow-up in home or family living? I heard you say something about Miss Wells being away. What happened during the year Miss Wells was away?

SEVERAL

We had regular English and history.

U.V.

I felt sorry for those teachers.

BETTY

I think that was a test in itself.

SEVERAL

It was!

GINNY

We rebelled. Here was someone telling us, "We're going to do this today."

INTERVIEWER
Why was that? Wouldn't it have been a relief to have someone tell you what to do?

SEVERAL
Oh no, not at that stage of the game.

JIM
When we came into English at Wayne, taking a required English course, I remember this professor. I told him I had never had regular English. He wanted to know what I had and when I said core he just said "Oh, that." But we did well in English and were as capable as other students. There was a fellow from Cass who had English all the way through and he flunked English in the university.

FRANCES
I think we were afraid to go into the regular English classes but we found we did better than we thought once we got into it.

JIM
I remember when we were writing for a schedule Miss Jamison said I would never do well in college English, that I'd fall flat on my face.

GINNY
You learn basic English in grade school and when you get to college it's review. If you never had any trouble in the mechanics of English, it's more of a review.

JIM
In Scotland, they teach grammar differently. When we got here we didn't have a lot of basic grammar and I was glad for the review. Miss Wells marked up our papers pretty well.

FRANCES
Another thing, in speech she would correct us if we used poor English grammar.

INTERVIEWER
So she was at work all right.

GINNY
In our evaluation, they would say something about our diction, how you presented your topic, posture, if your English was poor, and everything.

INTERVIEWER
You mean the class evaluation?

GINNY

They would tell you about it. It was fun.

INTERVIEWER

Do any of you have any unhappy remembrances of that?

BETTY

I don't think it bothered anyone because of the fact that we had always worked together.

JIM

Sue was sensitive to it. She used to resent it sometimes.

MARGE

But that was her personality.

INTERVIEWER

She was defensive?

GINNY

But everyone criticized everyone else so it didn't make any difference.

FRANCES

We didn't feel they were doing it to be brutal. It was more of a help.

WALTER

It was constructive more than anything else.

INTERVIEWER

If you were doing it over, if you had youngsters going to school, would you like them to have this?

JIM

Right after you get in core, for a year it's not so good, until you get organized. So, if you put our youngsters in core after it was rolling, it would be okay.

GINNY

You waste a lot of time getting organized. It would be better if you didn't have to spend all that time getting organized.

BETTY

But that helps you to learn to organize.

DAN

If you could have it along with English and history, then core would just be a matter of learning how to get along.

GINNY

I know you can but you don't learn history in core. It's because you don't want to do it. If someone made you do it you would, and I think you should have history in high school.

INTERVIEWER

What would you lose?

FRANCES

If you had straight English and history class combined with core, you would lose something because core isn't English and history straight.

GINNY

I think core should be a separate class.

INTERVIEWER

Now, let's see. Were those two periods important or should we cut it down to one?

WALTER

Two periods are important because sometimes you'd just get started and the bell would ring.

INTERVIEWER

You said if you could figure things to get your youngsters in core after it gets rolling that would be all right. Would you say that was hard work the first year?

MARGE

You have to learn how to make it roll, to get it organized.

WALTER

I don't see how you could do it any other way.

JIM

When you think about it, maybe that was one of the best parts of core. Maybe we're talking that first year down too much. Maybe that was where we learned more about core than anything else.

GINNY

I don't think it's necessary to have core for four years.

INTERVIEWER

How would you know when you were through with it?

JEAN

I think the last two because you are going out to meet the public . . .

MARGE

You are coming from a grade school to high school and Denby is bigger than most high schools, but in any high school it's quite a jump.

Core helps you to make that change. So, I think it's important in the first two years, too.

INTERVIEWER

So, if we could cut out the awkwardness in the first two years . . . Well, is there something we have overlooked? Who should have been in core and should not have been in core? Would you be able to recognize somebody who ought not to be in core?

BETTY

If you could point out someone who should not be in core, actually, that is the one who should be. The person who is rebelling against that type of learning is the one who needs to be in core because he needs more help because that one is going to have trouble later on.

INTERVIEWER

I'm checking the notes to see if we've covered everything. Do you think you have a scientific attitude? That's an open question. Pick it up any way you want to.

GINNY

Do you mean do you do things by a scientific method the way they do in chemistry?

INTERVIEWER

You were saying you listed things on the board and chose what you wanted and you had criteria to decide. These were things that I suppose were pretty important in the way Miss Wells worked with you. Do you suppose this is a way, or thing, you developed that you still use?

MARGE

We had that criteria we had to meet, certain objective things, but there were interests too—something you would like to do, too.

INTERVIEWER

So that interests, feelings, emotions were there, too. Well, I think we have pretty well covered everything, Miss Wells.

(Miss Wells *joins the group.*)

MISS WELLS

I was interested in what was said about core being easy. Does that mean core is a snap?

BETTY

You could get by. But then you had an evaluation and you marked yourself and everyone had a guilty conscience. So, after you graded yourself everyone tried to do better and you didn't want to get by with so much, so you did more because you didn't feel like saying you deserved a "B" if you had earned a "C."

INTERVIEWER

And what about anyone who survived in core and didn't outside?

BETTY

They didn't have quite enough core.

MARGE

They get special help in core but it can't work miracles. I think core couldn't solve the problem but it could give them a helping hand . . . In other classes you just throw them in with everyone else.

JEAN

Shouldn't core be for special people? Those who are having trouble?

WALTER

Don't you remember the time Jeff made that projector and a lot of us admired it? If we had all in a class like Jeff, how many would go up to him like that?

MARGE

In the rest of their lives they're not going to be in special groups. They have to work with people who aren't going to be special people.

FRANCES

If you have only people of that type, you would feel as if core were only a refuse dump.

INTERVIEWER

Is core a snap? You answer, "When we evaluate ourselves we get a guilty conscience," and that's personal. Those people would be evaluating themselves too, and pushing themselves too. It's individual. So it's only a snap according to whether you have a high grade or low grade conscience, and whether you expect anything of yourself.

MISS WELLS

I was listening to what you said about the tedium of that first year. What would you suggest be left out of that year? The first year you're setting up goals and so forth.

GINNY

Everything comes at you at once. First you have to set up your goals. Then you set up your criteria. There's too much planning all at once.

FRANCES

I think it is a matter of making too many decisions, too.

GINNY

You just can't do it because everything is coming up all at once. You start all these things and you don't know where you are going or what you're doing them for.

INTERVIEWER

Did your parents ask what you learned, or what you did? Was it easy to answer that? What was the hardest one?

SEVERAL

What did you learn today?

FRANCES

I don't think you could so much say what you did or what you learned, but I think you showed it.

INTERVIEWER

Some of the things you learned became a part of you?

FRANCES

Yes. More as a matter of your own personality—leadership, this business of making decisions, knowing what you wanted to do and doing it.

INTERVIEWER

How about it, not only planning but there were too many decisions to make?

MISS WELLS

Too many at one time right at the beginning. I think you're right, and I think it's one of the things I have been working toward in my own teaching. I am not sure that it's solving the problem, because you are missing having that experience to work with.

FRANCES

I am sure that if they felt they could stick to what they decided whatever it was, I think that would help. Not that they had so many decisions to make but the decisions they made, they should be important.

MISS WELLS

In that first year, for example, one of the things you had to learn to do was just to work together—just the togetherness. Was that easy? In connection with combining the three groups I think the person I remember most on that creative project was Jean. She just didn't like what she was doing.

JEAN

That's right.

INTERVIEWER

As you reminisce a bit about it, did you find yourself dreading to go to core sometimes? Were there other classes you dreaded to go to?

GINNY

I was always anxious to go to core.

JEAN

I was too.

FRANCES

Yes, I was too.

MARGE

It was a relief to get away from running into a class and opening your books and getting ready for a test.

FRANCES

I was always anxious to get to core. I don't think it was the subject so much as the people with whom you were going. Even in that English class I didn't mind so much because the same people were there even though we were having a straight English class.

INTERVIEWER

Well, you know I am very privileged to have a chance to sit down and talk to you like this.

At this point the interview, as recorded on the tape, was concluded, although it was followed for some time by miscellaneous remarks by the participants.

Index